Language Arts *for* Intermediate Students

by Katherine Weitz

BARDS & POETS I

Student Book

Acknowledgements

The art on the cover is "The Constitution and the Guerriere" by 19th century British painter Thomas Chambers. Other images courtesy of The Graphics Fairy (thegraphicsfairy.com) and Dreamstime (dreamstime.com). Most selections at the beginning of lessons are in the public domain, besides the full length excerpts of the progymnasmata translations, which are used by permission of the Society for Biblical Literature in Atlanta, Georgia (see Bibliography).

I owe a debt of gratitude to several folks for their help on the Cottage Press Language Arts Curriculum. The gorgeous cover designs are the craftsmanship of my friend Jayme Metzgar. Many other dear friends have helped with both editing and content: in particular, Cheryl Turner, Kimberlynn Curles, Dovey Elliott, Kathy Whitmore, Summer Wilkes, Hannah Taylor, Melissa Turner, and all the other exceptional teachers, moms, and students of Providence Prep. My daughter Grace Weitz has spent many hours editing the project, and contributed significantly to the content of Teaching Helps. As always, the main source of help and encouragement in myriad ways – from design consultation to field testing to laundry, dinner, and dish duty – has always come from my dear husband and my wonderful children.—kpw

BARDS & POETS I

Contents

Writer's Journal

Commonplace Book

Vocabulary Study

Grammar Flashcards

Quizlet Quizzes

Theon's Six Narrative Elements

Eloquent Expression Through Copia

Grammar Terms & Definitions

Bibliography

MATERIALS NEEDED

All materials, resources, and links listed below are available at Cottage Press:

cottagepresspublishing.net

Required Books and Resources

❧ BARDS & POETS I TEACHING HELPS Features an answer key for all exercises that warrant it, tips on teaching, and additional notes and information on more advanced grammar topics and enrichment ideas. Please note if you are using this in a co-op situation, each teacher at home will also need a copy of the Teacher Manual.

❧ SENTENCE SENSE The grammar handbook from Cottage Press for terms & definitions, sentence diagramming and parsing. Lessons from the 1878 classic *Harvey's Revised English Grammar* are included in *Sentence Sense*, and scheduled in *Bards & Poets I* and *II*. This comprehensive and concise grammar reference will also be used through *Poetics & Progym* (*Language Arts for Upper School*).

❧ FLASHCARDS A free flashcard PDF for drilling grammar concepts is available at the website. Each student will also need an index card box with index card dividers. If you prefer to have students make their own flashcards, you will need index cards as well.

❧ TWO COMPOSITION BOOKS Each student will need two sewn composition books (100 pages). These lay flat, and pages tend to stay in better than they do in spiral-bound notebooks. One will be used for a Commonplace Book and one for a Writer's Journal. See instructions for setting up and using these in the Appendix.

Recommended Literature

❧ POETRY ANTHOLOGY Students will be prompted in each lesson to read and copy poems into their Commonplace Books. There are several excellent anthologies linked from the Cottage Press website, but my personal favorite for this purpose is *Favorite Poems Old and New* by Helen Ferris.

❧ BOOKS, BOOKS, BOOKS! Excellence in writing is inextricably linked to excellence in reading choices. Cottage Press has long-term plans to republish worthy books for students. Visit us often to check our progress!

Recommended Resources

✦ BOOK OF CENTURIES A blank timeline book for students, from Cottage Press. We provide suggestions in the lessons for entries that should be added to the Book of Centuries. When adding entries to the Book of Centuries, students should include authors and works of literature as well as events and other historical events. For works of literature, format the work properly (poems in quotations, book titles underlined) and include the name of the author and date of compositon and/or publication.

✦ QUIZLET An online flashcard review site. Cottage Press provides free flashcards here for *Bards & Poets I*. Access this resource from our webpage.

✦ A KEY TO HARVEY'S PRACTICAL ENGLISH GRAMMAR We provide an answer key in *Bards & Poets I Teaching Helps* for all assigned exercises, but you may wish to access this free online answer key in case you want to use additional exercises for extra review. Look for the link on the *Bards & Poets I* page at cottagepresspublishing.net. This is the correct key to the exercises from *Harvey's Revised English Grammar* in *Sentence Sense*, even though the name is slightly different.

✦ A PRINT DICTIONARY Vocabulary Study is best completed with a big, old-fashioned comprehensive dictionary—the fatter, the better. I recommend an older collegiate dictionary. These generally have not been afflicted with the modern malady of political correctness, and better yet, can often be had for pennies at a used bookstore or thrift store.

✦ A THESAURUS Indispensable for Vocabulary Study and Eloquent Expression lessons. Free online versions, like thesaurus.com work well also, but beware the ads!

✦ A RHYMING DICTIONARY Very helpful for Poetry Observation and Classical Composition lessons. Also look for free online versions, like rhymezone.com.

INTRODUCTION FOR STUDENTS & TEACHERS

My heart overflows with a pleasing theme;
I address my verses to the king;
my tongue is like the pen of a ready scribe.
— Psalm 45:1, ESV

The aim of Language Arts at Cottage Press is to develop ready scribes who pen pleasing themes flowing from a heart of truth, goodness, and beauty. Our methods are based on a classical tradition beginning with the ancient Greeks and Romans, and embraced in the educational practices of Western Civilization—Christendom—over the past two thousand years. The ancient Greek and Roman orators and rhetoricians, who developed and articulated many of the methods that we have adopted, considered training in effective communication to be inseparable from training in virtue. We agree wholeheartedly.

Cottage Press Language Arts courses are organized around the ancient Greek Progymnasmata (Progym) because it is a comprehensive pedagogy, aimed at developing rhetorical skill and love of virtue. Students trained by the Progym are prepared for ALL of life's writing requirements including—but not limited to—academic and college-level composition. Literature and poetry studies along with a strong emphasis on grammar round out our Language Arts instruction.

The Greek word *progymnasmata* (pronounced proh-jim-naz-MAH-tuh) literally means *exercises before*. These fourteen successive exercises are designed to train students in elegant and effective composition. As they worked through these exercises progressively, ancient Greek and Roman scholars imitated great orators and authors of their past. With the knowledge gained from each level, they would then write their own compositions. This training was intended to produce men who were able

to think and speak persuasively and virtuously on any given topic in the public forum and in the court of law. The need for virtuous and persuasive articulation of truth is certainly as great today as it has ever been.

For a more detailed explanation of each level of the Progymnasmata, visit the Cottage Press website: cottagepresspublishing.net.

The composition exercises in *Bards & Poets I* are primarily based on the progymnasma Narrative, beginning with a short fable retelling; the length and complexity of the narrative increases somewhat over the course of the lessons. The writing sequence is emphasized: Plan, Write, Revise. The aim of poetry lessons in *Bards & Poets I* is first and foremost to delight in the poems. Beyond that, students are taught to scan poems, to identify rhyme and stanza forms, and to recognize other literary devices.

In all lessons, students practice a variety of applied grammar and vocabulary exercises, including extensive sentence diagramming. They learn to identify figures of speech and figures of description, and to use them in their own writing. All of these exercises are designed to supply the student with *copia*—an abundant stockpile of language, ready at hand. Read more about this in Lesson 1.

One word of caution: *Bards & Poets I* (and all of our Language Arts books) is intended to accompany the student's broad and generous curriculum of reading. We teach students to observe these particular stories and poems in a very detailed way, but please do not attempt to do this with every poem and story the student reads. Most of your student's reading should be unencumbered by analysis and "comprehension" exercises, which are often little more than busywork. Instead, a student should form the habit of narrating (telling back) what he has read with very little intervention on the part of the teacher. Narration is a vital component of composition and critical thinking for all students, and should be practiced across the curriculum, even in subjects like math, science, and logic where composition is not generally emphasized. For more details on this, consult the many excellent resources online that explain Charlotte Mason's completely classical method of narration.

Bards & Poets I is designed for the needs and abilities of an intermediate writer, from 6th grade and up. Adjust the pace according to the needs and abilities of the student.

The instruction in the Student Book is written directly to students, yet the material is intended to be actively taught by a teacher. *Bards & Poets I* works well in home-school, classroom, and co-op settings. In any case, the student should have either parental or teacher oversight for **each day's** work. For composition lessons, students are instructed to work with a writing mentor. This is the person who works one-on-one with the individual student. It may be the teacher, the parent, or an outside tutor employed for the purpose. There are online services that provide writing mentorship. See the Cottage Press website for links.

STUDENT PREPARATION

Bards & Poets I contains twenty-eight lessons. Each lesson is centered around a classic literary selection—either a poem, or a retelling of a historical or literary narrative. Each lesson has five sub-lessons. The format is flexible, so that each sub-lesson may be completed in as little as one day, or at a more leisurely pace over several days. This may also be varied from lesson to lesson.

Lesson components include:

- Commonplace Book
- Prose & Poetry (literary observation)
- Language Logic (word usage and grammar)
- Eloquent Expression (developing style)
- Classical Composition (retell a fable or parable)
- Dictation

You will be instructed to complete most written work in your Writer's Journal. You will also enter passages from literary selections into your Commonplace Book. The Appendix has instructions for setting up and using these composition books. These images indicate that the work is to be completed in one or the other:

Work to be completed on the computer is indicated by this image:

This image indicates grammar lessons to be completed in *Sentence Sense* (See Materials Needed for *Bards & Poets I*).

Grammar flashcards will be added throughout the lessons, and should be reviewed regularly. The Appendix has instructions for setting up and using a *Bards & Poets I* Grammar Flashcard review system. This symbol indicates that flashcards are to be reviewed and quizzed, or that new flashcards are to be added.

Before you begin Lesson 1, gather and set up your materials. First, read each of these sections in the Appendix; then, follow the instructions to set up your notebooks and flashcard review system.

- Writer's Journal
- Commonplace Book
- Grammar Flashcards

Familiarize yourself with the layout of *Sentence Sense*:

A. Read the Preface and Introduction.

B. Study the Table of Contents.

C. Turn to each of the five chapters and get a bird's eye view of the content of each.

Lesson 1

CR

THE BUNDLE OF STICKS

from THE AESOP FOR CHILDREN with pictures by Milo Winter

A certain Father had a family of Sons, who were forever quarreling among themselves. No words he could say did the least good, so he cast about in his mind for some very striking example that should make them see that discord would lead them to misfortune.

One day when the quarreling had been much more violent than usual and each of the Sons was moping in a surly manner, he asked one of them to bring him a bundle of sticks. Then handing the bundle to each of his Sons in turn he told them to try to break it. But although each one tried his best, none was able to do so.

The Father then untied the bundle and gave the sticks to his Sons to break one by one. This they did very easily.

"My Sons," said the Father, "do you not see how certain it is that if you agree with each other and help each other, it will be impossible for your enemies to injure you? But if you are divided among yourselves, you will be no stronger than a single stick in that bundle."

In unity is strength.

CR

Lesson 1.1

Prose & Poetry

A LOOK AT LITERARY ELEMENTS IN THE FABLE

1 Read

◆ Listen carefully as your teacher reads the selection aloud. **Delight** in the story.

2 Inquire

◆ Does the **title** give any hint as to the content or message of the story? If this story was published by the author in a larger book or an anthology, does that title give any hint?

◆ Discuss the meaning of these words in the context of the story: *cast, striking, discord, violent, unity,* and any unfamiliar words.

3 Observe the Content

◆ **Setting** When and where does this story take place?

◆ **Characters** Who is (are) the main character(s) in this story?

◆ **Conflict** What is the main problem or crisis for the character(s)?

◆ **Resolution** Is the problem solved? If so, how? If not, why not?

4 Investigate the Context

Aesop was a Greek storyteller who lived from around 620 – 564 B.C. According to the ancient Greek historian, Herodotus, Aesop was a slave. As a reward for his wit and wisdom, Aesop's master gave him his freedom. To further his learning, Aesop visited the rulers of many countries, especially those who were known to be patrons of learning. His keen wit is reputed to have caused his death at Delphi. He so offended the people there that they hurled him from a rock into the sea. Aesop is most famous for his fables, which are really short narratives, portraying animals who speak, act, and have the characteristics of people while still retaining their animal traits. These stories are brief and conclude with simple, commonsense

truths that we call morals. Aesop's fables are so famous that they are often quoted or alluded to in literature. Some have even become part of our everyday language. For example, a liar is commonly referred to as someone who *cries wolf*, as in Aesop's fable *The Shepherd Boy and the Wolf.*

5 **Connect the Thoughts**
   ◆ Does this fable remind you of other fables, or of stories with similar plots, messages, or characters?
   ◆ Does this fable remind you of any proverbs or other well-known quotations? If so, make a note to enter these in your Commonplace Book once it is set up at the end of Lesson 1.1.

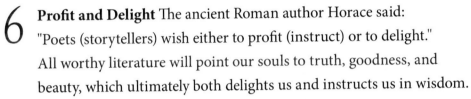

6 **Profit and Delight** The ancient Roman author Horace said: "Poets (storytellers) wish either to profit (instruct) or to delight." All worthy literature will point our souls to truth, goodness, and beauty, which ultimately both delights us and instructs us in wisdom.
   ◆ **Delight** What are the sources of delight in this story?
   ◆ **Wisdom** What wisdom does this story furnish?
   ◆ **Read** the fable aloud to your teacher with expression and with proper pauses.
   ◆ **Record** in your Book of Centuries: Aesop and his fables. For more information on the Book of Centuries, and how to add entries, see Materials Needed for *Bards & Poets I* in the Introduction.

Language Logic

THE SENTENCE

Stories and fables are made up of sentences. In *Bards & Poets I* we will devote much time to reading and writing excellent sentences. With few exceptions, an excellent sentence follows the rules of English grammar, so learn these lessons well.

If you completed *Fable & Song* from Cottage Press, many of the grammar concepts we cover in *Bards & Poets I* will be somewhat familiar. *Sentence Sense: A Grammar and Parsing Handbook* from Cottage Press (a required resource for *Bards & Poets I*) provides explanations and examples of the grammar terms and definitions covered in all levels of Cottage Press Language Arts.

⚜ Read and discuss the following sections in *Sentence Sense* with your teacher. Please note, if a section contains more than one point (A, B, C, etc.), you should only study the point listed here. The other points (including the Remarks) will be covered in future Language Logic lessons.

Begin by looking over the Table of Contents to familiarize yourself with the layout of the book. Then, read the Preface and Introduction.

II. Syntax: The Sentence
◆ Lesson 9.1A Sentence Definition

Read the instructions for Grammar Flashcards and Quizlet Quizzes in the Appendix with your teacher. Then set up your flashcard review system. Add this flashcard, which summarizes the grammar concepts you just reviewed in *Sentence Sense*, behind the Daily tab. For now, simply memorize these characteristics of a sentence, even if you do not fully understand what each one means.

◆ Sentence

Read "The Bundle of Sticks" once more with your teacher. In the original fable, show your teacher several capital letters and several lower case letters.

Look at the beginning of each sentence in the original fable. Note that capital letters are used at the beginning of the first word of each sentence. Look at the end of each sentence. Notice the end punctuation. Answer the following questions orally with your teacher.

◆ What type of punctuation is used for each sentence in this fable?
◆ How many sentences are there in this fable?

This sentence from the fable begins with a capital letter, ends with end punctuation, and expresses a complete thought:

One day when the quarreling had been much more violent than usual and each of the Sons was moping in a surly manner, he asked one of them to bring him a bundle of sticks.

The following examples are not sentences because neither expresses a complete thought. Instead of finishing what they start, they simply leave the reader hanging. Discuss with your teacher how you could make these into complete sentences.

One day when the quarreling had been much more violent than usual

To bring him a bundle of sticks

Writer's Journal

❁ Write a sentence telling what happened when the sons tried to break the bundle of sticks. Make sure your sentence begins with a capital letter, ends with end punctuation, and expresses a complete thought.

Commonplace

Commonplace Book

YOUR COMMONPLACE BOOK

❁ In the *Bards & Poets I* Appendix, read the section on Commonplace Book. Study the example entries. Set up your Commonplace Book, and make a title page for it. You will make your first commonplace entry in Lesson 1.2.

Lesson 1.2

Prose & Poetry

FABLE PLOT OBSERVATION

The sequence of actions in a story is called the **plot**. The plot generally includes a beginning, a middle, and an end. Usually, we are introduced to most of the **main characters** and the **conflict** in the beginning. In the middle, as the story unfolds, we get to know the characters better, and the conflict mounts. The ending shows the **resolution** of the conflict and all the attendant consequences. There are many variations on this basic plot structure as we will see in later lessons.

The first step in plot observation, then, is to simply list the sequence of actions. Study this example plot observation for "The Crow and the Pitcher," a well-known fable from Aesop. The straight lines represent pencil marks dividing the plot of the fable into segments of action. Below the fable is an example of a simple outline capturing the sequence of actions in the fable.

A thirsty Crow found a Pitcher with some water in it, | but so little was there that, try as she might, she could not reach it with her beak, | and it seemed as though she would die of thirst within sight of the remedy. | At last she hit upon a clever plan. | She began dropping pebbles into the Pitcher, | and with each pebble the water rose a little higher until at last it reached the brim, | and the knowing bird was enabled to quench her thirst. |

Plot Observation for "The Crow and the Pitcher"

1. thirsty Crow found Pitcher of water
2. too low to reach with beak
3. die in sight of remedy?
4. hit upon a plan
5. began dropping pebbles
6. water rose to brim
7. thirst quenched

Observe the plot of "The Bundle of Sticks."

◆ Place short pencil marks on the fable (copied below) to divide the plot into a series of action.

A certain Father had a family of Sons, who were forever quarreling among themselves. No words he could say did the least good, so he cast about in his mind for some very striking example that should make them see that discord would lead them to misfortune.

One day when the quarreling had been much more violent than usual and each of the Sons was moping in a surly manner, he asked one of them to bring him a bundle of sticks. Then handing the bundle to each of his Sons in turn he told them to try to break it. But although each one tried his best, none was able to do so.

The Father then untied the bundle and gave the sticks to his Sons to break one by one. This they did very easily.

"My Sons," said the Father, "do you not see how certain it is that if you agree with each other and help each other, it will be impossible for your enemies to injure you? But if you are divided among yourselves, you will be no stronger than a single stick in that bundle."

◆ In your Writer's Journal, write a short outline to capture the **plot** (sequence of actions) of this fable. For each action you marked in the fable, write a few words or phrases.

Language Logic

GRAMMAR TERMS & DEFINITIONS
Review your grammar flashcard.

THE SENTENCE: CAPITALIZATION

 Read and discuss the following sections in *Sentence Sense* with your teacher.

II. Syntax: Capitalization and Punctuation
◆ 11.1A Basic Capitalization Rules

V. Exercises (Note that these Exercises, located in the final section of *Sentence Sense*, are taken from the original lessons in *Harvey's Revised Grammar*. Answers to all exercises assigned in *Bards & Poets I* are found in the Teaching Helps lesson where they are assigned.)
◆ Optional oral or written practice with capitalization: *Harvey's* 12, #1, #6, #7, #15.

 Add this flashcard behind the Daily tab. Review all flashcards according to tabs.

◆ Capitalization Rules

Read again the first three reasons to capitalize a word in *Sentence Sense* 11.1A. Then read through "The Bundle of Sticks" again with your teacher. Discuss the capitalization:

◆ Notice all of the capital letters at the beginning of sentences.

◆ You may have noticed that the words *Father* and *Sons* are capitalized, even though we do not always think of them as actual names. This is often done in Aesop's fables, and in many other stories written long ago. Sometimes the author gives animals or objects a human or living personality. Sometimes the author simply wants us to know how important these words are to the story.

In your Writer's Journal:

Writer's Journal

A. Copy the title of the fable: The Bundle of Sticks"

Notice that the word *of* is not capitalized in this title. This is because little words in the middle of a title are not usually capitalized. However, the first word of a title is always capitalized, so the word *The* at the beginning follows this rule.

B. Write the first names of three of your relatives. Use proper capitalization.

C. Write the names of three cities. Use proper capitalization.

D. Write the names of two rivers and two mountains. Use proper capitalization.

E. Write the titles of two books on your bookshelf. Use proper capitalization.

Eloquent Expression

COPIA

Our lessons in Eloquent Expression aim to teach you to write — and speak!— with "fluency, propriety, elegance, and animation" (from Noah Webster's 1828 definition of *eloquent*). Writing that is eloquent is pleasing and winsome to your readers, and it goes a long way toward helping persuade others to your point of view.

Erasmus of Rotterdam was a famous rhetorician and teacher in the late Middle Ages. A *rhetorician* is one who studies and practices the effective use of language. Erasmus taught his students the importance of crafting sentences with copia, by which he meant an abundant stockpile of language, ready at hand.

In his book *Copia: Foundations of the Abundant Style*, Erasmus showed his students how to create copia by beginning with the simple sentence *Your letter pleased me greatly*. He rewrote that same sentence in other words more than 150 times to express the same idea in an abundance of ways. Here are a just a few examples:

> Your letter was very sweet to me. By your letter I was mightily pleased. Your lines conveyed to me the greatest joy. I was singularly delighted by your epistle. How overjoyed I was by your letter! Heavens, what causes for joy your letter did provide! I rejoiced greatly at your letter. Your missive showered a wealth of gladness upon me. Not unpleasing to me was your letter. Your by no means disagreeable letter has come to me. Your writing, in no way displeasing to me, has come.[1]

Of course, not every one of Erasmus' rewritten sentences is clear and eloquent, but the exercise of expressing the same thought in different ways is valuable, even if some of the variations are less than eloquent. Writing is a process, and in the process, all writers sometimes write duds! The important thing is to practice constantly and diligently. Further, as you work through the exercises, evaluate your sentences. Notice when you write a sentence that is a dud and figure out why it is a dud. This will give you extra practice in editing, and help you quickly catch and fix errors in your writing.

In Eloquent Expression, we follow Erasmus' excellent method for developing copia. The Sentence Style exercises apply Language Logic lessons to sentences from the narrative selection. By imitating excellent writers of the past in this way, you will begin to build your own eloquence of expression. In later lessons, the Sentence Style lessons will apply Language Logic to your own writing and you will begin to develop your own **voice**, enhanced and enriched by the influence of those worthy writers of the past.

COPIA OF WORDS: VOCABULARY STUDY

Our first task in developing eloquence of expression is to observe and analyze this wealth by studying vocabulary taken from the literary selection. First, review the use of the print dictionary and its organization with your teacher.

> dictionary (dik' shə nēr ē), n. a reference book containing an alphabetical selection of the words of a language, giving information about their meanings, pronunciations, and other features.

Every student should have a big, fat, old-fashioned, comprehensive dictionary on hand. It is a thoroughly enjoyable pastime to simply peruse a dictionary. Dictionaries contain an abundance of information about words. You can find the correct spelling and pronunciation of a word and

---

1. Erasmus, *On Copia of Words and Ideas*, tr. Donald King, 38-42.

all of its meanings. In larger dictionaries, you will also find synonyms, antonyms, etymology (how the word came into our language), notes about word usage, and quotations using the word. Some dictionaries have pictures and illustrations of selected words.

With your teacher, inspect your dictionary and learn how it is organized. First, notice that the words are listed alphabetically. Many larger dictionaries have thumb indexes for each letter of the alphabet. In order to look up the word *unity*, you must go to the section of the dictionary that has words beginning with the letter U.

There are many, many words that begin with the letter U, so you will need to look at the second and following letters to get closer to the word you are looking for. Most dictionaries have **guide words** at the top of each page to help you locate words more easily. For example, in my dictionary, the guide word on the top of the left-hand page is *Unimak Island*, which is the first word listed on that page. The guide word at the top of the right-hand page is *universe*. These guide words let you know that the word you are looking for, *unity*, will probably be on the right-hand page.

Read and discuss these Vocabulary Study steps in the Appendix with your teacher. We will study the rest of the steps in upcoming lessons. When instructed to complete Vocabulary Study, use your print dictionary, and work in your Writer's Journal.

A. Literary Context

B. Spelling Analysis

C. Part of Speech Identification

D. Definition

Writer's Journal

Conduct a vocabulary study for "The Bundle of Sticks."

A. Choose at least two unfamiliar words to study. If you need suggestions, see the list under Inquire in Literary Elements above. Work in your Writer's Journal.

B. Complete Vocabulary Study steps A-D for each word (see *Appendix*).

Commonplace

FABLE

In each lesson of *Bards & Poets I*, you will have three separate sessions for entering a selection into your Commonplace Book, either from the poem or narrative featured in the lesson, or from a related literary selection. Each of these commonplace sessions should last about 5-10 minutes, and never longer than 10 minutes. Discuss the length of time you should spend on each session with your teacher and use a timer. You may be able to copy the complete selection during that time, or you may not. You should aim for quality in each session, not quantity. If you are in the middle of a sentence or a phrase when the timer sounds, you should finish it.

Session one of three commonplace sessions for this lesson. Literary selection: "The Bundle of Sticks."

Commonplace Book

🏵 Set your timer and begin copying. When you finish, check your work carefully, word by word, against the original. Check spelling, capitalization, and punctuation for accuracy.

Lesson 1.3

Language Logic

GRAMMAR FLASHCARDS

GRAMMAR TERMS & DEFINITIONS
🏵 Review all flashcards according to tabs.

THE SENTENCE: PUNCTUATION
🏵 Read and discuss the following sections in *Sentence Sense* with your teacher.

SENTENCE SENSE

II. Syntax: Capitalization and Punctuation
- ◆ 11.2A Punctuation
- ◆ 11.3A-B The Comma *You will learn more about commas and conjunctions in a later lesson. For now, just memorize the rule.*

Add the indicated flashcard behind the Daily tab.

◆ Basic Comma Rules

THE SENTENCE: REVIEW

 Which of the following are sentences? Tell your teacher why the others are not sentences: *Does it begin with a capital letter? Does it end with end punctuation? Does it express a complete thought?* For each one that you did not mark as a sentence, tell your teacher orally how to make it a complete sentence.

1. A certain Father had a family of Sons.

2. Although each one tried his best.

3. He told them to try to break it

4. This they did very easily.

5. in unity is strength.

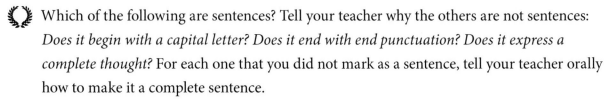
Eloquent Expression

COPIA OF WORDS: VOCABULARY STUDY

 Conduct a vocabulary study for "The Bundle of Sticks."

A. Choose at least two more unfamiliar words to study. If you need suggestions, see the list under Inquire in Literary Elements above. Work in your Writer's Journal.

B. Complete Vocabulary Study steps A-D for each word (see *Appendix*).

Writer's Journal

Commonplace

FABLE

Session two of three commonplace sessions for this lesson.
Literary selection: "The Bundle of Sticks."

 Set your timer and begin where you stopped in the last session. When you finish, check your work carefully against the original for accuracy.

Commonplace Book

Lesson 1.4

Language Logic

GRAMMAR FLASHCARDS

GRAMMAR TERMS & DEFINITIONS

 Review all flashcards according to tabs.

SENTENCE CLASSIFICATION BY USE

Sentences can be classified in several ways. Here we learn to classify sentences by the way that they are used to express our meaning.

 Read and discuss the following sections in *Sentence Sense* with your teacher.

SENTENCE SENSE

II. Syntax: The Sentence
  ◆ 9.14A Sentence Classification by Use
V. Exercises
  ◆ Oral exercise: Identify sentence classes by use in *Harvey's* 156.
    Nota Bene: *All oral exercises should be completed with your teacher.*

Study these examples of sentence classification by use.

Declarative Sentence: A certain Father had a family of Sons.
Interrogative Sentence: Must you quarrel amongst yourselves?

Exclamatory Sentence: My sons are always quarreling!

Imperative Sentence: Sons, stop quarreling. Sons, stop quarreling!

Add the indicated flashcards behind the Daily tab. Review all flashcards according to tabs.

GRAMMAR FLASHCARDS

- ◆ Declarative Sentence
- ◆ Interrogative Sentence
- ◆ Exclamatory Sentence
- ◆ Imperative Sentence

In your Writer's Journal, copy these sentences. Next to each, note its sentence classification by use. You should learn to spell these classifications, so write them out in full each time. A hint on spelling *interrogative*: This comes from the Latin words *inter + rogo*, which means *I ask*. If you know these Latin roots, it is easier to remember that there is only one *g*, but there are two *r*'s.

1. Were they not forever quarreling?

2. Each of the sons was moping in a surly manner.

3. Bring me a bundle of sticks.

4. The sticks broke easily!

5. Where do wars and fights come from among you? — James 4:1

Writer's Journal

Eloquent Expression

SENTENCE STYLE – COPIA OF CONSTRUCTION: SENTENCE CLASS BY USE

Read these four sentences. Classify each as Declarative, Interrogative, Exclamatory, or Imperative.

Your letter pleased me greatly.

Your letter pleased me greatly!

Did not your letter please me greatly?

Dear friend, please me greatly with your letter.

As you can see, a sentence can be rewritten as any of the other four classes by use. Sometimes the word order will have to be altered or the verb will have to be changed in order for the sentence to remain grammatically correct. Imperative sentences will probably have to change the most.

Writer's Journal

Copy these sentences into your Writer's Journal, and then paraphrase it as each of the other classifications.

1. Were they not forever quarreling?

2. Each of the sons was moping in a surly manner.

Classical Composition

PLOT OBSERVATION: ORAL NARRATION

Without reading the fable again, narrate orally "The Bundle of Sticks" to your teacher from the outline you constructed in Lesson 1.2.

Commonplace

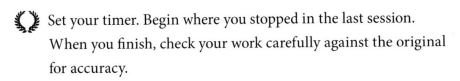

FABLE

Session three of three commonplace sessions for this lesson. Literary selection: "The Bundle of Sticks."

Commonplace Book

Set your timer. Begin where you stopped in the last session. When you finish, check your work carefully against the original for accuracy.

Lesson 1.5

Language Logic

GRAMMAR TERMS & DEFINITIONS

❧ Ask your teacher to quiz you with the grammar flashcards. Alternately, use the test feature in the Cottage Press *Bards & Poets I* Quizlet Classroom for an online or printed quiz for Lesson 1.

DICTATION: FABLE

❧ Work in your Writer's Journal. Write as your teacher dictates a passage to you from your Commonplace Book. When you are done, check your work carefully, word by word, against the original. Check for accurate spelling, capitalization, and punctuation.

Eloquent Expression

SENTENCE STYLE REVIEW

❧ Copy these sentences into your Writer's Journal, and then paraphrase it as each of the other classifications.

1. Bring me a bundle of sticks.

2. In unity is strength.

Classical Composition

THE WRITING SEQUENCE

Composition is rarely a "one and done" deal. A three-step sequence is fairly standard practice for most compositions: plan, write, revise. *Bards & Poets* makes this a bit easier by spreading out the steps for you across different lesson sessions. Writing begins, before you put pen to paper for the actual composition, with some kind of plan or **outline** for what you are going to say. After your composition is complete, you must revise. Your first draft will almost never be your final draft.

Follow this sequence, whether you are writing an academic essay, a personal letter, or a blog post. Aside from personal journaling, and some electronic correspondence, there are very few times in our lives when we simply dash off some words on paper and are done with it.

WRITING SEQUENCE FOR BARDS & POETS I

- ♦ **Plan**: Outline
- ♦ **Write**: Retell
- ♦ **Revise**: with your **Editor's Pen**
  - ✓ Big Picture
  - ✓ Zoom 5x: Paragraphs
  - ✓ Zoom 10x: Sentences
  - ✓ Fine Focus: Words

Notice that the Revise step is broken into smaller sequential steps. The photography theme here should help you "picture" the sequence. First, read over your composition, making sure you have said all that you mean to say; you are looking at the Big Picture. Next, zoom in a bit closer to look at paragraphs. Zoom in again to look at sentences. Finally, focus in on the fine details of spelling, grammar, and word choice. Following these steps in sequence will yield the best results with the least frustration.

NARRATIVE RETELLING

This is a simple composition exercise, but it is foundational for every type of writing. Nearly all writing you will do in life, including your academic career, will require some level of narrative skill.

The plot observation you completed in Lesson 1.2 was the first step, as you captured the sequence of action in an outline.

Now your assignment is to draft a retelling of the fable "The Bundle of Sticks" without referring back to the original. Although you should do your best to use proper grammar and spelling, keep in mind that you will have opportunity to edit before you finalize your retelling.

Writer's Journal

A. At the top left of the page, write a heading. The attribution *From the Original Fable by Aesop* is included to give proper credit to the author of the original fable. Your finished heading should look like this:

> The Bundle of Sticks
> Retold by ___ (fill in with your name)
> From the Original Fable by Aesop

B. Retell the fable "The Bundle of Sticks" (from the selection at the beginning of this lesson) in writing, keeping the same characters, setting, and sequence of action. Refer to your simple outline, but do not review the narrative again before you write. Indent each paragraph, and leave every other line blank. Include in this retelling:

   ◆ at least one new direct quotation (one that is not in the original fable)

C. Ask your writing mentor (see *Bards & Poets I* Introduction) to check that the assignment is complete.

D. Type your retelling on the computer with spell-check turned off, or ask your writing mentor to type it exactly as you wrote it. Save, print, and file this draft in your writing binder.

Commonplace

FROM YOUR READING

Find selections in a book or poem to enter in your Commonplace Book. Include the name of the book or poem, properly formatted. Label the item with the grammar feature or as a favorite passage.

Commonplace
Book

◉ Grammar Features

   ◆ A declarative sentence
   ◆ An imperative sentence
   ◆ An exclamatory sentence
   ◆ An interrogative sentence

◉ Favorite Passage: This is where you begin to really make your Commonplace Book your own. Add at least one passage of one to three sentences or several lines of poetry that captured your attention in your reading this week. It may be something you found beautiful, thought-provoking, funny, or interesting.

Lesson 2

ℭℛ

WHEN MOTHER READS ALOUD

When Mother reads aloud, the past
Seems real as every day;
I hear the tramp of armies vast,
I see the spears and lances cast,
I join the thrilling fray;
Brave knights and ladies fair and proud
I meet when Mother reads aloud.

When Mother reads aloud, far lands
Seem very near and true;
I cross the desert's gleaming sands,
Or hunt the jungle's prowling bands,
Or sail the ocean blue.
Far heights, whose peaks the cold mists shroud,
I scale, when Mother reads aloud.

When Mother reads aloud, I long
For noble deeds to do —
To help the right, redress the wrong;
It seems so easy to be strong,
So simple to be true.
Oh, thick and fast the visions crowd
My eyes, when Mother reads aloud.

— AUTHOR UNKNOWN

ℭℛ

Lesson 2.1

Prose & Poetry

INTRODUCTION TO POETRY

"A poem is a metrical composition, with an aim to please by addressing the imagination and sensibilities."[1] A rather un-poetical definition of poetry, yet its three points will serve us well.

1. **Poetry is metrical**. The poetry of western civilization is traditionally metrical, which means it has some kind of patterned or rhythmic sound. In English poetry, this has usually been produced by using prescribed numbers of syllables along with a pattern of regular stress on certain of those syllables.
2. **Poetry seeks to please**. Rhythmic sound, rhyming words, poetic expression, and figures of speech delight readers of all ages. Poets aim to charm their readers by making them see ordinary things in extraordinary ways.
3. **Poetry addresses the imagination and sensibilities**. Poetry captivates our imaginations, very often by engaging our senses—making us see, feel, hear, touch, and taste things in new and memorable ways. In the words of poet Percy Shelley, it "makes familiar objects... as if they were not familiar."

A LOOK AT LITERARY ELEMENTS IN THE POEM

1 **Read**
◆ Follow along and listen carefully as the poem is read aloud, OR read it aloud yourself. Read it at least two or three times. **Delight** in the meter, the rhyme, and the images.

2 **Inquire**
◆ Does the **title** give any hint as to the content or message of the poem?
◆ Are there any other unfamiliar persons, places, or things mentioned in the poem? Discuss these with your teacher.
◆ Discuss the meaning of these words in the context of the story: *vast, fray, fair, shroud, scale, redress,* and any unfamiliar words.
◆ Was there any part of the poem you did not understand? If so, discuss this with your teacher and classmates.

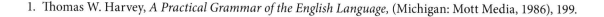

1. Thomas W. Harvey, *A Practical Grammar of the English Language,* (Michigan: Mott Media, 1986), 199.

3 **Observe the Content**
  ◆ **Lyrical Elements**
    ▪ What does the poet describe?
    ▪ Does the poet make you see, hear, smell, taste, or touch anything?
    ▪ Does the poet compare something in the poem to some other thing?
  ◆ **Narrative Elements** Does this poem tell a story? If so, observe the
    ▪ **Setting** When and where does this story take place?
    ▪ **Characters** Who is (are) the main character(s) in this story?
    ▪ **Conflict** What is the main problem or crisis for the character(s)?
    ▪ **Resolution** Is the problem solved? If so, how? If not, why not?

4 **Investigate the Context**
  This author of this poem is unknown, so we cannot know much about the context, aside from the fact that it is written in English.

5 **Connect the Thoughts**
  ◆ Does this poem remind you of other poems, or of stories with similar plots, messages, or characters?
  ◆ Does this poem remind you of any proverbs or other well-known quotations? If so, enter these in your Commonplace Book.

Commonplace Book

6 **Profit and Delight**
  ◆ **Delight** What are the sources of delight in this poem?
  ◆ **Wisdom** What wisdom does this poem furnish?
  ◆ **Read** the poem aloud to your teacher with expression and with proper pauses. Pause ONLY where you see punctuation marks, not necessarily at the end of each line. Commas get a short pause; end punctuation gets a longer pause. This may take some practice, as the tempation to pause at the end of each line is great!
  ◆ **Memorize** this poem and **recite** it before an audience.

Eloquent Expression

COPIA OF WORDS: VOCABULARY STUDY

In this lesson, you will add another step to your Vocabulary Study routine. A **synonym**, from the Greek *syn* (*same*) + *onoma* (*name*), is a word that is very close in meaning to another word. An **antonym**, from the Greek *anti* (*opposite*) + *onoma* (*name*), is a word that is opposite in meaning.

Both synonyms and antonyms are excellent tools to help us better comprehend the meanings of a particular word that we are studying.

Writer's Journal

🏵 Read and discuss this Vocabulary Study Step F in the Appendix with your teacher. From now on, include this step in your Vocabulary Study routine.

🏵 Conduct a vocabulary study for "When Mother Reads Aloud."

A. Choose at least two unfamiliar words to study. If you need suggestions, see the list under **Inquire** in Literary Elements above. Work in your Writer's Journal.

B. Complete Vocabulary Study steps A-D and F for each word (see *Appendix*).

Classical Composition

EDITOR'S PEN – THE BIG PICTURE

When you get out your editor's pen, it is so tempting to zero in immediately on misspelled words and grammar errors. Avoiding this temptation will probably be very challenging for your teacher. It may also be very challenging for you if you are a perfectionist. But trust me! It is vital to step back for a panoramic view of your retelling before you do any of that.

🏵 Edit your retelling from Lesson 1:

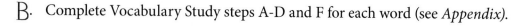

Editor's Pen – The Big Picture
✔ All important plot elements included
✔ All characters represented correctly
✔ Sequence: *same as the original*
✔ Length: *similar to the original*

A. Read aloud exactly what you have written—not what you THINK you have written! This is an important distinction, as it is so easy for us to overlook our own errors. After all, we know exactly what we MEANT to write. As you carefully read the actual words you have written, you may find errors. Mark any corrections on your first draft.

B. Next, work through the Big Picture checklist above with your writing mentor.

C. Transfer all additions and corrections from your print copy of
the retelling to your file on the computer. Print and file this
edited version in your binder along with your marked-up editing
copy of the first draft.

Commonplace

Commonplace
Book

POETRY

Session one of three commonplace sessions for this lesson. Literary
selection: "When Mother Reads Aloud."

 Set your timer and begin copying. When finished, check your
work carefully against the original for accuracy.

Lesson 2.2

Prose & Poetry

FIGURES OF SPEECH: RHYME

The great Roman orator and teacher Quintilian defined a **figure of speech** as "speech artfully
varied"[2] from our usual way of speaking or talking. Virtually all authors and poets use figures of
speech. There are hundreds of figures of speech that teachers of rhetoric have classified in dozens
of ways. In *Bards & Poets I,* we will study quite a few figures, and you will begin to experiment
with these in your writing. Most of these were introduced in *Fable & Song,* and even *Primer Two,*
so they may be familiar to you.

RHYME

Rhyme is "a correspondence of sound in the last syllables of two or more lines, succeeding each
other immediately, or at no great distance."[3] It is certainly artful, requiring some thought and
effort to do it well. And, unless you are a *Princess Bride* character, you probably do not make your
words rhyme in everyday conversation. Rhyme is "artfully varied" from common speech.

Every poem does not need to rhyme, but **end-rhyme** is traditionally associated with poetry

2. Corbett, *Classical Rhetoric,* 424-458.
3. Harvey, *A Practical Grammar of the English Language,* 253.

written in our English language. Rhyming words please the ear. They also aid the memory. Think of how many things we learn by way of rhyme:

Thirty days hath September, April, June, and November...

In 1492 Columbus sailed the ocean blue...

I before E, except after C...

To analyze end-rhyme, place corresponding capital letters at the end of each rhyming line. In the poem below (*The Swing*, by Robert Louis Stevenson) *swing* and *thing* rhyme, so we place an **A** at the end of those two lines; *blue* and *do* rhyme, so we place a **B** at the end of those two lines; and so on to the end of the poem.

How do you like to go up in a swing?	A
Up in the air so blue?	B
Oh, I do think it the pleasantest thing	A
Ever a child can do!	B
Up in the air and over the wall	C
Till I can see so wide,	D
Rivers and trees and cattle and all	C
Over the countryside—	D
Till I look down on the garden green	E
Down on the roof so brown—	F
Up in the air I go flying again,	E
Up in the air and down!	F

The rhyme scheme of "The Swing" is denoted as ABAB. Notice the spelling of each rhyming pair. Often, the rhyming words are spelled similarly, like *swing* and *thing*. But what about *blue* and *do*? They sound the same, but the letters used to spell those sounds are different. Discuss the spelling of each word with your teacher. According to your spelling curriculum, is there a rule that governs the spelling of the word?

🏅 Mark the end rhyme in the stanzas below.

When Mother reads aloud, the past

Seems real as every day;

I hear the tramp of armies vast,

I see the spears and lances cast,

I join the thrilling fray;

Brave knights and ladies fair and proud

I meet when Mother reads aloud.

When Mother reads aloud, far lands

Seem very near and true;

I cross the desert's gleaming sands,

Or hunt the jungle's prowling bands,

Or sail the ocean blue.

Far heights, whose peaks the cold mists shroud,

I scale, when Mother reads aloud.

When Mother reads aloud, I long

For noble deeds to do —

To help the right, redress the wrong;

It seems so easy to be strong,

So simple to be true.

Oh, thick and fast the visions crowd

My eyes, when Mother reads aloud.

Language Logic

DIRECT QUOTATIONS

 Read and discuss the following sections in *Sentence Sense* with your teacher.

II. Syntax: The Sentence
- ◆ 9.16A Direct Quotations

II. Syntax: Capitalization & Punctuation
- ◆ 11.1B Capitalization, Rule IV
- ◆ 11.3C The Comma, Rule XI

Add the indicated flashcard behind the Daily tab. Review your grammar flashcards from the last lesson. When you have finished, divide the flashcards that you have mastered equally between the Even and Odd tabs. Leave any that you have not mastered behind the Daily tab and continue to review them until you have!

◆ Direct Quotation

Eloquent Expression

SENTENCE STYLE – COPIA OF WORDS & CONSTRUCTION: DIALOGUE

Dialogue adds interest to a story by allowing the narrator to show the reader what the characters say or think. The exact words of the character are repeated in **direct quotations**.

"Your letter pleased me greatly," said Erasmus.

Erasmus said, "Your letter pleased me greatly."

"Your letter," said Erasmus, "pleased me greatly."

In the sentences above, the words *said Erasmus* are called **dialogue tags**. They can be placed at different points in the direct quotation – beginning, middle, or end. Look closely at the punctuation in the sentences. In each, at least one comma is needed to set off the dialogue tag. Study the placement of the comma and quotation marks for each. Notice that the punctuation mark at the end of each quoted section is always inside the quotation marks.

Now observe the use of capital letters inside the quotation marks. All three of these sentences follow the first rule of a sentence: *Capitalize the first word of a sentence.* In the second sentence, notice that the first word of the direct quotation is also capitalized. If you think about it, this makes perfect sense. A direct quotation is really a sentence within a sentence, and both of the sentences must follow the rule.

In the third sentence, the first word of the second part of the direct quotation is not capitalized. This is because that second part is not the beginning of a new sentence, but it is a continuation of a sentence begun earlier in the sentence. Again, it makes perfect sense.

⟨⟩ Copy this direct quotation into your Writer's Journal. Paraphrase it twice, moving the dialogue tag to a new position each time.

The father said, "If you are divided among yourselves, you will be no stronger than a single stick."

Classical Composition

EDITOR'S PEN – ZOOM 5X: PARAGRAPHS

⟨⟩ Now that the Big Picture is set, begin to zoom in for a close look at the paragraph(s) in your retelling with your writing mentor.

> ### Editor's Pen – Zoom 5x: Paragraphs
> ✔ Formatting: *proper indentation*
> ✔ Length: *neither too wordy nor too short*
> ✔ Sentence class by use: *effective use*
> ✔ Dialogue: *effective use*

A. Read aloud your most recently edited version. Check each item in the Editor's Pen checklist to identify possible changes. Mark these on your print copy.

B. Transfer all additions and corrections from your print copy to the computer file. Print this version and file it in your binder along with your other versions.

Lesson 2.3

Language Logic

PARTS OF SPEECH

"English grammar teaches us how to speak and write the English language correctly."[4]

4. Harvey, *Elementary Grammar,* 8.

The English language is made up of words that are combined into sentences in order to express thoughts. When you look at the words that make up a sentence, you must understand what each word means to make sense of it. But you also must understand how each word is used within the sentence, and that is why we study English grammar.

When you look up a word in the dictionary, its **definition** tells what that word means, while its **part of speech** tells how the word can be used in a sentence. In the upcoming lessons, we will learn what each of these parts of speech means, and how to identify the parts of speech within a sentence.

 Read and discuss the following section in *Sentence Sense* with your teacher.

I. Etymology: The Parts of Speech
   ◆ The Parts of Speech – An Introduction.

 Add the indicated flashcard behind the Daily tab. Review all flashcards according to tabs.

   ◆ Parts of Speech

Eloquent Expression

SENTENCE STYLE – COPIA OF WORDS: SYNONYMS

These are foundational treasures for your "storehouse" of copia. Erasmus used quite a few synonyms even in our short sampling of his sentences. For example, in place of the word *letter*, he used *missive*, *epistle*, and *lines*. Others from the complete list of variations included *note*, *communication*, *words*, and others.

To find a synonym for a particular word, start by thinking aloud—brainstorming—with your teacher, and make a list of synonyms that come to mind. When you have exhausted your own supply, look for more in the dictionary and/or the thesaurus. Look up synonyms for your "brainstormed" synonyms in addition to the original word. Aim to have at least five or six strong synonyms for each word—this is copia! As you write your own compositions, you will be glad to have this ready supply of synonyms at your command.

Writer's Journal

Copy the sentence below into your Writer's Journal, and list as many synonyms as you can for each of the underlined words. Paraphrase the sentence twice, using your favorite synonyms. Compare your rewritten sentences with the original.

If you are <u>divided</u> among yourselves, you will be no <u>stronger</u> than a <u>single</u> <u>stick</u>.

Classical Composition

EDITOR'S PEN – ZOOM 10X: SENTENCES

Now it is time to zoom in even closer as you check the sentences in your retelling. Work with your writing mentor.

Editor's Pen – Zoom 10x: Sentences
✓ Complete thought expressed
✓ Subject and predicate agree in number
✓ Correct capitalization and punctuation

A. Read aloud your your most recently edited version. Use the Editor's Pen checklist to identify changes you need to make. Mark all changes on your print copy.

B. Transfer all additions and corrections from your print copy to the computer file. Print this version and file it in your binder along with your other versions.

Commonplace

POETRY

Session two of three commonplace sessions for this lesson. Literary selection: "When Mother Reads Aloud."

Commonplace
Book

 Set your timer. Begin where you stopped in the last session. When you finish, check your work carefully against the original for accuracy.

Lesson 2.4

Language Logic

GRAMMAR
FLASHCARDS

GRAMMAR TERMS & DEFINITIONS

 Review all flashcards according to tabs.

Eloquent Expression

SENTENCE STYLE – COPIA OF WORDS: DIALOGUE TAGS

Study the sentences below.

"Your letter pleased me greatly," wrote Erasmus.

Erasmus smiled, "Your letter pleased me greatly."

"Your letter," cried Erasmus, "pleased me greatly."

In the first sentence, the dialogue tag *said* is replaced by *wrote*. In the second sentence, *said* is replaced by *smiled*. In the third sentence, *said* is replaced by *cried*. *Wrote, smiled,* and *cried* are all synonyms for *said*. Notice how using different tags creates a slightly different feeling in each sentence.

Said and *asked* are the most frequently used dialogue tags, and therefore they are comfortable (or even "invisible") to most readers; good writers use them freely. But the occasional use of a synonym for *said* or *asked* can bring extra emphasis to a direct quotation.

Writing dialogue with varied tags requires you to exercise your imagination. You may even want to get up from your desk, and act out the dialogue, and put yourself in the place of the person speaking. Think about

- the expression on your face
- what you are doing with your hands
- what you are doing with the rest of your body
- how your voice would sound
- what other sounds you might be making

Writer's Journal

❦ Spend some time with your teacher (or your class) making a list entitled **Dialogue Tags** on the last page or two of your Writer's Journal. Add to this list often and refer to it whenever you need a synonym for *said*.

❦ Copy the direct quotation below in your Writer's Journal. Paraphrase it twice, varying your dialogue tags and their position in the sentence each time.

The father said, "If you are divided among yourselves, you will be no stronger than a single stick."

Classical Composition

EDITOR'S PEN – FINE FOCUS: WORDS

The final checks dwell on the details of your word usage. The list below includes things that you have studied. These will become a natural part of your writing over time. Keep in mind that even the best writers, before they submit any final work, often run through a personal editing checklist to correct particular errors they commonly make. The fact is that none of us ever outgrow our need for editing.

Editor's Pen – Fine Focus: Words
- ✓ Word choices varied; word meanings clear
  - ◆ Dialogue: *dialogue tags varied if appropriate*
- ✓ Correct spelling
- ✓ Final read-through

A. Read aloud your most recent version. Identify changes you need
   to make with the Editor's Pen checklist. Mark these on your
   print copy.

B. Transfer all additions and corrections from your print copy to the
   computer file. Print this final version and file it in your binder
   along with your other versions.

Commonplace

Commonplace
Book

POETRY

Session three of three commonplace sessions for this lesson. Literary
selection: "When Mother Reads Aloud."

 Set your timer and begin copying. When you finish, check your
work carefully against the original for accuracy.

Lesson 2.5

Prose & Poetry

RHYME

Read and enjoy a few poems in your poetry anthology. Identify the rhyme schemes of several.
Read one or two poems aloud with expression and proper pauses. Pause at punctuation, but not
necessarily at the ends of lines.

 Choose a rhyming poem in your anthology. Determine its rhyme
scheme.

Writer's
Journal

◆ In your Writer's Journal, write the title of the poem and the
  author. Make note of its rhyme scheme.

◆ Write the rhyming words from the poem in two lists: one
  list for those spelled the same, and one list for those spelled
  differently.

◆ Choose one of the rhyming words from the spelled differently list, and try to come up
  with several additional rhymes. Look especially for varied spellings.

Language Logic

GRAMMAR TERMS & DEFINITIONS

❂ Ask your teacher to quiz you with the grammar flashcards. Alternately, use the test feature in Cottage Press *Bards & Poets I* Quizlet Classroom for an online or printed quiz for Lesson 2.

DICTATION: POETRY

❂ Work in your Writer's Journal. Write as your teacher dictates a passage to you from your Commonplace Book. When you are done, check your work carefully, word by word, against the original. Check for accurate spelling, capitalization, and punctuation.

Eloquent Expression

RHYMING WORDS

❂ Do these exercises in your Writer's Journal.

A. Read "When Mother Reads Aloud" aloud once more.

B. List pairs (and triplets) of rhyming words in the poem spelled the same.

C. List pairs (and triplets) of rhyming words in the poem spelled differently.

D. Write several other words that rhyme with *true*. At least one of them should have an ending that is spelled differently.

SENTENCE STYLE REVIEW

❂ Copy the first sentence into your Writer's Journal, and then paraphrase it as each of the other classifications. Replace at least three words with synonyms. Copy the second sentence, then rewrite it two times, varying the dialogue tags and placement in each one.

I see the spears and lances cast.

Aesop said, "In unity is strength."

Classical Composition

NARRATIVE RETELLING – FINAL DRAFT

🏵 Read over the final version of your retelling one last time and make any needed changes. Save it on your computer; print and file with all the other drafts in your writing binder.

Commonplace

FROM YOUR READING

Find selections in a book or poem to add to your Commonplace Book. Include the name of the book or poem, properly formatted. Label the entry with the grammar or poetry feature or as a favorite passage. Aim for a minimum of three entries, with at least one from each category.

Commonplace Book

🏵 Grammar Features (choose any)

- ◆ An interesting dialogue tag (add to your Dialogue Tags list)
- ◆ An interrogative, exclamatory, or imperative sentence (most sentences in a narrative or poem are declarative, so we are not including those on this list!)

🏵 Poetry Features

- ◆ Rhyme (note name of the rhyme scheme)

🏵 Favorite Passage: Add at least one passage of one to three sentences or several lines of poetry that captured your attention in your reading this week. It may be something you found beautiful, thought-provoking, funny, or interesting.

Lesson 3

ℭℛ

THE REAL PRINCESS
by Hans Christian Anderson

There was once a Prince who wished to marry a Princess; but then she must be a real Princess. He travelled all over the world in hopes of finding such a lady; but there was always something wrong. Princesses he found in plenty; but whether they were real Princesses it was impossible for him to decide, for now one thing, now another, seemed to him not quite right about the ladies. At last he returned to his palace quite cast down, because he wished so much to have a real Princess for his wife.

One evening a fearful tempest arose, it thundered and lightened, and the rain poured down from the sky in torrents: besides, it was as dark as pitch. All at once there was heard a violent knocking at the door, and the old King, the Prince's father, went out himself to open it.

It was a Princess who was standing outside the door. What with the rain and the wind, she was in a sad condition; the water trickled down from her hair, and her clothes clung to her body. She said she was a real Princess.

"Ah! we shall soon see that!" thought the old Queen-mother; however, she said not a word of what she was going to do; but went quietly into the bedroom, took all the bed-clothes off the bed, and put three little peas on the bedstead. She then laid twenty mattresses one upon another over the three peas, and put twenty feather beds over the mattresses.

Upon this bed the Princess was to pass the night.

The next morning she was asked how she had slept. "Oh, very badly indeed!" she replied. "I have scarcely closed my eyes the whole night through. I do not know what was in my bed, but I had something hard under me, and am all over black and blue. It has hurt me so much!"

Now it was plain that the lady must be a real Princess, since she had been able to feel the three little peas through the twenty mattresses and twenty feather beds. None but a real Princess could have had such a delicate sense of feeling.

The Prince accordingly made her his wife; being now convinced that he had found a real Princess. The three peas were however put into the cabinet of curiosities, where they are still to be seen, provided they are not lost.

Wasn't this a lady of real delicacy?

CR

Lesson 3.1

Prose & Poetry

A LOOK AT LITERARY ELEMENTS IN THE NARRATIVE

1 Read
 ◆ Listen carefully as your teacher reads the selection aloud. **Delight** in the story.

2 Inquire
 ◆ Does the **title** give any hint as to the content or message of the story? If this story was published by the author in a larger book or an anthology, does that title give any hint?
 ◆ Discuss the meaning of these words in the context of the story: *plenty, tempest, pitch, condition, scarcely, delicate, curiosities,* and any unfamiliar words. Note the use of the word *lightened* in the narrative; you can easily tell what it means by the context even though you would probably use a slightly different word for this phenomenon. So, is it a misspelling or a misuse of the word in the narrative? Check the listing in your dictionary to see!

3 Observe the Content
 ◆ **Setting** When and where does this story take place?
 ◆ **Characters** Who is (are) the main character(s) in this story?

◆ **Conflict** What is the main problem or crisis for the character(s)?

◆ **Resolution** Is the problem solved? If so, how? If not, why not?

4 **Investigate the Context**

Hans Christian Andersen was born in 1805 in Denmark. Andersen's formal schooling was very sparse, but he was always convinced he would be a famous author someday. He worked very hard in Copenhagen writing books, plays, and poems, yet success did not come.

But while he was doing work of the most ordinary merit in this line, he had one admirable talent which he never even dreamed of taking seriously. Odense, his birthplace, was a rich treasure house of legends and folk lore, and sometimes, just to amuse the children of his friends, he would gather the little ones about him and weave these old legends into the most wonderful tales in the liveliest manner, never bothering about grammar, but using childish words, and as he talked he would act and jump about and make remarkable faces.

Perceiving all this, Andersen's friends at length suggested to him that he should write these stories down to make a book. At first, he laughed at such an idea, but finally, more in fun that in earnest, he consented to the plan and wrote the stories down exactly as he had told them. . .In this lay their peculiar charm. . . Little did he dream that it was to be his fairy tales and nothing else which should win him his lasting fame.

. . . The recognition thus won by Andersen after so many years of struggle was, to him, a source of constant wonder and delight. That he, the son of a poor washerwoman and a cobbler, should now be the friend of princes and kings, seemed to him more marvelous than any story of Cinderella. — *My Book House: Halls of Fame*, ed. Olive Beaupré Miller

5 **Connect the Thoughts**

◆ Does this story remind you of other stories with similar plots, messages, or characters?

◆ Does this story remind you of any fables?

◆ Does this story remind you of any proverbs or other well-known quotations? If so, enter these in your Commonplace Book.

Commonplace Book

6 **Profit and Delight**

◆ **Delight** What are the sources of delight in this story?

◆ **Wisdom** What wisdom does this story furnish?

◆ **Read** the narrative aloud to your teacher with expression and with proper pauses.

◆ **Record** in your Book of Centuries: Hans Christian Andersen.

Language Logic

GRAMMAR FLASHCARDS

GRAMMAR TERMS & DEFINITIONS

 Review all flashcards according to tabs.

Commonplace

NARRATIVE

Session one of three commonplace sessions for this lesson. Literary selection: "The Real Princess."

Commonplace Book

 Set your timer and begin copying. When you finish, check your work carefully, word by word, against the original.

Lesson 3.2

Prose & Poetry

NARRATIVE PLOT OBSERVATION

If needed, review plot observation in Lesson 1.2. For a short narrative like this, we can use the same procedure that we used for a fable.

Observe the plot of "The Real Princess."

◆ Place short pencil marks on the narrative (copied below) to divide the plot into a series of action.

There was once a Prince who wished to marry a Princess; but then she must be a real Princess. He travelled all over the world in hopes of finding such a lady; but there was always something wrong. Princesses he found in plenty; but whether they were real Princesses it was impossible for him to decide, for now one thing, now another, seemed to him not quite right about the ladies. At last he returned to his palace quite cast down, because he wished so much to have a real Princess for his wife.

One evening a fearful tempest arose, it thundered and lightened, and the rain poured down from the sky in torrents: besides, it was as dark as pitch. All at once there was heard a violent knocking at the door, and the old King, the Prince's father, went out himself to open it.

It was a Princess who was standing outside the door. What with the rain and the wind, she was in a sad condition; the water trickled down from her hair, and her clothes clung to her body. She said she was a real Princess.

"Ah! we shall soon see that!" thought the old Queen-mother; however, she said not a word of what she was going to do; but went quietly into the bedroom, took all the bed-clothes off the bed, and put three little peas on the bedstead. She then laid twenty mattresses one upon another over the three peas, and put twenty feather beds over the mattresses.

Upon this bed the Princess was to pass the night.

The next morning she was asked how she had slept. "Oh, very badly indeed!" she replied. "I have scarcely closed my eyes the whole night through. I do not know what was in my bed, but I had something hard under me, and am all over black and blue. It has hurt me so much!"

Now it was plain that the lady must be a real Princess, since she had been able to feel the three little peas through the twenty mattresses and twenty feather beds. None but a real Princess could have had such a delicate sense of feeling.

The Prince accordingly made her his wife; being now convinced that he had found a real Princess. The three peas were however put into the cabinet of curiosities, where they are still to be seen, provided they are not lost.

Wasn't this a lady of real delicacy?

◆ In your Writer's Journal, write a short outline to capture the **plot** (sequence of actions) of this fairy tale. For each action you marked in the fairy tale, write a few words or phrases.

Language Logic

THE NOUN

A noun names a person, place, thing, or idea. *George Washington*, *grandmother*, and *shopkeeper* are nouns that **name persons**. *Virginia*, *river*, and *kitchen* are nouns that **name places**. *Blackboard*, *tail*, and *blanket* are nouns that **name things**. *Life*, *love*, and *happiness* are nouns that **name ideas**.

Words like *he*, *she*, *it*, *we*, *you*, and *they* also may refer to a person, place, thing, or idea, but these are not nouns, because they do not **name** the person, place, thing, or idea. Instead, they stand in for a noun, and are called **pronouns**. We will learn about pronouns in a later lesson.

 Read and discuss the following sections in *Sentence Sense* with your teacher.

I. Etymology: The Noun
 ◆ 1.1 Noun Definition
V. Exercises
 ◆ Oral Exercise: Point out the nouns in the sentences from *Harvey's* 19.3.

 Add the indicated flashcard behind the Daily tab. Review all flashcards according to tabs.

◆ Noun

In your Writer's Journal:

A. Write four nouns from "The Real Princess" which name persons.

B. Write four nouns that name places.

C. Write four nouns that name things.

D. Write a noun that names an idea.

Eloquent Expression

COPIA OF WORDS: VOCABULARY STUDY

The English language contains a wonderful mix of words, many of which originated in other languages. The history of the English language is a delightful study, which we hope you will pursue someday. In the meantime, a real understanding of any particular word requires a closer look at where it came from, and how it was used in bygone days. The study of the history of a word is called **etymology**. This is the step we will now add to your Vocabulary Study routine.

Read and discuss this Vocabulary Study Step E in the Appendix with your teacher. From now on, include this in your Vocabulary Study routine.

Conduct a vocabulary study for "The Real Princess."

A. Choose at least two unfamiliar words to study. If you need suggestions, see the list under **Inquire** in Literary Elements above. Work in your Writer's Journal.

B. Complete Vocabulary Study steps A-F for each word (see *Appendix*).

Classical Composition

PLOT OBSERVATION: ORAL NARRATION

 Without reading "The Real Princess" again, retell the **plot** orally to your teacher. Refer to your outline if needed.

Commonplace

NARRATIVE

Session two of three commonplace sessions for this lesson. Literary selection: "The Real Princess."

Commonplace Book

 Set your timer and begin copying. When you finish, check your work carefully, word by word, against the original. Check spelling, capitalization, and punctuation for accuracy.

Lesson 3.3

Language Logic

THE VERB

 Read and discuss the following sections in *Sentence Sense* with your teacher.

SENTENCE SENSE

    I. Etymology: The Verb

- 3.1 Verb Definition

- 3.4 Auxiliaries [Helping Verbs] Often, two verbs will work together in a sentence to form a **verb phrase** that shows action, being, or state. In the verb phrase, an **auxiliary** or **helping verb** is paired with a main (or principal) verb. Memorize the list of auxiliaries so that you can easily recognize them in verb phrases.

    V. Exercises

- Oral Exercise: Point out the verbs in the sentences from *Harvey's* 19.4. Discuss with your teacher whether each verb or verb phrase you marked shows action, or whether it shows being/state.

Add the indicated flashcards behind the Daily tab. Review all flashcards according to tabs.

- Verb
- Auxiliaries (Helping Verbs)

Practice identifying the parts of speech you have learned. Underline each noun in the sentences below, and double underline the verb or verb phrase. Discuss with your teacher whether each verb or verb phrase you marked shows action, or whether it shows being/state. Finally, for each noun, tell your teacher whether it names a person, place, thing, or idea.

1. A Prince was searching for a Princess.

2. One evening, a fearful tempest arose.

3. A Princess was standing outside the door.

4. The Queen-mother had put three little peas in the bed.

5. The Princess slept very badly.

6. The Prince married the Princess.

7. The peas are in the cabinet.

Eloquent Expression

SENTENCE STYLE – COPIA OF WORDS: ANTONYMS

Like synonyms, antonyms are an effective way to express an idea in other words. Several of Erasmus's example sentences use antonyms. Consider the underlined words in these three:

> Not unpleasing to me was your letter. Your by no means disagreeable letter has come to me. Your writing, in no way displeasing to me, has come.

In order to express the idea of how pleasing the letter was to him, Erasmus takes the antonyms *unpleasing*, *disagreeable*, and *displeasing*, and he **negates** them by putting words or phrases like *not*, *by no means*, and *in no way* in front of them.

Antonyms used in this manner will not always provide the best sentences, so it is a device you should use very sparingly in your writing. However, it is an excellent exercise for building copia.

So, once you have a list of synonyms for a particular word, think of some antonyms and consider how you might use them to express a similar thought either by negating the antonym, or by rewording the sentence. If you need help, check the dictionary and/or the thesaurus. Remember to look up synonyms for your antonyms!

 Copy the sentences below into your Writer's Journal, and list antonyms for each of the underlined words or phrases. Paraphrase each sentence twice, using a negated antonym in each. Compare your rewritten sentences with the original.

Writer's Journal

1. She went <u>quietly</u> in to the bedroom.

2. It has hurt me <u>so much</u>!

Classical Composition

THE WRITING SEQUENCE

Recall the basic steps of the writing sequence we will follow in *Bards & Poets*:

> ## WRITING SEQUENCE FOR BARDS & POETS
>
> ◆ **Plan**: Outline
> ◆ **Write**: Retell
> ◆ **Revise**: with your **Editor's Pen**
>   ✓ Big Picture
>   ✓ Zoom 5x: Paragraphs
>   ✓ Zoom 10x: Sentences
>   ✓ Fine Focus: Words

NARRATIVE RETELLING – BEGIN FIRST DRAFT

The plot observation you completed in Lesson 3.2 was the first step, particularly the notes you made for **action**. As you write your retelling, do your best to use proper grammar and spelling, but keep in mind that you will have opportunity to edit before you finalize it. Do as much as you are able in this session; you will have another writing session in the next lesson segment.

 Retell "The Real Princess" in writing, keeping the same characters, setting, and sequence of action. Refer to your outline if needed, but do not review the original narrative before you write.

Writer's Journal

A. At the top left of the page, write a heading. The attribution *From the Original Fairy Tale by Anderson* is included to give proper credit to the author of the original fable. Your finished heading should look like this:

> The Real Princess
> Retold by ___ (fill in with your name)
> From the Original Fairy Tale by Anderson

B. Ask your writing mentor to check that the assignment is complete.

Lesson 3.4

Language Logic

SENTENCE DIAGRAMMING: SUBJECTS AND PREDICATES

◯ Read and discuss the following sections in *Sentence Sense* with your teacher.

SENTENCE SENSE

II. Syntax: The Sentence
   ◆ 9.4A Subjects
   ◆ 9.5A Predicates

III. Sentence Diagrammming: Sentence Patterns
   ◆ 12.1 Basic Pattern: Subject – Predicate
   ◆ 12.2 Pattern: Subject – Verb

◯ Add these flashcards behind the Daily tab. Review all flashcards according to tabs.

GRAMMAR FLASHCARDS

◆ Subject
◆ Predicate

◯ In your Writer's Journal, copy these sentences. Analyze each sentence by marking the simple subject (who or what the sentence is about) with a single underline, and the verb or verb phrase with a double underline. Then diagram the sentence. Refer to *Sentence Sense* as needed. When you diagram, you may just ignore any additional words in the sentence which are not the simple subject or the verb.[1]

Writer's Journal

1. The Prince was searching.

2. A tempest arose.

3. The Princess was standing.

4. The Queen-mother thought.

5. Those peas can be seen.

Eloquent Expression

VERBS IN YOUR WRITING

Good writers use fitting (appropriate) and strong verbs in their sentences. Look at these sentences:

The Father implored his sons to stop quarreling. "You must stop quarreling," he pleaded.

The words *implored* and *pleaded* are stronger substitutes for the word *asked*. Notice how they give extra urgency and desperation to the plight of the father. When you are writing a story, always look at each sentence to see if you can use a stronger, more descriptive verb. As you can see, we have already been practicing this as we have worked with dialogue tags.

For each of the underlined verbs below from "The Real Princess," list several substitutes in your Writer's Journal. They should fit the context of the story. Make your verbs strong and descriptive.

Writer's Journal

1. The Prince <u>wished</u> to marry a real Princess.

2. A Princess <u>knocked</u> at the door.

3. She <u>said</u> she was a real Princess.

4. It <u>hurt</u> me so much!

1. Students who have completed *Fable & Song* may diagram all the words in the sentence.

Classical Composition

Writer's Journal

NARRATIVE RETELLING – FINISH FIRST DRAFT

🏅 Finish the first draft of your narrative retelling. Review the instructions in Lesson 3.3 as needed.

Commonplace

NARRATIVE

Session three of three commonplace sessions for this lesson. Literary selection: "The Real Princess."

Commonplace Book

🏅 Set your timer. Begin where you stopped in the last session. When you finish, check your work carefully against the original for accuracy.

Lesson 3.5

Prose & Poetry

POETRY APPRECIATION

🏅 Read and enjoy a few poems in your poetry anthology. Identify the rhyme schemes of several. Read one or two poems aloud with expression and proper pauses.

Language Logic

GRAMMAR TERMS & DEFINITIONS

GRAMMAR FLASHCARDS

🏅 Ask your teacher to quiz you with the grammar flashcards. Alternately, use the test feature in the Cottage Press *Bards & Poets I* Quizlet Classroom for an online or printed quiz for Lesson 3.

DICTATION: NARRATIVE PASSAGE

Writer's Journal

Work in your Writer's Journal. Write as your teacher dictates a passage to you from your Commonplace Book. When you are done, check your work carefully, word by word, against the original. Check for accurate spelling, capitalization, and punctuation.

Eloquent Expression

SENTENCE STYLE REVIEW

Writer's Journal

Copy this sentence into your Writer's Journal, and then paraphrase it as each of the other classifications. Replace at least three words with synonyms and/or negated antonyms.

He travelled all over the world in hopes of finding such a lady.

Copy this sentence into your Writer's Journal, and then rewrite it two times, varying the dialogue tags and placement in each one.

"Oh, very badly indeed!" she replied. "I have scarcely closed my eyes the whole night through."

Classical Composition

NARRATIVE RETELLING: TYPE DRAFT

Type your retelling on the computer with spell-check turned off, or ask your writing mentor to type it exactly as you wrote it. Save, print, and file this draft in your writing binder.

Commonplace

FROM YOUR READING

Find selections in a book or poem to add to your Commonplace Book. Include the name of the book or poem, properly formatted. Label the entry with the grammar or poetry feature, the figure of speech, or as a favorite passage. Aim for a minimum of three entries, with at least one from each category.

Commonplace Book

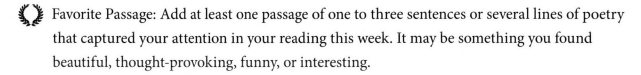 Grammar Features (choose any)

- ◆ A sentence that has a strong and fitting verb
- ◆ An interesting dialogue tag (add to your Dialogue Tags list)
- ◆ An interrogative, exclamatory, or imperative sentence

Poetry Features (choose any)

- ◆ Rhyme (note name of the rhyme scheme)

Favorite Passage: Add at least one passage of one to three sentences or several lines of poetry that captured your attention in your reading this week. It may be something you found beautiful, thought-provoking, funny, or interesting.

Lesson 4

☙

ROBERT BRUCE'S MARCH TO BANNOCKBURN

At Bannockburn the English lay,—
The Scots they were na far away,
But waited for the break o' day
    That glinted in the east.

But soon the sun broke through the heath
And lighted up that field of death,
When Bruce, wi' saul-inspiring[1] breath,
    His heralds thus addressed:—

Scots, wha[2] hae wi' Wallace bled,
Scots, wham[3] Bruce has aften led,
Welcome to your gory bed,[4]
    Or to Victorie!

Now's the day, and now's the hour;
See the front o' battle lour;[5]
See approach proud Edward's power—
    Chains and Slaverie!

1. saul-inspiring *soul-inspiring; courage-inspiring*
2. wha *who*
3. wham *whom*
4. bed *grave*
5. lour *threaten, crouch*

Wha will be a traitor knave?[6]

Wha can fill a coward's grave?

Wha sae base as be a Slave?

    Let him turn and flee!

Wha, for Scotland's King and Law,

Freedom's sword will strongly draw,

Free-man stand, or Free-man fa',

    Let him on wi' me!

By Oppression's woes and pains!

By your Sons in servile chains!

We sill[7] drain our dearest veins,

    But they shall be free!

Lay the proud Usurpers low!

Tyrants fall in every foe!

Liberty's in every blow!—

    Let us Do or Die![8]

                      — ROBERT BURNS

6. knave *lad*

7. sill *shall*

8. die (pronounced *dee*)

Lesson 4.1

Prose & Poetry

A LOOK AT LITERARY ELEMENTS IN THE POEM

1 Read
- Follow along and listen carefully as the poem is read aloud, OR read it aloud yourself. Read it at least two or three times. **Delight** in the meter, the rhyme, and the images.

2 Inquire
- Does the **title** give any hint as to the content or message of the poem?
- Are there any other unfamiliar persons, places, or things mentioned in the poem? Discuss these with your teacher.
- Discuss the meaning of these words in the context of the story: *heath, lour (lower), knave, oppression, servile, usurper,* and any unfamiliar words.
- Was there any part of the poem you did not understand? If so, discuss this with your teacher and classmates.

3 Observe the Content
- **Lyrical Elements**
  - What does the poet describe?
  - Does the poet make you see, hear, smell, taste, or touch anything?
  - Does the poet compare something in the poem to some other thing?
- **Narrative Elements** Does this poem tell a story? If so, observe the
  - **Setting** When and where does this story take place?
  - **Characters** Who is (are) the main character(s) in this story?
  - **Conflict** What is the main problem or crisis for the character(s)?
  - **Resolution** Is the problem solved? If so, how? If not, why not?

4 Investigate the Context
Robert Burns (1759-1796) was born at Alloway, Scotland. His poetry celebrates the beautiful places and people of his beloved Scotland. "Robbie" Burns composed his poetry in the broad Scotch dialect that was a hallmark of his homeland, and did much to restore the love of impoverished and oppressed Scots — and the rest of the world — for the simple, homey joys of rural life in Scotland. We catch some glimpses of his early life

. . . in his poems and in his Common-place Book. Here we see the boy at school; for like most Scotch peasants, the father gave his boys the best education he possibly could. We see him following the plow, not like a slave, but like a free man, crooning over an old Scotch song and making a better one to match the melody. We see him stop the plow to listen to what the wind is saying, or turn aside lest he disturb the birds at their singing and nest making. At supper we see the family about the table, happy notwithstanding their scant fare, each child with a spoon in one hand and a book in the other. — William J. Long, *English Literature, Its History and Its Significance for the English-Speaking World*

As a young man, Robert went away from his home to study surveying, but he fell into bad company, and developed many destructive habits, which were a lifelong snare and sorrow to him. He eventually gained some literary notoriety in his late twenties, not just among scholars, but even among "plowboys and maid servants."[9]

All the fine ladies and gentlemen were eager to see the plowman poet. The fuss they made over him was enough to turn the head of a lesser man. But in spite of all the flattery, Burns, though pleased and glad, remained as simple as before. He moved among the grand people in their silks and velvets clad in homespun clothes "like a farmer dressed in his best to dine with the laird"[10] as easily as he had moved among his humble friends. . .— Henrietta Marshall, *English Literature for Boys and Girls*

In this midst of this, Burns realized he must return home again, where he married a country lass and settled down to farm life. His old habits followed him, however, and even as he penned some of the most beautiful and inspiring poetry of all time, Robbie Burns died a disappointed and broken man at age thirty-seven. His legacy did not die, however; Burns inspired a new generation of poets, including the venerable Walter Scott, whom we will meet later in this book.

5 Connect the Thoughts

Commonplace Book

◆ Does this poem remind you of other poems, or of stories with similar plots, messages, or characters?

◆ Does this poem remind you of any proverbs or other well-known quotations? If so, enter these in your Commonplace Book.

9. Robert Heron, *A Memoir of the Life of the Late Robert Burns*
10. Sir Walter Scott, *Life of Burns*

6 Profit and Delight

- **Delight** What are the sources of delight in this poem?
- **Wisdom** What wisdom does this poem furnish?
- **Read** the poem aloud to your teacher with expression and with proper pauses.
- **Record** in your Book of Centuries: Robert Burns, Robert Bruce, Battle of Bannockburn.
- **Memorize** this poem and **recite** it before an audience.

Language Logic

GRAMMAR FLASHCARDS

GRAMMAR TERMS & DEFINITIONS
Review all flashcards according to tabs.

GRAMMAR PRACTICE AND REVIEW

In your Writer's Journal, copy these sentences. Analyze each sentence by marking the simple subject with a single underline, and the verb or verb phrase with a double underline. For each noun, tell your teacher whether it names a person, place, thing, or idea. Then diagram the sentence. Refer to *Sentence Sense* as needed.

Writer's Journal

1. The English lay.
2. The Scots waited.
3. The sun rose.
4. A battle threatens.
5. Tyrants fall.

Eloquent Expression

COPIA OF WORDS: VOCABULARY STUDY

We come to the final step for our Vocabulary Study: Literary Quotation. Comparing the ways that the word has been used in other literary settings will give you a better understanding of its meaning and its proper usage. These may also give you ideas for your Commonplace Book!

Read and discuss this Vocabulary Study Step G in the Appendix with your teacher. From now on, include this in your Vocabulary Study routine.

⚜ Conduct a vocabulary study for "Robert Bruce's March to Bannockburn."

Writer's Journal

A. Choose at least two unfamiliar words to study. If you need suggestions, see the list under **Inquire** in Literary Elements above. Work in your Writer's Journal.

B. Complete Vocabulary Study steps A–G for each word (see *Appendix*).

Classical Composition

EDITOR'S PEN – THE BIG PICTURE
Remember to save the grammar and spelling errors for later.

⚜ Edit your retelling from Lesson 3:

Editor's Pen – The Big Picture
✓ All important plot elements included
✓ All characters represented correctly
✓ Sequence: *same as the original*
✓ Length: *similar to the original*

A. Read aloud exactly what you have written—not what you THINK you have written! Mark any corrections on your first draft.

B. Next, work through the Big Picture checklist above with your writing mentor.

C. Transfer all additions and corrections from your print copy of the retelling to your file on the computer. Print and file this edited version in your binder along with your marked-up editing copy of the first draft.

Commonplace

Commonplace Book

POETRY
Session one of three commonplace sessions for this lesson. Literary selection: "Robert Bruce's March to Bannockburn."

Set your timer and begin copying. When finished, check your work carefully against the original for accuracy.

Lesson 4.2

Prose & Poetry

RHYME SCHEME

The rhyme in "Robert Bruce's March to Bannockburn" is a little tricky, since some of the rhymes are based on the Scots pronunciation, rather than the spelling. You will also notice a few imperfect rhyming pairs or triplets where the endings look the same, but sound slightly different. Be sure to check the footnotes in the model again for pronunciation reminders.

 Mark the end rhyme in the stanzas below.

> At Bannockburn the English lay,—
>
> The Scots they were na far away,
>
> But waited for the break o' day
>
> > That glinted in the east.

> But soon the sun broke through the heath
>
> And lighted up that field of death,
>
> When Bruce, wi' saul-inspiring breath,
>
> > His heralds thus addressed:—

> Scots, wha hae wi' Wallace bled,
>
> Scots, wham Bruce has aften led,
>
> Welcome to your gory bed,
>
> > Or to Victorie!

> Now's the day, and now's the hour;
>
> See the front o' battle lour;

See approach proud Edward's power—

  Chains and Slaverie!

Wha will be a traitor knave?

Wha can fill a coward's grave?

Wha sae base as be a Slave?

  Let him turn and flee!

Wha, for Scotland's King and Law,

Freedom's sword will strongly draw,

Free-man stand, or Free-man fa',

  Let him on wi' me!

By Oppression's woes and pains!

By your Sons in servile chains!

We sill drain our dearest veins,

  But they shall be free!

Lay the proud Usurpers low!

Tyrants fall in every foe!

Liberty's in every blow!—

  Let us Do or Die!

Language Logic

NOUN CLASSES

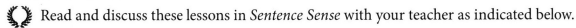 Read and discuss these lessons in *Sentence Sense* with your teacher as indicated below.

I. Etymology: The Noun

- ◆ 1.2A Noun Classes
- ◆ 1.3 Noun Properties *Memorize all of the noun properties, but note that we will only study number, gender, and person.*

❂ Add these flashcards to your box behind the Daily Tab, and begin to memorize them. Review all flashcards according to tabs.

- ◆ Noun Classes
- ◆ Noun Properties

❂ In your Writer's Journal, from "Robert Bruce's March to Bannockburn" by Burns:

A. Write four proper nouns which name persons, and two common nouns which name persons.

B. Write two proper nouns that name places, and two common nouns which name places.

C. You will notice the poet has capitalized several nouns that name things. Before English was standardized, this was not uncommon. In this case, we will classify these as common nouns, even though they are capitalized. Write four common nouns from the poem that name things. Think of three proper nouns not in the poem that name things, and add them to your list.

D. Again, you will notice that several nouns that we today would consider common are capitalized. Here, we might well consider at least some of these as proper nouns. *Victorie*,[11] *Oppression*, and *Liberty* are all given properties of persons; this is a figure of speech we call personification. Because of this, we classify these as proper nouns. Write down these three as proper nouns that name ideas. Think of three common nouns not in the poem that name ideas, and add them to your list.

Classical Composition

EDITOR'S PEN – ZOOM 5X: PARAGRAPHS

❂ Now that the Big Picture is set, begin to zoom in for a close look at the paragraph(s) in your retelling with your writing mentor.

11. *Victorie* is the spelling Burns used; today we would spell it *victory*.

Editor's Pen – Zoom 5x: Paragraphs

✔ Formatting: *proper indentation*
✔ Length: *neither too wordy nor too short*
✔ Sentence class by use: *effective use*
✔ Dialogue: *effective use*

A. Read aloud your most recently edited version. Check each item in the Editor's Pen checklist to identify possible changes. Mark these on your print copy.

B. Transfer all additions and corrections from your print copy to the computer file. Print this version and file it in your binder along with your other versions.

Lesson 4.3

Prose & Poetry

POETIC METER – IAMBIC

In addition to rhyme, another feature of much poetry is **meter**—the rhythmical pattern of sound made by the poet's arrangement of words. In English poems the meter is usually produced by a pattern of stressed and unstressed syllables. Read the lines below, and pay attention to the stressed syllables that are indicated by the italic type.

From *break*-fast *on* through *all* the *day*

At *home* a-*mong* my *friends* I *stay*

We **scan** poetry by analyzing the stressed and unstressed syllables and naming the patterns these form. Here are the same lines, scanned.

    ∪   / ∪ /   ∪   / ∪ /
From *break* fast *on* through *all* the *day*

    ∪ / ∪ / ∪   / ∪ /
At *home* a *mong* my *friends* I *stay*

This pattern (unstressed-stressed, unstressed-stressed, . . .) is called **iambic meter**. The first two stanzas of "Robert Bruce's March to Bannockburn" are written in iambic meter. The rest of the verses are written in trochaic meter, which we will study in a later lesson.

Scan these four lines by marking each syllable as either stressed (/) or unstressed (∪). Read each line several times until you get a feel for the rhythm. It sometimes helps to exaggerate the accented syllables in a sing-song way when you are scanning poetry. Just remember that this is never the proper way to read poetry any other time!

At Bannockburn the English lay,—

The Scots they were na far away,

But waited for the break o' day

That glinted in the east.

Language Logic

NOUN NUMBER

Read and discuss these lessons in *Sentence Sense* with your teacher at home as indicated below.

I. Etymology: The Noun
- ◆ 1.4A Property: Number
- ◆ 1.4B Formation of the Plural #1, #2, #3, #4, #5, and #6

Add this flashcard to your box behind the Daily Tab, and begin to memorize them. Review all flashcards according to tabs.

- ◆ Property: Number

In your Writer's Journal, from "Robert Bruce's March to Bannockburn":

A. Write four plural nouns, and four singular nouns.

B. Copy these words, then write the plural form beside each:

ox, city, desk, alley, street, school, girl, fish, road, child, house, money, boy, man, folly, wind, pencil, wagon, calf, rose, book, knife, vessel, woman, box, plow, chair, fence, potato, monkey

Writer's
Journal

Eloquent Expression

SENTENCE STYLE REVIEW

Copy this sentence into your Writer's Journal, and then paraphrase it as each of the other classifications. Replace at least two words with synonyms and/or negated antonyms. In doing this, you will probably turn the poetry into prose.

Now's the day, and now's the hour;

See the front o' battle lour;

See approach proud Edward's power—

Chains and Slaverie!

Writer's
Journal

Classical Composition

EDITOR'S PEN – ZOOM 10X: SENTENCES

Now it is time to zoom in even closer as you check the sentences in your retelling. Work with your writing mentor.

Editor's Pen – Zoom 10x: Sentences
✔ Complete thought expressed
✔ Subject and predicate agree in number
✔ Correct capitalization and punctuation

A. Read aloud your your most recently edited version. Use the Editor's Pen checklist to identify changes you need to make. Mark all changes on your print copy.

B. Transfer all additions and corrections from your print copy to the computer file. Print this version and file it in your binder along with your other versions.

Commonplace

POETRY

Session two of three commonplace sessions for this lesson. Literary selection: "Robert Bruce's March to Bannockburn."

Commonplace Book

Set your timer. Begin where you stopped in the last session. When you finish, check your work carefully against the original for accuracy.

Lesson 4.4

Prose & Poetry

POETIC METER – IAMBIC

Scan these lines by marking each syllable as either stressed (/) or unstressed (∪), as you learned in Lesson 4.3.

But soon the sun broke through the heath

And lighted up that field of death,

When Bruce, wi' saul-inspiring breath,

His heralds thus addressed:—

Language Logic

GRAMMAR TERMS & DEFINITIONS

◯ Review all flashcards according to tabs.

SENTENCE DIAGRAMMING: DIRECT OBJECTS

◯ Read and discuss the following section in *Sentence Sense* with your teacher.

III. Sentence Diagrammming: Sentence Patterns
- ◆ 12.3 Pattern: Subject – Verb – Direct Object

◯ In your Writer's Journal, copy these sentences. Analyze each sentence by marking the simple subject (who or what the sentence is about) with a single underline, and the verb or verb phrase with a double underline. Write DO over the direct object. Then diagram the sentence. Refer to *Sentence Sense* as needed. When you diagram, you may just ignore any additional words in the sentence which are not the simple subject, the verb, or the direct object.[12]

1. The sun lighted the field.

2. Bruce addressed his heralds.

3. The peas hurt the Princess.

4. I see the spears.

5. The Father untied the bundle.

Writer's Journal

---

12. Students who have completed *Fable & Song* may diagram all the words in the sentence if they prefer.

Eloquent Expression

NOUNS IN YOUR WRITING

In Lesson 1, we worked with synonyms and antonyms very generally. In this lesson, we will specifically consider how to use these in retellings. Any time you write, nouns and verbs are the most important word choices you will make. Clear, descriptive nouns and strong, fitting verbs should be your first concern as you choose the words you will use to retell a story. This lesson is a brief review from *Fable & Song*, where we worked quite a bit with nouns and verbs in composition. As we progress through *Bards & Poets I*, we will be adding to this concept with more specific grammar terms.

SENTENCE STYLE – COPIA OF WORDS: NOUNS

Aesop's fable "The Blacksmith and His Dog" could be written like this—

> A Blacksmith had a little Dog, which used to sleep when the dog's blacksmith was at work, but the dog was very wide awake indeed when it was time for meals. One day the blacksmith pretended to be disgusted at this, and when the blacksmith had thrown the dog a bone as usual, the blacksmith said, "What on earth is the good of a lazy dog like you? When the blacksmith is hammering away at the blacksmith's anvil, the dog just curls up and goes to sleep: but no sooner does the blacksmith stop for a mouthful of food than the dog wakes up and wags the dog's tail to be fed."

but instead, the translator made it much more interesting:

> A Blacksmith had a little Dog, which used to sleep when his master was at work, but he was very wide awake indeed when it was time for meals. One day his master pretended to be disgusted at this, and when he had thrown him a bone as usual, he said, "What on earth is the good of a lazy cur like you? When I am hammering away at my anvil, you just curl up and go to sleep: but no sooner do I stop for a mouthful of food than you wake up and wag your tail to be fed."

The words *blacksmith* and *master* both refer to the same person, and the words *dog* and *cur* refer to the same animal. You can also see that instead of saying *the dog* over and over, the author also uses the pronouns *he* and *his*. The author's use of the noun substitutes *cur*, *he*, and *his* keep the story from sounding repetitive.

Find substitutes for the nouns listed below from "The Real Princess." For each noun in the list:

- List all the other nouns and pronouns used to refer to the same thing in the story.
- List more nouns and pronouns that could be substituted, keeping the context in mind. Check a thesaurus for synonyms. For a person, consider his or her moral character in choosing synonyms.

1. Princess 2. bed

Classical Composition

EDITOR'S PEN – FINE FOCUS: WORDS

The final checks dwell on the details of your word usage. As you work through this list with each retelling, compile for yourself a personal editing checklist to correct particular errors you commonly make. None of us ever outgrow our need for editing!

Editor's Pen – Fine Focus: Words

✓ Word choices varied; word meanings clear
- Verbs: *strong, fitting*
- Nouns: *clear, descriptive*
- Dialogue: *dialogue tags varied if appropriate*

✓ Correct spelling
✓ Final read-through

A. Read aloud your most recent version. Identify changes you need to make with the Editor's Pen checklist. Mark these on your print copy.

B. Transfer all additions and corrections from your print copy to the computer file. Print this final version and file it in your binder along with your other versions.

Commonplace

Commonplace
Book

POETRY

Session three of three commonplace sessions for this lesson. Literary selection: "Robert Bruce's March to Bannockburn."

 Set your timer and begin copying. When you finish, check your work carefully against the original for accuracy.

Lesson 4.5

Prose & Poetry

RHYME AND METER

Read and enjoy a few poems in your poetry anthology. Identify the rhyme schemes of several. Read one or two poems aloud with expression and proper pauses. Pause at punctuation, but not necessarily at the ends of lines. See if you can find another poem with iambic meter. To test this, try to read the poem aloud with this rhythm: da DUM da DUM da DUM . . .

Writer's
Journal

 Choose a rhyming poem in your anthology. Determine its rhyme scheme.

- In your Writer's Journal, write the title of the poem and the author. Make note of its rhyme scheme.
- Write the rhyming words from the poem in two lists: one list for those spelled the same, and one list for those spelled differently.
- Choose one of the rhyming words from the spelled differently list, and try to come up with several additional rhymes. Look especially for varied spellings.

Language Logic

GRAMMAR
FLASHCARDS

GRAMMAR TERMS & DEFINITIONS

 Ask your teacher to quiz you with the grammar flashcards. Alternately, use the test feature in Cottage Press *Bards & Poets I* Quizlet Classroom for an online or printed quiz for Lesson 4.

DICTATION: POETRY

Writer's Journal

Work in your Writer's Journal. Write as your teacher dictates a passage to you from your Commonplace Book. When you are done, check your work carefully, word by word, against the original. Check for accurate spelling, capitalization, and punctuation.

Eloquent Expression

RHYMING WORDS

Writer's Journal

Do these exercises in your Writer's Journal.

A. Read "Robert Bruce's March to Bannockburn" aloud once more.

B. List pairs of rhyming words in the poem spelled the same.

C. List pairs of rhyming words in the poem spelled differently.

D. Write several other words that rhyme with *chains*. At least one of them should have an ending that is spelled differently.

Classical Composition

POETRY

John Bunyan, in his classic work, *The Pilgrim's Progress*, ends each chapter with a few rhyming lines wrapping up the action and often commenting on its moral or spiritual significance. In the spirit of Bunyan, then, complete this creative assignment.

Writer's Journal

In your Writer's Journal, write two to four rhyming lines that summarize the action of "The True Princess." If you wish, include a poetic moral at the end. Consider including them at the end of your retelling as a brief summary of the story. You may find it easiest to imitate a few lines of the poetic selection for this lesson or a previous lesson.

NARRATIVE RETELLING – FINAL DRAFT

◉ Read over the final version of your retelling one last time and make any needed changes. Save it on your computer; print and file with all the other drafts in your writing binder.

Commonplace

FROM YOUR READING

Find selections in a book or poem to add to your Commonplace Book. Include the name of the book or poem, properly formatted. Label the entry with the grammar or poetry feature or as a favorite passage. Aim for a minimum of three entries, with at least one from each category.

Commonplace Book

◉ Grammar Features (choose any)

- ◆ A sentence that has an interesting or descriptive noun
- ◆ A sentence that has a strong and fitting verb
- ◆ An interesting dialogue tag (add to your Dialogue Tags list)
- ◆ An interrogative, exclamatory, or imperative sentence

◉ Poetry Features (choose any)

- ◆ Rhyme (note name of the rhyme scheme)
- ◆ Iambic meter (note name of the meter)

◉ Favorite Passage: Add at least one passage of one to three sentences or several lines of poetry that captured your attention in your reading this week. It may be something you found beautiful, thought-provoking, funny, or interesting.

☙

A Clever Slave

from Fifty Famous People by James Baldwin

A long time ago there lived a poor slave whose name was Aesop. He was a small man with a large head and long arms. His face was white, but very homely. His large eyes were bright and snappy.

When Aesop was about twenty years old his master lost a great deal of money and was obliged to sell his slaves. To do this, he had to take them to a large city where there was a slave market.

The city was far away, and the slaves must walk the whole distance. A number of bundles were made up for them to carry. Some of these bundles contained the things they would need on the road; some contained clothing; and some contained goods which the master would sell in the city.

"Choose your bundles, boys," said the master. "There is one for each of you."

Aesop at once chose the largest one. The other slaves laughed and said he was foolish. But he threw it upon his shoulders and seemed well satisfied. The next day, the laugh was the other way. For the bundle which he had chosen had contained the food for the whole party. After all had eaten three meals from it, it was very much lighter. And before the end of the journey Aesop had nothing to carry, while the other slaves were groaning under their heavy loads.

"Aesop is a wise fellow," said his master. "The man who buys him must pay a high price."

A very rich man, whose name was Xanthus,[1] came to the slave market to buy a servant. As the slaves stood before him he asked each one to tell what kind of work he could do. All were eager to be bought by Xanthus because they knew he would be a kind master. So each one boasted of his skill in doing some sort of labor. One was a fine gardener; another could take care of horses; a third was a good cook; a fourth could manage a household.

"And what can you do, Aesop?" asked Xanthus.

"Nothing," he answered.

"Nothing? How is that?"

"Because, since these other slaves do everything, there is nothing left for me to perform," said Aesop.

This answer pleased the rich man so well that he bought Aesop at once, and took him to his home on the island of Samos.

In Samos the little slave soon became known for his wisdom and courage. He often amused his master and his master's friends by telling droll fables about birds and beasts that could talk. They saw that all these fables taught some great truth, and they wondered how Aesop could have thought of them.

Many other stories are told of this wonderful slave. His master was so much pleased with him that he gave him his freedom. Many great men were glad to call him their friend, and even kings asked his advice and were amused by his fables.

CR

Lesson 5.1

Prose & Poetry

A LOOK AT LITERARY ELEMENTS IN THE NARRATIVE

1 Read
- Listen carefully as your teacher reads the selection aloud. **Delight** in the story.

2 Inquire
- Does the **title** give any hint as to the content or message of the story? If this story was published by the author in a larger book or an anthology, does that title give any hint?
- Discuss the meaning of these words in the context of the story: *homely, obliged, bundle, foolish, wise, boasted, droll,* and any unfamiliar words.

3 Observe the Content
- **Setting** When and where does this story take place?
- **Characters** Who is (are) the main character(s) in this story?
- **Conflict** What is the main problem or crisis for the character(s)?
- **Resolution** Is the problem solved? If so, how? If not, why not?

4 Investigate the Context

For biographical information on Aesop, please see Lesson 1. James Baldwin (1841-1925) was a largely self-educated teacher and school superintendent in Indiana. He loved the great stories of the Western tradition, and he wanted his students to love them too. Over the course of his lifetime he either edited or wrote more than fifty volumes, most of which were retellings of the best stories from literature and history for young people. These were standard fare in United States schoolrooms for many years. In fact, for several decades during the twentieth century, more than half of the books used in schools had been either edited or written by him. "A Clever Slave" is Baldwin's retelling of a story from the life of Aesop.

5 **Connect the Thoughts**
   ◆ Does this story remind you of other stories with similar plots, messages, or characters?
   ◆ Does this story remind you of any fables?
   ◆ Does this story remind you of any proverbs or other well-known quotations? If so, enter these in your Commonplace Book.

Commonplace Book

6 **Profit and Delight**
   ◆ **Delight** What are the sources of delight in this story?
   ◆ **Wisdom** What wisdom does this story furnish?
   ◆ **Read** the narrative aloud to your teacher with expression and with proper pauses.
   ◆ **Record** in your Book of Centuries: James Baldwin.

Language Logic

GRAMMAR FLASHCARDS

GRAMMAR TERMS & DEFINITIONS

🏵 Review all flashcards according to tabs.

GRAMMAR PRACTICE AND REVIEW

🏵 In your Writer's Journal, copy these sentences. Analyze each sentence by marking the simple subject (who or what the sentence is about) with a single underline, and the verb or verb phrase with a double underline. Write D.O. over the direct object, if there is one in the sentence. Then diagram the sentence. Refer to *Sentence Sense* as needed. When you diagram, you may just ignore any additional words in the sentence which are not the simple subject, the verb, or the direct object.[2]

Writer's Journal

1. The slave was named Aesop.

2. The slaves must walk.

3. Bundles were made.

4. Aesop chose a bundle.

5. Aesop told fables.

2. Students who have completed *Fable & Song* may diagram all the words in the sentence.

Eloquent Expression

COPIA OF WORDS: VOCABULARY STUDY

Writer's Journal

Conduct a vocabulary study for "A Clever Slave."

A. Choose at least two unfamiliar words to study. If you need suggestions, see the list under **Inquire** in Literary Elements above. Work in your Writer's Journal.

B. Complete Vocabulary Study steps A-G for each word (see Appendix).

Commonplace

NARRATIVE

Commonplace Book

Session one of three commonplace sessions for this lesson. Literary selection: "The Clever Slave."

 Set your timer and begin copying. When you finish, check your work carefully, word by word, against the original.

Lesson 5.2

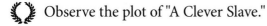

Prose & Poetry

NARRATIVE PLOT OBSERVATION

Observe the plot of "A Clever Slave."

◆ Place short pencil marks on the narrative (copied below) to divide the plot into a series of action.

A long time ago there lived a poor slave whose name was Aesop. He was a small man with a large head and long arms. His face was white, but very homely. His large eyes were bright and snappy.

When Aesop was about twenty years old his master lost a great deal of money and was obliged to sell his slaves. To do this, he had to take them to a large city where there was a slave market.

The city was far away, and the slaves must walk the whole distance. A number of bundles were made up for them to carry. Some of these bundles contained the things they would need on the road; some contained clothing; and some contained goods which the master would sell in the city.

"Choose your bundles, boys," said the master. "There is one for each of you."

Aesop at once chose the largest one. The other slaves laughed and said he was foolish. But he threw it upon his shoulders and seemed well satisfied. The next day, the laugh was the other way. For the bundle which he had chosen had contained the food for the whole party. After all had eaten three meals from it, it was very much lighter. And before the end of the journey Aesop had nothing to carry, while the other slaves were groaning under their heavy loads.

"Aesop is a wise fellow," said his master. "The man who buys him must pay a high price."

A very rich man, whose name was Xanthus, came to the slave market to buy a servant. As the slaves stood before him he asked each one to tell what kind of work he could do. All were eager to be bought by Xanthus because they knew he would be a kind master. So each one boasted of his skill in doing some sort of labor. One was a fine gardener; another could take care of horses; a third was a good cook; a fourth could manage a household.

"And what can you do, Aesop?" asked Xanthus.

"Nothing," he answered.

"Nothing? How is that?"

"Because, since these other slaves do everything, there is nothing left for me to perform," said Aesop.

This answer pleased the rich man so well that he bought Aesop at once, and took him to his home on the island of Samos.

In Samos the little slave soon became known for his wisdom and courage. He often amused his master and his master's friends by telling droll fables about birds and beasts that could talk. They saw that all these fables taught some great truth, and they wondered how Aesop could have thought of them.

Many other stories are told of this wonderful slave. His master was so much pleased with him that he gave him his freedom. Many great men were glad to call him their friend, and even kings asked his advice and were amused by his fables.

Writer's Journal

◆ In your Writer's Journal, write a short outline to capture the **plot** (sequence of actions) of this narrative. For each action you marked on the selection, write a few words or phrases.

Language Logic

THE ADJECTIVE

◎ Read and discuss these lessons in *Sentence Sense* with your teacher as indicated below.

     I. Etymology: The Adjective

         ◆ 4.0A Oral Lesson

         ◆ 4.1 Adjective Definition

     V. Exercises

         ◆ Oral exercise: Identify the adjectives in *Harvey's* 55, sentences 1, 2, 8, and 12. Tell which noun each adjective modifies.

◎ Add this flashcard to your box behind the Daily Tab, and begin to memorize it. Review all flashcards according to tabs.

GRAMMAR FLASHCARDS

       ◆ Adjective

Classical Composition

PLOT OBSERVATION: ORAL NARRATION

 Without reading "The Clever Slave" again, retell the **plot** orally to your teacher. Refer to your outline if needed.

Commonplace

NARRATIVE

Session two of three commonplace sessions for this lesson. Literary selection: "The Clever Slave."

 Set your timer and begin copying. When you finish, check your work carefully, word by word, against the original. Check spelling, capitalization, and punctuation for accuracy.

Commonplace Book

Lesson 5.3

Language Logic

ADJECTIVE CLASSES

Read and discuss these lessons in *Sentence Sense* with your teacher as indicated below.

I. Etymology: The Adjective
- ◆ 4.0B Oral Lesson
- ◆ 4.2A Adjective Classes

V. Exercises
- ◆ Oral exercise: For each adjective you identified in *Harvey's* 55, sentences 1, 2, 8, and 12, tell whether it is descriptive or definitive. The key to distinguishing between definitive and descriptive adjectives is determining which of the adjective questions is being answered. Learn those questions well!

Add this flashcard to your box behind the Daily Tab, and begin to memorize it. Review all flashcards according to tabs.

GRAMMAR FLASHCARDS

◆ Adjective Classes

Eloquent Expression

SENTENCE STYLE REVIEW

Writer's Journal

❁ Copy this sentence into your Writer's Journal, and then paraphrase it as each of the other classifications. Replace at least three words with synonyms and negated antonyms.

A very rich man, whose name was Xanthus, came to the slave market to buy a servant.

❁ Copy this sentence into your Writer's Journal, and then rewrite it two times, varying the dialogue tags and placement in each one. Replace at least two words with synonyms and/or negated antonyms.

"And what can you do, Aesop?" asked Xanthus.

Classical Composition

NARRATIVE RETELLING – FIRST DRAFT

You will have two sessions to work on this retelling. Begin here, and plan to finish in Lesson 5.4. As you write your retelling, do your best to use proper grammar and spelling, but keep in mind that you will have opportunity to edit before you finalize it.

❁ Retell "A Clever Slave" in writing, keeping the same characters, setting, and sequence of action. Refer to your outline if needed, but do not review the original narrative before you write. Include a heading, properly formatted (Refer back to Lesson 5. 5 as needed.)

Writer's Journal

Lesson 5.4

Language Logic

GRAMMAR TERMS & DEFINITIONS
◊ Review all flashcards according to tabs.

SENTENCE DIAGRAMMING: ADJECTIVES
◊ Read and discuss the following sections in *Sentence Sense* with your teacher.

III. Sentence Diagrammming: Modifiers
- ◆ 13.1 Adjectives *Skip the second sentence and its explanation. We will come back to that when we study linking verbs in Lesson 6.*

◊ In your Writer's Journal, copy these sentences. Analyze each sentence by marking the simple subject (who or what the sentence is about) with a single underline, and the verb or verb phrase with a double underline. Write D.O. over the direct object. Then diagram the sentence. Refer to *Sentence Sense* as needed. You should be able to diagram each word in the sentence now.

1. The poor slaves carried the heavy bundles.

2. Wise Aesop had a lighter bundle.

3. Aesop gave a clever answer.

4. This answer pleased the rich man.

5. The droll fables express wonderful truths.

Writer's Journal

Eloquent Expression

SENTENCE STYLE – COPIA OF WORDS: ADJECTIVES

You may also wish to add adjectives to bring additional clarity and description to your sentences. Make sure that they fit the context of the story. For example, a fox would not generally be a kind and compassionate animal who wants to be friends with the chickens.

If you wish to describe a character, think about what the character looks like. Consider how he or she is feeling, and what kind of moral character he or she has. Here are a few questions you might ask yourself:

- How big or small is he? Is she young or old? Is he clean or dirty?
- Is she angry, overjoyed, nervous, hesitant, quiet, bossy, sweet?
- Is he prideful, foolish, wise, grateful, careful, heedless, courageous?

Once you have come up with a few adjectives, check the dictionary for possible synonyms for those adjectives. A synonym is a word that has the same, or close to the same, meaning. Most dictionaries have a list of synonyms at the end of each entry.

Find substitutes for nouns from "A Clever Slave" for the nouns listed below. Also find adjectives you could pair with the nouns you have chosen. For each noun:

Writer's Journal

- List all the other nouns and pronouns used to refer to the same thing in the fable.
- List more nouns and pronouns that could be substituted, keeping the context in mind. Check a thesaurus for synonyms. For a person, consider his or her moral character in choosing synonyms.
- List any adjectives used to describe these nouns in the selection, then list others that fit the context of the fable. Check a thesaurus for synonyms.
- Write down several of your favorite adjective-noun combinations.

    1. Aesop   2. bundle

For each of the following verbs from "A Clever Slave":

- List several substitutions that fit the context. Make your verbs strong and fitting. Use the dictionary for synonyms if you wish.

◆ Paraphrase each sentence, substituting different verbs for the underlined words.

1. The slaves must <u>walk</u> the whole distance.

2. The other slaves <u>laughed</u> and <u>said</u> he was foolish.

3. A very rich man <u>came</u> to the slave market to <u>buy</u> a servant.

4. Even kings <u>asked</u> his advice and were <u>amused</u> by his fables.

Classical Composition

Writer's
Journal

NARRATIVE RETELLING – FINISH FIRST DRAFT

Finish the first draft of your narrative retelling. Review the instructions in Lesson 5.3 as needed.

Commonplace

NARRATIVE

Session three of three commonplace sessions for this lesson. Literary selection: "The Clever Slave."

Commonplace
Book

Set your timer. Begin where you stopped in the last session. When you finish, check your work carefully against the original for accuracy.

Lesson 5.5

Prose & Poetry

POETRY APPRECIATION

Read and enjoy a few poems in your poetry anthology. Identify the rhyme schemes of several. Read one or two poems aloud with expression and proper pauses. Pause at punctuation, but not necessarily at the ends of lines. See if you can find another poem with iambic meter.

Language Logic

GRAMMAR TERMS & DEFINITIONS

Writer's Journal

❦ Ask your teacher to quiz you with the grammar flashcards. Alternately, use the test feature in the Cottage Press *Bards & Poets I* Quizlet Classroom for an online or printed quiz for Lesson 5.

DICTATION: NARRATIVE PASSAGE

❦ Work in your Writer's Journal. Write as your teacher dictates a passage to you from your Commonplace Book. When you are done, check your work carefully, word by word, against the original. Check for accurate spelling, capitalization, and punctuation.

Classical Composition

NARRATIVE RETELLING: TYPE DRAFT

❦ Type your retelling on the computer with spell-check turned off, or ask your writing mentor to type it exactly as you wrote it. Save, print, and file this draft in your writing binder.

Commonplace

FROM YOUR READING

Find selections in a book or poem to add to your Commonplace Book. Include the name of the book or poem, properly formatted. Label the entry with the grammar or poetry feature or as a favorite passage. Aim for a minimum of three entries, with at least one from each category.

Commonplace Book

❦ Grammar Features (choose any)

 ◆ A sentence that has an interesting or descriptive noun

- ◆ A sentence that has a strong and fitting verb
- ◆ A sentence that has a well-chosen adjective
- ◆ A sentence with one or more prepositional phrases
- ◆ An interesting dialogue tag (add to your Dialogue Tags list)
- ◆ An interrogative, exclamatory, or imperative sentence

Poetry Features (choose any)

- ◆ Rhyme (note name of the rhyme scheme)
- ◆ Iambic meter (note name of the meter)

Favorite Passage: Add at least one passage of one to three sentences or several lines of poetry that captured your attention in your reading this week. It may be something you found beautiful, thought-provoking, funny, or interesting.

Lesson 6

_c&_

COLUMBUS

Behind him lay the gray Azores,

Behind the Gates of Hercules;

Before him not the ghost of shores,

Before him only shoreless seas.

The good mate said: "Now we must pray,

For lo! the very stars are gone.

Brave Admiral, speak, what shall I say?"

"Why, say, 'Sail on! sail on! and on!'"

"My men grow mutinous day by day;

My men grow ghastly wan and weak."

The stout mate thought of home; a spray

Of salt wave washed his swarthy cheek.

"What shall I say, brave Admiral, say,

If we sight naught but seas at dawn?"

"Why, you shall say at break of day,

'Sail on! sail on! and on!'"

They sailed and sailed, as winds might blow,

Until at last the blanched mate said:

"Why, now not even God would know

Should I and all my men fall dead.

These very winds forget their way,

For God from these dead seas is gone.

Now speak, brave Admiral, speak and say" --

He said, "Sail on! sail on! and on!"

They sailed. They sailed. Then spake the mate:

"This mad sea shows his teeth tonight.

He curls his lip, he lies in wait,

With lifted teeth, as if to bite!

Brave Admiral, say but one good word:

What shall we do when hope is gone?"

The words leapt like a leaping sword:

"Sail on! sail on! sail on! and on!"

Then pale and worn, he kept his deck,

And peered through darkness. Ah, that night

Of all dark nights! And then a speck --

A light! a light! at last a light!

It grew, a starlit flag unfurled!

It grew to be Time's burst of dawn.

He gained a world; he gave that world

Its grandest lesson: "On! sail on!"

— JOAQUIN MILLER

ℭℜ

Lesson 6.1

Prose & Poetry

A LOOK AT LITERARY ELEMENTS IN THE POEM

1 **Read**

♦ Follow along and listen carefully as the poem is read aloud, OR read it
aloud yourself. Read it at least two or three times. **Delight** in the meter,
the rhyme, and the images.

2 Inquire

- Does the **title** give any hint as to the content or message of the poem?
- Are there any other unfamiliar persons, places, or things mentioned in the poem? Discuss these with your teacher.
- Discuss the meaning of these words in the context of the story: *mutinous, ghastly, wan, naught, blanched,* and any unfamiliar words.
- Was there any part of the poem you did not understand? If so, discuss this with your teacher and classmates.

3 Observe the Content

- **Lyrical Elements**
  - What does the poet describe?
  - Does the poet make you see, hear, smell, taste, or touch anything?
  - Does the poet compare something in the poem to some other thing?
- **Narrative Elements** Does this poem tell a story? If so, observe the
  - **Setting** When and where does this story take place?
  - **Characters** Who is (are) the main character(s) in this story?
  - **Conflict** What is the main problem or crisis for the character(s)?
  - **Resolution** Is the problem solved? If so, how? If not, why not?

4 Investigate the Context

Joaquin Miller (1841-1913), born Cincinnatus Heine, joined the California Gold Rush of the mid-nineteenth century as a boy. He saw first hand the colorful life of the miners and the cowboy culture of the Old West. As a young man, he owned both a Pony Express route and a newspaper.

Somewhere about this time, Cincinnatus made the acquaintance of a famous Mexican bandit named Joaquin (Walkeen) Murietta This boy he regarded with pity as a brave and ill-used young fellow who had been driven to desperation by wrongs inflicted in his own country too brutal to be told. His sympathy was aroused, his love of daring and romance, and he cast away his burdensome appellation of Cincinnatus, replacing it forever with the far more picturesque name of Joaquin.

It was in a little cabin which he had built with his own hands on land given him by the Shasta Chief, that Joaquin first began serious writing. By and by he had saved enough money to cross the ocean to London . . . Presently he caused to be printed with his own hard-earned dollars a thin little volume of poems which fortunately attracted the attention of the famous Rossetti family and their literary friends. They were struck by the breezy freedom of the poet from the west and with their help he brought out a book called *Songs of the Sierras.* Suddenly Miller awakened to find himself famous...So it was England which first recognized Joaquin Miller's genius and he returned to America in the full noontide of his glory, to remain the most unique and picturesque figure in all the field of American letters—tall, broad-shouldered, long-haired and bearded like a pard, always in his big sombrero, his high-top boots, and coat to match. — *My Book House: Halls of Fame,* ed. Olive Beaupré Miller

Joaquin Miller has given to the world some of the best-known and best-loved poetry of the American West. "Columbus" has been a perennial favorite, and has been a staple in poetry anthologies for generations of children.

5 Connect the Thoughts
◆ Does this poem remind you of other poems, or of stories with similar plots, messages, or characters?
◆ Does this poem remind you of any proverbs or other well-known quotations? If so, enter these in your Commonplace Book.

Commonplace Book

6 Profit and Delight
◆ **Delight** What are the sources of delight in this poem?
◆ **Wisdom** What wisdom does this poem furnish?
◆ **Read** the poem aloud to your teacher with expression and with proper pauses.
◆ **Record** in your Book of Centuries: Joaquin Miller, Columbus.
◆ **Memorize** this poem and **recite** it before an audience.

Language Logic

GRAMMAR TERMS & DEFINITIONS
◯ Review all flashcards according to tabs.

GRAMMAR PRACTICE AND REVIEW
◯ In your Writer's Journal, copy these sentences. Analyze each sentence by marking the simple subject (who or what the sentence is about) with a single underline, and the verb or verb phrase with a double underline. Write D.O. over the direct object, if there is one in the sentence. Then diagram the sentence. Refer to *Sentence Sense* as needed. When you diagram, you may just ignore any additional words in the sentence which are not the simple subject, the verb, or the direct object.[1]

1. We must pray.

2. A spray washed his swarthy cheek.

3. These very winds forget their way.

4. He curls his lip.

5. A starlit flag unfurled.

Eloquent Expression

COPIA OF WORDS: VOCABULARY STUDY
◯ Conduct a vocabulary study for "Columbus."

A. Choose at least two unfamiliar words to study. If you need suggestions, see the list under **Inquire** in Literary Elements above. Work in your Writer's Journal.

B. Complete Vocabulary Study steps A-G for each word (see Appendix).

1. Students who have completed *Fable & Song* may diagram all the words in the sentence if they prefer.

Classical Composition

EDITOR'S PEN – THE BIG PICTURE

Remember to save the grammar and spelling errors for later.

⬡ Edit your retelling from Lesson 5:

Editor's Pen – The Big Picture

✔ All important plot elements included
✔ All characters represented correctly
✔ Sequence: *same as the original*
✔ Length: *similar to the original*

A. Read aloud exactly what you have written—not what you THINK you have written! Mark any corrections on your first draft.

B. Next, work through the Big Picture checklist above with your writing mentor.

C. Transfer all additions and corrections from your print copy of the retelling to your file on the computer. Print and file this edited version in your binder along with your marked-up editing copy of the first draft.

Commonplace

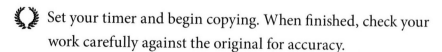

Commonplace Book

POETRY

Session one of three commonplace sessions for this lesson. Literary selection: "Columbus."

⬡ Set your timer and begin copying. When finished, check your work carefully against the original for accuracy.

Lesson 6.2

Prose & Poetry

RHYME SCHEME

Mark the end rhyme in the stanzas below. You will find at least one imperfect rhyming pair where the endings look the same, but sound slightly different.

Behind him lay the gray Azores,

Behind the Gates of Hercules;

Before him not the ghost of shores,

Before him only shoreless seas.

The good mate said: "Now we must pray,

For lo! the very stars are gone.

Brave Admiral, speak, what shall I say?"

"Why, say, 'Sail on! sail on! and on!' "

"My men grow mutinous day by day;

My men grow ghastly wan and weak."

The stout mate thought of home; a spray

Of salt wave washed his swarthy cheek.

"What shall I say, brave Admiral, say,

If we sight naught but seas at dawn?"

"Why, you shall say at break of day,

'Sail on! sail on! and on!' "

They sailed and sailed, as winds might blow,

Until at last the blanched mate said:

"Why, now not even God would know

Should I and all my men fall dead.

These very winds forget their way,

For God from these dead seas is gone.

Now speak, brave Admiral, speak and say" --

He said, "Sail on! sail on! and on!"

They sailed. They sailed. Then spake the mate:

"This mad sea shows his teeth tonight.

He curls his lip, he lies in wait,

With lifted teeth, as if to bite!

Brave Admiral, say but one good word:

What shall we do when hope is gone?"

The words leapt like a leaping sword:

"Sail on! sail on! sail on! and on!"

Then pale and worn, he kept his deck,

And peered through darkness. Ah, that night

Of all dark nights! And then a speck --

A light! a light! at last a light!

It grew, a starlit flag unfurled!

It grew to be Time's burst of dawn.

He gained a world; he gave that world

Its grandest lesson: "On! sail on!"

STANZA FORM

A poet chooses both the words and the form of a poem to communicate the message. A **stanza** is a grouping of verses (lines) in a pattern, which is often repeated throughout the poem. The word **verse** correctly refers to a single line of the poem. Although many people commonly use **stanza** and **verse** interchangeably, this is not technically correct when you are analyzing a poem.

Stanza Forms are named according to the number of lines that are grouped together. For example, if the stanza has two lines, it is called a **couplet**.[2] Most of these are named using Latin derivatives for numbers:

# OF LINES	STANZA FORM
2	Couplet
3	Tercet
4	Quatrain
5	Quintain (also called cinquain or quintet)
6	Sextet (also called sextain, sixain, sexain, sestet, or my favorite—hexastich!)
7	Septet
8	Octave (also called octet)

What is the stanza name for "Columbus"? Review the other poems we have studied thus far. Identify the stanza name of each one.

Language Logic

THE PRONOUN

Read and discuss these lessons in *Sentence Sense* with your teacher as indicated below.

I. Etymology: The Pronoun

- 2.0A Oral Lesson
- 2.0B Oral Lesson
- 2.1 Pronoun Definition
- 2.2 Antecedent #1 *Study the definition only.*

V. Exercises

- Oral exercise: Identify the pronouns in *Harvey's* 65. Tell which noun the pronoun is standing in for (the antecedent).

Move the flashcards that you have mastered backwards in your file system. Leave any that you have not mastered behind the **Daily** tab. Add these flashcards to your box behind the Daily tab, and begin to memorize them:

- Pronoun
- Antecedent

✦ Review all flashcards according to tabs.

Classical Composition

EDITOR'S PEN – ZOOM 5X: PARAGRAPHS

✦ Now that the Big Picture is set, begin to zoom in for a close look at the paragraph(s) in your retelling with your writing mentor.

> ### Editor's Pen – Zoom 5x: Paragraphs
> ✓ Formatting: *proper indentation*
> ✓ Length: *neither too wordy nor too short*
> ✓ Sentence class by use: *effective use*
> ✓ Dialogue: *effective use*

A. Read aloud your most recently edited version. Check each item in the Editor's Pen checklist to identify possible changes. Mark these on your print copy.

B. Transfer all additions and corrections from your print copy to the computer file. Print this version and file it in your binder along with your other versions.

Lesson 6.3

Prose & Poetry

POETIC METER – IAMBIC

In Lesson 4.3, we learned that meter in English poems is usually produced by a pattern of stressed and unstressed syllables. Read the lines below, and pay attention to the stressed syllables that are indicated by the italic type.

> Be *hind* him *lay* the *gray* A *zores*,
> Be *hind* the *Gates* of *Her* cu *les*

Recall that we **scan** poetry by analyzing the stressed and unstressed syllables and naming the patterns these form. Here are the same lines, scanned.

∪　／　∪　／　∪　／　∪　／

Be hind him lay the gray A zores

∪　／　∪　／　∪　／　∪　／

Be hind the Gates of Her cu les

"Columbus" keeps this pattern of unstressed-stressed syllables pretty consistently throughout. This pattern (unstressed-stressed, unstressed-stressed, . . .) is called **iambic meter**.

 Scan these lines by marking each syllable as either stressed (/) or unstressed (∪). Read each line several times until you get a feel for the rhythm. In the second to last line, pronounce and mark the word Admiral with only two syllables: *Ad m'ral*, to keep the iambic meter.

Before him not the ghost of shores,

Before him only shoreless seas.

The good mate said: "Now we must pray,

For lo! the very stars are gone.

Brave Admiral, speak, what shall I say?"

"Why, say, 'Sail on! sail on! and on!' "

Language Logic

SENTENCE DIAGRAMMING: LINKING VERBS

 Read and discuss the following sections in *Sentence Sense* with your teacher.

I. Etymology: The Verb
  ◆ 3.0C Oral Lesson
  ◆ 3.2C Verb Classes by Use: Linking Verbs
III. Sentence Diagrammming: Sentence Patterns
  ◆ 12.4 Pattern: Subject-Verb-Subject Complement

In your Writer's Journal, copy these sentences. Analyze each sentence by marking the simple subject (who or what the sentence is about) with a single underline, and the verb or verb phrase with a double underline. Write DO over a direct object, LV over a linking verb, PA over a predicate adjective, and PN over a predicate nominative. Then diagram the sentence. Refer to *Sentence Sense* as needed. You should be able to diagram each word in the sentence now.

1. The Admiral was brave.

2. My men grow mutinous.

3. The seas seem dead.

4. A speck became a light.

5. The answer was a lesson.

 Add the indicated flashcard behind the Daily tab. Review all flashcards according to tabs.

♦ Linking Verb

Eloquent Expression

FIGURES OF SPEECH

The great Roman orator and teacher Quintilian defined a **figure of speech** as "a form of speech artfully varied" from our usual way of speaking or talking. Virtually all authors and poets use figures of speech. There are hundreds of figures of speech that teachers of rhetoric have classified in dozens of ways. In *Bards & Poets I,* we will study quite a few figures, and you will begin to experiment with these in your writing. Some of these were introduced in *Fable & Song,* and even *Primer One* and *Primer Two,* so they may be familiar to you.

FIGURE OF SPEECH: SIMILE

A **simile** is a figure of speech that directly compares two things of unlike nature using the words *like*, *as*, or *than*. Choosing an appropriate and engaging comparison is the "artful" part; expressing that comparison with the words *like*, *as*, or *than* is the "variation" part.

> His cheeks were like cherries.

> His cheeks were as ruddy as cherries.

> His cheeks were brighter than cherries.

What kind of picture do you see in your mind? In these examples, *his cheek* are compared to *cherries*. These comparisons meet the requirements of a simile:

1. Compares two things of unlike nature (*his cheeks* are made up of flesh and located on his face; *cherries* are a fruit found on a tree).
2. Expresses a direct comparison using the words *like*, *as*, or *than*.

When you see the words *like*, *as*, or *than*, they may be clues that the author or poet is using a simile. Pay attention to the context, though. Not every use of *like*, *as*, or *than* indicates a simile. Consider these non-similes:

> The dog likes his bone. (*Like* is used to express action, not a comparison.)

> The girl is as pretty as her mother. (*Girl* and *mother* have a like nature—they both are people.)

> Israel loved Joseph more than any of his children. (*Joseph* and *children* have a like nature— they both are humans.)

Here are a few examples of simile from literature. Discuss the comparison made by each with your teacher.

> The sagacious animal . . . uttered a deep growl, which sounded from his chest like distant thunder. — Sir Walter Scott, *The Talisman*

> All flesh is as grass. — I Peter 1:24

> Saul and Jonathan . . . were swifter than eagles, they were stronger than lions. — II Samuel 1:23

Look for similes in these selections and list them in your Writer's Journal. Discuss them with your teacher.

- "Columbus"
- "The Real Princess"
- "The Bundle of Sticks"

Classical Composition

EDITOR'S PEN – ZOOM 10X: SENTENCES

Now it is time to zoom in even closer as you check the sentences in your retelling. Work with your writing mentor.

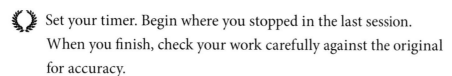

Editor's Pen – Zoom 10x: Sentences
✓ Complete thought expressed
✓ Subject and predicate agree in number
✓ Correct capitalization and punctuation

A. Read aloud your most recent version. Identify changes you need to make with the Editor's Pen checklist. Mark these on your print copy.

B. Transfer all additions and corrections from your print copy to the computer file. Print this final version and file it in your binder along with your other versions.

Commonplace

POETRY

Session two of three commonplace sessions for this lesson. Literary selection: "Columbus."

Set your timer. Begin where you stopped in the last session. When you finish, check your work carefully against the original for accuracy.

Lesson 6.4

Prose & Poetry

POETIC METER – IAMBIC

 Scan these lines by marking each syllable as either stressed (/) or unstressed (∪). Read each line several times until you get a feel for the rhythm. In the first line, pronounce and mark the word *mutinous* with only two syllables: *mu t'nous*, in order to keep the iambic meter.

"My men grow mutinous day by day;

My men grow ghastly wan and weak."

The stout mate thought of home; a spray

Of salt wave washed his swarthy cheek.

"What shall I say, brave Admiral, say,

If we sight naught but seas at dawn?"

"Why, you shall say at break of day,

'Sail on! sail on! and on!' "

Language Logic

GRAMMAR FLASHCARDS

GRAMMAR TERMS & DEFINITIONS
  Review all flashcards according to tabs.

VERBS – PERSON, NUMBER, AND TENSE
  Read and discuss the following sections in *Sentence Sense* with your teacher.

I. Etymology: The Verb
- ◆ 3.6A Verb Properties – Person and Number
- ◆ 3.7A Verb Property – Tense

V. Exercises
- ◆ Oral exercise: Identify the verbs in *Harvey's* 132, #1, 5, 7, 9, 14, 15, 16, 17, 18. For each verb, name the person, number, and tense.

SENTENCE DIAGRAMMING

In your Writer's Journal, copy these sentences. Analyze each sentence by marking the simple subject (who or what the sentence is about) with a single underline, and the verb or verb phrase with a double underline. Write D.O. over the direct object, or L.V. over the linking verb; write PA over a predicate adjective and PN over a predicate nominative. Then diagram the sentence. Refer to *Sentence Sense* as needed.

1. You should be diligent.

2. Men may be imprudent.

3. I had seen the stars.

4. You are the people.

5. Brave Columbus discovered the New World.

Writer's Journal

Tell your teacher the person and number of each verb or verb phrase in the sentences which you just diagrammed. Tell the tense for sentences #3-5.

Eloquent Expression

SENTENCE STYLE REVIEW

Copy this sentence into your Writer's Journal, and then paraphrase it as each of the other classifications. Replace at least three words with synonyms and/or negated antonyms.

Writer's Journal

This answer pleased the rich man so well that he bought Aesop at once, and took him to his home on the island of Samos.

Copy this sentence into your Writer's Journal, and then rewrite it two times, varying the dialogue tags and placement in each one. Replace at least two words with synonyms and/or negated antonyms.

"Since these other slaves do everything, there is nothing left for me to perform," said Aesop.

Classical Composition

EDITOR'S PEN – FINE FOCUS: WORDS

The final checks dwell on the details of your word usage. Continue to compile your personal editing checklist to use in editing all of your work across the curriculum.

Editor's Pen – Fine Focus: Words

✓ Word choices varied; word meanings clear
- Verbs: *strong, fitting*
- Nouns: *clear, descriptive; appropriate adjectives if needed*
- Dialogue: *dialogue tags varied if appropriate*

✓ Correct spelling

✓ Final read-through

A. Read aloud your most recent version. Identify changes you need to make with the Editor's Pen checklist. Mark these on your print copy.

B. Transfer all additions and corrections from your print copy to the computer file. Print this final version and file it in your binder along with your other versions.

Commonplace

POETRY

Session three of three commonplace sessions for this lesson. Literary selection: "Columbus."

Commonplace Book

 Set your timer and begin copying. When you finish, check your work carefully against the original for accuracy.

Lesson 6.5

Prose & Poetry

POETRY APPRECIATION

Read and enjoy a few poems in your poetry anthology. Try to find one of each kind of stanza. See if you can find another poem with iambic meter. Read one or two poems aloud with expression and proper pauses. Pause at punctuation, but not necessarily at the ends of lines. Look for similes in the poems you read, and make note of any you find for a future Commonplace Book entry. Finally, choose a rhyming poem in your anthology. Determine its rhyme scheme.

Writer's Journal

- In your Writer's Journal, write the title of the poem and the author. Make note of its rhyme scheme and stanza form.
- Write the rhyming words from the poem in two lists: one list for those spelled the same, and one list for those spelled differently.
- Choose one of the rhyming words from the spelled differently list, and try to come up with several additional rhymes. Look especially for varied spellings.

Language Logic

GRAMMAR TERMS & DEFINITIONS

GRAMMAR FLASHCARDS

Ask your teacher to quiz you with the grammar flashcards. Alternately, use the test feature in the Cottage Press *Bards & Poets I* Quizlet Classroom for an online or printed quiz for Lesson 6.

DICTATION: POETRY

Writer's Journal

Work in your Writer's Journal. Write as your teacher dictates a passage to you from your Commonplace Book. When you are done, check your work carefully, word by word, against the original. Check for accurate spelling, capitalization, and punctuation.

Eloquent Expression

RHYMING WORDS

Writer's Journal

🏵 Do these exercises in your Writer's Journal.

A. Read "Columbus" aloud once more.

B. List pairs of rhyming words in the poem spelled the same.

C. List pairs of rhyming words in the poem spelled differently.

D. Write several other words that rhyme with *dawn*. At least one of them should have an ending that is spelled differently.

Classical Composition

Writer's Journal

POETRY

🏵 In your Writer's Journal, write two to four rhyming lines that summarize the action of "The Clever Slave." If you wish, include a poetic **moral** at the end. Consider including them at the end of your retelling as a brief summary of the story. You may find it easiest to imitate the rhyme and meter of a few lines of the poetic selection for this lesson or a previous lesson.

NARRATIVE RETELLING – FINAL DRAFT

🏵 Read over the final version of your retelling one last time and make any needed changes. Save it on your computer; print and file with all the other drafts in your writing binder.

Commonplace

Commonplace Book

FROM YOUR READING

Find selections in a book or poem to add to your Commonplace Book. Include the name of the book or poem, properly formatted. Label the entry with the grammar or poetry feature, the figure of speech, or as a favorite passage. Aim for a minimum of three entries, with at least one from each category.

❂ Grammar Features (choose any)

- ◆ A sentence that has an interesting or descriptive noun
- ◆ A sentence that has a strong and fitting verb
- ◆ A sentence that has a well-chosen adjective
- ◆ A sentence that has a vivid adverb
- ◆ An interesting dialogue tag (add to your Dialogue Tags list)
- ◆ An interrogative, exclamatory, or imperative sentence

❂ Figure of Speech (choose any)

- ◆ A simile

❂ Poetry Features (choose any)

- ◆ Rhyme (note name of the rhyme scheme)
- ◆ Iambic meter (note name of the meter)
- ◆ Stanza (note name of stanza form)

❂ Favorite Passage: Add at least one passage of one to three sentences or several lines of poetry that captured your attention in your reading this week. It may be something you found beautiful, thought-provoking, funny, or interesting.

ॐ

The Sword of Damocles
from Fifty Famous Stories **by James Baldwin**

There was once a king whose name was Dionysius. He was so unjust and cruel that he won for himself the name of tyrant. He knew that almost everybody hated him, and so he was always in dread lest some one should take his life.

But he was very rich, and he lived in a fine palace where there were many beautiful and costly things, and he was waited upon by a host of servants who were always ready to do his bidding. One day a friend of his, whose name was Damocles, said to him,—

"How happy you must be! You have here everything that any man could wish."

"Perhaps you would like to change places with me," said the tyrant.

"No, not that, O king!" said Damocles; "but I think, that, if I could only have your riches and your pleasures for one day, I should not want any greater happiness."

"Very well," said the tyrant. "You shall have them."

And so, the next day, Damocles was led into the palace, and all the servants were bidden to treat him as their master. He sat down at a table in the banquet hall, and rich foods were placed before him. Nothing was wanting that could give him pleasure. There were costly wines, and beautiful flowers, and rare perfumes, and delightful music. He rested himself among soft cushions, and felt that he was the happiest man in all the world.

Then he chanced to raise his eyes toward the ceiling. What was it that was dangling above him, with its point almost touching his head? It was a sharp sword, and it was hung by only a single horse-hair. What if the hair should break? There was danger every moment that it would do so.

The smile faded from the lips of Damocles. His face became ashy pale. His hands trembled. He wanted no more food; he could drink no more wine; he took no more delight in the music. He longed to be out of the palace, and away, he cared not where.

"What is the matter?" said the tyrant.

"That sword! that sword!" cried Damocles. He was so badly frightened that he dared not move.

"Yes," said Dionysius, "I know there is a sword above your head, and that it may fall at any moment. But why should that trouble you? I have a sword over my head all the time. I am every moment in dread lest something may cause me to lose my life."

"Let me go," said Damocles. "I now see that I was mistaken, and that the rich and powerful are not so happy as they seem. Let me go back to my old home in the poor little cottage among the mountains."

And so long as he lived, he never again wanted to be rich, or to change places, even for a moment, with the king.

☙

Lesson 7.1

Prose & Poetry

A LOOK AT LITERARY ELEMENTS IN THE NARRATIVE

1 Read

◆ Listen carefully as your teacher reads the selection aloud. **Delight** in the story.

2 Inquire

◆ Does the **title** give any hint as to the content or message of the story? If this story was published by the author in a larger book or an anthology,

does that title give any hint?

◆ Discuss the meaning of these words in the context of the story: *dread, pleasures, bidden, wanting, rare, ashy,* and any unfamiliar words.

3 Observe the Content
◆ **Setting** When and where does this story take place?

◆ **Characters** Who is (are) the main character(s) in this story?

◆ **Conflict** What is the main problem or crisis for the character(s)?

◆ **Resolution** Is the problem solved? If so, how? If not, why not?

◆ **Figures** Can you identify any examples of simile in this narrative?

4 Investigate the Context
For biographical information on James Baldwin, please see Lesson 5.1. This is his retelling of a story told by Cicero, the great first century A.D. orator, who was probably retelling it from an earlier Greek source.

5 Connect the Thoughts
◆ Does this story remind you of other stories with similar plots, messages, or characters?

◆ Does this story remind you of any fables?

◆ Does this story remind you of any proverbs or other well-known quotations? If so, enter these in your Commonplace Book.

Commonplace Book

6 Profit and Delight
◆ **Delight** What are the sources of delight in this story?

◆ **Wisdom** What wisdom does this story furnish?

◆ **Read** the narrative aloud to your teacher with expression and with proper pauses.

◆ **Record** in your Book of Centuries: Dionysius and Damocles (4th century B.C. Sicily)

THEON'S SIX NARRATIVE ELEMENTS

You have probably heard of the questions that every newspaper reporter is taught to answer in a news story. They are often called the "Five W's and an H": **Who?**, **What?**, **Where?**, **When?**, **Why?**, and **How?** Rudyard Kipling, who started his career as a newspaper reporter, called these questions his "Six Honest Serving-Men"[1]:

I keep six honest serving-men

(They taught me all I knew);

1. Poem from "The Elephant's Story" in *Just So Stories*. Go there and read the rest of this delightful poem!

Their names are What and Why and When

And How and Where and Who.

I send them over land and sea,

I send them east and west...

Nothing is new under the sun! Aelius Theon was a Greek orator and teacher in the first century A.D. who had the same idea, only he used different words. He said every narrative will include six elements: **Person**, **Action**, **Place**, **Time**, **Manner**, and **Cause**. These line up perfectly with the "Five W's and an H":

Person	Who?
Action	What?
Place	Where?
Time	When?
Manner	How?
Cause	Why?

For each of these six elements, Theon developed questions to help his students thoroughly investigate a narrative. We have simplified these into a working list for *Bards & Poets I*. Later, in *Bards & Poets II*, you will study the full list. To keep from being repetitious, we will refer to these from now on as **Theon's Six**. In this lesson, we will study the first four.

The first two are **Person** and **Action**. Notice that there are several questions for Person. These will not all be addressed in every narrative. The list of questions is simply meant to get you thinking and to remind you of all the possibilities for that element.

PERSON   Who are the characters in this narrative? Make notes of anything significant you learn about each one, such as:
- ✓ Place of birth and parents or ancestors
- ✓ Physical appearance
- ✓ Personality
- ✓ Education
- ✓ Age
- ✓ Situation in life (social standing, job, etc.)

ACTION   What happened? List the actions in the narrative.

The third and fourth elements of Theon's Six, **Place** and **Time**, are often referred to as the **setting** of the story. You will note that these two elements relate to the narrative as a whole, as well as to the individual actions within the narrative.

PLACE   Where does this narrative (or action) take place? Inside or outside? Country,
               continent, planet, universe? Does the author describe its physical appearance?

TIME   When does this narrative (or action) take place?
               ✓ Date
               ✓ Season or time of year
               ✓ Time of day
               ✓ Other things happening in the same place at the same time
               ✓ Other things happening in other places at the same time

Notice that there are several questions for each of these. Again, this list of questions is simply meant to get you thinking and to remind you of all the possibilities for that element.

Nota Bene: The entire simplified list of questions for all of Theon's Six Narrative Elements is in the Appendix for easy reference.

Writer's Journal

Discuss Person, Action, Time, and Place with your teacher. Then, in your Writer's Journal, turn back two pages before the *Synonyms for Said* chart (Lesson 2.3). Title the page *Theon's Six Narrative Elements*. You will complete this entire chart in upcoming lessons, but for now, copy the sections for Person, Action, Place, and Time from the text above, including all of the questions for each. Leave the rest of this page blank until you are instructed to copy the other elements.

Language Logic

GRAMMAR FLASHCARDS

GRAMMAR TERMS & DEFINITIONS
Review all flashcards according to tabs.

GRAMMAR PRACTICE AND REVIEW
In your Writer's Journal, copy these sentences. Analyze each sentence by marking the simple subject (who or what the sentence is about) with a single underline, and the verb or verb phrase with a double underline. Write DO over the direct object, or LV over the linking verb; write PA over a predicate adjective and PN over a predicate nominative. Then diagram the sentence. Refer to *Sentence Sense* as needed.

1. Dionysius was an unjust tyrant.

2. You have everything.

3. He was the happiest man.

4. The face became pale.

5. The sword had frightened him.

Writer's Journal

Eloquent Expression

COPIA OF WORDS: VOCABULARY STUDY

Conduct a vocabulary study for "The Sword of Damocles."

A. Choose at least two unfamiliar words to study. If you need suggestions, see the list under **Inquire** in Literary Elements above. Work in your Writer's Journal.

B. Complete Vocabulary Study steps A-G for each word (see Appendix).

Writer's Journal

Commonplace

NARRATIVE

Session one of three commonplace sessions for this lesson. Literary selection: "The Sword of Damocles."

Set your timer and begin copying. When you finish, check your work carefully, word by word, against the original.

Commonplace Book

Lesson 7.2

Prose & Poetry

PLOT OBSERVATION — PERSON, ACTION, PLACE, AND TIME

Read the narrative below taken from from "The Frogs Desiring a King" in *Aesop's Fables* by Joseph Jacobs. Then, study the example observation using the first four elements of Theon's Six.

The Frogs were living as happy as could be in a marshy swamp that just suited them; they went splashing about caring for nobody and nobody troubling with them. But some of them thought that this was not right, that they should have a king and a proper constitution, so they determined to send up a petition to Jove to give them what they wanted. "Mighty Jove," they cried, "send unto us a king that will rule over us and keep us in order." Jove laughed at their croaking, and threw down into the swamp a huge Log, which came down with a splash. The Frogs were frightened out of their lives by the commotion made in their midst, and all rushed to the bank to look at the horrible monster; but after a time, seeing that it did not move, one or two of the boldest of them ventured out towards the Log, and even dared to touch it; still it did not move. Then the greatest hero of the Frogs jumped upon the Log and commenced dancing up and down upon it, thereupon all the Frogs came and did the same; and for some time the Frogs went about their business every day without taking the slightest notice of their new King Log lying in their midst. But this did not suit them, so they sent another petition to Jove, and said to him, "We want a real king; one that will really rule over us." Now this made Jove angry, so he sent among them a big Stork that soon set to work gobbling them all up. Then the Frogs repented when it was too late.

Better no rule than cruel rule.

Narrative Observation of "The Frogs Desiring a King"

Person

Frogs – ruled by Jove; some frightened, some bold, some brave
Jove – controls the Frogs and their circumstances

Action

1. The Frogs make a petition to Jove to be given a king and a government

2. Jove first sends them a Log to be their king as a joke

3. The Frogs continue to ask for a real king

4. Finally Jove sends them a Stork as king who proceeds to eat the Frogs all up

Place

in a marshy swamp – not many details

Time

In the (ancient) past – not many details

In your Writer's Journal, write down your own observation of "The Sword of Damocles" using Theon's Six. Use Theon's questions for Person, Action, Place, and Time as a guide, but do not worry if you cannot answer each. Remember they are just there to get you thinking. Under Action, make note of what happens first, second, third, etc.

Language Logic

ADVERBS

Read and discuss these lessons in *Sentence Sense* with your teacher as indicated below.

I. Etymology: The Adverb
   ◆ 5.0 Oral Lesson
   ◆ 5.1A Adverb Definition

V. Exercises
   ◆ Oral exercise: Identify the adverbs in *Harvey's* 132, Sentences 1, 2, 4, 5, 6, 8, 9, 10, 11, 13, 15, 17, and 18. Tell whether the adverb modifies a verb, an adjective, or another adverb.

Move the flashcards that you have mastered backwards in your file system. Leave any that you have not mastered behind the **Daily** tab. Add this flashcard to your box behind the Daily tab, and begin to memorize it:

◆ Adverb

🏵 Review all flashcards according to tabs.

Classical Composition

PLOT OBSERVATION: ORAL NARRATION

🏵 Without reading "The Sword of Damocles" again, retell the **plot** orally to your teacher. Refer to your Theon's Six notes if needed.

Commonplace

NARRATIVE

Commonplace Book

Session two of three commonplace sessions for this lesson. Literary selection: "The Sword of Damocles."

🏵 Set your timer and begin copying. When you finish, check your work carefully, word by word, against the original. Check spelling, capitalization, and punctuation for accuracy.

Lesson 7.3

Language Logic

GRAMMAR TERMS & DEFINITIONS
🏵 Review all flashcards according to tabs.

SENTENCE DIAGRAMMING: ADVERBS

Read and discuss the following sections in *Sentence Sense* with your teacher.

III. Sentence Diagrammming: Modifiers
- ◆ 13.2 Adverbs Which Modify Verbs
- ◆ 13.3 Adverbs Which Modify Adjectives
- ◆ 13.4 Adverbs Which Modify Other Adverbs

In your Writer's Journal, copy these sentences. Analyze each sentence by marking the simple subject (who or what the sentence is about) with a single underline, and the verb or verb phrase with a double underline. Write DO over a direct object, LV over a linking verb, PA over a predicate adjective, and PN over a predicate nominative. Then diagram the sentence. Refer to *Sentence Sense* as needed. You should be able to diagram each word in the sentence now.

1. Cruel Dionysius was very rich.

2. You have here everything.

3. Costly wines were served abundantly.

4. The aghast friend was so badly frightened.

5. Very powerful men are often not so happy.

Writer's Journal

Eloquent Expression

SENTENCE STYLE – VERB COPIA: TENSE

One more way to apply grammar in your writing is to consider a verb's property of **tense** (*Sentence Sense, 3.7B*). For example, a sentence written in present may be changed to past or future tense. This may require some adjustment to the rest of the sentence.

Your letter pleases Erasmus. (present)

Your letter pleased Erasums. (past)

Your letter will please Erasmus. (future)

Your letter has pleased Erasmus. (present perfect)

Your letter had pleased Erasmus. (past perfect)

Your letter will have pleased Erasmus. (future perfect)

Complete these exercises in your Writer's Journal.

Writer's Journal

🏆 Paraphrase these sentences in each of the other five tenses.

1. Damocles sat down at a table.

2. I have a sword over my head.

Classical Composition

NARRATIVE RETELLING – FIRST DRAFT

You will have two sessions to work on this retelling. Begin here, and plan to finish in Lesson 7.4. As you write your retelling, do your best to use proper grammar and spelling, but keep in mind that you will have opportunity to edit before you finalize it.

🏆 Retell "The Sword of Damocles" in writing, keeping the same characters, setting, and sequence of action. Refer to your plot observation of the narrative with Theon's Six, but do not review the original narrative before you write. Include:

Writer's Journal

- ◆ a heading, properly formatted (Refer back to Lesson 5. 5)
- ◆ at least one simile

Lesson 7.4

Language Logic

GRAMMAR FLASHCARDS

GRAMMAR TERMS & DEFINITIONS
🏆 Review all flashcards according to tabs.

SENTENCE DIAGRAMMING: ADVERBS

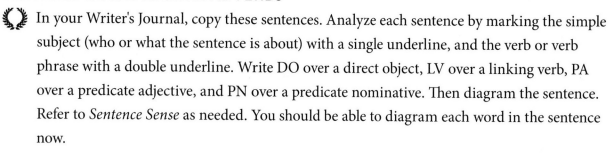 In your Writer's Journal, copy these sentences. Analyze each sentence by marking the simple subject (who or what the sentence is about) with a single underline, and the verb or verb phrase with a double underline. Write DO over a direct object, LV over a linking verb, PA over a predicate adjective, and PN over a predicate nominative. Then diagram the sentence. Refer to *Sentence Sense* as needed. You should be able to diagram each word in the sentence now.

Hints: In sentence #2, *away* is used as an adjective. For sentence #5, you will need to think very carefully about the function of each word in the sentence. You cannot rely on word order as you have been able to do with most sentences we have diagrammed thus far. This will become really important as we diagram more and more sentences taken directly from the selections with little or no change.

1. My men grow ghastly wan.

2. The city was far away.

3. He had finally found a real princess.

4. Far lands seem very near.

5. This they did very easily.

Eloquent Expression

SENTENCE STYLE – COPIA OF WORDS: ADVERBS

Just as adjectives used in a story can give more precise understanding of the nouns we use, so adverbs can bring better understanding of a particular action in a story by helping us see *how?* or *when?* or *to what extent?* or *where?* the action occured.

Use the adverb questions to help you think of appropriate adverbs to use with your verbs:

♦ How was the action done – *angrily, sweetly, nervously, sadly, stealthily*?
♦ When was the action done – *yesterday, earlier, then, now*?
♦ Where was the action done – *above, below, inside, yonder, here, there*?

In your own writing, look at the verbs you have used, and think of appropriate adverbs that could help make the action of your story more clear or interesting. Once you have listed a few adverbs, check the dictionary for possible synonyms for those adverbs.

Writer's
Journal

For each of the following verbs from "The Sword of Damocles":

♦ List several substitutions that fit the context. Make your verbs strong and fitting. Use the dictionary for synonyms if you wish.

♦ Paraphrase the sentence, replacing the verbs with substitutions from your list, and add adverbs to help clarify or intensify the action.

1. He <u>knew</u> that almost everybody hated him.

2. He <u>rested</u> himself among soft cushions.

3. I now <u>see</u> that I <u>was mistaken</u>.

4. He never again <u>wanted</u> to be rich.

Find substitutes for nouns from "The Sword of Damocles." Also find adjectives you could pair with the nouns you have chosen. For each noun in the list below:

♦ List all the other nouns and pronouns used to refer to the same thing in the fable.

♦ List more nouns and pronouns that could be substituted, keeping the context in mind. Check a thesaurus for synonyms. For a person, consider his or her moral character in choosing synonyms.

♦ List any adjectives used to describe these nouns in the selection, then list others that fit the context of the fable. Check a thesaurus for synonyms.

♦ Write down several of your favorite adjective-noun combinations.

1. Damocles   2. sword

Classical Composition

Writer's
Journal

NARRATIVE RETELLING – FINISH FIRST DRAFT

Finish the first draft of your narrative retelling. Review the instructions in Lesson 6.3 as needed.

Commonplace

Commonplace
Book

NARRATIVE

Session three of three commonplace sessions for this lesson. Literary selection: "The Sword of Damocles."

◯ Set your timer. Begin where you stopped in the last session. When you finish, check your work carefully against the original for accuracy.

Lesson 7.5

Prose & Poetry

POETRY APPRECIATION

◯ Read and enjoy a few poems in your poetry anthology. Identify rhyme schemes and stanza forms of one or two. Look for poems with iambic meter. Look for similes in the poems you read, and make note of any you find for a future Commonplace Book entry. Read one or two poems aloud with expression and proper pauses. Pause at punctuation, but not necessarily at the ends of lines.

Language Logic

GRAMMAR TERMS & DEFINITIONS

GRAMMAR
FLASHCARDS

◯ Ask your teacher to quiz you with the grammar flashcards. Alternately, use the test feature in the Cottage Press *Bards & Poets I* Quizlet Classroom for an online or printed quiz for Lesson 7.

DICTATION: NARRATIVE PASSAGE

Writer's
Journal

◯ Work in your Writer's Journal. Write as your teacher dictates a passage to you from your Commonplace Book. When you are done, check your work carefully, word by word, against the original. Check for accurate spelling, capitalization, and punctuation.

Classical Composition

NARRATIVE RETELLING: TYPE DRAFT

⟨⟩ Type your retelling on the computer with spell-check turned off, or ask your writing mentor to type it exactly as you wrote it. Save, print, and file this draft in your writing binder.

Commonplace

FROM YOUR READING

Commonplace Book

Find selections in a book or poem to add to your Commonplace Book. Include the name of the book or poem, properly formatted. Label the entry with the grammar or poetry feature, the figure of speech, or as a favorite passage. Aim for a minimum of three entries, with at least one from each category.

⟨⟩ Grammar Features (choose any)

- ◆ A sentence that has an interesting or descriptive noun, a strong and fitting verb, a well-chosen adjective, and/or a vivid adverb
- ◆ An interesting dialogue tag (add to your Dialogue Tags list)
- ◆ An interrogative, exclamatory, or imperative sentence

⟨⟩ Figure of Speech (choose any)

- ◆ A simile

⟨⟩ Poetry Features (choose any)

- ◆ Rhyme (note name of the rhyme scheme)
- ◆ Iambic meter (note name of the meter)
- ◆ Stanza (note name of stanza form)

⟨⟩ Favorite Passage: Add at least one passage of one to three sentences or several lines of poetry that captured your attention in your reading this week. It may be something you found beautiful, thought-provoking, funny, or interesting.

ℭℛ

JABBERWOCKY

'Twas brillig, and the slithy toves
  Did gyre and gimble in the wabe;
All mimsy were the borogoves,
  And the mome raths outgrabe.

"Beware the Jabberwock, my son
  The jaws that bite, the claws that catch!
Beware the Jubjub bird, and shun
  The frumious Bandersnatch!"

He took his vorpal sword in hand;
  Long time the manxome foe he sought—
So rested he by the Tumtum tree,
  And stood awhile in thought.

And, as in uffish thought he stood,
  The Jabberwock, with eyes of flame,
Came whiffling through the tulgey wood,
  And burbled as it came!

One, two! One, two! And through and through
  The vorpal blade went snicker-snack!
He left it dead, and with its head
  He went galumphing back.

"And hast thou slain the Jabberwock?

Come to my arms, my beamish boy!

O frabjous day! Callooh! Callay!"

He chortled in his joy.

'Twas brillig, and the slithy toves

Did gyre and gimble in the wabe;

All mimsy were the borogoves,

And the mome raths outgrabe.

— LEWIS CARROLL

ᘓ

Lesson 8.1

Prose & Poetry

A LOOK AT LITERARY ELEMENTS IN THE POEM

At first glance, this may seem like a nonsense poem, with so many made-up words. But listen carefully as your teacher reads it aloud with expression. You will hear a clear story being told!

1 Read
- Follow along and listen carefully as the poem is read aloud, OR read it aloud yourself. Read it at least two or three times. **Delight** in the meter, the rhyme, and the images.

2 Inquire
- Does the **title** give any hint as to the content or message of the poem?
- Are there any other unfamiliar persons, places, or things mentioned in the poem? Discuss these with your teacher.
- Though many of the words in the poem were invented, some of them were actually **archaic** (out of use) words. Discuss the meaning of these words in the context of the story: *gyre, gimble, shun, whiffling, burbled, mome,* and any unfamiliar words.

◆ Was there any part of the poem you did not understand? If so, discuss this with your teacher and classmates.

3 Observe the Content

◆ **Lyrical Elements**

■ What does the poet describe?

■ Does the poet make you see, hear, smell, taste, or touch anything?

■ Does the poet compare something in the poem to some other thing?

◆ **Narrative Elements** Does this poem tell a story? If so, observe the

■ **Setting** When and where does this story take place?

■ **Characters** Who is (are) the main character(s) in this story?

■ **Conflict** What is the main problem or crisis for the character(s)?

■ **Resolution** Is the problem solved? If so, how? If not, why not?

◆ **Figures** Can you identify any examples of simile in this poem?

4 Investigate the Context

Charles Lutwidge Dodgson (1832-1898) was an English mathemetician and logician. But the world knows him best as Lewis Carroll, creator and author of *Alice in Wonderland* and *Through the Looking-Glass*, two of the best-loved children's classics of all time. The son of a scholar and country vicar, Lewis Carroll was one of eleven children, all of whom survived to adulthood (very unusual for his day!) In the official biography commissioned by Carroll's siblings, his nephew writes:

In this quiet home the boy invented the strangest diversions for himself; he made pets of the most odd and unlikely animals, and numbered certain snails and toads among his intimate friends. He tried also to encourage civilised warfare among earthworms, by supplying them with small pieces of pipe, with which they might fight if so disposed. His notions of charity at this early age were somewhat rudimentary; he used to peel rushes with the idea that the pith would afterwards "be given to the poor," though what possible use they could put it to he never attempted to explain. Indeed he seems at this time to have actually lived in that charming "Wonderland" which he afterwards described so vividly; but for all that he was a thorough boy, and loved to climb the trees and to scramble about in the old marl-pits. — Stuart Dodgson Collingwood, *The Life and Letters of Lewis Carroll*

Encouraged by his parents, young Charles began writing at an early age. He was educated at Christ Church, Oxford and went on to hold the Mathematical Lectureship there for more than a quarter-century. Although he was a prolific writer and speaker, his nonsense poetry and fanciful children's stories are his true legacy. "Jabberwocky" is a poem which Alice finds in a mysterious book on her travels in *Through the Looking Glass.*

5 Connect the Thoughts

Commonplace Book

- ◆ Does this poem remind you of other poems, or of stories with similar plots, messages, or characters?
- ◆ Does this poem remind you of any proverbs or other well-known quotations? If so, enter these in your Commonplace Book.

6 Profit and Delight

- ◆ **Delight** What are the sources of delight in this poem?
- ◆ **Wisdom** What wisdom does this poem furnish?
- ◆ **Read** the poem aloud to your teacher with expression and with proper pauses.
- ◆ **Record** in your Book of Centuries: Lewis Carroll.
- ◆ **Memorize** this poem and **recite** it before an audience.

Language Logic

GRAMMAR FLASHCARDS

GRAMMAR TERMS & DEFINITIONS

◯ Review all flashcards according to tabs.

GRAMMAR PRACTICE AND REVIEW

◯ In your Writer's Journal, copy these sentences. Analyze each sentence by marking the simple subject (who or what the sentence is about) with a single underline, and the verb or verb phrase with a double underline. Write D.O. over the direct object, or L.V. over the linking verb; write PA over a predicate adjective and PN over a predicate nominative. Then diagram the sentence. Refer to *Sentence Sense* as needed.

Hint: Though these sentences employ nonsense words, you should be able to figure out how to diagram them. Consider the sense and the flow of the sentence, not the order of the words.

1. All mimsy were the borogoves.

2. The manxome foe he sought.

3. The vorpal blade went snicker-snack.

4. He went galumphing back.

Writer's Journal

Eloquent Expression

COPIA OF WORDS: VOCABULARY STUDY

Conduct a vocabulary study for words invented by Lewis Carroll.

Writer's Journal

A. Study the words *galumphing* and *chortled*. Work in your Writer's Journal.

B. Complete Vocabulary Study steps A-G for each word (see Appendix).

Classical Composition

EDITOR'S PEN – THE BIG PICTURE

Edit your retelling from Lesson 7:

Editor's Pen – The Big Picture

✔ All important plot elements included

✔ All characters represented correctly

✔ Sequence: *same as the original*

✔ Length: *similar to the original*

✔ Figure of Speech: *simile*

A. Read aloud exactly what you have written—not what you THINK you have written! Mark any corrections on your first draft.

B. Next, work through the Big Picture checklist above with your writing mentor.

C. Transfer all additions and corrections from your print copy of the retelling to your file on the computer. Print and file this edited version in your binder along with your marked-up editing copy of the first draft.

Commonplace

Commonplace Book

POETRY

Session one of three commonplace sessions for this lesson. Literary selection: "Jabberwocky."

 Set your timer and begin copying. When finished, check your work carefully against the original for accuracy.

Lesson 8.2

Prose & Poetry

RHYME SCHEME AND STANZA FORM

 Mark the end rhyme in the stanzas below.

'Twas brillig, and the slithy toves
  Did gyre and gimble in the wabe;
All mimsy were the borogoves,
  And the mome raths outgrabe.

"Beware the Jabberwock, my son
  The jaws that bite, the claws that catch!
Beware the Jubjub bird, and shun
  The frumious Bandersnatch!"

He took his vorpal sword in hand;

   Long time the manxome foe he sought—

So rested he by the Tumtum tree,

   And stood awhile in thought.

And, as in uffish thought he stood,

   The Jabberwock, with eyes of flame,

Came whiffling through the tulgey wood,

   And burbled as it came!

One, two! One, two! And through and through

   The vorpal blade went snicker-snack!

He left it dead, and with its head

   He went galumphing back.

"And hast thou slain the Jabberwock?

   Come to my arms, my beamish boy!

O frabjous day! Callooh! Callay!"

   He chortled in his joy.

'Twas brillig, and the slithy toves

   Did gyre and gimble in the wabe;

All mimsy were the borogoves,

   And the mome raths outgrabe.

❧ Is the rhyme scheme the same in all stanzas? Name the predominant rhyme scheme and the stanza form of this poem.

Language Logic

PREPOSITIONS

◆ Read and discuss these lessons in *Sentence Sense* with your teacher as indicated below.

I. Etymology: The Preposition
- ◆ 6.0 Oral Lesson
- ◆ 6.1A Preposition Definition
- ◆ 6.2 Common Prepositions

V. Exercises
- ◆ Oral exercise: Identify each preposition and its object in *Harvey's* 139, Sentences 1-5 and 7-9.

◆ Move the flashcards that you have mastered backwards in your file system. Leave any that you have not mastered behind the **Daily** tab. Add these flashcards to your box behind the Daily tab, and begin to memorize them:

- ◆ Prepositions
- ◆ Common Prepositions*

   It is easier to memorize the common prepositions if you chant them, or set them to a tune you are very familiar with, such as "Yankee Doodle." There are quite a few examples of this on YouTube.

◆ Review all flashcards according to tabs.

Eloquent Expression

FIGURE OF SPEECH: ONOMATOPOEIA

In the figure of speech **onomatopoeia**, the sound of the word echoes the sense. The easiest form of onomatopoeia to recognize is in the words we use to indicate animal sounds such as *bark*, *oink*, *cock-a-doodle-do*, etc. Other examples of onomatopoeia are words that sound like the sound they are describing: *ring*, *babble*, *crash*, *boom*, *bang*, *whoosh*, etc.

> Now, the only reason for making a buzzing-noise that I know of is because you're a bee!
> — A. A. Milne, *Winnie-the-Pooh*

> Baa, baa, black sheep, have you any wool? — Nursery Rhyme

I chatter over stony ways,

In little sharps and trebles,

I bubble into eddying bays,

I babble on the pebbles. —Alfred, Lord Tennyson, "The Brook"

How they tinkle, tinkle, tinkle,

In the icy air of night!

. . . To the tintinnabulation that so musically wells — Edgar Allen Poe, "The Bells"

Sometimes an author or poet will invent a word using onomatopoeia if the right one does not already exist, as Poe did with the word *tintinnabulation* in the final example.

Study and review this figure with your teacher.

A. Discuss the examples of onomatopoeia with your teacher.

B. Look in "Jabberwocky" for examples of onomatopoeia; discuss them with your teacher. Make a list of onomatopoeia from the poem in your Writer's Journal.

Writer's Journal

C. Look in "When Mother Reads Aloud" (Lesson 2) for more examples of onomatopoeia. Make note of some that you may wish to copy into your Commonplace Book. Check your poetry anthology as well!

Classical Composition

EDITOR'S PEN – ZOOM 5X: PARAGRAPHS

Now that the Big Picture is set, begin to zoom in for a close look at the paragraph(s) in your retelling with your writing mentor.

Editor's Pen – Zoom 5x: Paragraphs

✔ Formatting: *proper indentation*

✔ Length: *neither too wordy nor too short*

✔ Sentence class by use: *effective use*

✔ Dialogue: *effective use*

✔ Verb Tense: *consistent (do not jump between present and past tense in storytelling; dialogue may use present tense)*

A. Read aloud your most recently edited version. Check each item in the Editor's Pen checklist to identify possible changes. Mark these on your print copy.

B. Transfer all additions and corrections from your print copy to the computer file. Print this version and file it in your binder along with your other versions.

Lesson 8.3

Prose & Poetry

SCANSION – IAMBIC METER

In English poetry, there are four common meters – **iambic, trochaic, dactylic**, and **anapestic**. In Lesson 4, you were introduced to the the most common meter in English poetry, **iambic meter**.

Scansion is analysis of a poem's meter. We begin by looking at each **verse (line)** in the poem. As you learned, each syllable in the line is either **stressed** or **unstressed**. The **foot** is the basic unit used to scan a verse. It is made up of a prescribed number and order of stressed and unstressed syllables. An **iamb** is a foot made up of one unstressed syllable followed by one stressed syllable.[1]

Whew, that is a lot of terms! This will become simpler once you practice it a bit. Now, let us put all of it together and apply it to the first line from "A Book," by Emily Dickinson.

Step 1 Mark each syllable as either stressed (/) or unstressed (∪). Remember, you may need to say the line aloud several times to "get" the meter. Next, say the line aloud, emphasizing the stresses, as you mark the stresses only. Then go back and mark the unstress syllables, saying the line aloud again to check your work.

∪ / ∪ / ∪ / ∪ /
There is no frig ate like a book

Step 2 Insert dividers (|) to mark off the feet. In two of the most common English meters, there will only be one stress in each foot. Keeping that in mind, we can see that the pattern in this line is *unstress-stress*. So, the feet in this line are called **iambs**.

| ∪ / | ∪ / | ∪ / | ∪ / |
There is no frig ate like a book

1. Gayley, Young, and Kurtz, *English Poetry*, xxxiii.

Step 3 Give the metrical name of the line:

> a. Make the foot name (*iamb*) into an adjective ending in *-ic*: **iambic**.
>
> b. Count the number of feet: *four*. Then take the Greek word for the number four, *tetra*, and add it to the word *meter*: **tetrameter**. The stress is on the second syllable: teTRAMeter.

And as easy as that, you have scanned this line of poetry and identified the meter as **iambic tetrameter**. Usually, a poem will have a predominant meter that we can name. Sometimes a poet will switch meter in the middle of a poem to create a certain effect. It is not at all unusual for a poem to have some stray syllables that do not fit the predominant pattern very well, particularly unstressed syllables at the beginning or end of a line. For now, when you scan a poem, you should look for and name the predominant meter. In *Poetics & Progym,* we will learn more about intentional metrical variations in poetry.

The only other thing you need to know for now is the rest of the Greek words we use as prefixes for -meter.

NUMBER OF FEET	METER NAME	PRONUNCIATION
1	monometer	moNOMeter
2	dimeter	DIMeter
3	trimeter	TRIMeter
4	tetrameter	teTRAMeter
5	pentameter	penTAMeter
6	hexameter	hexAMeter
7	heptameter	hepTAMeter
8	octameter	ocTAMeter

 Scan these stanzas, following the three steps you have learned.

Step 1 Mark each syllable as either stressed (/) or unstressed (∪). Say the line aloud several times to "get" the meter. Next, say the line aloud emphasizing the stresses as you mark the stresses only. Then go back and mark the unstressed syllables, saying the line aloud once more to check your work. Hint: in the final line, you will need to stress the word *the* to keep the rhythm, even though you would not do so were this sentence written in prose.

Step 2 Insert dividers (|) to mark off the feet.

Step 3 Name the poem's meter:

'Twas brillig, and the slithy toves

   Did gyre and gimble in the wabe;

All mimsy were the borogoves,

   And the mome raths outgrabe.

Language Logic

GRAMMAR TERMS & DEFINITIONS
⚜ Review all flashcards according to tabs.

SENTENCE DIAGRAMMING: PREPOSITIONS
⚜ Read and discuss the following section in *Sentence Sense* with your teacher.

III. Sentence Diagrammming: Modifiers
   ◆ 13.5 Prepositional Phrases *Read just the first four paragraphs (through Nota Bene), and study the example after the second paragraph. We will study the rest of this section in Lesson 8.4.*

⚜ In your Writer's Journal, copy these sentences. Analyze each sentence by marking the simple subject (who or what the sentence is about) with a single underline, and the verb or verb phrase with a double underline. Write DO over a direct object, LV over a linking verb, PA over a predicate adjective, and PN over a predicate nominative. Put parentheses around each prepositional phrase. Then diagram the sentence. Refer to *Sentence Sense* as needed. You should be able to diagram each word in the sentence now.

1. The slithy toves did gimble in the wabe.

2. He took his vorpal sword in hand.

3. So rested he by the tum-tum tree.

4. He chortled in his joy.

Writer's Journal

Classical Composition

EDITOR'S PEN – ZOOM 10X: SENTENCES

Now it is time to zoom in even closer as you check the sentences in your retelling. Work with your writing mentor.

> ### Editor's Pen – Zoom 10x: Sentences
> ✔ Complete thought expressed
> ✔ Subject and predicate agree in number
> ✔ Correct capitalization and punctuation

A. Read aloud your your most recently edited version. Use the Editor's Pen checklist to identify changes you need to make. Mark all changes on your print copy.

B. Transfer all additions and corrections from your print copy to the computer file. Print this version and file it in your binder along with your other versions.

Commonplace

POETRY

Session two of three commonplace sessions for this lesson. Literary selection: "Jabberwocky."

Set your timer. Begin where you stopped in the last session. When you finish, check your work carefully against the original for accuracy.

Commonplace Book

Lesson 8.4

Prose & Poetry

SCANSION – IAMBIC METER

Scan this stanza, following the three steps you have learned.

Step 1 Mark each syllable as either stressed (/) or unstressed (∪). In the fourth line of the first stanza below, pronounce frumious with two syllables: *fru mious.*

Step 2 Insert dividers (|) to mark off the feet.

Step 3 Name the poem's meter:

"Beware the Jabberwock, my son

   The jaws that bite, the claws that catch!

Beware the Jubjub bird, and shun

   The frumious Bandersnatch!"

He took his vorpal sword in hand;

   Long time the manxome foe he sought—

So rested he by the Tumtum tree,

   And stood awhile in thought.

Language Logic

GRAMMAR TERMS & DEFINITIONS
Review all flashcards according to tabs.

SENTENCE DIAGRAMMING: PREPOSITIONS
Read and discuss the following section in *Sentence Sense* with your teacher.

III. Sentence Diagrammming: Modifiers
* 13.5 Prepositional Phrases *Read the rest of this section.*

In your Writer's Journal, copy these sentences. Analyze each sentence by marking the simple subject (who or what the sentence is about) with a single underline, and the verb or verb phrase with a double underline. Write DO over a direct object, LV over a linking verb, PA over a predicate adjective, and PN over a predicate nominative. Put parentheses around each prepositional phrase. Then diagram the sentence. Refer to *Sentence Sense* as needed. You should be able to diagram each word in the sentence now.

1. Dionysius won for himself the name of tyrant.

2. A host of servants waited upon him.

3. Damocles sat down at a table in the banquet hall.

4. The smile faded from the lips of Damocles.

5. I will go back to my old home in the poor little cottage among

   the mountains.

Eloquent Expression

PARAGRAPH STYLE – PARAPHRASE WITH COPIA

To paraphrase means "to tell in other words" (from the Greek *paraphrazein*). This is what you have already been doing in the Sentence Style exercises. Now you will paraphrase an entire paragraph from "The Sword of Damocles" using the copia devices you have learned.

In your Writer's Journal, paraphrase this paragraph. Change the verb tense to present throughout the paragraph. Use synonym substitution for as many other words as you can. Make notes on the paragraph below before you begin.

The smile faded from the lips of Damocles. His face

became ashy pale. His hands trembled. He wanted no

more food; he could drink no more wine; he took no

more delight in the music. He longed to be out of the

palace, and away, he cared not where.

Writer's Journal

Classical Composition

EDITOR'S PEN – FINE FOCUS: WORDS

The final checks dwell on the details of your word usage. Continue to compile your personal editing checklist to use in editing all of your work across the curriculum.

Editor's Pen – Fine Focus: Words

✓ Word choices varied; word meanings clear
  - Verbs: *strong, fitting; appropriate adverbs if needed*
  - Nouns: *clear, descriptive; appropriate adjectives if needed*
  - Dialogue: *dialogue tags varied if appropriate*

✓ Correct spelling

✓ Final read-through

A. Read aloud your most recent version. Identify changes you need to make with the Editor's Pen checklist. Mark these on your print copy.

B. Transfer all additions and corrections from your print copy to the computer file. Print this final version and file it in your binder along with your other versions.

Commonplace

POETRY

Session three of three commonplace sessions for this lesson. Literary selection: "Jabberwocky."

 Set your timer and begin copying. When you finish, check your work carefully against the original for accuracy.

Commonplace Book

Lesson 8.5

Prose & Poetry

POETRY APPRECIATION

 Read and enjoy a few poems in your poetry anthology. Try to find one of each kind of stanza. Read one or two poems aloud with expression and proper pauses. See if you can find another poem with iambic meter. Look for figures of speech and figures of description in the poems you read, and make note of any you find for future Commonplace Book entries. Finally, choose a rhyming poem with iambic meter to observe.

Writer's Journal

- In your Writer's Journal, write the title of the poem and the author. Make note of its meter, rhyme scheme, and stanza form.
- Write the rhyming words from the poem in two lists: one list for those spelled the same, and one list for those spelled differently.
- Choose one of the rhyming words from the spelled differently list, and try to come up with several additional rhymes. Look especially for varied spellings.

Language Logic

GRAMMAR TERMS & DEFINITIONS

◯ Ask your teacher to quiz you with the grammar flashcards. Alternately, use the test feature in the Cottage Press *Bards & Poets I* Quizlet Classroom for an online or printed quiz for Lesson 8.

DICTATION: POETRY

◯ Work in your Writer's Journal. Write as your teacher dictates a passage to you from your Commonplace Book. When you are done, check your work carefully, word by word, against the original. Check for accurate spelling, capitalization, and punctuation.

Classical Composition

POETRY

◯ In your Writer's Journal, write two to four rhyming lines that summarize the action of "The Sword of Damocles." If you wish, include a poetic **moral** at the end. Consider including them at the end of your retelling as a brief summary of the story. You may find it easiest to imitate the rhyme and meter of a few lines of the poetic selection for this lesson or a previous lesson.

NARRATIVE RETELLING – FINAL DRAFT

◯ Read over the final version of your retelling one last time and make any needed changes. Save it on your computer; print and file with all the other drafts in your writing binder.

Commonplace

Commonplace Book

FROM YOUR READING

Find selections in a book or poem to add to your Commonplace Book. Include the name of the book or poem, properly formatted. Label the entry with the grammar or poetry feature, the figure of speech, or as a favorite passage. Aim for a minimum of three entries, with at least one from each category.

Grammar Features (choose any)

- A sentence that has an interesting or descriptive noun, a strong and fitting verb, a well-chosen adjective, and/or a vivid adverb
- A sentence with one or more prepositional phrases
- An interesting dialogue tag (add to your Dialogue Tags list)
- An interrogative, exclamatory, or imperative sentence

Figure of Speech (choose any)

- A simile
- An example of onomatopoeia

Poetry Features (choose any)

- Rhyme (note name of the rhyme scheme)
- Iambic meter (note name of the meter)
- Stanza (note name of stanza form)

Favorite Passage: Add at least one passage of one to three sentences or several lines of poetry that captured your attention in your reading this week. It may be something you found beautiful, thought-provoking, funny, or interesting.

Lesson 9

CR

STORY OF DAEDALUS AND ICARUS
from THE STORY OF THE GREEKS by Helene Guerber

Among all those mortals who grew so wise that they learned the secrets of the gods, none was more cunning than Daedalus.

He once built, for King Minos of Crete, a wonderful Labyrinth of winding ways so cunningly tangled up and twisted around that, once inside, you could never find your way out again without a magic clue. But the king's favor veered with the wind, and one day he had his master architect imprisoned in a tower. Daedalus managed to escape from his cell; but it seemed impossible to leave the island, since every ship that came or went was well guarded by order of the king.

At length, watching the sea-gulls in the air,—the only creatures that were sure of liberty,—he thought of a plan for himself and his young son Icarus, who was captive with him.

Little by little, he gathered a store of feathers great and small. He fastened these together with thread, moulded them in with wax, and so fashioned two great wings like those of a bird. When they were done, Daedalus fitted them to his own shoulders, and after one or two efforts, he found that by waving his arms he could winnow the air and cleave it, as a swimmer does the sea. He held himself aloft, wavered this way and that with the wind, and at last, like a great fledgling, he learned to fly.

Without delay, he fell to work on a pair of wings for the boy Icarus, and taught him carefully how to use them, bidding him beware of rash adventures among the stars. "Remember," said the father, "never to fly very low or very high, for the fogs about the earth would weigh you down, but the blaze of the sun will surely melt your feathers apart if you go too near."

For Icarus, these cautions went in at one ear and out by the other. Who could remember to be careful when he was to fly for the first time?

Are birds careful? Not they! And not an idea remained in the boy's head but the one joy of escape.

The day came, and the fair wind that was to set them free. The father bird put on his wings, and, while the light urged them to be gone, he waited to see that all was well with Icarus, for the two could not fly hand in hand. Up they rose, the boy after his father. The hateful ground of Crete sank beneath them; and the country folk, who caught a glimpse of them when they were high above the tree-tops, took it for a vision of the gods,—Apollo, perhaps, with Cupid after him.

At first there was a terror in the joy. The wide vacancy of the air dazed them,—a glance downward made their brains reel. But when a great wind filled their wings, and Icarus felt himself sustained, like a halcyon-bird in the hollow of a wave, like a child uplifted by his mother, he forgot everything in the world but joy. He forgot Crete and the other islands that he had passed over: he saw but vaguely that winged thing in the distance before him that was his father Daedalus. He longed for one draught of flight to quench the thirst of his captivity: he stretched out his arms to the sky and made towards the highest heavens.

Alas for him! Warmer and warmer grew the air. Those arms, that had seemed to uphold him, relaxed. His wings wavered, drooped. He fluttered his young hands vainly,—he was falling,—and in that terror he remembered. The heat of the sun had melted the wax from his wings; the feathers were falling, one by one, like snowflakes; and there was none to help.

He fell like a leaf tossed down the wind, down, down, with one cry that overtook Daedalus far away. When he returned, and sought high and low for the poor boy, he saw nothing but the bird-like feathers afloat on the water, and he knew that Icarus was drowned.

The nearest island he named Icaria, in memory of the child; but he, in heavy grief, went to the temple of Apollo in Sicily, and there hung up his wings as an offering. Never again did he attempt to fly.

☙

Lesson 9.1

Prose & Poetry

A LOOK AT LITERARY ELEMENTS IN THE NARRATIVE

1 **Read**
- Listen carefully as your teacher reads the selection aloud. **Delight** in the story.

2 **Inquire**
- Does the **title** give any hint as to the content or message of the story? If this story was published by the author in a larger book or an anthology, does that title give any hint?
- Discuss the meaning of these words in the context of the story: *mortals, cunning, labyrinth, architect, captive, aloft, cautions, halcyon,* and any unfamiliar words.

3 **Observe the Content**
- **Setting** When and where does this story take place?
- **Characters** Who is (are) the main character(s) in this story?
- **Conflict** What is the main problem or crisis for the character(s)?
- **Resolution** Is the problem solved? If so, how? If not, why not?
- **Figures** Can you identify any examples of simile or onomatopoeia in this narrative?

4 **Investigate the Context**
The story of Daedalus and Icarus comes to us from Ovid, the ancient author who chronicled the lives of the Greek gods. The famous Labyrinth of Daedalus figures prominently in several famous stories from ancient Greece. Thomas Bulfinch tells this tale as a sequel to the one you just read:

Daedalus was so proud of his achievements that he could not bear the idea of a rival. His sister had placed her son Perdix under his charge to be taught the mechanical arts. He was an apt scholar and gave striking evidences of ingenuity. Walking on the seashore he picked up the spine of a fish. Imitating it, he took a piece of iron and notched it on the edge, and thus invented the saw. He put two pieces of iron together, connecting them at one end with a rivet, and sharpening the other ends, and made a pair of compasses. Daedalus was so envious of his nephew's performances that he took an opportunity, when they were together one day on the top of a high tower to push him off. But Minerva, who favours ingenuity, saw him falling, and arrested his fate by changing him into a bird called after his name, the Partridge. This bird does not build his nest in the trees, nor take lofty flights, but nestles in the hedges, and mindful of his fall, avoids high places. — Thomas Bulfinch, *Bulfinch's Mythology*

The retelling of Daedalus and Icarus we have used for this lesson comes from nineteenth century British historian Helene Adeline Guerber (1859-1929) in her *Story of the Greeks*, a wonderful narrative history for grammar-school students. The illustration above is taken from her text.

5 Connect the Thoughts

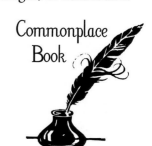

Commonplace Book

- Does this story remind you of other stories with similar plots, messages, or characters?
- Does this story remind you of any fables?
- Does this story remind you of any proverbs or other well-known quotations? If so, enter these in your Commonplace Book.
- The story of Daedalus and Icarus inspired a beautiful and famous Dutch painting by Pieter Brueghel the Elder called "Landscape with the Fall of Icarus." You can view this painting in the Pieter Brueghel the Elder Picture Study PDF on the Cottage Press website: cottagepresspublishing.net.

6 Profit and Delight

- **Delight** What are the sources of delight in this story?
- **Wisdom** What wisdom does this story furnish?
- **Read** the narrative aloud to your teacher with expression and with proper pauses.
- **Record** in your Book of Centuries: King Minos, Daedalus, and Icarus to a Greek mythology section somewhere around the 8th century B. C.

PLOT OBSERVATION — THEON'S SIX

Each of Theon's Six elements is important, but Action is particularly so because the entire narrative "is a clarification of an action."[1] Under Person, we name the story's characters. Under Action, we give the story's plot. Theon's other elements will add detail about the the plot. When we retell a story orally, we naturally recount the plot by telling which character does what action. Our written retellings should begin there also, as we have been doing with our brief outlines. Theon's Six helps us add more detail.

1. George A. Kennedy, *Progymnasmata*, 184.

In the narrative for this lesson, the author begins with a brief, two-paragraph **Prologue** that gives context to the story and sets up the coming action. She then proceeds to the main Action of the narrative. The final paragraph is an **Epilogue** that wraps up the story. We have identified four main actions in this narrative. Dividing the narrative into actions is not an exact science, and there may be several good schemes for doing so. In later lessons, you will begin to divide a narrative's action on your own, but for now, we will identify divisions for you.

Quickly read through the narrative once more. In the margin of the narrative at the beginning of this lesson, number the paragraphs and then mark the story as follows:

A. Beside the first paragraph, write **Prologue**.

B. Beside the third paragraph, write **Action A**.

C. Beside the fifth paragraph, write **Action B**.

D. Beside the seventh paragraph, write **Action C**.

E. Beside the ninth paragraph, write **Action D**.

F. Beside the final paragraph, write **Epilogue**.

In your Writer's Journal, write down your own observation of "The Story of Daedalus and Icarus" using Theon's Six. Use Theon's questions for Person, Action, Place, and Time as a guide, but do not worry if you cannot answer each. Remember, they are just there to get you thinking. Under Action, list A-D with a brief description of the action in each section identified above.

Writer's Journal

Language Logic

GRAMMAR FLASHCARDS

GRAMMAR TERMS & DEFINITIONS
Review all flashcards according to tabs.

GRAMMAR PRACTICE AND REVIEW
In your Writer's Journal, copy these sentences. Analyze each sentence by marking the simple subject (who or what the sentence is about) with a single underline, and the verb or verb

phrase with a double underline. Write DO over a direct object, LV over a linking verb, PA over a predicate adjective, and PN over a predicate nominative. Put parentheses around each prepositional phrase. Then diagram the sentence. Refer to *Sentence Sense* as needed.

1. The king's favor veered with the wind.

2. Daedalus held himself aloft.

3. The father cautioned the son against rash adventures among the stars.

4. The fogs about the earth would weigh you down.

5. The heat of the sun had melted the wax from his wings.

Writer's Journal

Eloquent Expression

COPIA OF WORDS: VOCABULARY STUDY

Conduct a vocabulary study for "The Story of Daedalus and Icarus."

A. Choose at least two unfamiliar words to study. If you need suggestions, see the list under **Inquire** in Literary Elements above. Work in your Writer's Journal.

B. Complete Vocabulary Study steps A-G for each word (see Appendix).

Writer's Journal

Commonplace

NARRATIVE

Session one of three commonplace sessions for this lesson. Literary selection: "The Story of Daedalus and Icarus."

Set your timer and begin copying. When you finish, check your work carefully, word by word, against the original.

Commonplace Book

Lesson 9.2

Prose & Poetry

PLOT OBSERVATION — MANNER AND CAUSE

The final two elements of Theon's Six are **Manner** and **Cause**. Manner and Cause are a bit more challenging because they are not always answered directly, but must be gleaned from a careful and informed reading of the narrative. They generally relate to individual actions within the narrative.

MANNER   How was the action done? Was it done willingly or unwillingly?
   ✓ If unwillingly – was it done in ignorance, by accident, or from necessity?
   ✓ If willingly – was it done by force, by deceit, or in secret?

CAUSE   Why was the action done?
   ✓ To acquire goods?
   ✓ To escape evil?
   ✓ From friendship?
   ✓ Because of relationship: wife, husband, children, father, mother, friend, etc.?
   ✓ Out of the passions: love, hate, envy, pity, drunkenness, etc.?

Once more, this list of questions is simply meant to get you thinking and to remind you of all the possibilities for each element.

Returning to our model, "The Frogs Desiring a King," we could add these details to our observation, based on the questions for Manner and Cause:

Narrative Observation of The Frogs Desiring a King

Manner

Frogs – asked willingly for a king

Jove – gave the king unwillingly, but with a purpose in mind

Cause

Frogs – wanted to do things "properly"; they were discontent

Jove – gave the Log as a joke; gave the Stork in anger

Writer's
Journal

⚜ Discuss Manner and Cause with your teacher. Then, in your
Journal, copy the sections Manner and Cause from Theon's Six
into your Writer's Journal on the page entitled *Theon's Six
Narrative Elements* below the questions for Person, Action, Place,
and Time.

⚜ In your Writer's Journal, add your own observation of Manner
and Cause for "The Story of Daedalus and Icarus" using Theon's Six to the observation you
did in Lesson 9.1 for Person, Action, Place, and Time. Use Theon's questions as a guide, but
do not worry if you cannot answer each. Remember they are just there to get you thinking.

Language Logic

CONJUNCTIONS

⚜ Read and discuss these lessons in *Sentence Sense* with your teacher as indicated below.

I. Etymology: The Conjunction
  ◆ 7.0 Oral Lesson *Read this entire exercise, but we will only be
     dealing with coordinate conjunctions in this lesson.*
  ◆ 7.1 Conjunction Definition
V. Exercises
  ◆ Oral Exercise: Identify each conjunction in *Harvey's* 146,
     Sentences 1, 3, 6, 7, 9, and 12.

⚜ Move the flashcards that you have mastered backwards in your file system. Leave any that
you have not mastered behind the **Daily** tab. Add this flashcard to your box behind the
Daily tab, and begin to memorize it:

GRAMMAR
FLASHCARDS

◆ Conjunctions

⚜ Review all flashcards according to tabs.

Classical Composition

PLOT OBSERVATION: ORAL NARRATION

⚜ Without reading "The Story of Daedalus" again, retell the **plot** orally to your teacher. Refer to your Theon's Six notes if needed.

Commonplace

NARRATIVE

Session two of three commonplace sessions for this lesson. Literary selection: "The Story of Daedalus and Icarus."

⚜ Set your timer and begin copying. When you finish, check your work carefully, word by word, against the original. Check spelling, capitalization, and punctuation for accuracy.

Commonplace Book

Lesson 9.3

Language Logic

GRAMMAR FLASHCARDS

GRAMMAR TERMS & DEFINITIONS

⚜ Review all flashcards according to tabs.

SENTENCE DIAGRAMMING: COMPOUNDS

⚜ Read and discuss the following sections in *Sentence Sense* with your teacher.

SENTENCE SENSE

III. Sentence Diagrammming: Compounds
- ◆ 19.1 Compound Subjects
- ◆ 19.2 Compound Verbs
- ◆ 19.3 Compound Direct Objects
- ◆ 19.6 Compound Objects of Prepositions

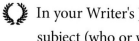 In your Writer's Journal, copy these sentences. Analyze each sentence by marking the simple subject (who or what the sentence is about) with a single underline, and the verb or verb phrase with a double underline. Write DO over a direct object, LV over a linking verb, PA over a predicate adjective, and PN over a predicate nominative. Put parentheses around each prepositional phrase. Then diagram the sentence. Refer to *Sentence Sense* as needed. You should be able to diagram each word in the sentence now.

1. Daedalus thought of a plan for himself and his young son.

2. He could winnow the air and cleave it.

3. The father bird and his son put on their wings.

4. He forgot Crete and the other islands.

Eloquent Expression

SENTENCE STYLE – COPIA OF CONSTRUCTION: COMPOUND ELEMENTS I

When you retell a narrative, it is often necessary to refer to a given character, event, object, etc. repeatedly. Consider these **simple** sentences:

> Erasmus received a letter from a friend. Erasmus read the letter many times. Erasmus wrote a reply. Erasmus sent the reply to his friend.

Of course, you already know one way to improve this series of sentences—substitute other nouns and pronouns and possibly add adjectives to avoid too much repetition.

> Erasmus received a letter from a friend. He read it many times. The delighted scholar wrote a reply. He sent it to his friend.

You could also combine these sentences using conjunctions and compounds. Because each sentence has the same subject, you could combine them by creating a **compound predicate**:

> Erasmus received a letter from a friend, read it many times, wrote a reply, and sent it to his friend.

Any elements of a sentence can be compounded in this way: **subjects, objects, adjectives, adverbs.** Consider these simple sentences:

> The friend sent kind greetings. He related interesting news. He promised to visit.

Erasmus was filled with joy.

These could be combined by creating a **compound subject**:

Kind greetings, interesting news, and the promise of a visit brought Erasmus great joy.

or **compound object of a preposition**:

Erasmus was filled with great joy by the kind greetings, the interesting news, and the promise of a visit.

 Read and discuss the lesson in *Sentence Sense* with your teacher as indicated below. This lesson teaches the proper use of commas when writing a series of nouns, verbs, adjectives, etc.

II. Syntax: Capitalization and Punctuation
♦ 11.3C The Comma, Rule I

Complete these exercises in your Writer's Journal.

 Paraphrase each series of sentences into one simple sentence with compound elements using commas and conjunctions.

1. Daedalus gathered a great store of feathers. He fastened the feathers with thread. He molded them with wax.

2. Daedalus rose in the air. Icarus rose in the air.

Writer's Journal

Classical Composition

NARRATIVE RETELLING – FIRST DRAFT

You will have two sessions to work on this retelling. Begin here, and plan to finish in Lesson 9.4. As you write your retelling, do your best to use proper grammar and spelling, but keep in mind that you will have opportunity to edit before you finalize it.

Retell "The Story of Daedalus and Icarus " in writing, keeping the same characters, setting, and sequence of action. Refer to your plot observation of the narrative with Theon's Six, but do not review the original narrative before you write. Include:

Writer's Journal

- ◆ a heading, properly formatted
- ◆ at least one simile
- ◆ at least one onomatopoeic word

Lesson 9.4

Language Logic

GRAMMAR TERMS & DEFINITIONS
Review all flashcards according to tabs.

SENTENCE DIAGRAMMING: COMPOUNDS
Read and discuss the following sections in *Sentence Sense* with your teacher.

III. Sentence Diagrammming: Compounds
- ◆ 19.4 Compound Adjectives
- ◆ 19.5 Compound Adverbs

In your Writer's Journal, copy these sentences. Analyze each sentence by marking the simple subject (who or what the sentence is about) with a single underline, and the verb or verb phrase with a double underline. Write DO over a direct object, LV over a linking verb, PA over a predicate adjective, and PN over a predicate nominative. Put parentheses around each prepositional phrase. Then diagram the sentence. Refer to *Sentence Sense* as needed. You should be able to diagram each word in the sentence now.

1. Daedalus gathered a store of feathers great and small.

2. They should not fly too high or too low.

3. The slithy toves did gyre and gimble in the wabe.

4. Dionysius lived in a fine palace with many beautiful and costly things.

5. The other slaves laughed and mocked Aesop.

Eloquent Expression

SENTENCE STYLE – COPIA OF WORDS: STRONG VERBS AND FITTING NOUNS

For each of the following verbs from "The Story of Daedalus and Icarus":

- ◆ List several substitutions that fit the context. Make your verbs strong and fitting. Use a thesaurus for synonyms if you wish.
- ◆ Paraphrase the sentence, replacing the verbs with substitutions from your list, and add adverbs to help clarify or intensify the action.

1. He once <u>built</u>, for King Minos of Crete, a wonderful Laby-rinth.

2. Every ship that <u>came</u> or <u>went</u> was well <u>guarded</u> by order of the king.

3. When he <u>returned</u>, and <u>sought</u> high and low for the poor boy, he <u>saw</u> nothing but the bird-like feathers afloat on the water, and he <u>knew</u> that Icarus was drowned.

Find substitutes for each noun in the list below from "The Story of Daedalus and Icarus." Also find adjectives you could pair with the nouns you have chosen. For each noun:

- ◆ List all the other nouns and pronouns used to refer to the same thing in the fable.
- ◆ List more nouns and pronouns that could be substituted, keeping the context in mind. Check a thesaurus for synonyms. For a person, consider his or her moral character in

choosing synonyms.

- List any adjectives used to describe these nouns in the selection, then list others that fit the context of the fable. Check a thesaurus for synonyms.
- Write down several of your favorite adjective-noun combinations.

1. Icarus   2. cautions

Classical Composition

Writer's Journal

NARRATIVE RETELLING – FINISH FIRST DRAFT

Finish the first draft of your narrative retelling. Review the instructions in Lesson 9.3 as needed.

Commonplace

Commonplace Book

NARRATIVE

Session three of three commonplace sessions for this lesson. Literary selection: "The Story of Daedalus and Icarus."

Set your timer. Begin where you stopped in the last session. When you finish, check your work carefully against the original for accuracy.

Lesson 9.5

Prose & Poetry

POETRY APPRECIATION

Read and enjoy a few poems in your poetry anthology. Identify rhyme schemes and stanza forms of one or two. Look for poems with iambic meter. Look for figures of speech and figures of description in the poems you read, and make note of any you find for future Commonplace Book entries. Read one or two poems aloud with expression and proper pauses. Pause at punctuation, but not necessarily at the ends of lines.

Language Logic

GRAMMAR TERMS & DEFINITIONS

🏵 Ask your teacher to quiz you with the grammar flashcards. Alternately, use the test feature in the Cottage Press *Bards & Poets I* Quizlet Classroom for an online or printed quiz for Lesson 9.

DICTATION: NARRATIVE PASSAGE

🏵 Work in your Writer's Journal. Write as your teacher dictates a passage to you from your Commonplace Book. When you are done, check your work carefully, word by word, against the original. Check for accurate spelling, capitalization, and punctuation.

Eloquent Expression

PARAGRAPH STYLE – PARAPHRASE WITH COPIA

To paraphrase means "to tell in other words" (from the Greek *paraphrazein*). This is what you have already been doing in the Sentence Style exercises. Now you will paraphrase an entire paragraph using the copia devices you have learned.

🏵 In your Writer's Journal, paraphrase this paragraph. Change the verb tense to future tense (except inside the quotation). Change one sentence to another classification by use. Reposition the dialogue tag. Use synonym substitution for the dialogue tag and as many other words as you can. Make notes on the paragraph below before you begin.

Without delay, he fell to work on a pair of wings for the boy

Icarus, and taught him carefully how to use them, bidding him

beware of rash adventures among the stars. "Remember," said

the father, "never to fly very low or very high, for the fogs about the earth would weigh

you down, but the blaze of the sun will surely melt your feathers apart if you go too near."

Classical Composition

NARRATIVE RETELLING: TYPE DRAFT

Type your retelling on the computer with spell-check turned off, or ask your writing mentor to type it exactly as you wrote it. Save, print, and file this draft in your writing binder.

Commonplace

FROM YOUR READING

Find selections in a book or poem to add to your Commonplace Book. Include the name of the book or poem, properly formatted. Label the entry with the grammar or poetry feature, the figure of speech, or as a favorite passage. Aim for a minimum of three entries, with at least one from each category.

Commonplace Book

Grammar Features (choose any)

- A sentence that has an interesting or descriptive noun, a strong and fitting verb, a well-chosen adjective, and/or a vivid adverb
- A sentence with one or more prepositional phrases
- A sentence that has a conjunction to join words, phrases, or clauses
- An interesting dialogue tag (add to your Dialogue Tags list)
- An interrogative, exclamatory, or imperative sentence

Figure of Speech (choose any)

- A simile
- An example of onomatopoeia

◉ Poetry Features (choose any)

- ◆ Rhyme (note name of the rhyme scheme)
- ◆ Iambic (note name of the meter)
- ◆ Stanza (note name of stanza form)

◉ Favorite Passage: Add at least one passage of one to three sentences or several lines of poetry that captured your attention in your reading this week. It may be something you found beautiful, thought-provoking, funny, or interesting.

℃Ω

THE NEW ENGLAND BOY'S SONG
ABOUT THANKSGIVING DAY

Over the river, and through the wood,

To grandfather's house we go;

The horse knows the way

To carry the sleigh

Through the white and drifted snow.

Over the river, and through the wood—

Oh, how the wind does blow!

It stings the toes

And bites the nose

As over the ground we go.

Over the river, and through the wood,

To have a first-rate play.

Hear the bells ring

"Ting-a-ling-ding",

Hurrah for Thanksgiving Day!

Over the river, and through the wood

Trot fast, my dapple-gray!

Spring over the ground,

Like a hunting-hound!

For this is Thanksgiving Day.

Over the river, and through the wood,

And straight through the barn-yard gate.

We seem to go

Extremely slow,—

It is so hard to wait!

Over the river and through the wood—

Now grandmother's cap I spy!

Hurrah for the fun!

Is the pudding done?

Hurrah for the pumpkin-pie!

— LYDIA MARIA CHILD

Lesson 10.1

Prose & Poetry

A LOOK AT LITERARY ELEMENTS IN THE POEM

1 Read
◆ Follow along and listen carefully as the poem is read aloud, OR read it aloud yourself. Read it at least two or three times. **Delight** in the meter, the rhyme, and the images.

2 Inquire
◆ Does the **title** give any hint as to the content or message of the poem?

◆ Are there any other unfamiliar persons, places, or things mentioned in the poem? Discuss these with your teacher.

◆ Discuss the meaning of these words in the context of the story: *sleigh, Thanksgiving, dapple, extremely, spy, hurrah,* and any unfamiliar words.

◆ Was there any part of the poem you did not understand? If so, discuss this with your teacher and classmates.

3 Observe the Content

◆ **Lyrical Elements** What does the poet describe?

  ▪ What does the poet describe?

  ▪ Does the poet make you see, hear, smell, taste, or touch anything?

  ▪ Does the poet compare something in the poem to some other thing?

◆ **Narrative Elements** Does this poem tell a story? If so, observe the

  ▪ **Setting** When and where does this story take place?

  ▪ **Characters** Who is (are) the main character(s) in this story?

  ▪ **Conflict** What is the main problem or crisis for the character(s)?

  ▪ **Resolution** Is the problem solved? If so, how? If not, why not?

◆ **Figures** Can you identify any examples of simile or onomatopoeia in this poem?

4 Investigate the Context

Lydia Maria Child (1802-1880) was an American teacher, author, and journalist with strong ties to the the abolitionist and women's suffrage movements of the mid-nineteenth century. The *American Frugal Housewife* was her most successful book, but "The New England Boy's Song About Thanksgiving Day," often called "Over the River and Through the Wood" after the poem's first line, was her most famous work. It was published in Volume II of an anthology of stories and poems for children called *Flowers for Children*.

5 Connect the Thoughts

◆ Does this poem remind you of other poems, or of stories with similar plots, messages, or characters?

◆ Does this poem remind you of any proverbs or other well-known quotations? If so, enter these in your Commonplace Book.

Commonplace Book

6 Profit and Delight

◆ **Delight** What are the sources of delight in this poem?

◆ **Wisdom** What wisdom does this poem furnish?

◆ **Read** the poem aloud to your teacher with expression and with proper pauses.

◆ **Record** in your Book of Centuries: Lydia Maria Child.

◆ **Memorize** this poem and **recite** it before an audience.

Language Logic

GRAMMAR
FLASHCARDS

GRAMMAR TERMS & DEFINITIONS
◉ Review all flashcards according to tabs.

GRAMMAR PRACTICE AND REVIEW
◉ In your Writer's Journal, copy these sentences. Analyze each sentence by marking the simple subject (who or what the sentence is about) with a single underline, and the verb or verb phrase with a double underline. Write D.O. over the direct object, or L.V. over the linking verb; write PA over a predicate adjective and PN over a predicate nominative. Put parentheses around each prepositional phrase. Then diagram the sentence. Refer to *Sentence Sense* as needed.

1. Over the river, and through the wood, to grandfather's house we go.

2. It stings the toes and bites the nose.

3. They sailed and sailed.

4. He was unjust and cruel.

5. In Samos, the little slave soon was known for his wisdom and courage.

Writer's
Journal

Eloquent Expression

COPIA OF WORDS: VOCABULARY STUDY
◉ Conduct a vocabulary study for "New England Boy's Song."

A. Choose at least two unfamiliar words to study. If you need suggestions, see the list under **Inquire** in Literary Elements above. Work in your Writer's Journal.

B. Complete Vocabulary Study steps A-G for each word (see Appendix).

Writer's
Journal

Classical Composition

EDITOR'S PEN – THE BIG PICTURE

 Edit your retelling from Lesson 9:

Editor's Pen – The Big Picture

✓ All important plot elements included
✓ All characters represented correctly
✓ Sequence: *same as the original*
✓ Length: similar to the original
✓ Figure of Speech: *simile, onomatopoeia*
✓ Figure of Description: *anemographia* (will be added in Lesson 10.2)

A. Read aloud exactly what you have written—not what you THINK you have written! Mark any corrections on your first draft.

B. Next, work through the Big Picture checklist above with your writing mentor.

C. Transfer all additions and corrections from your print copy of the retelling to your file on the computer. Print and file this edited version in your binder along with your marked-up editing copy of the first draft.

Commonplace

Commonplace
Book

POETRY

Session one of three commonplace sessions for this lesson. Literary selection: "New England Boy's Song."

 Set your timer and begin copying. When finished, check your work carefully against the original for accuracy.

Lesson 10.2

Prose & Poetry

RHYME SCHEME AND STANZA FORM

🏆 Mark the end rhyme in the stanzas below.

Over the river, and through the wood,

  To grandfather's house we go;

    The horse knows the way

    To carry the sleighs Through the

white and drifted snow.

Over the river, and through the wood—

  Oh, how the wind does blow!

    It stings the toes

    And bites the nose

As over the ground we go.

Over the river, and through the wood,

  To have a first-rate play.

    Hear the bells ring

    "Ting-a-ling-ding",

Hurrah for Thanksgiving Day!

Over the river, and through the wood

  Trot fast, my dapple-gray!

    Spring over the ground,

    Like a hunting-hound!

For this is Thanksgiving Day.

Over the river, and through the wood,

  And straight through the barn-yard gate.

    We seem to go

    Extremely slow,—

It is so hard to wait!

Over the river and through the wood—

  Now grandmother's cap I spy!

    Hurrah for the fun!

    Is the pudding done?

Hurrah for the pumpkin-pie!

🏆 Name the predominant rhyme scheme and the stanza form of this poem.

Language Logic

INTERJECTIONS

🏆 Read and discuss these lessons in *Sentence Sense* with your teacher as indicated below.

I. Etymology: The Interjection
- ◆ 8.1 Interjection Definition

V. Exercises
- ◆ Oral Exercise: Identify each interjection in *Harvey's* 151.

Move the flashcards that you have mastered backwards in your file system. Leave any that you have not mastered behind the **Daily** tab. Add this flashcard to your box behind the Daily tab, and begin to memorize it:

- ◆ Interjections

Review all flashcards according to tabs.

Eloquent Expression

FIGURES OF DESCRIPTION

Figures of description bring a narrative to life "before the eyes" of your reader or hearer. We will learn several figures of description that the ancient Greeks identified and that are used very often in narrative writing, and then you will practice using them in your own retellings.

FIGURE OF DESCRIPTION – ANEMOGRAPHIA

Anemographia (an Ā mō graf i a) is a vivid description of the wind. In Greek, the word *anemographia* literally means "writing about the wind."

Figures of speech are often used to produce figures of description. Look for **simile** in these examples of **anemographia** from literature:

> It came clear and cold, with a touch in the air like frost, and a northerly wind that blew the clouds away and made the stars bright. — Robert Louis Stevenson, *Kidnapped*

The night was dark, and a cold wind blew, driving the clouds, furiously and fast, before it. There was one black, gloomy mass that seemed to follow him: not hurrying in the wild chase with the others, but lingering sullenly behind, and gliding darkly and stealthily on. He often looked back at this, and, more than once, stopped to let it pass over; but, somehow, when he went forward again, it was still behind him, coming mournfully and slowly up, like a shadowy funeral train. — Charles Dickens, *Nicholas Nickleby*

The winds drove the raft to and fro—the South wind tossed it to the North to bear along, and the East wind tossed it to the West to chase. — Padraic Colum, *The Children's Homer*

⚜ Study and practice the figure of anemographia with your teacher.

A. Discuss the examples of anemographia with your teacher.

B. Look in this week's poem for examples of anemographia. Discuss this with your teacher. Look through your poetry anthology, or in stories you are reading, for more examples of anemographia. Make note of some that you may wish to copy into your Commonplace Book.

C. In your Writer's Journal, write a sentence or two of your own anemographia, vividly describing the wind as Daedalus and Icarus flew.

D. Add your figure of anemographia to the narrative retelling by writing it in the appropriate place on your print copy of our current draft.

Classical Composition

EDITOR'S PEN – ZOOM 5X: PARAGRAPHS

⚜ Now that the Big Picture is set, begin to zoom in for a close look at the paragraph(s) in your retelling with your writing mentor.

> ### Editor's Pen – Zoom 5x: Paragraphs
> ✓ Formatting: *proper indentation*
> ✓ Length: *neither too wordy nor too short*

✔ Sentence class by use: *effective use*
✔ Dialogue: *effective use*
✔ Verb Tense: *consistent (do not jump between present and past tense in storytelling; dialogue may use present tense)*

A. Read aloud your most recently edited version. Check each item in the Editor's Pen checklist to identify possible changes. Mark these on your print copy.

B. Transfer all additions and corrections from your print copy to the computer file. Print this version and file it in your binder along with your other versions.

Lesson 10.3

Prose & Poetry

SCANSION – DACTYLIC METER

A **dactyl** is a foot with three beats: stress-unstress-unstress. Say these dactylic words aloud to get a feel for the rhythm: *elephant, buffalo, merrily, alphabet, poetry.* Can you think of any other dactylic words?

Dactylic meter is not very common in English poetry, but is common in ancient epic poetry, like Homer's *Iliad* and *Odyssey.* Because this meter is not so natural to the English language, you will often find variations in the meter when it is used. Here is the first line of our selection for this lesson, scanned with the first two feet following the dactylic meter stress-unstress-unstress pattern.

```
|╱ ∪  ∪|╱ ∪ ∪|   ╱   ∪|  ╱ |
 O ver the riv er and through the wood
```

The third foot is missing the second unstressed syllable, but if you read it aloud as it is marked, you will probably read it with a pause on *through* that makes up that missing beat. Also, notice the stressed syllable at the end of the line all by itself with no unstressed syllables. This is a typical variation in lines of dactylic meter, both in English and in the ancient languages. Say this line in a sing-song way, and you will understand why Child used this meter for this line. You can actually hear the galloping hoofbeats in the meter!

A dactyl has three syllables in its pronunciation as well as in its pattern. A good way to remember both is the pronounce the word emphasizing its associated pattern, putting the stress on the first syllable: **DAC tyl ic.**

Now, let's take a look at the other lines in the first stanza. They scan like this:

|∪   ╱ | ∪ ∪   ╱ |∪ ╱ |

To grand fath er's house we go;

|∪   ╱ | ∪   ∪ ╱ |

The horse knows the way

|∪ ╱|∪ ∪   ╱ |

To car ry the sleigh

| ∪   ∪   ╱ |∪ ╱ |∪ ╱ |

Through the white and drift ed snow.

There are several metrical patterns going on in this stanza; you do not need to learn the names of these just yet. For now, you will just mark the stressed and unstressed syllables, and divide the lines into feet. *This should be a teacher-led exercise guided by the scansion key in Teaching Helps.*

With your teacher, scan these stanzas, following the three steps you have learned. First scan line one of each stanza like line one of the example stanza above. Then, scan lines two, three, and four of each stanza. Finally, scan the last line of each stanza as your teacher instructs using the scansion key in Teaching Helps.

Step 1 Mark each syllable as either stressed (╱) or unstressed (∪). Say the line aloud several times to "get" the meter. Next, say the line aloud emphasizing the stresses as you mark the stresses only. Then go back and mark the unstressed syllables, saying the line aloud once more to check your work. *Teachers, please use the scansion key in Teaching Helps to help your students mark the stresses.*

Step 2 Insert dividers (|) to mark off the feet. Remember that you will only have one stress in each foot for this poem. *Teachers, please use the scansion key in Teaching Helps to help your students mark the feet, particularly in the irregular lines.*

Step 3 Name the meter of each line ONLY IF it is iambic or dactylic:

Over the river, and through the wood—

Oh, how the wind does blow!

It stings the toes

And bites the nose

As over the ground we go.

Over the river, and through the wood,

To have a first-rate play.

Hear the bells ring

"Ting-a-ling-ding",

Hurrah for Thanksgiving Day!

Language Logic

GRAMMAR TERMS & DEFINITIONS
◉ Review all flashcards according to tabs.

SENTENCE DIAGRAMMING: SENTENCE CLASS BY USE
◉ Read and discuss the following sections in *Sentence Sense* with your teacher.

III. Sentence Diagrammming: Sentence Class By Use
- ◆ 22.1 Declarative Senences
- ◆ 22.3 Exclamatory Sentences
- ◆ 22.4 Imperative Sentences

III. Sentence Diagrammming: Independent Elements
- ◆ 24.2 Interjections

◉ In your Writer's Journal, copy these sentences. Analyze each sentence by marking the simple subject (who or what the sentence is about) with a single underline, and the verb or verb phrase with a double underline. Write DO over a direct object, LV over a linking verb, PA over a predicate adjective, and PN over a predicate nominative. Put parentheses around each prepositional phrase. Then diagram the sentence. Refer to *Sentence Sense* as needed. You should be able to diagram each word in the sentence now.

1. Oh, how the wind does blow!

2. Trot fast, my dapple-gray!

3. Spring over the ground, like an Irish hound!

4. Now Grandmother's cap I spy!

5. Sail on!

Writer's Journal

Classical Composition

EDITOR'S PEN – ZOOM 10X: SENTENCES

Now it is time to zoom in even closer as you check the sentences in your retelling. Work with your writing mentor.

> ## Editor's Pen – Zoom 10x: Sentences
> ✓ Complete thought expressed
> ✓ Subject and predicate agree in number
> ✓ Correct capitalization and punctuation
> ♦ Commas correctly used for words in a series

A. Read aloud your your most recently edited version. Use the Editor's Pen checklist to identify changes you need to make. Mark all changes on your print copy.

B. Transfer all additions and corrections from your print copy to the computer file. Print this version and file it in your binder along with your other versions.

Eloquent Expression

SENTENCE STYLE – YOUR STYLE!

❂ Craft copia for sentences from your own retelling using Sentence Style devices we have studied.

A. Work with your writing mentor to choose three sentences from your retelling that could be improved.

B. Copy the first in your Writer's Journal. Underline every important word in the sentence and jot down synonyms for each.

Writer's Journal

C. Use the list of Sentence Style devices below as you write several new versions of the sentence. New devices from this lesson are listed in bold type. You may use more than one device in each sentence.

D. Repeat the instructions above for the second and third sentences.

E. Choose your favorite paraphrase of each sentence. Replace the original sentences in your retelling before you edit again.

COPIA OF WORDS
✓ Synonyms and Antonyms
✓ Dialogue Tags - synonyms for *said*
✓ Nouns – varied and descriptive
  ◆ switch noun/pronouns
✓ Verbs – strong and fitting
✓ Modifiers
  ◆ add adjective
  ◆ add adverb

COPIA OF CONSTRUCTION
✓ Sentence class by use
✓ Dialogue
  ◆ Tag line position
✓ Verb Tense
✓ **Sentence Combination**
  ◆ **compound elements**

Commonplace

Commonplace Book

POETRY

Session two of three commonplace sessions for this lesson. Literary selection: "New England Boy's Song."

Set your timer. Begin where you stopped in the last session. When you finish, check your work carefully against the original for accuracy.

Lesson 10.4

Prose & Poetry

SCANSION

Here is the scansion for stanza three:

| / ∪ ∪ | / ∪ ∪ | /   ∪ | / |
O ver the riv er and through the wood

| ∪   / | ∪ / | ∪ / |
Trot fast, my dap ple - gray!

| ∪ / | ∪ ∪ / |
Spring o ver the ground,

| ∪ ∪ / | ∪ / |
Like a hunt ing-hound!

| ∪ / | ∪   ∪ / | ∪ / |
For this is Thanks giv ing Day.

As you can see, this stanza has quite a few variations! These next stanzas we will scan have some similar patterns.

With your teacher, scan the stanzas below, following the three steps you have learned. First scan line one of each stanza like line one of the example stanza above. Next, scan lines three through five of stanza five (first one below). Finally, scan the rest of the lines as your teacher instructs using the scansion key in Teaching Helps.

Step 1 Mark each syllable as either stressed (/) or unstressed (∪). Say the line aloud several times to "get" the meter. Next, say the line aloud emphasizing the stresses as you mark the stresses only. Then go back and mark the unstressed syllables, saying the line aloud once more to check your work. *Teachers, please use the scansion key in Teaching Helps to help your students mark the stresses.*

Step 2 Insert dividers (|) to mark off the feet. Remember that you will only have one stress in each foot for this poem. *Teachers, please use the scansion key in Teaching Helps to help your students mark the feet, particularly in the irregular lines.*

Step 3 Name the meter of each line ONLY IF it is iambic or dactylic:

Over the river, and through the wood,

And straight through the barn-yard gate.

   We seem to go

   Extremely slow,—

It is so hard to wait!

Over the river and through the wood—

Now grandmother's cap I spy!

   Hurrah for the fun!

   Is the pudding done?

Hurrah for the pumpkin-pie!

And now, you have scanned the whole poem, challenging as the meter is! Go back and read the entire poem once more. You can see how all those variations in meter actually help us imagine this . At times, the horse and sleigh glide along regularly, but other times, you experience bumps and starts and fits as the way takes you up hill, down hill, through the wood, and over the river. The meter communicates the message along with the words.

Language Logic

GRAMMAR TERMS & DEFINITIONS
❧ Review all flashcards according to tabs.

SENTENCE DIAGRAMMING: SENTENCE CLASS BY USE

Read and discuss the following section in *Sentence Sense* with your teacher.

III. Sentence Diagrammming: Sentence Class By Use
- ◆ 22.2 Interrogative Sentences

In your Writer's Journal, copy these sentences. Analyze each sentence by marking the simple subject (who or what the sentence is about) with a single underline, and the verb or verb phrase with a double underline. Write DO over a direct object, LV over a linking verb, PA over a predicate adjective, and PN over a predicate nominative. Put parentheses around each prepositional phrase. Then diagram the sentence. Refer to *Sentence Sense* as needed. You should be able to diagram each word in the sentence now.

1. Is the pudding done?

2. Are birds careful?

3. Why should that sword trouble you?

4. Will you go with me into the garden?

Writer's Journal

Eloquent Expression

PARAGRAPH STYLE – PARAPHRASE WITH COPIA

For this exercise, choose from all of the copia devices you have learned so far. See the copia chart in Lesson 10.3. New devices are in bold type.

In your Writer's Journal, paraphrase this paragraph. Change each sentence opener, and change at least one sentence class by use. Use as many synonym substitutions as possible. Use as many of the other copia devices as you are able. Make notes on the paragraph below before you begin.

Writer's Journal

The day came, and the fair wind that was to set them free. The father bird had put on his wings, and, while the light urged them to be gone, he waited to see that all was well with Icarus, for the two could not fly hand in hand. Up they rose, the boy after his father. The hateful ground of Crete sank beneath them; and the country folk, who caught a glimpse of them when they were high above the tree-tops, took it for a vision of the gods.

Classical Composition

EDITOR'S PEN – FINE FOCUS: WORDS

The final checks dwell on the details of your word usage. Continue to compile your personal editing checklist to use in editing all of your work across the curriculum.

Editor's Pen – Fine Focus: Words

✓ Word choices varied; word meanings clear
- ◆ Verbs: *strong, fitting; appropriate adverbs if needed*
- ◆ Nouns: *clear, descriptive; appropriate adjectives if needed*
- ◆ Dialogue: *dialogue tags varied if appropriate*

✓ Correct spelling
✓ Final read-through

A. Read aloud your most recent version. Identify changes you need to make with the Editor's Pen checklist. Mark these on your print copy.

B. Transfer all additions and corrections from your print copy to the computer file. Print this final version and file it in your binder along with your other versions.

Commonplace

Commonplace
Book

POETRY

Session three of three commonplace sessions for this lesson. Literary selection: "New England Boy's Song."

 Set your timer and begin copying. When you finish, check your work carefully against the original for accuracy.

Lesson 10.5

Prose & Poetry

POETRY APPRECIATION

 Read and enjoy a few poems in your poetry anthology. Try to find one of each stanza form. Read one or two poems aloud with expression and proper pauses. Perhaps you can even spot one with some dactylic lines. Look for figures of speech and figures of description in the poems you read, and make note of any you find for future Commonplace Book entries. Finally, choose a rhyming poem with dactylic or iambic meter to observe.

Writer's
Journal

- In your Writer's Journal, write the title of the poem and the author. Make note of its meter, rhyme scheme, and stanza form.
- Write the rhyming words from the poem in two lists: one list for those spelled the same, and one list for those spelled differently.
- Choose one of the rhyming words from the spelled differently list, and try to come up with several additional rhymes. Look especially for varied spellings.

Language Logic

GRAMMAR TERMS & DEFINITIONS

⚜ Ask your teacher to quiz you with the grammar flashcards. Alternately, use the test feature in the Cottage Press *Bards & Poets I* Quizlet Classroom for an online or printed quiz for Lesson 10.

DICTATION: POETRY

⚜ Work in your Writer's Journal. Write as your teacher dictates a passage to you from your Commonplace Book. When you are done, check your work carefully, word by word, against the original. Check for accurate spelling, capitalization, and punctuation.

Classical Composition

POETRY

⚜ In your Writer's Journal, write two to four rhyming lines that summarize the action of "The Story of Daedalus and Icarus." If you wish, include a poetic **moral** at the end. Consider including them at the end of your retelling as a brief summary of the story. You may find it easiest to imitate the rhyme and meter of a few lines of the poetic selection for this lesson or a previous lesson.

NARRATIVE RETELLING – FINAL DRAFT

⚜ Read over the final version of your retelling one last time and make any needed changes. Save it on your computer; print and file with all the other drafts in your writing binder.

Commonplace

FROM YOUR READING

Find selections in a book or poem to add to your Commonplace Book. Include the name of the book or poem, properly formatted. Label the entry with the grammar or poetry feature, the figure of speech, or as a favorite passage. Aim for a minimum of three entries, with at least one from each category.

Commonplace Book

◉ Grammar Features (choose any)

- ◆ A sentence that has an interesting or descriptive noun, a strong and fitting verb, a well-chosen adjective, and/or a vivid adverb
- ◆ A sentence with one or more prepositional phrases
- ◆ A sentence that has a conjunction to join words, phrases, or clauses
- ◆ An interesting dialogue tag (add to your Dialogue Tags list)
- ◆ An interrogative, exclamatory, or imperative sentence

◉ Figures (choose any)

- ◆ Figures of Speech: simile and/or onomatopoeia
- ◆ Figures of Description: anemographia

◉ Poetry Features (choose any)

- ◆ Rhyme (note name of the rhyme scheme)
- ◆ Iambic or dactylic meter (note name of the meter)
- ◆ Stanza (note name of stanza form)

◉ Favorite Passage: Add at least one passage of one to three sentences or several lines of poetry that captured your attention in your reading this week. It may be something you found beautiful, thought-provoking, funny, or interesting.

☙

THE LADY ROMA

from THE STORY OF ROME by Mary Macgregor

Long, long years ago, Troy, one of the great cities in Asia Minor, was taken by the Greeks.

Many mighty Trojans had defended their city well, and among them all none had fought more bravely than the prince Æneas.

But when Æneas saw that the Greeks had set fire to the city, he fled, carrying, it is said, his father on his shoulders, and grasping by the hand his son Ascanius.

Moreover, so precious to him was the sacred image of the goddess Pallas, that he saved it from the burning city.

The gods, pleased with his reverence, helped him in his flight by building a ship. So when Æneas reached the sea he at once embarked in it, with his followers and their wives, and sailed away to seek for a new land in which to build a new city.

As the Trojans sailed they saw a bright star shining above them. Day and night the star was always to be seen, showing the seafarers the direction in which to steer.

At length the Trojans reached the western shore of Italy, and here, at a town called Latium, they disembarked.

The women were weary of the sea, and no sooner had they landed than they began to wonder how they could persuade their husbands to journey no farther, but to settle in the pleasant country which they had reached.

Among these women was a lady of noble birth, who was wise as she was good.

Roma, for that was the lady's name, proposed that they should burn the ship in which they had sailed. Then it would be impossible for their husbands to go any farther in search of a new home.

The other women agreed to Roma's daring plan, and with mingled hope and fear the ship was set on fire.

When the men saw the flames devouring the vessel they were troubled, but when they found out how it had been set on fire, they were angry.

Yet, as anger could not give them back their ship, and as Italy was a pleasant land, the men did as the women wished. They settled near a hill called Mount Palatine, and there they built a city.

Some old stories tell that the city was called Rome after Roma, the noble lady who had first thought of setting the ship on fire.

But other stories say that the country in which Æneas landed belonged to a king named Latinus, who welcomed the Trojan, and gave him ground on which to build. Æneas married Lavinia, the daughter of the king, and called the city which he built after her Lavinium.

Soon after this, King Latinus was killed in battle, and then for three years Æneas ruled well and wisely not only over his own Trojan followers, but also over the subjects of his royal father-in-law. His people he now called Latins, in memory of King Latinus.

When the three years were passed, war broke out against the Etruscans, who were at that time the most powerful tribe in Italy.

One day a terrible storm overtook the armies on the battlefield; so dark grew the clouds that the soldiers could not see each other.

When at length the sky cleared Æneas had disappeared, and was seen no more on earth.

"The gods have taken him away," said the Latins. So they built an altar, and henceforth worshipped their king as the god Jupiter.

Ascanius, who had escaped from Troy with his father, now ruled in Lavinium. But he soon found that the city was not large enough for all his people; so, leaving Lavinium, he built a new city, and called it Alba Longa, or the Long White City.

Alba Longa stood in the midst of the Alban hills, not far from the site on which Rome itself was soon to be built.

ॐ

Lesson 11.1

Prose & Poetry

A LOOK AT LITERARY ELEMENTS IN THE NARRATIVE

1 Read
- ◆ Listen carefully as your teacher reads the selection aloud. **Delight** in the story.

2 Inquire
- ◆ Does the **title** give any hint as to the content or message of the story? If this story was published by the author in a larger book or an anthology, does that title give any hint?
- ◆ Discuss the meaning of these words in the context of the story: *sacred, reverence, embarked (disembarked), seafarers, noble, devouring, henceforth,* and any unfamiliar words.

3 Observe the Content
- ◆ **Setting** When and where does this story take place?
- ◆ **Characters** Who is (are) the main character(s) in this story?
- ◆ **Conflict** What is the main problem or crisis for the character(s)?
- ◆ **Resolution** Is the problem solved? If so, how? If not, why not?
- ◆ **Figures** Can you identify any examples of simile, onomatopoeia, or anemographia in this narrative?

4 Investigate the Context
Mary McGregor (1874-1961) wrote a number of narrative history books, as well as myth, legend, and fairy tale anthologies for children during the first half of the 19th century. The details on her life are scarce, but perhaps the introductory letter she wrote to "Ian and

Willie" at the beginning of *The Story of Rome* in 1912 will give you a bit of insight into her life and interests:

> *The Story of Rome* has been written, as you know, in your beautiful, quiet old garden. And as the story grew, the short cold days of winter passed and the long warm days of summer were here. In the garden a miracle had been wrought. It had become alive. After slow, persistent struggle with storm and frost, the delicate bare branches were no longer bare, but clothed in living green. The hard black earth too had stirred, and shoots and blades appeared, until at length the garden was ablaze with gold, purple, crimson.
>
> Sometimes I dreamed that, in its own different way, the *Story of Rome* too was a miracle, wrought out of the tears and throes of a brave and ambitious people. For the story tells of the birth of a city and of its growth through storm and struggle, until it became a great world empire. The city which Romulus founded was built upon a single hill; soon seven hills were not great enough to contain her. And when Augustus, the first Emperor of Rome, began to reign, part of Europe, Asia Minor, Egypt, Syria, and a large portion of Africa formed his kingdom.
>
> Although the story was written in the quiet of your garden, little of its peace has stolen into the tale, and for that you boys may care for it the more. As you read, fierce battle-cries will ring in your ears, and the clash of arms will startle you. You will hear the tramp of armies marching to new lands to conquer them and their treasures for Rome, the city of their love. Sometimes you will catch your breath in horror as you read of terrible and cruel deeds, for the Romans were often pitiless, showing little mercy to those they conquered. But at other times your breath will come quick with wonder as you read of the dauntless courage, the rare endurance of these mighty men of old.
>
> And if there are many things which you do not admire in the people of Rome, yet they possess one virtue which you and every British boy and girl may not only admire, but gladly imitate. What that virtue is I will leave you to find out for yourselves as you read *The Story of Rome*.
>
> —Yours affectionately,
> MARY MACGREGOR.

5 Connect the Thoughts
- Does this story remind you of other stories with similar plots, messages, or characters?
- Does this story remind you of any fables?

◆ Does this story remind you of any proverbs or other well-known quotations? If so, enter these in your Commonplace Book.

6 Profit and Delight

- **Delight** What are the sources of delight in this story?
- **Wisdom** What wisdom does this story furnish?
- **Read** the narrative aloud to your teacher with expression and with proper pauses.
- **Record** in your Book of Centuries: Aeneas Sails to Rome (c. 1200 B. C.).

PLOT OBSERVATION: IDENTIFYING ACTIONS

To identify actions in a narrative, it is helpful to remember that the start of a new action is sometimes signaled by a change in one of Theon's Six, particularly Person, Time, or Place.

You might notice a shift in focus from one character or set of characters to another. This is not completely failproof; one or two person(s) leaving or entering the story does not necessarily indicate a change in action when there are other characters who remain constant.

Beginnings and endings can be helpful indicators to the actions that form the plot. For example, one action may end with preparations for a big battle and the next action may begin with the battle itself. One action may end with a conversation and the next detail a new action that the conversation set in motion.

Time and place shifts can also be helpful in deciding how to divide the plot into a series of actions. Sometimes, though, a single action may last for a long time; for example, a journey may be completed over several days or months and involve a number of place changes. An entire war lasting many years with battles in different regions may be treated as a single action.

An action may be contained in one paragraph or it may span many. In many of the narratives we will read, actions usually begin at the beginning of a paragraph, but sometimes a new action will begin in the middle of a paragraph, or even in the middle of a sentence. **Theon's Six** provide us with a framework to evaluate these changes.

In "The Lady Roma," there is one paragraph that gives a **Summary**, adding a bit of information about the preceding actions, and a quick overview of intervening years in the life of Æneas.

Quickly read through the narrative once more. In the margin of the narrative at the beginning of this lesson, number the paragraphs, and then mark the story as follows:

A. Beside the first paragraph, write **Prologue.**

B. Beside the third paragraph, write **Action A.**

C. Beside the fifth paragraph, write **Action B.**

D. Beside the eighth paragraph, write **Action C.**

E. Beside the fourteenth paragraph, write **Summary.**

F. Beside the sixteenth paragraph, write **Action D.**

G. Beside the seventeenth paragraph, write **Action E.**

H. Beside the second paragraph from the end, write **Prologue.**

Review the narrative. Make notes in the margin indicating which of Theon's Six changed to with each action. Discuss this with your teacher.

Language Logic

GRAMMAR
FLASHCARDS

GRAMMAR TERMS & DEFINITIONS
Review all flashcards according to tabs.

GRAMMAR PRACTICE AND REVIEW

In your Writer's Journal, copy these sentences. Analyze each sentence by marking the simple subject (who or what the sentence is about) with a single underline, and the verb or verb phrase with a double underline. Write D.O. over the direct object, or L.V. over the linking verb; write PA over a predicate adjective and PN over a predicate predicate nominative. Put parentheses around each prepositional phrase. Then diagram the sentence. Refer to *Sentence Sense* as needed.

Writer's Journal

1. Among them all, none had fought more bravely.

2. With a mix of hope and fear the ship was set on fire.

3. Did Jupiter take Aeneas away?

4. They built an altar, and henceforth worshipped their king.

5. Ascanius, build the new city of Alba Longa.

Eloquent Expression

Writer's
Journal

COPIA OF WORDS: VOCABULARY STUDY

 Conduct a vocabulary study for "The Lady Roma."

A. Choose at least two unfamiliar words to study. If you need
suggestions, see the list under **Inquire** in Literary Elements
above. Work in your Writer's Journal.

B. Complete Vocabulary Study steps A-G for each word (see
Appendix).

Commonplace

Commonplace
Book

NARRATIVE

Session one of three commonplace sessions for this lesson. Literary
selection: "The Lady Roma."

Set your timer and begin copying. When you finish, check your
work carefully, word by word, against the original.

Lesson 11.2

Prose & Poetry

Writer's
Journal

PLOT OBSERVATION: THEON'S SIX

In your Writer's Journal, write down your own observation of
"The Lady Roma" using Theon's Six. List each major action, then

make notes using all six of Theon's questions as a guide. Do not worry if you cannot answer each one. Remember they are just there to get you thinking. Under Action, list A. followed by a brief description of the action, then B. followed by a brief description of the action, etc.

Language Logic

GRAMMAR TERMS & DEFINITIONS
◆ Review all flashcards according to tabs.

COMPOUND SENTENCES
◆ Read and discuss the lesson in *Sentence Sense* with your teacher as indicated below.

III. Sentence Diagramming: Compounds
  ◆ 19.7 Compound Sentences

◆ In your Writer's Journal, copy these sentences. Analyze each sentence by marking the simple subject (who or what the sentence is about) with a single underline, and the verb or verb phrase with a double underline. Write DO over a direct object, LV over a linking verb, PA over a predicate adjective, and PN over a predicate nominative. Put parentheses around each prepositional phrase. Then diagram the sentence. Refer to *Sentence Sense* as needed. You should be able to diagram each word in the sentence now.

Writer's Journal

1. Many mighty Trojans had defended their city well, and Aeneas had fought most bravely.

2. Italy was a pleasant land, so they settled near a hill, and there they built a city.

3. Aeneas had disappeared, and he was seen no more on earth.

4. He kept his deck, and peered through darkness.

Classical Composition

PLOT OBSERVATION: ORAL NARRATION

🏅 Without reading "The Lady Roma" again, retell the **plot** orally to your teacher. Refer to your Theon's Six notes if needed.

Commonplace

NARRATIVE

Commonplace Book

Session two of three commonplace sessions for this lesson. Literary selection: "The Lady Roma."

🏅 Set your timer and begin copying. When you finish, check your work carefully, word by word, against the original. Check spelling, capitalization, and punctuation for accuracy.

Lesson 11.3

Language Logic

GRAMMAR FLASHCARDS

GRAMMAR TERMS & DEFINITIONS

🏅 Review all flashcards according to tabs.

CONJUNCTIONS INTRODUCING SENTENCES

🏅 Read and discuss the lesson in *Sentence Sense* with your teacher as indicated below.

SENTENCE SENSE

III. Sentence Diagramming: Independent Elements
◆ 24.1 Conjunctions Introducing Sentences

In your Writer's Journal, copy these sentences. Analyze each sentence by marking the simple subject (who or what the sentence is about) with a single underline, and the verb or verb phrase with a double underline. Write DO over a direct object, LV over a linking verb, PA over a predicate adjective, and PN over a predicate nominative. Put parentheses around each prepositional phrase. Then diagram the sentence. Refer to *Sentence Sense* as needed. You should be able to diagram each word in the sentence now.

1. But the king's favor veered with the wind, and soon he imprisoned the master architect in a tower.

2. And hast thou slain the Jabberwock?

3. And so, Damocles was led into the palace.

4. But he was very rich, and he lived in a fine palace.

Writer's
Journal

Eloquent Expression

SENTENCE STYLE – COMBINING SENTENCES: COMPOUND ELEMENTS II

Let us look again at the series of sentences from Lesson 9.3.

> Erasmus received a letter from a friend. Erasmus read the letter many times. Erasmus wrote a reply. Erasmus sent the reply to his friend.

In that lesson, we saw that these can be combined with **compound elements**. Another way to combine them would be to create **compound sentences** from the original simple sentences by combining those simple sentences with conjunctions.

> Erasmus received a letter from a friend, and he read it many times. He wrote a reply, then he sent it to his friend.

Caution: Avoid these two common errors when combining sentences:

1. **Run-on Sentence**: *Erasmus received a letter from a friend he was delighted.*

This is corrected by using a comma and conjunction: *Erasmus received a letter from a friend, and he was delighted.*

2. **Comma Splice**: *The delighted scholar wrote a reply, he sent it to his friend.*

Two simple sentences cannot be combined into a compound sentence by just sticking a comma between them. You must either use a comma and conjunction, or you must use a semi-colon. *The delighted scholar wrote a reply, and he sent it to his friend. The delighted scholar wrote a reply; he sent it to his friend.*

If you learn to recognize and conquer the dreaded comma splice now, your college professors will likely rise up and call you blessed.

Nota Bene: There are fashions is writing, just as in clothing. Comma splices have not always been considered poor style. Many great authors of the past used them quite often. But the comma splice is definitely considered an error in academic writing, so we want to make sure that you know what it is and how to avoid it.

Also, in order to create a particular figure of speech, a good writer sometimes will use a comma splice on purpose. We will learn such a figure in a later course. Once you know and consistently follow the rules, you will be able to break some of them occasionally—but always by intention, never by mistake.

Read and discuss the lesson in *Sentence Sense* with your teacher as indicated below. This lesson teaches the proper use of commas with compound sentences.

II. Syntax: Capitalization and Punctuation
   ◆ 11.3C The Comma, Rule II

Paraphrase these sentences, combining them with conjunctions.

1. The Greeks burned the city of Troy. Aeneas fled with his son and his father.

2. The women were weary of the sea. They wanted to journey no further.

Writer's Journal

Classical Composition

NARRATIVE RETELLING – FIRST DRAFT

You will have two sessions to work on this retelling. Begin here, and plan to finish in Lesson 11.4. As you write your retelling, do your best to use proper grammar and spelling, but keep in mind that you will have opportunity to edit before you finalize it.

Retell "The Lady Roma" in writing, keeping the same characters, setting, and sequence of action. Refer to your plot observation of the narrative with Theon's Six, but do not review the original narrative before you write. Include:

Writer's Journal

- ◆ a heading, properly formatted
- ◆ at least one simile
- ◆ at least one onomatopoeic word
- ◆ (optional figure of description) anemographia

Lesson 11.4

Language Logic

GRAMMAR FLASHCARDS

GRAMMAR TERMS & DEFINITIONS
Review all flashcards according to tabs.

Classical Composition

NARRATIVE RETELLING – FINISH FIRST DRAFT
Finish the first draft of your narrative retelling. Review the instructions in Lesson 11.3 as needed.

Writer's Journal

Commonplace

NARRATIVE

Session three of three commonplace sessions for this lesson. Literary selection: "The Lady Roma."

Commonplace Book

🏅 Set your timer. Begin where you stopped in the last session. When you finish, check your work carefully against the original for accuracy.

Lesson 11.5

Prose & Poetry

POETRY APPRECIATION

🏅 Read and enjoy a few poems in your poetry anthology. Identify rhyme schemes and stanza forms of one or two. Look for poems with iambic meter. Look for figures of speech and figures of description in the poems you read, and make note of any you find for future Commonplace Book entries. Read one or two poems aloud with expression and proper pauses. Pause at punctuation, but not necessarily at the ends of lines.

Language Logic

GRAMMAR TERMS & DEFINITIONS

GRAMMAR FLASHCARDS

🏅 Ask your teacher to quiz you with the grammar flashcards. Alternately, use the test feature in the Cottage Press *Bards & Poets I* Quizlet Classroom for an online or printed quiz for Lesson 11.

DICTATION: NARRATIVE PASSAGE

Writer's Journal

🏅 Work in your Writer's Journal. Write as your teacher dictates a passage to you from your Commonplace Book. When you are done, check your work carefully, word by word, against the original. Check for accurate spelling, capitalization, and punctuation.

Classical Composition

NARRATIVE RETELLING: TYPE DRAFT

🏅 Type your retelling on the computer with spell-check turned off, or ask your writing mentor to type it exactly as you wrote it. Save, print, and file this draft in your writing binder.

Commonplace

FROM YOUR READING

Find selections in a book or poem to add to your Commonplace Book. Include the name of the book or poem, properly formatted. Label the entry with the grammar or poetry feature, the figure of speech, or as a favorite passage. Aim for a minimum of three entries, with at least one from each category.

Commonplace Book

🏅 Grammar Features (choose any)

- ◆ A sentence that has an interesting or descriptive noun, a strong and fitting verb, a well-chosen adjective, and/or a vivid adverb
- ◆ A sentence with one or more prepositional phrases
- ◆ A sentence that has a conjunction to join words, phrases, or clauses
- ◆ An interesting dialogue tag (add to your Dialogue Tags list)
- ◆ An interrogative, exclamatory, or imperative sentence

🏅 Figures (choose any)

- ◆ Figures of Speech: simile and/or onomatopoeia
- ◆ Figures of Description: anemographia

🏅 Poetry Features (choose any)

- ◆ Rhyme (note name of the rhyme scheme)
- ◆ Iambic or dactylic meter (note name of the meter)
- ◆ Stanza (note name of stanza form)

🏅 Favorite Passage: Add at least one passage of one to three sentences or several lines of poetry that captured your attention in your reading this week. It may be something you found beautiful, thought-provoking, funny, or interesting.

Lesson 12

❦

GOD OF OUR FATHERS

God of our fathers, whose almighty hand
Leads forth in beauty all the starry band
Of shining worlds in splendor through the skies,
Our grateful songs before Thy throne arise.

Thy love divine hath led us in the past;
In this free land by Thee our lot is cast;
Be Thou our Ruler, Guardian, Guide, and Stay;
Thy Word our law, Thy paths our chosen way.

From war's alarms, from deadly pestilence,
Be Thy strong arm our ever sure defence;
Thy true religion in our hearts increase,
Thy bounteous goodness nourish us in peace.

Refresh Thy people on their toilsome way,
Lead us from night to never-ending day;
Fill all our lives with love and grace divine,
And glory, laud, and praise be ever Thine.

— DANIEL C. ROBERTS

❦

Lesson 12.1

Prose & Poetry

A LOOK AT LITERARY ELEMENTS IN THE POEM

1 Read

◆ Follow along and listen carefully as the poem is read aloud, OR read it aloud yourself. Read it at least two or three times. **Delight** in the meter, the rhyme, and the images.

2 Inquire

◆ Does the **title** give any hint as to the content or message of the poem?

◆ Are there any other unfamiliar persons, places, or things mentioned in the poem? Discuss these with your teacher.

◆ Discuss the meaning of these words in the context of the story: *almighty, splendor, divine, guardian, stay, pestilence, nourish, toilsome,* and any unfamiliar words.

◆ Was there any part of the poem you did not understand? If so, discuss this with your teacher and classmates.

3 Observe the Content

◆ **Lyrical Elements**
   ■ What does the poet describe?
   ■ Does the poet make you see, hear, smell, taste, or touch anything?
   ■ Does the poet compare something in the poem to some other thing?

◆ **Narrative Elements** Does this poem tell a story? If so, observe the
   ■ **Setting** When and where does this story take place?
   ■ **Characters** Who is (are) the main character(s) in this story?
   ■ **Conflict** What is the main problem or crisis for the character(s)?
   ■ **Resolution** Is the problem solved? If so, how? If not, why not?

◆ **Figures** Can you identify any examples of simile, onomatopoeia, or anemographia in this poem?

4 Investigate the Context

Daniel Crane Roberts (1841-1907), rector of a small New England Episcopal parish, wrote this hymn in

1876 to commemorate the Centennial celebration of the Declaration of Independence in his New England town. Later, it was chosen as the official hymn of the national Constitution Centennial celebration. In 1901 Roberts wrote, "I remain a country parson, known only in my small world . . . My little hymn has thus had a very flattering official recognition. But that which would really gladden my heart, popular recognition, it has not received." By the time of his death, however, the hymn had received recognition, and had earned him an honorary doctorate from Norwich University. Today, it is a well-known and well-loved staple of American hymnody.

5 Connect the Thoughts

◆ Does this poem remind you of other poems, or of stories with similar plots, messages, or characters?

◆ Does this poem remind you of any proverbs or other well-known quotations? If so, enter these in your Commonplace Book.

Commonplace Book

6 Profit and Delight

◆ **Delight** What are the sources of delight in this poem?

◆ **Wisdom** What wisdom does this poem furnish?

◆ **Read** the poem aloud to your teacher with expression and with proper pauses.

◆ **Record** in your Book of Centuries: Daniel C. Roberts.

◆ **Memorize** this poem and **recite** it before an audience.

Language Logic

GRAMMAR FLASHCARDS

GRAMMAR TERMS & DEFINITIONS
❧ Review all flashcards according to tabs.

GRAMMAR PRACTICE AND REVIEW
❧ In your Writer's Journal, copy these sentences. Analyze each sentence by marking the simple subject (who or what the sentence is about) with a single underline, and the verb or verb phrase with a double underline. Write D.O. over the direct object, or L.V. over the linking verb; write PA over a predicate adjective and PN over a predicate nominative. Put parentheses around each prepositional phrase. Then diagram the sentence. Refer to *Sentence Sense* as needed.

1. Our grateful songs before thy throne arise.

2. Thy love divine hath led us in the past; in this free land by Thee our lot is cast.

3. From war's alarms, from deadly pestilence, be Thy strong arm our ever sure defence.

4. Refresh Thy people on their toilsome way.

5. Fill all our lives with love and grace divine, and glory, laud, and praise be ever Thine.

Writer's Journal

COPIA OF WORDS: VOCABULARY STUDY

Conduct a vocabulary study for "God of Our Fathers."

A. Choose at least two unfamiliar words to study. If you need suggestions, see the list under **Inquire** in Literary Elements above. Work in your Writer's Journal.

B. Complete Vocabulary Study steps A-G for each word (see Appendix).

Writer's Journal

Classical Composition

EDITOR'S PEN – THE BIG PICTURE

Edit your retelling from Lesson 11:

Editor's Pen – The Big Picture
✓ All important plot elements included
✓ All characters represented correctly
✓ Sequence: *same as the original*
✓ Length: *similar to the original*
✓ Figure of Speech: *simile, onomatopoeia*
✓ Figure of Description (optional): *anemographia*

A. Read aloud exactly what you have written—not what you THINK you have written! Mark any corrections on your first draft.

B. Next, work through the Big Picture checklist above with your writing mentor.

C. Transfer all additions and corrections from your print copy of the retelling to your file on the computer. Print and file this edited version in your binder along with your marked-up editing copy of the first draft.

Commonplace

Commonplace Book

POETRY

Session one of three commonplace sessions for this lesson. Literary selection: "God of Our Fathers."

 Set your timer and begin copying. When finished, check your work carefully against the original for accuracy.

Lesson 12.2

Prose & Poetry

RHYME SCHEME AND STANZA FORM

 Mark the end rhyme in the stanzas below.

God of our fathers, whose almighty hand
Leads forth in beauty all the starry band
Of shining worlds in splendor through the skies,
Our grateful songs before thy throne arise.

Thy love divine hath led us in the past;
In this free land by thee our lot is cast;
Be thou our Ruler, Guardian, Guide, and Stay;
Thy Word our law, thy paths our chosen way.

From war's alarms, from deadly pestilence,

Be thy strong arm our ever sure defence;

Thy true religion in our hearts increase,

Thy bounteous goodness nourish us in peace.

Refresh thy people on their toilsome way,

Lead us from night to never-ending day;

Fill all our lives with love and grace divine,

And glory, laud, and praise be ever thine.

◉ Name the predominant rhyme scheme and the stanza form of this poem.

Language Logic

GRAMMAR TERMS & DEFINITIONS
◉ Review all flashcards according to tabs.

SENTENCE DIAGRAMMING
◉ Read and discuss the following section in *Sentence Sense* with your teacher.

III. Sentence Diagrammming: Modifiers
  ◆ 13.7 Adverbial Nouns

◉ In your Writer's Journal, copy these sentences. Analyze each sentence by marking the simple subject (who or what the sentence is about) with a single underline, and the verb or verb phrase with a double underline. Write DO over a direct object, LV over a linking verb, PA over a predicate adjective, and PN over a predicate nominative. Put parentheses around each prepositional phrase. Then diagram the sentence. Refer to *Sentence Sense* as needed. You should be able to diagram each word in the sentence now.

Writer's Journal

1. Aeneas fled his homeland with his father and his young son.

2. The Trojans saw a bright star day and night.

3. Damocles went home to the poor little cottage among the mountains.

4. My men grow mutinous today.

5. Yesterday, the quarrels were much more violent.

Eloquent Expression

FIGURE OF SPEECH: ANASTROPHE

Anastrophe is an inversion of the usual or expected word order in a sentence.

Whose woods these are I think I know.
His house is in the village though. — Robert Frost, "Stopping By Woods"

Did ever dragon keep so fair a cave? — William Shakespeare, *Romeo and Juliet*

Sure I am of this, that you have only to endure to conquer. — Winston Churchill

The normal sentence pattern of Subject – Verb – Object (or Complement) may be inverted by putting the object or the verb first. Or a noun may precede its adjective, instead of the expected adjective – noun order. Any "artful deviation" from the usual or expected word order may be classified as anastrophe. Full of anastrophe is poetry!

Study and review figures of speech with your teacher.

A. Discuss the examples of anastrophe with your teacher and try to paraphrase them in the usual or expected order. Your practice with sentence diagramming (particularly interrogative sentences) will pay off here.

B. Look in "God of Our Fathers" for examples of anastrophe; discuss them with your teacher. Make a list of figures from the poem in your Writer's Journal.

Writer's Journal

C. Look through other poems we have studied in *Bards & Poets I* for more examples of anastrophe. Make note of some that you may wish to copy into your Commonplace Book.

Classical Composition

EDITOR'S PEN – ZOOM 5X: PARAGRAPHS

Now that the Big Picture is set, begin to zoom in for a close look at the paragraph(s) in your retelling with your writing mentor.

> ### Editor's Pen – Zoom 5x: Paragraphs
> ✓ Formatting: *proper indentation*
> ✓ Length: *neither too wordy nor too short*
> ✓ Sentence class by use: *effective use*
> ✓ Dialogue: *effective use*
> ✓ Verb Tense: *consistent*

A. Read aloud your most recently edited version. Check each item in the Editor's Pen checklist to identify possible changes. Mark these on your print copy.

B. Transfer all additions and corrections from your print copy to the computer file. Print this version and file it in your binder along with your other versions.

Lesson 12.3

Prose & Poetry

SCANSION

If you are familiar with this hymn, you will probably be tempted to try to scan it while singing the melody in your head. This will not work! Instead, read it as a poem, and mark the stresses that you hear in a natural reading.

Scan these stanzas, following the three steps you have learned.

Step 1 Mark each syllable as either stressed (/) or unstressed (∪). Say the line aloud several times to "get" the meter. Next, say the line aloud emphasizing the stresses as you mark the stresses only. Then go back and mark the unstressed syllables, saying the line aloud once more to check your work. You should find this meter very regular, with these exception: read *Guardian* as two syllables: *Guard ian.*

Step 2 Insert dividers (|) to mark off the feet.

Step 3 Name the poem's meter:

God of our fathers, whose almighty hand

Leads forth in beauty all the starry band

Of shining worlds in splendor through the skies,

Our grateful songs before thy throne arise.

Thy love divine hath led us in the past;

In this free land by thee our lot is cast;

Be thou our Ruler, Guardian, Guide, and Stay;

Thy Word our law, thy paths our chosen way.

Language Logic

GRAMMAR TERMS & DEFINITIONS
Review all flashcards according to tabs.

SENTENCE DIAGRAMMING

In your Writer's Journal, copy these sentences. Analyze each sentence by marking the simple subject (who or what the sentence is about) with a single underline, and the verb or verb phrase with a double underline. Write DO over a direct object, LV over a linking verb, PA over a predicate adjective, and PN over a predicate nominative. Put parentheses around each prepositional phrase. Then diagram the sentence. Refer to *Sentence Sense* as needed. You should be able to diagram each word in the sentence now.

1. Aeneas at once embarked in the ship with his followers.

2. Warmer and warmer grew the air.

3. Beware the Jubjub bird, and shun the frumious Bandersnatch!

4. And so, the next day, Damocles was led into the palace.

5. Damocles wanted no more food; he could drink no more
   wine; he took no more delight in the music.

Eloquent Expression

SENTENCE STYLE – YOUR STYLE!

Craft copia for sentences from your own retelling using Sentence Style devices we have
studied.

A. Work with your writing mentor to choose three sentences from your retelling that
   could be improved.

B. Copy the first in your Writer's Journal. Underline every
   important word in the sentence and jot down synonyms for
   each.

C. Use the list of Sentence Style devices below as you write
   several new versions of the sentence. New devices from this
   lesson are listed in bold type. You may use more than one
   device in each sentence.

D. Repeat the instructions above for the second and third sentences.

E. Choose your favorite paraphrase of each sentence. Replace the original sentences in
   your retelling before you edit again.

COPIA OF WORDS	COPIA OF CONSTRUCTION
✓ Synonyms and Antonyms	✓ Sentence class by use
✓ Dialogue Tags - synonyms for *said*	✓ Dialogue
✓ Nouns – varied and descriptive	◆ Tag line position
◆ switch noun/pronouns	✓ Verb Tense

✓ Verbs – strong and fitting
✓ Modifiers
   ◆ add adjective
   ◆ add adverb

✓ Sentence Combination
   ◆ **compound elements**

Classical Composition

EDITOR'S PEN – ZOOM 10X: SENTENCES

Now it is time to zoom in even closer as you check the sentences in your retelling. Work with your writing mentor.

Editor's Pen – Zoom 10x: Sentences

✓ Complete thought expressed
✓ Subject and predicate agree in number
✓ Correct capitalization and punctuation
   ◆ Commas correctly used for words in a series
   ◆ No comma splices or run-on sentences!

A. Read aloud your your most recently edited version. Use the Editor's Pen checklist to identify changes you need to make. Mark all changes on your print copy.

B. Transfer all additions and corrections from your print copy to the computer file. Print this version and file it in ysour binder along with your other versions.

Commonplace

POETRY

Session two of three commonplace sessions for this lesson. Literary selection: "God of Our Fathers."

Commonplace Book

Set your timer. Begin where you stopped in the last session. When you finish, check your work carefully against the original for accuracy.

Lesson 12.4

Prose & Poetry

SCANSION

 Scan these stanzas, following the three steps you have learned.

Step 1 Mark each syllable as either stressed (/) or unstressed (∪). Say the line aloud several times to "get" the meter. Next, say the line aloud emphasizing the stresses as you mark the stresses only. Then go back and mark the unstressed syllables, saying the line aloud once more to check your work. You should find this meter very regular, with this exception: read *bounteous* as two syllables: *boun teous.*

Step 2 Insert dividers (|) to mark off the feet.

Step 3 Name the poem's meter:

From war's alarms, from deadly pestilence,

Be thy strong arm our ever sure defence;

Thy true religion in our hearts increase,

Thy bounteous goodness nourish us in peace.

Refresh thy people on their toilsome way,

Lead us from night to never-ending day;

Fill all our lives with love and grace divine,

And glory, laud, and praise be ever thine.

Language Logic

GRAMMAR FLASHCARDS

GRAMMAR TERMS & DEFINITIONS

◉ Review all flashcards according to tabs.

Eloquent Expression

PARAGRAPH STYLE – PARAPHRASE WITH COPIA

For this exercise, choose from all of the copia devices you have learned so far. See the copia chart in Lesson 12.3. New devices are in bold type.

◉ In your Writer's Journal, paraphrase this paragraph. Change each sentence opener, and change at least one sentence class by use. Use as many synonym substitutions as possible. Use as many of the other copia devices as you are able. Make notes on the paragraph below before you begin.

Writer's Journal

Without delay, he fell to work on a pair of wings for the boy Icarus,

and taught him carefully how to use them, bidding him beware of rash

adventures among the stars. "Remember," said the father, "never to fly

very low or very high, for the fogs about the earth would weigh you

down, but the blaze of the sun will surely melt your feathers apart if you go too near."

Classical Composition

EDITOR'S PEN – FINE FOCUS: WORDS

The final checks dwell on the details of your word usage. Continue to compile your personal editing checklist to use in editing all of your work across the curriculum.

Editor's Pen – Fine Focus: Words
✔ Word choices varied; word meanings clear
  ◆ Verbs: *strong, fitting; appropriate adverbs if needed*
  ◆ Nouns: *clear, descriptive; appropriate adjectives if needed*
  ◆ Dialogue: *dialogue tags varied if appropriate*
✔ Correct spelling
✔ Final read-through

A. Read aloud your most recent version. Identify changes you need to make with the Editor's Pen checklist. Mark these on your print copy.

B. Transfer all additions and corrections from your print copy to the computer file. Print this final version and file it in your binder along with your other versions.

Commonplace

Commonplace Book

POETRY
Session three of three commonplace sessions for this lesson. Literary selection: "God of Our Fathers."

 Set your timer and begin copying. When you finish, check your work carefully against the original for accuracy.

Lesson 12.5

Prose & Poetry

POETRY APPRECIATION
 Read and enjoy a few poems in your poetry anthology. Try to find one of each kind of stanza. Read one or two poems aloud with expression and proper pauses. Look for figures of speech and figures of description in the poems you read, and make note of any you find for future Commonplace Book entries. Finally, choose a rhyming poem with iambic or dactylic meter to observe.

- In your Writer's Journal, write the title of the poem and the author. Make note of its meter, rhyme scheme, and stanza form.
- Write the rhyming words from the poem in two lists: one list for those spelled the same, and one list for those spelled differently.
- Choose one of the rhyming words from the spelled differently list, and try to come up with several additional rhymes. Look especially for varied spellings.

Language Logic

GRAMMAR TERMS & DEFINITIONS

GRAMMAR FLASHCARDS

Ⓤ Ask your teacher to quiz you with the grammar flashcards. Alternately, use the test feature in the Cottage Press *Bards & Poets I* Quizlet Classroom for an online or printed quiz for Lesson 12.

DICTATION: POETRY

Ⓤ Work in your Writer's Journal. Write as your teacher dictates a passage to you from your Commonplace Book. When you are done, check your work carefully, word by word, against the original. Check for accurate spelling, capitalization, and punctuation.

Classical Composition

POETRY

Ⓤ In your Writer's Journal, write two to four rhyming lines that summarize the action of "The Lady Roma." If you wish, include a poetic **moral** at the end. Consider including them at the end of your retelling as a brief summary of the story. You may find it easiest to imitate the rhyme and meter of a few lines of the poetic selection for this lesson or a previous lesson.

NARRATIVE RETELLING – FINAL DRAFT

❧ Read over the final version of your retelling one last time and make any needed changes. Save it on your computer; print and file with all the other drafts in your writing binder.

Commonplace

FROM YOUR READING

Find selections in a book or poem to add to your Commonplace Book. Include the name of the book or poem, properly formatted. Label the entry with the grammar or poetry feature, the figure of speech, or as a favorite passage. Aim for a minimum of three entries, with at least one from each category.

Commonplace Book

❧ Grammar Features (choose any)

- ◆ A sentence that has an interesting or descriptive noun, a strong and fitting verb, a well-chosen adjective, and/or a vivid adverb
- ◆ A sentence with one or more prepositional phrases
- ◆ A sentence that has a conjunction to join words, phrases, or clauses
- ◆ An interesting dialogue tag (add to your Dialogue Tags list)
- ◆ An interrogative, exclamatory, or imperative sentence

❧ Figures (choose any)

- ◆ Figures of Speech: simile, onomatopoeia, and/or anastrophe
- ◆ Figures of Description: anemographia

❧ Poetry Features (choose any)

- ◆ Rhyme (note name of the rhyme scheme)
- ◆ Iambic or dactylic meter (note name of the meter)
- ◆ Stanza (note name of stanza form)

❧ Favorite Passage: Add at least one passage of one to three sentences or several lines of poetry that captured your attention in your reading this week. It may be something you found beautiful, thought-provoking, funny, or interesting.

Lesson 13

CR

THE TWINS

from THE CHILDREN'S PLUTARCH by F. J. Gould

The cattle were feeding on the pasture, but the master was not there. He was going toward the river, and he was carrying a burden in his arms. When he reached the edge of the stream he paused. The water ran toward the Mediterranean Sea, rough and noisy.

"I shall not put them straight into the water," he said to himself; "I will leave them here, and perhaps the river will rise and carry them away."

It did. As the flood crept round the wooden trough or cradle, it rocked and then floated. Inside the trough lay two lovely and chubby boy-babes—twins—princes. Their uncle had taken their father's land and theirs, and had bidden the herdsman drown the twins.

The flood of the river Tiber carried the cradle to a green spot, where grew a wild fig-tree. The box lay on the grass, and when the flood went down it still stayed on land. And behold (or you will behold these things if you believe the ancient tale!), a big she-wolf came and gazed at the babes with her fierce and shifty eyes, and she seemed to think they were little cubs that needed her milk, and so she fed them. As they grew older, and were able to toddle about, and were too old for wolf's milk, they got food from a friendly woodpecker. I cannot say whether the woodpecker, with his long beak and tongue, brought the boys food such as he ate himself (that would be insects and grubs), or whether he was good enough to bring berries and other fruits. After a while, however, the herdsman took charge of the boys altogether, and saved the woodpecker any further trouble.

The twins became stout, tall, and strong young fellows, who minded cattle for the chieftain Amulius. One day a loud cry was heard.

"Our cattle have been stolen!"

"Who has taken them?"

"The herdsmen of the chieftain Numitor."

"Follow us!" shouted the tall twins; "we will get them back again!"

A furious fight took place. The twins won. The cattle were brought back in triumph. Then the brothers knew that more war would follow. They joined company with runaway slaves and other people who had no settled homes. These people looked upon the twins—Romulus and Remus—as captains. But Remus was captured, and taken to the house of Numitor.

The herdsman went to Romulus and said:

"Your brother is in danger of death. He will perhaps be killed by his grandfather Numitor."

"I never knew Numitor was our grandfather," replied Romulus.

"Yet it is so. Your mother was his daughter. But Amulius took the power, and wanted to get rid of you two boys, and bade me leave you in the cradle on the river Tiber, where you would soon have been drowned. But it happened otherwise, and I brought you up after a wolf and a woodpecker had fed you."

"I can hardly believe you."

"Well, here is the box you and Remus sailed in. Take it at once to Numitor. Tell him who you are. Perhaps he will spare Remus's life."

Romulus ran straightway to the house of the chief, burst into the room where he was questioning poor Remus, showed the cradle, and told all the strange story. And Numitor, looking at the faces of the young men, saw a likeness to his daughter, and felt sure the tale was true. The two brothers went off with a band of armed men to punish their great-uncle Amulius. Before the little army walked several standard-bearers, carrying poles, on the tops of which were fastened bunches of grass and shrubs. An attack was made on the tyrant's house, and Amulius was slain.

The two young chiefs—for such they now were—made up their minds to build a city of their own. They ploughed with a share or blade drawn by an ox, and ploughed a furrow in a sort of circle. This circle was the line on which the walls were built. But Remus never builded. He had told Romulus that the city ought to be built in another and safer spot.

"If you build here," he said, "the enemy will easily enter—as easily as this."

So saying, he jumped over the ploughed line in a mocking manner.

In anger Romulus and his friends fell upon Remus and struck him, and he died. When his passion cooled, great was the sorrow of Romulus; but it was too late; his brother was dead. The city that was being built would now be called after the brother who was left alive—Rome.

ॐ

Lesson 13.1

Prose & Poetry

A LOOK AT LITERARY ELEMENTS IN THE NARRATIVE

1 Read
- ◆ Listen carefully as your teacher reads the selection aloud. **Delight** in the story.

2 Inquire
- ◆ Does the **title** give any hint as to the content or message of the story? If this story was published by the author in a larger book or an anthology, does that title give any hint?
- ◆ Discuss the meaning of these words in the context of the story: *Mediterranean, trough, stout, bade, standard-bearers, passion,* and any unfamiliar words.

3 Observe the Content
- ◆ **Setting** When and where does this story take place?
- ◆ **Characters** Who is (are) the main character(s) in this story?
- ◆ **Conflict** What is the main problem or crisis for the character(s)?
- ◆ **Resolution** Is the problem solved? If so, how? If not, why not?
- ◆ **Figures** Can you identify any examples of simile, onomatopoeia, anemographia, or anastrophe in this narrative?

4 **Investigate the Context**

Lucius Mestrius Plutarchus (AD 42– AD 127), though a
Roman citizen, was a Greek historian and biographer.
Plutarch examines the lives of famous Greek and Roman
men in pairs, highlighting their moral virtues and vices in
his *Parallel Lives of the Noble Grecians and Romans*,
popularly known as *Plutarch's Lives*. Dr. George Grant
writes:

> It was the primary textbook of the Greek and
> Roman world for generations of students throughout
> Christendom. It was the historical source for many of
> Shakespeare's finest plays. It forever set the pattern for
> the biographical arts. It was the inspiration for many of the ideas of the American
> political pioneers—evidenced by liberal quotations in the articles, speeches, and
> sermons of Samuel Adams, Peyton Randolph, Patrick Henry, Samuel Davies,
> Alexander Hamilton, James Madison, Henry Lee, John Jay, George Mason,
> Gouverneur Morris, and Thomas Jefferson. Indeed, after the Bible it was the most
> frequently referenced source during the Founding era. For these and a myriad of
> other reasons, Plutarch's *Lives* is one of the most vital and consequential of all the
> ancient classics.[1]

F. J. Gould (1855-1938) was a British author and teacher. He wrote several history and
literature books for children, including two retellings of Plutarch, one with Greek lives, and
one with Roman lives from which our selection was drawn.

5 **Connect the Thoughts**

◆ Does this story remind you of other stories with similar plots, messages, or characters?

◆ Does this story remind you of any fables?

◆ Does this story remind you of any proverbs or other well-
known quotations? If so, enter these in your Commonplace
Book.

Commonplace Book

6 **Profit and Delight**

◆ **Delight** What are the sources of delight in this story?

◆ **Wisdom** What wisdom does this story furnish?

◆ **Read** the narrative aloud to your teacher with expression and with proper pauses.

◆ **Record** in your Book of Centuries: F. J. Gould, Plutarch, Birth of Romulus and Remus (c.
800 B.C.).

1. George Grant, "Why Read Plutarch?" Ambleside Online.

PLOT OBSERVATION: IDENTIFYING ACTIONS

"The Twins" has no Prologue; it simply plunges right into the main action. Also, in this narrative, we have several action changes that occur within paragraphs.

Quickly read through the narrative once more. In the margin of the narrative at the beginning of this lesson, mark the story as follows:

A. Beside the first paragraph, write **Action A.**

B. Beside the fourth paragraph, write **Action B.**

C. Beside the fifth paragraph, write **Summary**. A new action starts in the final sentence of this paragraph. Write **Action C** next to the final sentence of this paragraph.

D. Beside the fourth sentence of the tenth paragraph, write **Summary**. Beside the final sentence of the tenth paragraph, write **Action D.**

E. Beside the seventeenth paragraph, write **Action E.** A new action begins in the third sentence. Write **Action F** beside this sentence.

G. Beside the eighteenth paragraph, write **Action G.**

H. Beside the final sentence of the final paragraph, write **Epilogue.**

Review the narrative. Make notes in the margin indicating if any of the rest of Theon's Six changed with each action. You should definitely have notes about Person. Ask the questions for the other four, but do not worry too much if you can only add notes for two or three others.

Discuss your work with your teacher.

Language Logic

GRAMMAR FLASHCARDS

GRAMMAR TERMS & DEFINITIONS

Review all flashcards according to tabs.

GRAMMAR PRACTICE AND REVIEW

In your Writer's Journal, copy these sentences. Analyze each sentence by marking the simple subject (who or what the sentence is about) with a single underline, and the verb or verb phrase with a double underline. Write DO over the direct object, or LV over the linking verb; write PA over a predicate adjective and PN over a predicate nominative. Put parentheses around each prepositional phrase. Then diagram the sentence. Refer to *Sentence Sense* as needed.

1. The cattle were feeding on the pasture, but the master was not there.

2. And behold, a big she-wolf came and gazed at the babes with her fierce and shifty eyes.

3. Romulus and Remus became stout, tall, and strong young fellows.

4. Take it at once to Numitor.

5. In anger Romulus and his friends fell upon Remus and struck him, and he died.

Eloquent Expression

COPIA OF WORDS: VOCABULARY STUDY

Conduct a vocabulary study for "The Twins."

A. Choose at least two unfamiliar words to study. If you need suggestions, see the list under **Inquire** in Literary Elements above. Work in your Writer's Journal.

B. Complete Vocabulary Study steps A-G for each word (see Appendix).

Commonplace

Commonplace
Book

NARRATIVE

Session one of three commonplace sessions for this lesson. Literary selection: "The Twins."

 Set your timer and begin copying. When you finish, check your work carefully, word by word, against the original.

Lesson 13.2

Prose & Poetry

PLOT OBSERVATION: OUTLINE WITH CAPTIONS

The next task is to write a caption for each action, as well as the Prologue, Epilogue, and Summaries. Format each caption as a title, using capital letters for all words except some articles and prepositions. The first word will always be capitalized, even if it is an article or a preposition.

These captions should be *parallel*—each with the same grammatical format. Study these sample captions for "The Story of Daedalus and Icarus" (Lesson 9).

Prologue: The Plight of Daedalus
Action A: The Plan of Daedalus
Action B: The Warning to Icarus
Action C: The Flight of Icarus
Action D: The Fall of Icarus
Epilogue: The Sorrow of Daedalus

Notice that each of these captions follows the same pattern: Article – Noun – Preposition – Noun. They are *parallel*.

The captions could also be written as a short sentence.

Prologue: Minos Imprisons Daedalus
Action A: Daedalus Makes a Plan
Action B: Icarus Receives a Warning
Action C: Icarus Forgets the Warning
Action D: Sun Melts the Wings
Epilogue: Daedalus Relinquishes His Wings

Again, each of these captions follows the same pattern: Noun – Verb – Direct Object. Even though several of the direct objects are modified by an article or a pronoun showing possession, these captions are still *parallel*. Sometimes a few little extra words cannot be avoided when you write sentences.

Writer's Journal

◯ In your Writer's Journal, write a short caption for each action, as well as the Prologue, Epilogue, and Summaries.

A. Jot down a quick title for each action.

B. Review your captions, and choose a parallel format.

C. Revise all captions to conform to the format you have chosen.

Language Logic

GRAMMAR FLASHCARDS

GRAMMAR TERMS & DEFINITIONS
◯ Review all flashcards according to tabs.

SENTENCE DIAGRAMMING: INDIRECT OBJECTS
◯ Read and discuss the following section in *Sentence Sense* with your teacher.

SENTENCE SENSE

III. Sentence Diagrammming: Objects & Complements
◆ 16.1 Indirect Objects

◯ In your Writer's Journal, copy these sentences. Analyze each sentence by marking the simple subject (who or what the sentence is about) with a single underline, and the verb or verb phrase with a double underline. Write DO over a direct object, LV over a linking verb, PA over a predicate adjective, and PN over a predicate nominative. Put parentheses around each prepositional phrase. Then diagram the sentence. Refer to *Sentence Sense* as needed. You should be able to diagram each word in the sentence now.

1. Latinus welcomed the Trojan, and gave him ground.

2. I am telling you the truth.

3. Anger could not give them back their ship.

4. Daedalus made Icarus a pair of wings.

5. Discord would cause them misfortune.

Writer's Journal

Classical Composition

PLOT OBSERVATION: ORAL NARRATION

 Without reading "The Twins" again, retell the **plot** orally to your teacher. Refer to your plot observation of the narrative with Theon's Six if needed.

Commonplace

NARRATIVE

Session two of three commonplace sessions for this lesson. Literary selection: "The Twins."

 Set your timer and begin copying. When you finish, check your work carefully, word by word, against the original. Check spelling, capitalization, and punctuation for accuracy.

Commonplace Book

Lesson 13.3

Language Logic

GRAMMAR FLASHCARDS

GRAMMAR TERMS & DEFINITIONS
 Review all flashcards according to tabs.

SENTENCE DIAGRAMMING

In your Writer's Journal, copy these sentences. Analyze each sentence by marking the simple subject (who or what the sentence is about) with a single underline, and the verb or verb phrase with a double underline. Write DO over a direct object, LV over a linking verb, PA over a predicate adjective, and PN over a predicate nominative. Put parentheses around each prepositional phrase. Then diagram the sentence. Refer to *Sentence Sense* as needed. You should be able to diagram each word in the sentence now.

1. He was going toward the river, and he was carrying a burden in his arms.

2. Did the woodpecker, with his long beak and tongue, bring the boys insects and grubs, or did he bring them berries and other fruits?

3. Romulus ran straightway to the house of the chief, burst into the room, showed him the cradle, and told all the strange story.

4. Great was the sorrow of Romulus; his brother was dead.

5. He was unjust and cruel, and everyone hated him, so he was always in dread for his life.

Writer's Journal

Eloquent Expression

SENTENCE STYLE – COPIA: PERSON AND POINT OF VIEW

Another way to apply grammar in your writing is to consider the noun and pronoun property of **person** (*Sentence Sense*, 2.0B). For example, a sentence written in third person may be changed to first or second person. Again, you will probably need to adjust the rest of the sentence.

Erasmus was pleased by your letter. (3rd person)

I was pleased by your letter. (1st person)

You pleased me by your letter. (2nd person)

The noun property of person is used most often to create dialogue, but it can also be used to change the **point of view** (speaker) of an entire paragraph or narrative. We will practice with paragraphs in an upcoming lesson, and later apply it to a retelling.

Writer's Journal

🏵 Paraphrase each sentence twice, changing the person each time.

1. Amulius took the power, and wanted to get rid of the boys.

2. I can hardly believe you.

Classical Composition

NARRATIVE RETELLING – FIRST DRAFT

You will have two sessions to work on this retelling. Begin here, and plan to finish in Lesson 13.4. As you write your retelling, do your best to use proper grammar and spelling, but keep in mind that you will have opportunity to edit before you finalize it.

Writer's Journal

🏵 Retell "The Twins" in writing, keeping the same characters, setting, and sequence of action. Refer to your plot observation of the narrative with Theon's Six, but do not review the original narrative before you write. Include:

- ◆ a heading, properly formatted
- ◆ at least one onomatopoeic word
- ◆ at least one instance of anastrophe
- ◆ (optional figure of speech) simile
- ◆ (optional figure of description) anemographia

Lesson 13.4

Language Logic

GRAMMAR FLASHCARDS

GRAMMAR TERMS & DEFINITIONS
🏵 Review all flashcards according to tabs.

Classical Composition

Writer's Journal

NARRATIVE RETELLING – FINISH FIRST DRAFT

Finish the first draft of your narrative retelling. Review the instructions in Lesson 13.3 as needed.

Commonplace

NARRATIVE

Session three of three commonplace sessions for this lesson. Literary selection: "The Twins."

Commonplace Book

Set your timer. Begin where you stopped in the last session. When you finish, check your work carefully against the original for accuracy.

Lesson 13.5

Prose & Poetry

POETRY APPRECIATION

Read and enjoy a few poems in your poetry anthology. Identify rhyme schemes and stanza forms of one or two. Look for poems with iambic or dactylic meter. Look for figures of speech and figures of description in the poems you read, and make note of any you find for future Commonplace Book entries. Read one or two poems aloud with expression and proper pauses. Pause at punctuation, but not necessarily at the ends of lines.

Language Logic

GRAMMAR TERMS & DEFINITIONS

⚜ Ask your teacher to quiz you with the grammar flashcards. Alternately, use the test feature in the Cottage Press *Bards & Poets I* Quizlet Classroom for an online or printed quiz for Lesson 13.

DICTATION: NARRATIVE PASSAGE

⚜ Work in your Writer's Journal. Write as your teacher dictates a passage to you from your Commonplace Book. When you are done, check your work carefully, word by word, against the original. Check for accurate spelling, capitalization, and punctuation.

Classical Composition

NARRATIVE RETELLING: TYPE FINAL DRAFT

⚜ Type your retelling on the computer with spell-check turned off, or ask your writing mentor to type it exactly as you wrote it. Save, print, and file this draft in your writing binder.

Commonplace

FROM YOUR READING

Find selections in a book or poem to add to your Commonplace Book. Include the name of the book or poem, properly formatted. Label the entry with the grammar or poetry feature, the figure of speech, or as a favorite passage. Aim for a minimum of three entries, with at least one from each category.

⚜ Grammar Features (choose any)

   ◆ A sentence that has an interesting or descriptive noun, a strong and fitting verb, a well-chosen adjective, and/or a vivid adverb

- ◆ A sentence with one or more prepositional phrases or indirect objects
- ◆ A sentence that has a conjunction to join words, phrases, or clauses
- ◆ An interesting dialogue tag (add to your Dialogue Tags list)
- ◆ An interrogative, exclamatory, or imperative sentence

Figures (choose any)

- ◆ Figures of Speech: simile, onomatopoeia, and/or anastrophe
- ◆ Figures of Description: anemographia

Poetry Features (choose any)

- ◆ Rhyme (note name of the rhyme scheme)
- ◆ Iambic, dactylic, or anapestic meter (note name of the meter)
- ◆ Stanza (note name of stanza form)

Favorite Passage: Add at least one passage of one to three sentences or several lines of poetry that captured your attention in your reading this week. It may be something you found beautiful, thought-provoking, funny, or interesting.

CR

THE STAR-SPANGLED BANNER

O say can you see, by the dawn's early light,

What so proudly we hail'd at the twilight's last gleaming,

Whose broad stripes and bright stars through the perilous fight

O'er the ramparts we watch'd were so gallantly streaming?

And the rocket's red glare, the bombs bursting in air,

Gave proof through the night that our flag was still there,

O say does that star-spangled banner yet wave

O'er the land of the free and the home of the brave?

On the shore dimly seen through the mists of the deep

Where the foe's haughty host in dread silence reposes,

What is that which the breeze, o'er the towering steep,

As it fitfully blows, half conceals, half discloses?

Now it catches the gleam of the morning's first beam,

In full glory reflected now shines in the stream,

'Tis the star-spangled banner - O long may it wave

O'er the land of the free and the home of the brave!

And where is that band who so vauntingly swore,

That the havoc of war and the battle's confusion

A home and a Country should leave us no more?

Their blood has wash'd out their foul footstep's pollution.

No refuge could save the hireling and slave

From the terror of flight or the gloom of the grave,

And the star-spangled banner in triumph doth wave

O'er the land of the free and the home of the brave.

O thus be it ever when freemen shall stand

Between their lov'd home and the war's desolation!

Blest with vict'ry and peace may the heav'n rescued land

Praise the power that hath made and preserv'd us a nation!

Then conquer we must, when our cause it is just,

And this be our motto - "In God is our trust,"

And the star-spangled banner in triumph shall wave

O'er the land of the free and the home of the brave.

— FRANCIS SCOTT KEY

℆

Lesson 14.1

Prose & Poetry

A LOOK AT LITERARY ELEMENTS IN THE POEM

1 Read
- Follow along and listen carefully as the poem is read aloud, OR read it aloud yourself. Read it at least two or three times. **Delight** in the meter, the rhyme, and the images.

2 Inquire
- Does the **title** give any hint as to the content or message of the poem?
- Are there any other unfamiliar persons, places, or things mentioned in the poem? Discuss these with your teacher.
- Discuss the meaning of these words in the context of the story: *hailed, perilous, ramparts, reposes, conceals, discloses, vauntingly, havoc, hireling, desolation, preserved,* and any unfamiliar words.
- Was there any part of the poem you did not understand? If so, discuss this with your teacher and classmates.

3 Observe the Content

◆ **Lyrical Elements**

- What does the poet describe?
- Does the poet make you see, hear, smell, taste, or touch anything?
- Does the poet compare something in the poem to some other thing?

◆ **Narrative Elements** Does this poem tell a story? If so, observe the

- **Setting** When and where does this story take place?
- **Characters** Who is (are) the main character(s) in this story?
- **Conflict** What is the main problem or crisis for the character(s)?
- **Resolution** Is the problem solved? If so, how? If not, why not?

◆ **Point of View** Who is speaking in the poem? Is it first-person or third-person?

◆ **Figures** Can you identify any examples of simile, onomatopoeia, anemographia, or anastrophe in this poem?

4 Investigate the Context

Francis Scott Key (1779-1843) was a Maryland lawyer. Though only an occasional poet, he gave us our National Anthem. The story of its composition during the War of 1812 is inspiring:

> The British were about to attack Baltimore when Francis Scott Key, hearing that one of his friends had been taken prisoner, rowed out to the British fleet under a flag of truce to beg his release. The British Admiral consented to his release. He said, however, that both Key and his friend must wait until the attack was over.

> So, from the British fleet, Key watched the bombardment of Fort McHenry which guarded the town. All through the night the guns roared and flashed, and in the lurid light Key could see the flag on Fort McHenry fluttering proudly. But before dawn the firing ceased.

> "What had happened," he asked himself, "was the fort taken?"

> Eagerly he waited for the dawn. And when at last the sun rose he saw with joy that the Stars and Stripes still floated over the fort. There and then on the back of an old letter he wrote "The Star Spangled Banner." People hailed it with delight, soon it was sung throughout the length and breadth of the States, and at length became the National Anthem. — Henrietta E. Marshall, *This Country of Ours*

5 Connect the Thoughts

- ♦ Does this poem remind you of other poems, or of stories with similar plots, messages, or characters?

- ♦ Does this poem remind you of any proverbs or other well-known quotations? If so, enter these in your Commonplace Book.

Commonplace Book

6 Profit and Delight

- ♦ **Delight** What are the sources of delight in this poem?

- ♦ **Wisdom** What wisdom does this poem furnish?

- ♦ **Read** the poem aloud to your teacher with expression and with proper pauses.

- ♦ **Record** in your Book of Centuries: Francis Scott Key, Battle of Fort McHenry.

- ♦ **Memorize** this poem and **recite** it before an audience.

Language Logic

GRAMMAR FLASHCARDS

GRAMMAR TERMS & DEFINITIONS

❂ Review all flashcards according to tabs.

GRAMMAR PRACTICE AND REVIEW

❂ In your Writer's Journal, copy these sentences. Analyze each sentence by marking the simple subject (who or what the sentence is about) with a single underline, and the verb or verb phrase with a double underline. Write D.O. over the direct object, or L.V. over the linking verb; write PA over a predicate adjective and PN over a predicate nominative. Put parentheses around each prepositional phrase. Then diagram the sentence. Refer to *Sentence Sense* as needed.

1. No refuge could save the hireling and slave from the terror of flight or the gloom of the grave.

2. In God is our trust.

3. That evening, the bombs burst in air; next morning, the flag was still there.

4. Francis Scott Key gave us our National Anthem.

Writer's Journal

Eloquent Expression

COPIA OF WORDS: VOCABULARY STUDY

🏵 Conduct a vocabulary study for "The Star-Spangled Banner."

Writer's Journal

A. Choose at least two unfamiliar words to study. If you need suggestions, see the list under **Inquire** in Literary Elements above. Work in your Writer's Journal.

B. Complete Vocabulary Study steps A-G for each word (see Appendix).

Classical Composition

EDITOR'S PEN – THE BIG PICTURE

🏵 Edit your retelling from Lesson 13:

Editor's Pen – The Big Picture

✔ All important plot elements included
✔ All characters represented correctly
✔ Sequence: *same as the original*
✔ Length: *similar to the original*
✔ Figure of Speech: *onomatopoeia, anastrophe*; optional: *simile*
✔ Figure of Description (optional): *anemographia*

A. Read aloud exactly what you have written—not what you THINK you have written! Mark any corrections on your first draft.

B. Next, work through the Big Picture checklist above with your writing mentor.

C. Transfer all additions and corrections from your print copy of the retelling to your file on the computer. Print and file this edited version in your binder along with your marked-up editing copy of the first draft.

Commonplace

Commonplace
Book

POETRY

Session one of three commonplace sessions for this lesson. Literary
selection: "The Star-Spangled Banner."

 Set your timer and begin copying. When finished, check your
work carefully against the original for accuracy.

Lesson 14.2

Prose & Poetry

RHYME SCHEME AND STANZA FORM

 Mark the end rhyme in the stanzas below.

> O say can you see, by the dawn's early light,
>
> What so proudly we hail'd at the twilight's last gleaming,
>
> Whose broad stripes and bright stars through the perilous fight
>
> O'er the ramparts we watch'd were so gallantly streaming?
>
> And the rocket's red glare, the bombs bursting in air,
>
> Gave proof through the night that our flag was still there,
>
> O say does that star-spangled banner yet wave
>
> O'er the land of the free and the home of the brave?

> On the shore dimly seen through the mists of the deep
>
> Where the foe's haughty host in dread silence reposes,
>
> What is that which the breeze, o'er the towering steep,
>
> As it fitfully blows, half conceals, half discloses?
>
> Now it catches the gleam of the morning's first beam,
>
> In full glory reflected now shines in the stream,

'Tis the star-spangled banner - O long may it wave

O'er the land of the free and the home of the brave!

And where is that band who so vauntingly swore,

That the havoc of war and the battle's confusion

A home and a Country should leave us no more?

Their blood has wash'd out their foul footstep's pollution.

No refuge could save the hireling and slave

From the terror of flight or the gloom of the grave,

And the star-spangled banner in triumph doth wave

O'er the land of the free and the home of the brave.

O thus be it ever when freemen shall stand

Between their lov'd home and the war's desolation!

Blest with vict'ry and peace may the heav'n rescued land

Praise the power that hath made and preserv'd us a nation!

Then conquer we must, when our cause it is just,

And this be our motto - "In God is our trust,"

And the star-spangled banner in triumph shall wave

O'er the land of the free and the home of the brave.

Name the predominant rhyme scheme and the stanza form of this poem. Notice the repeated line at the end of each stanza, along with the repeated word in the line preceding the final one. This repetition is a figure of speech called a **refrain**, or sometimes in music, a **chorus**. Many hymns and songs use this figure. We have had another poem in this book that had such a repetition. Look back over the selections and find it.

Language Logic

GRAMMAR TERMS & DEFINITIONS

Review all flashcards according to tabs.

SENTENCE DIAGRAMMING

 Read and discuss the following section in *Sentence Sense* with your teacher.

III. Sentence Diagrammming: Modifiers
* 13.6 Adjectives as Substantives

 In your Writer's Journal, copy these sentences. Analyze each sentence by marking the simple subject (who or what the sentence is about) with a single underline, and the verb or verb phrase with a double underline. Write DO over a direct object, LV over a linking verb, PA over a predicate adjective, and PN over a predicate nominative. Put parentheses around each prepositional phrase. Then diagram the sentence. Refer to *Sentence Sense* as needed. You should be able to diagram each word in the sentence now.

1. O say, does that star-spangled banner yet wave o'er the land of the free and the home of the brave?

2. The blind receive their sight and the lame walk; the lepers are cleansed and the deaf hear. – Matthew 11:5

3. God resisteth the proud, but giveth grace to the humble. – James 4:1

Eloquent Expression

FIGURE OF SPEECH: ALLITERATION

This is another figure of speech, like onomatopoeia, which has to do with the way words *sound*. **Alliteration** is the repetition of beginning sounds in words that are adjacent or very close to each other. There are many examples of alliteration in names like Krispy Kreme or Fred Flintstone.

Diddle, diddle, dumpling, my son John... — Mother Goose

Peter Piper picked a peck of pickled peppers. — Mother Goose

With many a curve my banks I fret
By many a field and fallow,
And many a fairy foreland set
With willow-weed and mallow. — Alfred, Lord Tennyson, "The Brook"

. . the Cottage of content [is] better than the Palace of cold splendour . . . — Charles
Dickens, *David Copperfield*

Four score and seven years ago our fathers brought forth on this continent a new nation.
— Abraham Lincoln, "Gettysburg Address"

Study and review figures of speech with your teacher.

A. Discuss the examples of alliteration with your teacher.

B. Look in "The Star-Spangled Banner" for examples of alliteration and discuss them with your teacher. In your Writer's Journal, make a list of alliterative words you find in this poem.

Writer's Journal

C. Look through other poems we have studied in *Bards & Poets I* for more examples of alliteration. Make note of some that you may wish to copy into your Commonplace Book.

Classical Composition

EDITOR'S PEN – ZOOM 5X: PARAGRAPHS

Now that the Big Picture is set, begin to zoom in for a close look at the paragraph(s) in your retelling with your writing mentor.

Editor's Pen – Zoom 5x: Paragraphs
✔ Formatting: *proper indentation*
✔ Length: *neither too wordy nor too short*
✔ Sentence class by use: *effective use*
✔ Dialogue: *effective use*
✔ Verb Tense: *consistent*

A. Read aloud your most recently edited version. Check each item in the Editor's Pen checklist to identify possible changes. Mark these on your print copy.

B. Transfer all additions and corrections from your print copy to the computer file. Print this version and file it in your binder along with your other versions.

Lesson 14.3

Prose & Poetry

SCANSION – ANAPESTIC METER

An **anapest** is the opposite of a dactyl, a foot with three beats: unstress-unstress-stress. Say these anapestic words aloud to get a feel for the rhythm: *understand, overcome, interrupt.* Can you think of any other anapestic words?

Anapestic meter is not quite as common as iambic, but still is found quite often in English poetry. The word anapest is anapestic itself! It is helpful and fun to really emphasize the third syllable to remember the pattern: *an a PEST.*

Dr. Seuss uses anapestic meter extensively and masterfully, so we will use his classic *Horton Hears a Who* as our example for scanning. This selection is almost completely regular, except for one dropped unstress at the beginning of the final line. This is a common feature of anapestic lines.

|∪ ∪ /| ∪ ∪ / |∪∪ / |∪∪ / |
On the fif teenth of May, in the jun gle of Nool,

|∪∪ / | ∪∪ / |∪ ∪ / | ∪∪ / |
In the heat of the day, in the cool of the pool,

|∪ ∪ / | ∪ ∪ / |∪∪ / |∪ ∪ / |
He was splash ing... en joy ing the jun gle's great joys...

| ∪ / |∪ ∪ / |∪ ∪ / | ∪ ∪ / |
When Hor ton the el e phant heard a small noise.

Nota Bene: In line 4, the dactylic word *elephant* is used to form the second two anapestic feet because of the way it is arranged in the word order.

Scan these stanzas, following the three steps you have learned.

Step 1 Mark each syllable as either stressed (/) or unstressed (∪). Say the line aloud several times to "get" the meter. Next, say the line aloud emphasizing the stresses as you mark the stresses only. Then go back and mark the unstressed syllables, saying the line aloud once more to check your work.

Step 2 Insert dividers (|) to mark off the feet. Remember that you will only have one stress in each foot for this poem. Lines one, six, and seven drop out one unstress in the foot at the beginning of the line, another very common feature of anapestic meter. Lines two and four have an additional unstress at the end of the line, which is still part of the final foot.

Step 3 Name the poem's meter:

O say can you see, by the dawn's early light,

What so proudly we hail'd at the twilight's last gleaming,

Whose broad stripes and bright stars through the perilous fight

O'er the ramparts we watch'd were so gallantly streaming?

And the rocket's red glare, the bombs bursting in air,

Gave proof through the night that our flag was still there,

O say does that star-spangled banner yet wave

O'er the land of the free and the home of the brave?

Language Logic

GRAMMAR TERMS & DEFINITIONS
 Review all flashcards according to tabs.

SENTENCE DIAGRAMMING

In your Writer's Journal, copy these sentences. Analyze each sentence by marking the simple subject (who or what the sentence is about) with a single underline, and the verb or verb phrase with a double underline. Write DO over a direct object, LV over a linking verb, PA over a predicate adjective, and PN over a predicate nominative. Put parentheses around each prepositional phrase. Then diagram the sentence. Refer to *Sentence Sense* as needed. You should be able to diagram each word in the sentence now.

1. The broad stripes and bright stars through the perilous fight were so gallantly streaming.

2. A home and a country we shall leave you no more!

3. A great wind filled their wings, and Icarus forgot everything in the world but joy.

4. Do not pervert justice; do not show partiality to the poor or favoritism to the great, but judge your neighbor fairly. – Lev. 19:15

Eloquent Expression

SENTENCE STYLE – YOUR STYLE!

Craft copia for sentences from your own retelling using Sentence Style devices we have studied.

A. Work with your writing mentor to choose three sentences from your retelling that could be improved.

B. Copy the first in your Writer's Journal. Underline every important word in the sentence and jot down synonyms for each.

C. Use the list of Sentence Style devices below as you write several new versions of the sentence. You may use more than one device in each sentence.

D. Repeat the instructions above for the second and third sentences.

E. Choose your favorite paraphrase of each sentence. Replace the original sentences in your retelling before you edit again.

COPIA OF WORDS
✓ Synonyms and Antonyms
✓ Dialogue - synonyms for *said*
✓ Point of View
✓ Nouns – varied and descriptive
    ◆ switch noun/pronouns
✓ Verbs – strong and fitting
✓ Modifiers
    ◆ add adjective
    ◆ add adverb

COPIA OF CONSTRUCTION
✓ Sentence class by use
✓ Dialogue
    ◆ Tag line position
✓ Verb Tense
✓ Sentence Combination
    ◆ compound elements

Classical Composition

EDITOR'S PEN – ZOOM 10X: SENTENCES

Now it is time to zoom in even closer as you check the sentences in your retelling. Work with your writing mentor.

Editor's Pen – Zoom 10x: Sentences
✓ Complete thought expressed
✓ Subject and predicate agree in number
✓ Correct capitalization and punctuation
    ◆ Commas correctly used for words in a series
    ◆ No comma splices or run-on sentences!

A. Read aloud your your most recently edited version. Use the Editor's Pen checklist to identify changes you need to make. Mark all changes on your print copy.

B. Transfer all additions and corrections from your print copy to the computer file. Print this version and file it in your binder along with your other versions.

Commonplace

POETRY

Session two of three commonplace sessions for this lesson. Literary selection: "The Star-Spangled Banner."

Commonplace Book

 Set your timer. Begin where you stopped in the last session. When you finish, check your work carefully against the original for accuracy.

Lesson 14.4

Prose & Poetry

SCANSION

 Scan these stanzas, following the three steps you have learned.

Step 1 Mark each syllable as either stressed (/) or unstressed (∪). Say the line aloud several times to "get" the meter. Next, say the line aloud emphasizing the stresses as you mark the stresses only. Then go back and mark the unstressed syllables, saying the line aloud once more to check your work.

Step 2 Insert dividers (|) to mark off the feet. Remember that you will only have one stress in each foot for this poem. Lines one, two, five, and six drop an unstress in the foot at the beginning of the line. Lines two and four have an extra unstress in the final foot. Pronounce power as one syllable: *pow'r.*

Step 3 Name the poem's meter:

O thus be it ever when freemen shall stand

Between their lov'd home and the war's desolation!

Blest with vict'ry and peace may the heav'n rescued land

Praise the power that hath made and preserv'd us a nation!

Then conquer we must, when our cause it is just,

And this be our motto - "In God is our trust,"

And the star-spangled banner in triumph shall wave

O'er the land of the free and the home of the brave.

Language Logic

GRAMMAR TERMS & DEFINITIONS
Review all flashcards according to tabs.

Eloquent Expression

PARAGRAPH STYLE – PARAPHRASE WITH COPIA
For this exercise, choose from all of the copia devices you have learned so far. See the copia chart in Lesson 14.3. New devices are in bold type.

In your Writer's Journal, paraphrase this paragraph. Change each sentence opener, and change at least one sentence class by use. Use as many synonym substitutions as possible. Use as many of the other copia devices as you are able. Make notes on the paragraph below before you begin.

Writer's Journal

Romulus ran straightway to the house of the chief, burst into the room where he was questioning poor Remus, showed the cradle, and told all the strange story. And Numitor, looking at the faces of the young men, saw a likeness to his daughter, and felt sure the tale was true. The two brothers went off with a band of armed men to punish their great-uncle Amulius. Before the little army walked several standard-bearers, carrying poles, on the tops of which were fastened bunches of grass and shrubs. An attack was made on the

tyrant's house, and Amulius was slain.

Classical Composition

EDITOR'S PEN – FINE FOCUS: WORDS

The final checks dwell on the details of your word usage. Continue to compile your personal editing checklist to use in editing all of your work across the curriculum.

Editor's Pen – Fine Focus: Words
✓ Word choices varied; word meanings clear
   ◆ Verbs: *strong, fitting; appropriate adverbs if needed*
   ◆ Nouns: *clear, descriptive; appropriate adjectives if needed*
   ◆ Dialogue: *dialogue tags varied if appropropriate*
✓ Correct spelling
✓ Final read-through

A. Read aloud your most recent version. Identify changes you need to make with the Editor's Pen checklist. Mark these on your print copy.

B. Transfer all additions and corrections from your print copy to the computer file. Print this final version and file it in your binder along with your other versions.

Commonplace

Commonplace Book

POETRY

Session three of three commonplace sessions for this lesson. Literary selection: "The Star-Spangled Banner."

 Set your timer and begin copying. When you finish, check your work carefully against the original for accuracy.

Lesson 14.5

Prose & Poetry

POETRY APPRECIATION

 Read and enjoy a few poems in your poetry anthology. Identify rhyme schemes and stanza forms of one or two. Look for figures of speech and figures of description in the poems you read, and make note of any you find for future Commonplace Book entries. Read one or two poems aloud with expression and proper pauses. Pause at punctuation, but not necessarily at the ends of lines. Finally, choose a rhyming poem with anapestic meter to observe.

- ◆ In your Writer's Journal, write the title of the poem and the author. Make note of its meter, rhyme scheme, and stanza form.

- ◆ Write the rhyming words from the poem in two lists: one list for those spelled the same, and one list for those spelled differently.

- ◆ Choose one of the rhyming words from the spelled differently list, and try to come up with several additional rhymes. Look especially for varied spellings.

Language Logic

GRAMMAR TERMS & DEFINITIONS

GRAMMAR FLASHCARDS

 Ask your teacher to quiz you with the grammar flashcards. Alternately, use the test feature in the Cottage Press *Bards & Poets I* Quizlet Classroom for an online or printed quiz for Lesson 14.

DICTATION: POETRY

 Work in your Writer's Journal. Write as your teacher dictates a passage to you from your Commonplace Book. When you are done, check your work carefully, word by word, against the original. Check for accurate spelling, capitalization, and punctuation.

Classical Composition

POETRY

 In your Writer's Journal, write two to four rhyming lines that summarize the action of "The Twins." If you wish, include a poetic **moral** at the end. Consider including them at the end of your retelling as a brief summary of the story. You may find it easiest to imitate the rhyme and meter of a few lines of the poetic selection for this lesson or a previous lesson.

Writer's Journal

NARRATIVE RETELLING – FINAL DRAFT

Read over the final version of your retelling one last time and make any needed changes. Save it on your computer; print and file with all the other drafts in your writing binder.

Commonplace

FROM YOUR READING

Find selections in a book or poem to add to your Commonplace Book. Include the name of the book or poem, properly formatted. Label the entry with the grammar or poetry feature, the figure of speech, or as a favorite passage. Aim for a minimum of three entries, with at least one from each category.

Commonplace Book

Grammar Features (choose any)

- ◆ A sentence that has an interesting or descriptive noun, a strong and fitting verb, a well-chosen adjective, and/or a vivid adverb
- ◆ A sentence with one or more prepositional phrases or indirect objects
- ◆ A sentence that has a conjunction to join words, phrases, or clauses
- ◆ An interesting dialogue tag (add to your Dialogue Tags list)
- ◆ An interrogative, exclamatory, or imperative sentence

Figures (choose any)

- ◆ Figures of Speech: simile, onomatopoeia, anastrophe, and/or alliteration
- ◆ Figures of Description: anemographia

◯ Poetry Features (choose any)

- ◆ Rhyme (note name of the rhyme scheme)
- ◆ Iambic, anapestic, or dactylic meter (note name of the meter)
- ◆ Stanza (note name of stanza form)

◯ Favorite Passage: Add at least one passage of one to three sentences or several lines of poetry that captured your attention in your reading this week. It may be something you found beautiful, thought-provoking, funny, or interesting.

Lesson 15

❧

HORATIUS

from FAMOUS MEN OF ROME by John H. Haaren & A. B. Poland

For a time Rome was ruled by Publius Valerius. He was a good man. He caused laws to be passed for the benefit of the people and was therefore called Publicola, which means the people's friend. He had to fight Tarquin frequently. The banished king was constantly trying to capture Rome and get back his throne. He got help from various nations and fought very hard, but was never successful in his efforts. At one time he was aided by Lars Porsena, king of Clusium, a city of Etruria, who gathered a large army and set out to attack Rome.

But Porsena could not enter the city without crossing the Tiber, and there was only one bridge. This was called the Sublician Bridge. It was so called from the Latin word *sublicæ*, which means wooden beams. When the Romans saw the great army of Etruscans in the distance, they were much alarmed. They were not prepared to fight so powerful a force. The consul thought for a while, and then he resolved to cut down the bridge as the only means of saving Rome. So a number of men were at once set to work with axes and hammers.

It was hard work, for the bridge was very strongly built. Before the beams supporting it were all cut away the army of Porsena was seen approaching the river. What was to be done? It would take a few minutes more to finish the work, and if the farther end of the bridge could be held against the Etruscans for those few minutes all would be well for Rome. But how was it to be held, and who would hold it? Suddenly from the ranks of the Roman soldiers the brave Horatius Cocles stepped out and cried to the consul:

"Give me two good men to help me, and I will hold the bridge and stop the enemy from coming over."

Immediately two brave men, Spurius Lartius and Titus Herminius, ran to his side. Then the three hurried over to the other end of the bridge, and stood ready to keep off the enemy.

When the army of Etruscans saw the three men standing to keep them back a shout of laughter went up among them. Three men to keep back thousands! How ridiculous! There the three brave Romans stood, however, at the entrance of the bridge, with determined faces and fearless eyes.

Very quickly three Etruscans—stout, able fighters—came forth from the army to give battle to the three Romans. After a sharp combat the Etruscans were killed. Three more came out and continued the fight, but they too were beaten by Horatius and his companions.

But now the bridge began to shake and crack. Horatius felt that it was about to fall, and he cried to Spurius and Titus to run back to the other side. While they did so he stood alone and defied the whole Etruscan army, which was now rushing upon him. A whole army against one man! Javelins were hurled at him, but he skillfully warded them off with his shield.

Just as the Etruscans reached him the last beam was cut away, and the bridge fell with a tremendous crash. As it was falling Horatius plunged into the Tiber, and praying to the gods for help, he swam to the other side in safety. The Romans received him with shouts of joy, and even the Etruscans could not help raising a cheer in admiration of his bravery.

The three Romans were well rewarded. A fine statue of Horatius was built in one of the squares of the city. On the base of the statue was placed a brass tablet, with an account of the heroic deed engraved on it. The Senate also gave Horatius as much land as he could plow around in a day.

CR

Lesson 15.1

Prose & Poetry

A LOOK AT LITERARY ELEMENTS IN THE NARRATIVE

1 Read
◆ Listen carefully as your teacher reads the selection aloud. **Delight** in the story.

2 Inquire
◆ Does the **title** give any hint as to the content or message of the story? If this story was published by the author in a larger book or an anthology, does that title give any hint?

◆ Discuss the meaning of these words in the context of the story: *banished, various, consul, hold, ridiculous, determined, combat, defied, javelins, admiration,* and any unfamiliar words.

3 Observe the Content
◆ **Setting** When and where does this story take place?

◆ **Characters** Who is (are) the main character(s) in this story?

◆ **Conflict** What is the main problem or crisis for the character(s)?

◆ **Resolution** Is the problem solved? If so, how? If not, why not?

◆ **Point of View** Who is telling the story? Is it first-person or third-person?

◆ **Figures** Can you identify any examples of simile, onomatopoeia, anemographia, anastrophe, or alliteration in this narrative?

4 Investigate the Context
The story of Publius Horatius Cocles is told by several ancient Roman historians, including Plutarch, Livy, and Polybius. The details vary, but this version of the story was immortalized in verse by Lord Macaulay. We will read part of that poem and learn about the poet in the next lesson.

Famous Men of Rome was published in 1904 by John H. Haaren, the District Supervisor of the New York Public School System, with contributions from his colleague A. B. Poland. The Preface gives their purpose in retelling these stories:

> The study of history, like the study of a landscape, should begin with the most conspicuous features. Not until these have been fixed in memory will the lesser features fall into their appropriate places and assume their right proportions . . . The former practice in many elementary schools of beginning the detailed study of American history without any previous knowledge of general history limited the pupil's range of vision, restricted his sympathies, and left him without material for comparisons. Moreover, it denied to him a knowledge of his inheritance from the Greek philosopher, the Roman lawgiver, the Teutonic lover of freedom. Hence the recommendation . . . that the study of Greek, Roman and modern European history in the form of biography should precede the study of detailed American history in our elementary schools.

5   Connect the Thoughts

- Does this story remind you of other stories with similar plots, messages, or characters?
- Does this story remind you of any fables?
- Does this story remind you of any proverbs or other well-known quotations? If so, enter these in your Commonplace Book.

Commonplace Book

6   Profit and Delight

- **Delight** What are the sources of delight in this story?
- **Wisdom** What wisdom does this story furnish?
- **Read** the narrative aloud to your teacher with expression and with proper pauses.
- **Record** in your Book of Centuries: Horatius, Lars Porsena, Battle Between Rome and Clusium.

PLOT OBSERVATION: IDENTIFYING ACTIONS

Now it is your turn to try your hand at identifying the actions in a narrative. Base your outline of actions on changes in Theon's elements—most often in person, action, time, and place—as the narrative progresses. Remember that there may be several good schemes for outlining the action for any given narrative. Just be sure to have good reasons for your decisions, and be prepared to explain them to your teacher.

Observe the plot of "Horatius." Work in pencil on the original narrative at the beginning of this lesson, marking and making notes in the margin as instructed below.

A. Quickly read through the narrative once more. Number the paragraphs.

B. Identify the main actions. The first paragraph begins the **Prologue**, and the first action begins within the second paragraph. The final paragraph is an **Epilogue**. You should identify five or six actions in this narrative. Mark them on the narrative.

C. Review the narrative. Make notes in the margin indicating if any of the rest of Theon's Six changed with each action. You should definitely have notes about Person. Ask the questions for the other four, but do not worry too much if you can only add notes for two or three others.

D. Discuss your work with your teacher.

Language Logic

GRAMMAR TERMS & DEFINITIONS
❂ Review all flashcards according to tabs.

GRAMMAR PRACTICE AND REVIEW

❂ In your Writer's Journal, copy these sentences. Analyze each sentence by marking the simple subject (who or what the sentence is about) with a single underline, and the verb or verb phrase with a double underline. Write DO over the direct object, or LV over the linking verb; write PA over a predicate adjective and PN over a predicate nominative. Put parentheses around each prepositional phrase. Then diagram the sentence. Refer to *Sentence Sense* as needed.

1. Suddenly from the ranks of the Roman soldiers the brave Horatius Cocles stepped out and cried to the consul.

2. Could three keep back thousands?

3. Javelins were hurled at him, but he skillfully warded them off with his shield.

4. The Romans received him with shouts of joy, and even the Etruscans raised a cheer in admiration of his bravery.

Writer's Journal

Eloquent Expression

COPIA OF WORDS: VOCABULARY STUDY

Writer's
Journal

❂ Conduct a vocabulary study for the story "Horatius."

A. Choose at least two unfamiliar words to study. If you need suggestions, see the list under **Inquire** in Literary Elements above. Work in your Writer's Journal.

B. Complete Vocabulary Study steps A-G for each word (see Appendix).

Commonplace

NARRATIVE

Commonplace
Book

Session one of three commonplace sessions for this lesson. Literary selection: "Horatius."

❂ Set your timer and begin copying. When you finish, check your work carefully, word by word, against the original.

Lesson 15.2

Prose & Poetry

PLOT OBSERVATION: OUTLINE WITH CAPTIONS

Writer's
Journal

❂ In your Writer's Journal, create an outline to capture your observations with parallel captions.

A. Jot down a quick title for the Prologue, each major action, and the Epilogue.

B. Review your captions, and choose a parallel format.

C. Revise all captions to conform to the format you have chosen.

Language Logic

GRAMMAR TERMS & DEFINITIONS
Review all flashcards according to tabs.

SENTENCE DIAGRAMMING: POSSESSIVE NOUNS AND PRONOUNS
Read and discuss the following sections in *Sentence Sense* with your teacher.

III. Sentence Diagrammming: Possessives
- ◆ 14.1 Nouns and Pronouns Showing Possession
- ◆ 14.2 Possessive Pronouns

In your Writer's Journal, copy these sentences. Analyze each sentence by marking the simple subject (who or what the sentence is about) with a single underline, and the verb or verb phrase with a double underline. Write DO over a direct object, LV over a linking verb, PA over a predicate adjective, and PN over a predicate nominative. Put parentheses around each prepositional phrase. Then diagram the sentence. Refer to *Sentence Sense* as needed. You should be able to diagram each word in the sentence now.

1. Publicola was the people's friend.

2. The foe's haughty host in dread silence reposes.

3. Your mother was his daughter.

4. This book is not mine; it must be his or hers.

5. Is that horse of yours lame yet?

Writer's Journal

Classical Composition

PLOT OBSERVATION: ORAL NARRATION

Without reading "Horatius" again, retell the **plot** orally to your teacher. Refer to your plot observation of the narrative with Theon's Six if needed.

Commonplace

Commonplace Book

NARRATIVE

Session two of three commonplace sessions for this lesson. Literary selection: "Horatius."

Set your timer and begin copying. When you finish, check your work carefully, word by word, against the original. Check spelling, capitalization, and punctuation for accuracy.

Lesson 15.3

Language Logic

GRAMMAR FLASHCARDS

GRAMMAR TERMS & DEFINITIONS

Review all flashcards according to tabs.

SENTENCE DIAGRAMMING

In your Writer's Journal, copy these sentences. Analyze each sentence by marking the simple subject (who or what the sentence is about) with a single underline, and the verb or verb phrase with a double underline. Write DO over a direct object, LV over a linking verb, PA over a predicate adjective, and PN over a predicate nominative. Put parentheses around each prepositional phrase. Then diagram the sentence. Refer to *Sentence Sense* as needed. You should be able to diagram each word in the sentence now.

Hint: For #4, see *Sentence Sense* 19.8 Compounds with Correlative Conjunctions.

1. Three more came out and continued the fight, but they too were beaten by Horatius and his friends.

2. Their blood has wash'd out their foul footsteps' pollution.

3. Perhaps he will spare Remus's life.

4. The other women agreed to Roma's plan, and with both hope and fear the ship was set on fire.

Eloquent Expression

SENTENCE STYLE – COPIA OF CONSTRUCTION: OPENING WORDS

Most English sentences begin with a subject. That is the pattern most of the sentences in your writing will, and should, follow. But it is very tedious to read an entire paragraph, let alone an entire book, where every sentence begins with a subject.

Study the paragraph below:

> Peter had been looking along that little ridge and had discovered that it ended only a short distance from him. Now as he looked at it again, he saw the flat surface of the ground at the end of the ridge rise as if being pushed up from beneath, and that little ridge became just so much longer. Peter understood perfectly. Out of sight beneath the surface Miner the Mole was at work. He was digging a tunnel, and that ridge was simply the roof to that tunnel. It was so near the surface of the ground that Miner simply pushed up the loose soil as he bored his way along, and this made the little ridge over which Peter had stumbled. — Thornton Burgess, *The Bird Book for Children*

Notice that while most sentences in this paragraph do begin with a subject (*Peter, Peter, He, It*), two of the sentences begin differently. What part of speech does the author use to begin the second sentence? the fourth sentence?

There are some very specific grammatical ways to vary your sentence openers; you will learn several in this book. In this lesson, we give you one quick and easy way to get started immediately: just choose another word from the sentence and move it to the beginning. Adjust the rest of the sentence as needed so that it makes complete sense.

At last he returned to his palace quite cast down.
He returned to his palace at last quite cast down.
Quite cast down, he returned to his palace at last.

In your Writer's Journal, copy this sentence, then paraphrase it twice, changing the opening words each time.

When the army of Etruscans saw the three men standing to keep them back a shout of laughter went up among them.

Classical Composition

NARRATIVE RETELLING – FIRST DRAFT

You will have two sessions to work on this retelling. Begin here, and plan to finish in Lesson 15.4. As you write your retelling, do your best to use proper grammar and spelling, but keep in mind that you will have opportunity to edit before you finalize it.

Retell "Horatius" in writing, keeping the same characters, setting, and sequence of action, but **changing the point of view to first person**. You may choose to tell it from the perspective of Publius Valerius, or that of Horatius or one of his friends. This means you need to make sure that the pronouns are consistent, and pay close attention to subject/verb agreement. Refer to your plot observation of the narrative with Theon's Six, but do not review the original narrative before you write. Include:

- ◆ a heading, properly formatted
- ◆ at least one instance of anastrophe
- ◆ at least one instance of alliteration
- ◆ (optional figure of speech) simile, onomatopoeia
- ◆ (optional figure of description) anemographia

Lesson 15.4

Language Logic

GRAMMAR TERMS & DEFINITIONS

Review all flashcards according to tabs.

Classical Composition

Writer's Journal

NARRATIVE RETELLING – FINISH FIRST DRAFT

❀ Finish the first draft of your narrative retelling. Review the instructions in Lesson 15.3 as needed.

Commonplace

NARRATIVE

Session three of three commonplace sessions for this lesson. Literary selection: "Horatius."

Commonplace Book

❀ Set your timer. Begin where you stopped in the last session. When you finish, check your work carefully against the original for accuracy.

Lesson 15.5

Prose & Poetry

POETRY APPRECIATION

❀ Read and enjoy a few poems in your poetry anthology. Identify rhyme schemes and stanza forms of one or two. Look for poems with iambic, dactylic, or anapestic meter. Look for figures of speech and figures of description in the poems you read, and make note of any you find for future Commonplace Book entries. Read one or two poems aloud with expression and proper pauses. Pause at punctuation, but not necessarily at the ends of lines.

Language Logic

GRAMMAR TERMS & DEFINITIONS

GRAMMAR FLASHCARDS

❀ Ask your teacher to quiz you with the grammar flashcards. Alternately, use the test feature in the Cottage Press *Bards & Poets I* Quizlet Classroom for an online or printed quiz for Lesson 15.

DICTATION: NARRATIVE PASSAGE

Writer's Journal

⚜ Work in your Writer's Journal. Write as your teacher dictates a passage to you from your Commonplace Book. When you are done, check your work carefully, word by word, against the original. Check for accurate spelling, capitalization, and punctuation.

Classical Composition

NARRATIVE RETELLING: TYPE DRAFT

⚜ Type your retelling on the computer with spell-check turned off, or ask your writing mentor to type it exactly as you wrote it. Save, print, and file this draft in your writing binder.

Commonplace

FROM YOUR READING

Commonplace Book

Find selections in a book or poem to add to your Commonplace Book. Include the name of the book or poem, properly formatted. Label the entry with the grammar or poetry feature, the figure of speech, or as a favorite passage. Aim for a minimum of three entries, with at least one from each category.

⚜ Grammar Features (choose any)

- ◆ A sentence that has an interesting or descriptive noun, a strong and fitting verb, a well-chosen adjective, and/or a vivid adverb
- ◆ A sentence with one or more prepositional phrases or indirect objects
- ◆ A sentence that has a possessive noun or pronoun
- ◆ A sentence that has a conjunction to join words, phrases, or clauses
- ◆ An interesting dialogue tag (add to your Dialogue Tags list)
- ◆ An interrogative, exclamatory, or imperative sentence

⚜ Figures (choose any)

- ◆ Figures of Speech: simile, onomatopoeia, anastrophe, and/or alliteration

◆ Figures of Description: anemographia

❁ Poetry Features (choose any)

◆ Rhyme (note name of the rhyme scheme)

◆ Iambic, anapestic, or dactylic meter (note name of the meter)

◆ Stanza (note name of stanza form)

❁ Favorite Passage: Add at least one passage of one to three sentences or several lines of poetry that captured your attention in your reading this week. It may be something you found beautiful, thought-provoking, funny, or interesting.

Lesson 16

❧

from HORATIUS AT THE BRIDGE
A Lay Made About the Year Of The City CCCLX

XXIV

Fast by the royal standard,

O'erlooking all the war,

Lars Porsena of Clusium

Sat in his ivory car.

By the right wheel rode Mamilius,

Prince of the Latian name;

And by the left false Sextus,

That wrought the deed of shame.

XXV

But when the face of Sextus

Was seen among the foes,

A yell that rent the firmament

From all the town arose.

On the house-tops was no woman

But spat towards him and hissed,

No child but screamed out curses,

And shook its little fist.

XXVI

But the Consul's brow was sad,

And the Consul's speech was low,

And darkly looked he at the wall,

And darkly at the foe.

"Their van will be upon us
    Before the bridge goes down;
And if they once may win the bridge,
    What hope to save the town?"

XXVII

Then out spake brave Horatius,
    The Captain of the Gate:
"To every man upon this earth
    Death cometh soon or late.
And how can man die better
    Than facing fearful odds,
For the ashes of his fathers,
    And the temples of his gods,

XXVIII

"And for the tender mother
    Who dandled him to rest,
And for the wife who nurses
    His baby at her breast,
And for the holy maidens
    Who feed the eternal flame,
To save them from false Sextus
    That wrought the deed of shame?

XXIX

"Haul down the bridge, Sir Consul,
    With all the speed ye may;
I, with two more to help me,
    Will hold the foe in play.

In yon strait path a thousand
    May well be stopped by three.
Now who will stand on either hand,
    And keep the bridge with me?"

XXX

Then out spake Spurius Lartius;
    A Ramnian proud was he:
"Lo, I will stand at thy right hand,
    And keep the bridge with thee."
And out spake strong Herminius;
    Of Titian blood was he:
"I will abide on thy left side,
    And keep the bridge with thee."

XXXI

"Horatius," quoth the Consul,
    "As thou sayest, so let it be."
And straight against that great array
    Forth went the dauntless Three.
For Romans in Rome's quarrel
    Spared neither land nor gold,
Nor son nor wife, nor limb nor life,
    In the brave days of old.

— THOMAS BABBINGTON MACAULAY

Lesson 16.1

Prose & Poetry

A LOOK AT LITERARY ELEMENTS IN THE POEM

1 Read
- Follow along and listen carefully as the poem is read aloud, OR read it aloud yourself. Read it at least two or three times. **Delight** in the meter, the rhyme, and the images.

2 Inquire
- Does the **title** give any hint as to the content or message of the poem?
- Are there any other unfamiliar persons, places, or things mentioned in the poem? Discuss these with your teacher.
- Discuss the meaning of these words in the context of the story: *false, wrought, firmament, curses, spake, odds, eternal, abide, quoth, array, dauntless,* and any unfamiliar words.
- Was there any part of the poem you did not understand? If so, discuss this with your teacher and classmates.

3 Observe the Content
- **Lyrical Elements** What does the poet describe?
  - What does the poet describe?
  - Does the poet make you see, hear, smell, taste, or touch anything?
  - Does the poet compare something in the poem to some other thing?
- **Narrative Elements** Does this poem tell a story? If so, observe the
  - **Setting** When and where does this story take place?
  - **Characters** Who is (are) the main character(s) in this story?
  - **Conflict** What is the main problem or crisis for the character(s)?
  - **Resolution** Is the problem solved? If so, how? If not, why not?
- **Point of View** Who is speaking in the poem? Is it first-person or third-person?
- **Figures** Can you identify any examples of simile, onomatopoeia, anemographia, anastrophe, or alliteration in this poem?

4 Investigate the Context
In the last lesson, you read the narrative story of Horatius at the Bridge. A classic in its own right, Lord Thomas Babington Macaulay's nineteenth century retelling of this tale in verse is perhaps the most famous version of the story. Macaulay (1800-1859) was a British historian

and politician who served as Secretary of War for several years. His histories are considered literary masterpieces. In the Preface to his *Lays of Ancient Rome*, Macaulay laments the loss of an earlier poetic tradition of these stories, and seeks to set this to rights by versifying the prose narratives written by the ancient Roman historians:

> In the following poems the author speaks, not in his own person, but in the persons of ancient minstrels who know only what Roman citizen, born three or four hundred years before the Christian era, may be supposed to have known, and who are in no wise above the passions and prejudices of their age and nation. To these imaginary poets must be ascribed some blunders which are so obvious that is unnecessary to point them out. The real blunder would have been to represent these old poets as deeply versed in general history, and studious of chronological accuracy . . . The old Romans had some great virtues, fortitude, temperance, veracity, spirit to resist oppression, respect for legitimate authority, fidelity in the observing of contracts, disinterestedness, ardent patriotism; but Christian charity and chivalrous generosity were alike unknown to them.

5 Connect the Thoughts

◆ Does this poem remind you of other poems, or of stories with similar plots, messages, or characters?

◆ Does this poem remind you of any proverbs or other well-known quotations? If so, enter these in your Commonplace Book.

Commonplace Book

6 Profit and Delight

◆ **Delight** What are the sources of delight in this poem?

◆ **Wisdom** What wisdom does this poem furnish?

◆ **Read** the poem aloud to your teacher with expression and with proper pauses.

◆ **Memorize** this poem and **recite** it before an audience. Sir Winston Churchill did! He wrote to tell his father that he was memorizing 1000 lines, and had already learned 600. Later he found out that the prize for which he was competing actually required 1200 lines. Yet, he persevered:

It was thought incongruous that while I apparently stagnated in the lowest
form, I should gain a prize open to the whole school for reciting to the Headmaster
twelve hundred lines of Macaulay's "Lays of Ancient Rome" without making a single
mistake. — Winston Churchill, *My Early Life*

Language Logic

GRAMMAR
FLASHCARDS

GRAMMAR TERMS & DEFINITIONS
🏛 Review all flashcards according to tabs.

GRAMMAR PRACTICE AND REVIEW

🏛 In your Writer's Journal, copy these sentences. Analyze each sentence by marking the
simple subject (who or what the sentence is about) with a single underline, and the verb
or verb phrase with a double underline. Write D.O. over the direct object, or L.V. over the
linking verb; write PA over a predicate adjective and PN over a predicate nominative. Put
parentheses around each prepositional phrase. Then diagram the sentence. Refer to *Sentence
Sense* as needed.

1. But the Consul's brow was sad,

   And the Consul's speech was low,

   And darkly looked he at the wall,

   And darkly at the foe.

2. To every man upon this earth

   Death cometh soon or late.

3. Now who will stand on either hand,

   And keep the bridge with me?

4. For Romans in Rome's quarrel

   Spared neither land nor gold,

Writer's
Journal

Nor son nor wife, nor limb nor life,

In the brave days of old.

Eloquent Expression

COPIA OF WORDS: VOCABULARY STUDY

Writer's Journal

🏆 Conduct a vocabulary study for "Horatius at the Bridge."

A. Choose at least two unfamiliar words to study. If you need suggestions, see the list under **Inquire** in Literary Elements above. Work in your Writer's Journal.

B. Complete Vocabulary Study steps A-G for each word (see Appendix).

Classical Composition

EDITOR'S PEN – THE BIG PICTURE

🏆 Edit your retelling from Lesson 15:

Editor's Pen – The Big Picture

✓ All important plot elements included

✓ All characters represented correctly

✓ Sequence: *same as the original*

✓ Length: *similar to the original*

✓ Point of View: *1st person*

✓ Figure of Speech: *anastrophe, alliteration*; optional: *simile, onomatopoeia*

✓ Figure of Description: *hydrographia* (will be added in Lesson 16.2);
   optional: *anemographia*

A. Read aloud exactly what you have written—not what you THINK you have written! Mark any corrections on your first draft.

B. Next, work through the Big Picture checklist above with your writing mentor.

C.   Transfer all additions and corrections from your print copy of
     the retelling to your file on the computer. Print and file this
     edited version in your binder along with your marked-up editing
     copy of the first draft.

Commonplace

Commonplace
Book

POETRY

Session one of three commonplace sessions for this lesson. Literary
selection: "Horatius at the Bridge" (the poem).

 Set your timer and begin copying. When finished, check your
work carefully against the original for accuracy.

Lesson 16.2

Prose & Poetry

RHYME SCHEME AND STANZA FORM

 Mark the end rhyme in the stanzas below.

XXIV

    Fast by the royal standard,
        O'erlooking all the war,
    Lars Porsena of Clusium
        Sat in his ivory car.
    By the right wheel rode Mamilius,
        Prince of the Latian name;
    And by the left false Sextus,
        That wrought the deed of shame.

XXVI

    But the Consul's brow was sad,
        And the Consul's speech was low,
    And darkly looked he at the wall,
        And darkly at the foe.
    "Their van will be upon us
        Before the bridge goes down;
    And if they once may win the bridge,
        What hope to save the town?"

XXV

But when the face of Sextus
    Was seen among the foes,
A yell that rent the firmament
    From all the town arose.
On the house-tops was no woman
    But spat towards him and hissed,
No child but screamed out curses,
    And shook its little fist.

XXVII

Then out spake brave Horatius,
    The Captain of the Gate:
"To every man upon this earth
    Death cometh soon or late.
And how can man die better
    Than facing fearful odds,
For the ashes of his fathers,
    And the temples of his gods.

Check the original selection to see if this rhyme scheme and stanza form is continued throughout. Name the predominant rhyme scheme and the stanza form of this poem.

Language Logic

GRAMMAR TERMS & DEFINITIONS
Review all flashcards according to tabs.

SENTENCE DIAGRAMMING: APPOSITIVES
Read and discuss the following section in *Sentence Sense* with your teacher.

III. Sentence Diagrammming: Appositives
  ◆ 15.1 Appositives and Their Modifiers

In your Writer's Journal, copy these sentences. Analyze each sentence by marking the simple subject (who or what the sentence is about) with a single underline, and the verb or verb phrase with a double underline. Write DO over a direct object, LV over a linking verb, PA over a predicate adjective, and PN over a predicate nominative. Put parentheses around each prepositional phrase. Then diagram the sentence. Refer to *Sentence Sense* as needed. You should be able to diagram each word in the sentence now.

Writer's Journal

1. Then out spake brave Horatius,

   The Captain of the Gate.

2. At one time he was aided by Lars Porsena, king of Clusium, a city of Etruria.

3. He thought of a plan for himself and his young son Icarus.

4. The old King, the Prince's father, went to the door.

Eloquent Expression

FIGURES OF DESCRIPTION: HYDROGRAPHIA

Hydro is the Greek word for *water*; **hydrographia** is the vivid description of water. Recall that figures of speech are often used to produce figures of description. Look for **onamatopoeia** and other figures in these examples of hydrographia from literature:

I chatter over stony ways,
　In little sharps and trebles,
I bubble into eddying bays,
　I babble on the pebbles.

With many a curve my banks I fret
　By many a field and fallow,
And many a fairy foreland set
　With willow-weed and mallow.

I chatter, chatter, as I flow
　To join the brimming river,
For men may come and men may go,
　But I go on forever.

— Alfred, Lord Tennyson, "The Brook"

272 ◆ Lesson 16.2

Bards & Poets I

Mrs. Rachel Lynde lived just where the Avonlea main road dipped down into a little hollow, fringed with alders and ladies' eardrops and traversed by a brook that had its source away back in the woods of the old Cuthbert place; it was reputed to be an intricate, headlong brook in its earlier course through those woods, with dark secrets of pool and cascade; but by the time it reached Lynde's Hollow it was a quiet, well-conducted little stream, for not even a brook could run past Mrs. Rachel Lynde's door without due regard for decency and decorum — Lucy Maude Montgomery, *Anne of Green Gables*

By the time it came to the edge of the Forest, the stream had grown up, so that it was almost a river, and being grown-up, it did not run and jump and sparkle along as it used to do when it was younger, but moved more slowly. For it knew now where it was going, and it said to itself, "There is no hurry. We shall get there someday." But all the little streams higher up in the Forest went this way and that, quickly, eagerly, having so much to find out before it was too late. — A. A. Milne, *Winnie-the-Pooh*

Study and practice the figure of hydrographia with your teacher.

A. Discuss the examples of hydrographia with your teacher.

B. Look at the verses below, taken from a Stanza LVI of "Horatius at the Bridge," for an example of hydrographia. Discuss this with your teacher. Look through other selections we have studied in *Bards & Poets I* for examples of hydrographia. Make note of some that you may wish to copy into your Commonplace Book.

> And, like a horse unbroken
>   When first he feels the rein,
> The furious river struggled hard,
>   And tossed his tawny mane,
> And burst the curb and bounded,
>   Rejoicing to be free,
> And whirling down, in fierce career,
> Battlement, and plank, and pier,
>   Rushed headlong to the sea.

C. In your Writer's Journal, write a sentence or two of your own hydrographia, vividly describing the Tiber as the Etruscans are approaching the city.

D. Add your figure of hydrographia to the narrative retelling by writing it in the appropriate place on your print copy of our current draft.

Classical Composition

EDITOR'S PEN – ZOOM 5X: PARAGRAPHS

Now that the Big Picture is set, begin to zoom in for a close look at the paragraph(s) in your retelling with your writing mentor.

> ### Editor's Pen – Zoom 5x: Paragraphs
> ✔ Formatting: *proper indentation*
> ✔ Length: *neither too wordy nor too short*
> ✔ Sentence class by use: *effective use*
> ✔ Sentence openers: *varied*
> ✔ Dialogue: *effective use*
> ✔ Verb Tense: *consistent*
> ✔ Pronouns: *consistent with 1st person point of view*

A. Read aloud your most recently edited version. Check each item in the Editor's Pen checklist to identify possible changes. Mark these on your print copy.

B. Transfer all additions and corrections from your print copy to the computer file. Print this version and file it in your binder along with your other versions.

Lesson 16.3

Prose & Poetry

SCANSION

Scan these stanzas, following the three steps you have learned.

Step 1 Mark each syllable as either stressed (/) or unstressed (∪). Say the line aloud several times to "get" the meter. Next, say the line aloud emphasizing the stresses as you mark the stresses only. Then go back and mark the unstressed syllables, saying the line aloud once more to check your work. Pronounce *Clusium, ivory,* and *Latian* with two syllables, and *Mamilius* with three (*Mam i lius*). In the first, third, and sixth lines have an extra unstressed syllable in the final foot.

Step 2 Insert dividers (|) to mark off the feet.

Step 3 Name the poem's meter:

Fast by the royal standard,

    O'erlooking all the war,

  Lars Porsena of Clusium

    Sat in his ivory car.

  By the right wheel rode Mamilius,

    Prince of the Latian name;

And by the left false Sextus,

    That wrought the deed of shame.

Language Logic

GRAMMAR TERMS & DEFINITIONS
🏛 Review all flashcards according to tabs.

SENTENCE DIAGRAMMING

🏛 In your Writer's Journal, copy these sentences. Analyze each sentence by marking the simple subject (who or what the sentence is about) with a single underline, and the verb or verb phrase with a double underline. Write DO over a direct object, LV over a linking verb, PA over a predicate adjective, and PN over a predicate nominative. Put parentheses around each prepositional phrase. Then diagram the sentence. Refer to *Sentence Sense* as needed. You should be able to diagram each word in the sentence now.

1. Lo, I will stand at thy right hand,

    And keep the bridge with thee.

2. Haul down the bridge, Sir Consul.

3.   In yon strait path a thousand

Writer's Journal

May well be stopped by three.

4. The flood of the river Tiber carried the cradle to a green spot.

5. He will perhaps be killed by his grandfather Numitor.

Eloquent Expression

SENTENCE STYLE – YOUR STYLE!

Craft copia for sentences from your own retelling using Sentence Style devices we have studied.

A. Work with your writing mentor to choose three sentences from your retelling that could be improved.

B. Copy the first in your Writer's Journal. Underline every important word in the sentence and jot down synonyms for each.

Writer's Journal

C. Use the list of Sentence Style devices below as you write several new versions of the sentence. New devices from this lesson are listed in bold type. You may use more than one device in each sentence.

D. Repeat the instructions above for the second and third sentences.

E. Choose your favorite paraphrase of each sentence. Replace the original sentences in your retelling before you edit again.

COPIA OF WORDS
✓ Synonyms and Antonyms
✓ **Opening Words**
✓ Dialogue Tags - synonyms for *said*
✓ Point of View
✓ Nouns – varied and descriptive
  ◆ switch noun/pronouns
✓ Verbs – strong and fitting
✓ Modifiers
  ◆ add adjective
  ◆ add adverb

COPIA OF CONSTRUCTION
✓ Sentence class by use
✓ Dialogue
  ◆ Tag line position
✓ Verb Tense
✓ Sentence Combination
  ◆ compound elements

Classical Composition

EDITOR'S PEN – ZOOM 10X: SENTENCES

Now it is time to zoom in even closer as you check the sentences in your retelling. Work with your writing mentor.

Editor's Pen – Zoom 10x: Sentences

✓ Complete thought expressed

✓ Subject and predicate agree in number

✓ Correct capitalization and punctuation

- ◆ Commas correctly used for words in a series

- ◆ No comma splices or run-on sentences!

A. Read aloud your your most recently edited version. Use the Editor's Pen checklist to identify changes you need to make. Mark all changes on your print copy.

B. Transfer all additions and corrections from your print copy to the computer file. Print this version and file it in your binder along with your other versions.

Commonplace

POETRY

Session two of three commonplace sessions for this lesson. Literary selection: "Horatius at the Bridge" (the poem).

Set your timer. Begin where you stopped in the last session. When you finish, check your work carefully against the original for accuracy.

Commonplace Book

Lesson 16.4

Prose & Poetry

SCANSION

 Scan these stanzas, following the three steps you have learned.

Step 1 Mark each syllable as either stressed (/) or unstressed (∪). Say the line aloud several times to "get" the meter. Next, say the line aloud emphasizing the stresses as you mark the stresses only. Then go back and mark the unstressed syllables, saying the line aloud once more to check your work. In the fifth line, you will need to stress *the* to keep the meter.

Step 2 Insert dividers (|) to mark off the feet.

Step 3 Name the poem's predominant meter:

But when the face of Sextus

    Was seen among the foes,

A yell that rent the firmament

    From all the town arose.

On the house-tops was no woman

    But spat towards him and hissed,

No child but screamed out curses,

    And shook its little fist.

Language Logic

GRAMMAR
FLASHCARDS

GRAMMAR TERMS & DEFINITIONS
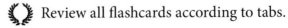 Review all flashcards according to tabs.

Eloquent Expression

PARAGRAPH STYLE – PARAPHRASE WITH COPIA

For this exercise, choose from all of the copia devices you have learned so far. See the copia chart in Lesson 16.3. New devices are in bold type.

In your Writer's Journal, paraphrase this paragraph. Change each sentence opener, and change at least one sentence class by use. Use as many synonym substitutions as possible. Use as many of the other copia devices as you are able. Make notes on the paragraph below before you begin.

Writer's Journal

It was hard work, for the bridge was very strongly built. Before the beams supporting it were all cut away the army of Porsena was seen approaching the river. What was to be done? It would take a few minutes more to finish the work, and if the farther end of the bridge could be held against the Etruscans for those few minutes all would be well for Rome. But how was it to be held, and who would hold it? Suddenly from the ranks of the Roman soldiers the brave Horatius Cocles stepped out and cried to the consul: "Give me two good men to help me, and I will hold the bridge and stop the enemy from coming over."

Classical Composition

EDITOR'S PEN – FINE FOCUS: WORDS

The final checks dwell on the details of your word usage. Continue to compile your personal editing checklist to use in editing all of your work across the curriculum.

Editor's Pen – Fine Focus: Words

✓ Word choices varied; word meanings clear
  ◆ Verbs: *strong, fitting; appropriate adverbs if needed*
  ◆ Nouns: *clear, descriptive; appropriate adjectives if needed*
  ◆ Dialogue: *dialogue tags varied if appropriate*
✓ Correct spelling
✓ Final read-through

A. Read aloud your most recent version. Identify changes you need to make with the Editor's Pen checklist. Mark these on your print copy.

B. Transfer all additions and corrections from your print copy to the computer file. Print this final version and file it in your binder along with your other versions.

Commonplace

Commonplace Book

POETRY

Session three of three commonplace sessions for this lesson. Literary selection: "Horatius at the Bridge" (the poem).

Set your timer and begin copying. When you finish, check your work carefully against the original for accuracy.

Lesson 16.5

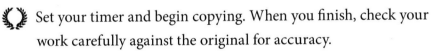

Prose & Poetry

POETRY APPRECIATION

Read and enjoy a few poems in your poetry anthology. Identify rhyme schemes and stanza forms of one or two. Look for figures of speech and figures of description in the poems you read, and make note of any you find for future Commonplace Book entries. Read one or two poems aloud with expression and proper pauses. Pause at punctuation, but not necessarily at the ends of lines. Finally, choose a rhyming poem with iambic, dactylic, or anapestic meter to observe.

Writer's Journal

- In your Writer's Journal, write the title of the poem and the author. Make note of its meter, rhyme scheme, and stanza form.
- Write the rhyming words from the poem in two lists: one list for those spelled the same, and one list for those spelled differently.
- Choose one of the rhyming words from the spelled differently list, and try to come up with several additional rhymes. Look for varied spellings.

Language Logic

GRAMMAR TERMS & DEFINITIONS

GRAMMAR FLASHCARDS

Ask your teacher to quiz you with the grammar flashcards. Alternately, use the test feature in the Cottage Press *Bards & Poets I* Quizlet Classroom for an online or printed quiz for Lesson 16.

DICTATION: POETRY

Writer's Journal

Work in your Writer's Journal. Write as your teacher dictates a passage to you from your Commonplace Book. When you are done, check your work carefully, word by word, against the original. Check for accurate spelling, capitalization, and punctuation.

Classical Composition

POETRY

Writer's Journal

In your Writer's Journal, write two to four rhyming lines that summarize the action of "Horatius at the Bridge." If you wish, include a poetic **moral** at the end. Consider including them at the end of your retelling as a brief summary of the story. You may find it easiest to imitate the rhyme and meter of a few lines of the poetic selection for this lesson or a previous lesson.

NARRATIVE RETELLING – FINAL DRAFT

🏆 Read over the final version of your retelling one last time and make any needed changes. Save it on your computer; print and file with all the other drafts in your writing binder.

Commonplace

FROM YOUR READING

Find selections in a book or poem to add to your Commonplace Book. Include the name of the book or poem, properly formatted. Label the entry with the grammar or poetry feature, the figure of speech, or as a favorite passage. Aim for a minimum of three entries, with at least one from each category.

Commonplace Book

🏆 Grammar Features (choose any)

- ◆ A sentence that has an interesting or descriptive noun, a strong and fitting verb, a well-chosen adjective, and/or a vivid adverb
- ◆ A sentence with one or more prepositional phrases or indirect objects
- ◆ A sentence that has a possessive noun or pronoun and/or an appositive
- ◆ A sentence that has a conjunction to join words, phrases, or clauses
- ◆ An interesting dialogue tag (add to your Dialogue Tags list)
- ◆ An interrogative, exclamatory, or imperative sentence

🏆 Figures (choose any)

- ◆ Figures of Speech: simile, onomatopoeia, anastrophe, and/or alliteration
- ◆ Figures of Description: anemographia and/or hydrographia

🏆 Poetry Features (choose any)

- ◆ Rhyme (note name of the rhyme scheme)
- ◆ Iambic, anapestic, or dactylic meter (note name of the meter)
- ◆ Stanza (note name of stanza form)

🏆 Favorite Passage: Add at least one passage of one to three sentences or several lines of poetry that captured your attention in your reading this week. It may be something you found beautiful, thought-provoking, funny, or interesting.

Lesson 17

❧

THE FARMER HERO
from THE STORY OF THE ROMANS by Helene Guerber

The Romans were so warlike a people that they were hardly ever at peace. As soon as one battle was ended, they prepared for the next, and after defeating one people they immediately tried their arms against another.

When not busy making war abroad, they often quarreled at home; for, as you have already heard, the patricians and plebeians were too jealous of each other to agree for any length of time. In all this fighting, many soldiers were slain, and when the people of Veii once began to rise up against Rome, the senate was dismayed to find that there was no army ready to meet them.

In this time of danger, a noble patrician, named Fabius, stood up in the senate, and said that he and his family would at once arm, and go forth and fight for the city. Early the next day, three hundred and six men, all related to one another, and all bearing the name of Fabius, marched out of Rome to meet the foe.

In the first battle the Fabii won a glorious victory; but later on in the campaign they were led into an ambush, and were all slain. When the news of their death was brought into the city the people burst into tears, and the gate through which they had passed was called the Unlucky.

The day of their death was marked in the Roman calendar as also unlucky, and the people publicly mourned the loss of such good and brave men, who had left only a few little children, too young to bear arms, for the defense of their country.

The Romans, however, soon won a great victory over the people of Veii, and the two cities made a long truce. But the wars with other peoples still went on, and among the worst enemies of Rome were the Æquians. On one occasion the Roman troops were led by a consul who had not had much experience. Before long his camp was surrounded by the Æquians, and his army was in great danger of suffering the same fate as the Fabii.

Five horsemen, however, managed to escape, and hurried to warn the senate of the army's peril. The people were horrified at these tidings, and, knowing that the second consul was no more of a general than the first, insisted that a dictator should be chosen.

Only one man seemed able to help them. This was Cincinnatus, an old soldier who had retired to a farm, where he spent all his time in plowing, sowing, and reaping. A party of senators went in search of him, and found him plowing in his fields.

In haste they told him of the army's danger, and implored him to take charge of the city, and do all he could to save the lives of their brave countrymen. Cincinnatus was weary of warfare, and would have preferred to remain on his farm; but as soon as he heard this news, he left his oxen standing in the furrow, and went back to Rome with the senators.

Arrived in the Forum, he called the citizens to arms. He bade every able-bodied man be on the Field of Mars before sundown, fully armed, and carrying enough food to last him five days. The Romans were so glad to have a good leader that they hastened to obey him; and, as the sun sank beneath the horizon, Cincinnatus, the new dictator, marched out of Rome, at the head of a little army of determined men.

By walking all night, Cincinnatus brought his men in the rear of the Æquians, who, at dawn, found that the tables were turned, and that they were now between two armies of angry Romans.

They soon saw that resistance would be useless, and, without striking a single blow, offered to surrender. Cincinnatus gladly accepted their offers of peace, but let them go only after they had given up their arms and spoil, and had gone through a ceremony called "passing under the yoke." This was considered a great disgrace, and the Æquians would never have submitted to it had they not been compelled to do so in order to save their lives.

The yoke was made by standing up two spears in the ground, and tying a third across their tops. The Roman soldiers were drawn up in two long lines facing each other, and the enemy marched between them and under the yoke, a prey to the taunts, and even to the blows, of their conquerors.

After thus rescuing the Roman army from certain death, Cincinnatus brought them back to the city, and enjoyed the honors of a triumph. Then, seeing that his country no longer needed him, he laid aside the title of dictator, which he had borne for only a few days. Joyfully hastening back to his farm, he took up his plowing where he had dropped it; and he went on living as quietly and simply as if he had never been called upon to serve as dictator, and to receive the honors of a grand triumph.

This man is admired quite as much for his simplicity and contentment as for his ability and courage. He was greatly esteemed by the Romans, and in this country his memory has been honored by giving his name to the thriving city of Cincinnati.

⊂℞

Lesson 17.1

Prose & Poetry

A LOOK AT LITERARY ELEMENTS IN THE NARRATIVE

1 **Read**
◆ Listen carefully as your teacher reads the selection aloud. **Delight** in the story.

2 **Inquire**
◆ Does the **title** give any hint as to the content or message of the story? If this story was published by the author in a larger book or an anthology, does that title give any hint?

◆ Discuss the meaning of these words in the context of the story: *patricians*, *plebeians*, *ambush*, *slain*, *tidings*, *senators*, *resistance*, *disgrace*, *compelled*, *taunts*, *dictator*, *triumph*, *esteemed*, and any unfamiliar words.

3 Observe the Content
◆ **Setting** When and where does this story take place?
◆ **Characters** Who is (are) the main character(s) in this story?
◆ **Conflict** What is the main problem or crisis for the character(s)?
◆ **Resolution** Is the problem solved? If so, how? If not, why not?
◆ **Point of View** Who is telling the story? Is it first-person or third-person?
◆ **Figures** Can you identify any examples of simile, onomatopoeia, anemographia, anastrophe, alliteration, or hydrographia in this narrative?

4 Investigate the Context
The moving story of the Roman statesman Quintus Cincinnatus was recounted by several ancient authors, most notably, Livy. Livy's history of Rome was a beloved book for our Founding Fathers; the lessons of his life, among many other noble Greeks and Romans, informed their shaping of our Republic. As we will see in later lessons, the story of Cincinnatus inspired George Washington in a particular way.

Our selection is another from nineteenth century British historian Helene Adeline Guerber (1859-1929), the author whom we met in Lesson 9. The narrative for this lesson is taken from her companion volume *The Story of the Romans*. The image at right was painted by French artist Alexandre Cabanel in 1843.

5 Connect the Thoughts
◆ Does this story remind you of other stories with similar plots, messages, or characters?
◆ Does this story remind you of any fables?
◆ Does this story remind you of any proverbs or other well-known quotations? If so, enter these in your Commonplace Book.

Commonplace Book

6 **Profit and Delight**
  ◆ **Delight** What are the sources of delight in this story?
  ◆ **Wisdom** What wisdom does this story furnish?
  ◆ **Read** the narrative aloud to your teacher with expression and with proper pauses.
  ◆ **Record** in your Book of Centuries: The Fabii, Cincinnatus.

PLOT OBSERVATION: IDENTIFYING ACTIONS

Most action in the narratives we have studied thus far has involved some type of physical act. But sometimes, a narrative action is made up primarily of **Dialogue** between two or more characters, or even inside a character's own **Thoughts**.

Often an author will include some additional details between actions or even in the middle of an action. These are often an integral part of the overall narrative, but they are not actually part of the plot. We have already encountered several of these so far: the **Prologue**, the **Summary**, and the **Epilogue**. In addition to these, a narrative may include **Explanation** of background or other needed information or **Description** that brings an action or a character or a setting "before the eyes" of the reader. Sometimes **Author Comments** are written directly to the reader. You may even find other types of transitions that we have not detailed here; you can name these creatively!

Observe the plot of "The Farmer Hero." Work in pencil on the original narrative at the beginning of this lesson, marking and making notes in the margin as instructed below.

A. Quickly read through the narrative once more. Number the paragraphs, and then mark the story as you have learned to do. Divide the narrative into actions. You should have a **Prologue**, six or seven main actions, a **Summary**, and an **Epilogue**. Several actions start in the middle of a paragraph.

B. Mark an x beside the sections that do not detail an action, and note what these are: **Prologue, Epilogue, Explanation, Description, Summary, Author Comments**.

C. Mark the major actions. Then, mark in the margin if the action is made up of **Dialogue** or **Thoughts**. Consider Theon's Six. Remember that action can change even in the middle of a paragraph. Feel free to change your mind often as you work through the entire narrative—this is why you must use a pencil! Keep in mind that there is not just one right way to divide narratives into actions. Just make sure you can explain why you divide them as you do, using Theon's Six.

D. Review the narrative. Make notes in the margin indicating if any of the rest of Theon's Six changed with each action. You should definitely have notes about Person. Ask the questions for the other four, but do not worry too much if you can only add notes for two or three others.

E. Discuss your work with your teacher.

Language Logic

GRAMMAR
FLASHCARDS

GRAMMAR TERMS & DEFINITIONS
◯ Review all flashcards according to tabs.

GRAMMAR PRACTICE AND REVIEW

◯ In your Writer's Journal, copy these sentences. Analyze each sentence by marking the simple subject (who or what the sentence is about) with a single underline, and the verb or verb phrase with a double underline. Write DO over the direct object, or LV over the linking verb; write PA over a predicate adjective and PN over a predicate nominative. Put parentheses around each prepositional phrase. Then diagram the sentence. Refer to *Sentence Sense* as needed.

1. In the first battle the Fabii won a glorious victory; but later in the campaign they were led into an ambush, and were all slain.

2. Five horsemen escaped and warned the senate.

3. Cincinnatus, the new dictator, marched out of Rome, at the head of a little army.

4. This man is admired for his simplicity and contentment, and for his ability and courage.

5. In his honor, our own country gave his name to the prosperous city of Cincinnati.

Writer's Journal

Eloquent Expression

COPIA OF WORDS: VOCABULARY STUDY

Conduct a vocabulary study for "The Farmer Hero."

Writer's
Journal

A. Choose at least two unfamiliar words to study. If you need suggestions, see the list under **Inquire** in Literary Elements above. Work in your Writer's Journal.

B. Complete Vocabulary Study steps A-G for each word (see *Appendix*).

Commonplace

NARRATIVE

Session one of three commonplace sessions for this lesson. Literary selection: "The Farmer Hero."

Commonplace
Book

Set your timer and begin copying. When you finish, check your work carefully, word by word, against the original.

Lesson 17.2

Prose & Poetry

PLOT OBSERVATION: OUTLINE WITH CAPTIONS

In your Writer's Journal, create an outline to capture your observations with parallel captions.

Writer's
Journal

A. Jot down a quick caption for each major action, as well as any of the following: Prologue, Epilogue, Explanation, Description, Summary, Author Comments.

B. Review your captions, and choose a parallel format.

C. Revise all captions to conform to the format you have chosen.

Language Logic

GRAMMAR TERMS & DEFINITIONS
◯ Review all flashcards according to tabs.

SENTENCE DIAGRAMMING
◯ Read and discuss the following section in *Sentence Sense* with your teacher.

III. Sentence Diagrammming: Objects & Complements
- ◆ 16.2 Objective Complements

◯ In your Writer's Journal, copy these sentences. Analyze each sentence by marking the simple subject (who or what the sentence is about) with a single underline, and the verb or verb phrase with a double underline. Write DO over a direct object, LV over a linking verb, PA over a predicate adjective, and PN over a predicate nominative. Put parentheses around each prepositional phrase. Then diagram the sentence. Refer to *Sentence Sense* as needed.

1. God called the light day.

2. The Romans considered Cincinnatus a hero.

3. These people made the twins, Romulus and Remus, captains.

4. His people he now called Latins, in memory of King Latinus.

5. The Prince accordingly made her his wife.

Writer's Journal

Classical Composition

PLOT OBSERVATION: ORAL NARRATION

❧ Without reading "The Farmer Hero" again, retell the **plot** orally to your teacher. Refer to your plot observation of the narrative with Theon's Six if needed.

Commonplace

NARRATIVE

Session two of three commonplace sessions for this lesson. Literary selection: "The Farmer Hero."

Commonplace Book

❧ Set your timer and begin copying. When you finish, check your work carefully, word by word, against the original. Check spelling, capitalization, and punctuation for accuracy.

Lesson 17.3

Language Logic

GRAMMAR FLASHCARDS

GRAMMAR TERMS & DEFINITIONS

❧ Review all flashcards according to tabs.

SENTENCE DIAGRAMMING

❧ In your Writer's Journal, copy these sentences. Analyze each sentence by marking the simple subject (who or what the sentence is about) with a single underline, and the verb or verb phrase with a double underline. Write DO over a direct object, LV over a linking verb, PA over a predicate adjective, and PN over a predicate nominative. Put parentheses around each prepositional phrase. Then diagram the sentence. Refer to *Sentence Sense* as needed.

1. The Romans, a warlike people, were hardly ever at peace.

2. The day of their death was marked in the Roman calendar as unlucky, and the people publicly mourned the loss of such good and brave men.

Writer's Journal

3. In haste they told him the army's danger.

4. The Senate named Cincinnatus dictator.

5. Cincinnatus brought them back to the city, and enjoyed the honors of a triumph.

Eloquent Expression

SENTENCE STYLE – COPIA OF CONSTRUCTION: POSSESSIVES AND "OF" PHRASES

Possessive nouns and pronouns function as adjectives in the sentence, (*Sentence Sense*, Sections 1.7C, 14.1). Either may be changed to an alternate possessive form using the preposition *of.*

Your letter pleased me greatly. That letter of yours pleased me greatly.

The contents of the letter pleased me. The letter's contents pleased me.

Complete these exercises in your Writer's Journal.

Writer's Journal

❧ Paraphrase these sentences, exchanging the underlined
possessive nouns and pronouns for an appropriate 'of' phrase,
and the underlined 'of' phrases for an appropriate possessive
form.

1. Five horsemen hurried to warn the senate of the army's peril.

2. Rome's fate was in the hands of one man.

Classical Composition

NARRATIVE RETELLING – FIRST DRAFT

You will have two sessions to work on this retelling. Begin here, and plan to finish in Lesson 17.4.
As you write your retelling, do your best to use proper grammar and spelling, but keep in mind
that you will have opportunity to edit before you finalize it.

Writer's Journal

❧ Retell "The Farmer Hero" in writing, keeping the same characters,
setting, and sequence of action. Choose either first or third
person point of view, but be consistent throughout. This means
you need to make sure that the pronouns are consistent, and pay
close attention to subject/verb agreement. Refer to your plot

observation of the narrative with Theon's Six, but do not review the original narrative before you write. Include:

- ◆ a heading, properly formatted
- ◆ at least one instance of anastrophe
- ◆ at least one instance of alliteration
- ◆ (optional figure of speech) simile, onomatopoeia
- ◆ (optional figure of description) anemographia, hydrographia

Lesson 17.4

Language Logic

GRAMMAR TERMS & DEFINITIONS
Review all flashcards according to tabs.

Classical Composition

Writer's Journal

NARRATIVE RETELLING – FINISH FIRST DRAFT
Finish the first draft of your narrative retelling. Review the instructions in Lesson 17.3 as needed.

Commonplace

NARRATIVE
Session three of three commonplace sessions for this lesson. Literary selection: "The Farmer Hero."

Commonplace Book

Set your timer. Begin where you stopped in the last session. When you finish, check your work carefully against the original for accuracy.

Lesson 17.5

Prose & Poetry

POETRY APPRECIATION

Read and enjoy a few poems in your poetry anthology. Identify rhyme schemes and stanza forms of one or two. Look for poems with iambic, dactylic, or anapestic meter. Look for figures of speech and figures of description in the poems you read, and make note of any you find for future Commonplace Book entries. Read one or two poems aloud with expression and proper pauses. Pause at punctuation, but not necessarily at the ends of lines.

Language Logic

GRAMMAR TERMS & DEFINITIONS

Ask your teacher to quiz you with the grammar flashcards. Alternately, use the test feature in the Cottage Press *Bards & Poets I* Quizlet Classroom for an online or printed quiz for Lesson 17.

DICTATION: NARRATIVE PASSAGE

Work in your Writer's Journal. Write as your teacher dictates a passage to you from your Commonplace Book. When you are done, check your work carefully, word by word, against the original. Check for accurate spelling, capitalization, and punctuation.

Classical Composition

NARRATIVE RETELLING: TYPE FINAL DRAFT

Type your retelling on the computer with spell-check turned off, or ask your writing mentor to type it exactly as you wrote it. Save, print, and file this draft in your writing binder.

Commonplace

FROM YOUR READING

Find selections in a book or poem to add to your Commonplace Book.
Include the name of the book or poem, properly formatted. Label the
entry with the grammar or poetry feature, the figure of speech, or as a
favorite passage. Aim for a minimum of three entries, with at least one
from each category.

Commonplace Book

⬭ Grammar Features (choose any)

- ◆ A sentence that has an interesting or descriptive noun, a strong and fitting verb, a well-chosen adjective, and/or a vivid adverb
- ◆ A sentence with one or more prepositional phrases or indirect objects
- ◆ A sentence that has a possessive noun or pronoun and/or an appositive
- ◆ A sentence that has a conjunction to join words, phrases, or clauses
- ◆ An interesting dialogue tag (add to your Dialogue Tags list)
- ◆ An interrogative, exclamatory, or imperative sentence

⬭ Figures (choose any)

- ◆ Figures of Speech: simile, onomatopoeia, anastrophe, and/or alliteration
- ◆ Figures of Description: anemographia and/or hydrographia

⬭ Poetry Features (choose any)

- ◆ Rhyme (note name of the rhyme scheme)
- ◆ Iambic, anapestic, dactylic, or trochaic meter (note name of the meter)
- ◆ Stanza (note name of stanza form)

⬭ Favorite Passage: Add at least one passage of one to three sentences or several lines of poetry
that captured your attention in your reading this week. It may be something you found
beautiful, thought-provoking, funny, or interesting.

Lesson 18

ℭℛ

THE BAREFOOT BOY

Blessings on thee, little man,

Barefoot boy, with cheek of tan!

With thy turned-up pantaloons,

And thy merry whistled tunes;

With thy red lip, redder still

Kissed by strawberries on the hill;

With the sunshine on thy face,

Through thy torn brim's jaunty grace;

From my heart I give thee joy, —

I was once a barefoot boy!

Prince thou art, — the grown-up man

Only is republican.

Let the million-dollared ride!

Barefoot, trudging at his side,

Thou hast more than he can buy

In the reach of ear and eye, —

Outward sunshine, inward joy:

Blessings on thee, barefoot boy!

Oh for boyhood's painless play,

Sleep that wakes in laughing day,

Health that mocks the doctor's rules,

Knowledge never learned of schools,

Of the wild bee's morning chase,

Of the wild-flower's time and place,

Flight of fowl and habitude

Of the tenants of the wood;

How the tortoise bears his shell,
How the woodchuck digs his cell,
And the ground-mole sinks his well;
How the robin feeds her young,
How the oriole's nest is hung;
Where the whitest lilies blow,
Where the freshest berries grow,
Where the ground-nut trails its vine,
Where the wood-grape's clusters shine;
Of the black wasp's cunning way,
Mason of his walls of clay,
And the architectural plans
Of gray hornet artisans!
For, eschewing books and tasks,
Nature answers all he asks;
Hand in hand with her he walks,
Face to face with her he talks,
Part and parcel of her joy, —
Blessings on the barefoot boy!

Oh for boyhood's time of June,
Crowding years in one brief moon,
When all things I heard or saw,
Me, their master, waited for.
I was rich in flowers and trees,
Humming-birds and honey-bees;
For my sport the squirrel played,
Plied the snouted mole his spade;
For my taste the blackberry cone
Purpled over hedge and stone;
Laughed the brook for my delight
Through the day and through the night,

Whispering at the garden wall,

Talked with me from fall to fall;

Mine the sand-rimmed pickerel pond,

Mine the walnut slopes beyond,

Mine, on bending orchard trees,

Apples of Hesperides!

Still as my horizon grew,

Larger grew my riches too;

All the world I saw or knew

Seemed a complex Chinese toy,

Fashioned for a barefoot boy!

Oh for festal dainties spread,

Like my bowl of milk and bread;

Pewter spoon and bowl of wood,

On the door-stone, gray and rude!

O'er me, like a regal tent,

Cloudy-ribbed, the sunset bent,

Purple-curtained, fringed with gold,

Looped in many a wind-swung fold;

While for music came the play

Of the pied frogs' orchestra;

And, to light the noisy choir,

Lit the fly his lamp of fire.

I was monarch: pomp and joy

Waited on the barefoot boy!

Cheerily, then, my little man,

Live and laugh, as boyhood can!

Though the flinty slopes be hard,

Stubble-speared the new-mown sward,

Every morn shall lead thee through

Fresh baptisms of the dew;

Every evening from thy feet

Shall the cool wind kiss the heat:

All too soon these feet must hide

In the prison cells of pride,

Lose the freedom of the sod,

Like a colt's for work be shod,

Made to tread the mills of toil,

Up and down in ceaseless moil:

Happy if their track be found

Never on forbidden ground;

Happy if they sink not in

Quick and treacherous sands of sin.

Ah! that thou couldst know thy joy,

Ere it passes, barefoot boy!

— JOHN GREENLEAF WHITTIER

Ꮽ

Lesson 18.1

Prose & Poetry

A LOOK AT LITERARY ELEMENTS IN THE POEM

1 Read

◆ Follow along and listen carefully as the poem is read aloud, OR read it aloud yourself. Read it at least two or three times. **Delight** in the meter, the rhyme, and the images.

2 Inquire

◆ Does the **title** give any hint as to the content or message of the poem?

◆ Are there any other unfamiliar persons, places, or things mentioned in

the poem? Discuss these with your teacher.

◆ Discuss the meaning of these words in the context of the story: *pantaloons, jaunty, republican, habitude, tenants, eschewing, Hesperides, festal, pied, monarch, baptisms, shod, moil,* and any unfamiliar words.

◆ Was there any part of the poem you did not understand? If so, discuss this with your teacher and classmates.

3 Observe the Content

◆ **Lyrical Elements**

- What does the poet describe?
- Does the poet make you see, hear, smell, taste, or touch anything?
- Does the poet compare something in the poem to some other thing?

◆ **Narrative Elements** Does this poem tell a story? If so, observe the

- **Setting** When and where does this story take place?
- **Characters** Who is (are) the main character(s) in this story?
- **Conflict** What is the main problem or crisis for the character(s)?
- **Resolution** Is the problem solved? If so, how? If not, why not?

◆ **Point of View** Who is speaking in the poem? Is it first-person or third-person?

◆ **Figures** Can you identify any examples of simile, onomatopoeia, anemographia, anastrophe, alliteration, or hydrographia in this poem?

4 Investigate the Context

American poet John Greenleaf Whittier (1807-1892) was one of the "Fireside Poets" of nineteenth century New England, along with Longfellow, Holmes, and Bryant. As a boy,

John was always writing poetry which he hid from everyone but his sister Mary. One day he was helping his father to mend a fence when the postman, passing his gate, tossed him a newspaper and what should he see but one of his very own verses in print! He could scarcely believe his eyes! His sister had secretly sent the poem to the Free Press, a paper published by that bold and sturdy foe to slavery, William Lloyd Garrison. Not long afterward Garrison came to see the poet while he was working in the cornfield and urged his father to send him to some higher school. Mr. Whittier had not the money for the purpose, but someone offered to teach the youth to make ladies' shoes and slippers during the winter. Thus he put himself through two years at Havehill Academy.

Whittier became, in time, the great poet of the anti-slavery movement and a writer of beautiful hymns still sung in churches today; but he was, first of all, the poet of New England farm life. He sang of corn and pumpkins and barefoot boys, of corn-huskings, of the homecoming of all the family at Thanksgiving, and the world of New Englnad snows, with cozy life indoors. — *My Book House: Halls of Fame,* ed. Olive Beaupré Miller

5 Connect the Thoughts

◆ Does this poem remind you of other poems, or of stories with similar plots, messages, or characters?

◆ Does this poem remind you of any proverbs or other well-known quotations? If so, enter these in your Commonplace Book.

Commonplace Book

6 Profit and Delight

◆ **Delight** What are the sources of delight in this poem?

◆ **Wisdom** What wisdom does this poem furnish?

◆ **Read** the poem aloud to your teacher with expression and with proper pauses.

◆ **Record** in your Book of Centuries: John Greenleaf Whittier.

◆ **Memorize** this poem and **recite** it before an audience.

Language Logic

GRAMMAR FLASHCARDS

GRAMMAR TERMS & DEFINITIONS

Ⓛ Review all flashcards according to tabs.

GRAMMAR PRACTICE AND REVIEW

Ⓛ In your Writer's Journal, copy these sentences. Analyze each sentence by marking the simple subject (who or what the sentence is about) with a single underline, and the verb or verb phrase with a double underline. Write DO over the direct object, or LV over the linking verb; write PA over a predicate adjective and PN over a predicate nominative. Put parentheses around each prepositional phrase. Then diagram the sentence. Refer to *Sentence Sense* as needed.

Writer's Journal

1. I was rich in flowers and trees,

   Humming-birds and honey-bees.

2. For my taste the blackberry cone

   Purpled over hedge and stone.

3. Laughed the brook for my delight

   Through the day and through the night.

4. I was monarch: pomp and joy

   Waited on the barefoot boy!

5. Every evening from thy feet

   Shall the cool wind kiss the heat.

Eloquent Expression

COPIA OF WORDS: VOCABULARY STUDY

Conduct a vocabulary study for "Barefoot Boy."

Writer's Journal

A. Choose at least two unfamiliar words to study. If you need suggestions, see the list under **Inquire** in Literary Elements above. Work in your Writer's Journal.

B. Complete Vocabulary Study steps A-G for each word (see Appendix).

Classical Composition

EDITOR'S PEN – THE BIG PICTURE

🏵 Edit your retelling from Lesson 17:

Editor's Pen – The Big Picture

✓ All important plot elements included

✓ All characters represented correctly

✓ Sequence: *same as the original*

✓ Length: *similar to the original*

✓ Point of View: *3rd person or 1st person*

✓ Figure of Speech: *anastrophe, alliteration;* optional: *simile, onomatopoeia*

✓ Figure of Description, optional: *anemographia, hydrographia*

A. Read aloud exactly what you have written—not what you THINK you have written! Mark any corrections on your first draft.

B. Next, work through the Big Picture checklist above with your writing mentor.

C. Transfer all additions and corrections from your print copy of the retelling to your file on the computer. Print and file this edited version in your binder along with your marked-up editing copy of the first draft.

Commonplace

Commonplace Book

POETRY

Session one of three commonplace sessions for this lesson. Literary selection: "Barefoot Boy."

🏵 Set your timer and begin copying. When finished, check your work carefully against the original for accuracy.

Lesson 18.2

Prose & Poetry

RHYME SCHEME AND STANZA FORM

◯ Mark the end rhyme in the stanzas below.

Blessings on thee, little man,

Barefoot boy, with cheek of tan!

With thy turned-up pantaloons,

And thy merry whistled tunes;

With thy red lip, redder still

Kissed by strawberries on the hill;

With the sunshine on thy face,

Through thy torn brim's jaunty grace;

From my heart I give thee joy, —

I was once a barefoot boy!

Prince thou art, — the grown-up man

Only is republican.

Let the million-dollared ride!

Barefoot, trudging at his side,

Thou hast more than he can buy

In the reach of ear and eye, —

Outward sunshine, inward joy:

Blessings on thee, barefoot boy!

◯ Name the rhyme scheme in this stanza. Look at the original selection; does it follow the same scheme? Go back to the original selection, and list the number of lines in each stanza. in order. Remember that not only the words, but the form of the poem communicates the poet's message. What do you think Whittier might be communicating with the irregular arrangement of stanzas?

Language Logic

GRAMMAR TERMS & DEFINITIONS

◯ Review all flashcards according to tabs.

THE PARTICIPLE

◯ Read and discuss the following sections in *Sentence Sense* with your teacher.

    I.   Etymology – The Verb

        ◆ 3.11A Verbals

        ◆ 3.11 B Verbal Classes *Read the entire section. In this lesson, we will only study participles. In upcoming lessons, we will study gerunds and infinitives.*

    V.   Exercises

        ◆ Oral exercise: Identify each participle in *Harvey's* 19.7.

◯ Move the flashcards that you have mastered backwards in your file system. Leave any that you have not mastered behind the **Daily** tab. Add these flashcards to your box behind the Daily tab, and begin to memorize them:

    ◆ Verbals

    ◆ Verbal Classes *Though we do not study gerunds and infinitives formally in this lesson, go ahead and begin memorizing all of these.*

◯ Review all flashcards according to tabs.

Eloquent Expression

FIGURES OF SPEECH – METAPHOR

The figure of speech **simile** directly compares two things of unlike nature, signaled by the use of the words like, as, or than:

Her hair was like silk.

Like simile, **metaphor** is a comparison between two things of unlike nature, but in metaphor the comparison is implied rather than stated directly:

Her hair was silk.

This example of metaphor represents the most straightforward kind of metaphor—a simple statement of x = y, where x and y are nouns, and the = represents a linking verb:

Laughter is the best medicine. The eye is a window to the soul.

Another kind of metaphor that is fairly easy to spot uses the preposition *of*:

Necessity is the mother of invention. Wise teaching is a fountain of life.

This kind of metaphor may also use a possesive form:

Necessity is invention's mother.

Adjectives or participles can also create metaphors:

He stood in stony silence. Her chilling glance broke his heart.

There are many other kinds of metaphor, some of which are not so easy to recognize. The more you practice (and the more widely you read!) the easier it will be to see and understand metaphor.

Here are some examples of metaphor from literature. Discuss what two things are being compared in each, and note the way in which they are compared.

I am the good shepherd . . . and I lay down my life for the sheep. — John 10:14-15

A mighty fortress is our God, a bulwark never failing. — Martin Luther

The blood of the martyrs is the seed of the church. — Tertullian

What sort of word escaped your teeth's barrier? — Homer, *Odyssey*

⚜ Study and review figures of speech with your teacher.

Writer's Journal

A. Discuss the examples of metaphor with your teacher.

B. Look in "The Barefoot Boy" for examples of metaphor and discuss them with your teacher. In your Writer's Journal, make a list of metaphors you find in this poem.

C. Look through other poems we have studied in *Bards & Poets I* for more examples of metaphor. Make note of some that you may wish to copy into your Commonplace Book.

Classical Composition

EDITOR'S PEN – ZOOM 5X: PARAGRAPHS

Now that the Big Picture is set, begin to zoom in for a close look at the paragraph(s) in your retelling with your writing mentor.

> ### Editor's Pen – Zoom 5x: Paragraphs
> ✓ Formatting: *proper indentation*
> ✓ Length: *neither too wordy nor too short*
> ✓ Sentence class by use: *effective use*
> ✓ Sentence openers: *varied*
> ✓ Dialogue: *effective use*
> ✓ Verb Tense: *consistent*
> ✓ Pronouns: *consistent with chosen point of view*

A. Read aloud your most recently edited version. Check each item in the Editor's Pen checklist to identify possible changes. Mark these on your print copy.

B. Transfer all additions and corrections from your print copy to the computer file. Print this version and file it in your binder along with your other versions.

Lesson 18.3

Prose & Poetry

SCANSION – TROCHAIC METER

Trochaic meter is also very common in English poetry. Like an iamb, a **trochee** is a poetic foot with two syllables, but the metrical pattern is reversed: stressed is followed by unstressed.

| / ∪| / ∪ | / ∪| / ∪ |
Dou ble, dou ble toil and trou ble

In a trochaic line, it is not uncommon for the final syllable to contain a single stressed syllable instead of a full trochee.

| / ∪| / ∪ |/∪| / |
Twin kle, twin kle lit tle star

Scan this stanza, following the three steps you have learned.

Step 1 Mark each syllable as either stressed (/) or unstressed (∪). Say the line aloud several times to "get" the meter. Next, say the line aloud emphasizing the stresses as you mark the stresses only. Then go back and mark the unstressed syllables, saying the line aloud once more to check your work. Pronounce *strawberries* with two syllables.

Step 2 Insert dividers (|) to mark off the feet.

Step 3 Name the poem's meter:

Blessings on thee, little man,

Barefoot boy, with cheek of tan!

With thy turned-up pantaloons,

And thy merry whistled tunes;

With thy red lip, redder still

Kissed by strawberries on the hill;

With the sunshine on thy face,

Through thy torn brim's jaunty grace;

From my heart I give thee joy, —

I was once a barefoot boy!

Prince thou art, — the grown-up man

Only is republican.

Let the million-dollared ride!

Barefoot, trudging at his side,

Thou hast more than he can buy

In the reach of ear and eye, —

Outward sunshine, inward joy:

Blessings on thee, barefoot boy!

Language Logic

GRAMMAR TERMS & DEFINITIONS
❧ Review all flashcards according to tabs.

SENTENCE DIAGRAMMING
❧ Read and discuss the following sections in *Sentence Sense* with your teacher.

III. Sentence Diagrammming: Verbals as Modifiers
- ◆ 17.1 Participles
- ◆ 17.2 Participial Phrases

❧ In your Writer's Journal, copy these sentences. Analyze each sentence by marking the simple subject (who or what the sentence is about) with a single underline, and the verb or verb phrase with a double underline. Write DO over a direct object, LV over a linking verb, PA over a predicate adjective, and PN over a predicate nominative. Put parentheses around each prepositional phrase. Then diagram the sentence. Refer to *Sentence Sense* as needed.

1. Sleep awakes in laughing day.

2. The Trojans saw a bright star shining above them.

3. The banished king was constantly seeking Rome's capture and his throne's recovery.

4. Praying to the gods for help, Horatius swam to the other side in safety.

5. They found Cincinnatus plowing his fields.

Eloquent Expression

SENTENCE STYLE – YOUR STYLE!

❦ Craft copia for sentences from your own retelling using Sentence Style devices we have studied.

A. Work with your writing mentor to choose three sentences from your retelling that could be improved.

B. Copy the first in your Writer's Journal. Underline every important word in the sentence and jot down synonyms for each.

C. Use the list of Sentence Style devices below as you write several new versions of the sentence. New devices from this lesson are listed in bold type. You may use more than one device in each sentence.

D. Repeat the instructions above for the second and third sentences.

E. Choose your favorite paraphrase of each sentence. Replace the original sentences in your retelling before you edit again.

COPIA OF WORDS	COPIA OF CONSTRUCTION
✓ Synonyms and Antonyms	✓ Sentence class by use
✓ Opening Words	✓ Dialogue
✓ Dialogue Tags - synonyms for *said*	◆ Tag line position
✓ Point of View	✓ Verb Tense
✓ Nouns – varied and descriptive	✓ Sentence Structure
◆ switch noun/pronouns	◆ **switch possessive/of phrases**
✓ Verbs – strong and fitting	✓ Sentence Combination
✓ Modifiers	◆ compound elements
◆ add adjective	
◆ add adverb	

EDITOR'S PEN – ZOOM 10X: SENTENCES

Now it is time to zoom in even closer as you check the sentences in your retelling. Work with your writing mentor.

Editor's Pen – Zoom 10x: Sentences

✓ Complete thought expressed

✓ Subject and predicate agree in number

✓ Correct capitalization and punctuation

    ◆ Commas correctly used for words in a series

    ◆ No comma splices or run-on sentences!

A. Read aloud your your most recently edited version. Use the Editor's Pen checklist to identify changes you need to make. Mark all changes on your print copy.

B. Transfer all additions and corrections from your print copy to the computer file. Print this version and file it in your binder along with your other versions.

Commonplace

Commonplace Book

POETRY

Session two of three commonplace sessions for this lesson. Literary selection: "Barefoot Boy."

Set your timer. Begin where you stopped in the last session. When you finish, check your work carefully against the original for accuracy.

Lesson 18.4

Prose & Poetry

SCANSION

 Scan this stanza, following the three steps you have learned.

Step 1 Mark each syllable as either stressed (/) or unstressed (∪). Say the line aloud several times to "get" the meter. Next, say the line aloud emphasizing the stresses as you mark the stresses only. Then go back and mark the unstressed syllables, saying the line aloud once more to check your work. Pronounce *blackberry, whispering,* and *pickerel* with two syllables.

Step 2 Insert dividers (|) to mark off the feet.

Step 3 Name the poem's predominant meter:

Oh for boyhood's time of June,

Crowding years in one brief moon,

When all things I heard or saw,

Me, their master, waited for.

I was rich in flowers and trees,

Humming-birds and honey-bees;

For my sport the squirrel played,

Plied the snouted mole his spade;

For my taste the blackberry cone

Purpled over hedge and stone;

Laughed the brook for my delight

Through the day and through the night,

Whispering at the garden wall,

Talked with me from fall to fall;

Mine the sand-rimmed pickerel pond,

Mine the walnut slopes beyond,

Mine, on bending orchard trees,

Apples of Hesperides!

Still as my horizon grew,

Larger grew my riches too;

All the world I saw or knew

Seemed a complex Chinese toy,

Fashioned for a barefoot boy.

Language Logic

GRAMMAR TERMS & DEFINITIONS
❦ Review all flashcards according to tabs.

SENTENCE DIAGRAMMING
❦ In your Writer's Journal, copy these sentences. Analyze each sentence by marking the simple subject (who or what the sentence is about) with a single underline, and the verb or verb phrase with a double underline. Write DO over a direct object, LV over a linking verb, PA over a predicate adjective, and PN over a predicate nominative. Put parentheses around each prepositional phrase. Then diagram the sentence. Refer to *Sentence Sense* as needed.

Writer's
Journal

1. All too soon these feet must hide

    In the prison cells of pride,

    Lose the freedom of the sod,

    Like a colt's for work be shod.

2. *Challenge (for classroom exercise)*

    Barefoot boy, with cheek of tan!

    With thy turned-up pantaloons,

    And thy merry whistled tunes;

    With thy red lip, redder still

    Kissed by strawberries on the hill;

    From my heart I give thee joy, —

    I was once a barefoot boy!

Eloquent Expression

PARAGRAPH STYLE – PARAPHRASE WITH COPIA

For this exercise, choose from all of the copia devices you have learned so far. See the copia chart in Lesson 18.3. New devices are in bold type.

In your Writer's Journal, paraphrase this paragraph. Change each sentence opener, and change at least one sentence class by use. Use as many synonym substitutions as possible. Use as many of the other copia devices as you are able. Make notes on the paragraph below before you begin.

Writer's
Journal

After thus rescuing the Roman army from certain death,

Cincinnatus brought them back to the city, and enjoyed the honors of a

triumph. Then, seeing that his country no longer needed him, he laid

aside the title of dictator, which he had borne for only a few days.

Joyfully hastening back to his farm, he took up his plowing where he

had dropped it; and he went on living as quietly and simply as if he had never been called upon to

serve as dictator, and to receive the honors of a grand triumph.

Classical Composition

EDITOR'S PEN – FINE FOCUS: WORDS
The final checks dwell on the details of your word usage. Continue to compile your personal
editing checklist to use in editing all of your work across the curriculum.

Editor's Pen – Fine Focus: Words
✓ Word choices varied; word meanings clear
   ◆ Verbs: *strong, fitting; appropriate adverbs if needed*
   ◆ Nouns: *clear, descriptive; appropriate adjectives if needed*
   ◆ Dialogue: *dialogue tags varied if appropropriate*
✓ Correct spelling
✓ Final read-through

A. Read aloud your most recent version. Identify changes you need
   to make with the Editor's Pen checklist. Mark these on your
   print copy.

B. Transfer all additions and corrections from your print copy to the
   computer file. Print this final version and file it in your binder
   along with your other versions.

Commonplace

Commonplace Book

POETRY

Session three of three commonplace sessions for this lesson. Literary selection: "Barefoot Boy."

 Set your timer and begin copying. When you finish, check your work carefully against the original for accuracy.

Lesson 18.5

Prose & Poetry

POETRY APPRECIATION

 Read and enjoy a few poems in your poetry anthology. Identify rhyme schemes and stanza forms of one or two. Look for figures of speech and figures of description in the poems you read, and make note of any you find for future Commonplace Book entries. Read one or two poems aloud with expression and proper pauses. Pause at punctuation, but not necessarily at the ends of lines. Finally, choose a rhyming poem with trochaic meter to observe.

Writer's Journal

- In your Writer's Journal, write the title of the poem and the author. Make note of its meter, rhyme scheme, and stanza form.
- Write the rhyming words from the poem in two lists: one list for those spelled the same, and one list for those spelled differently.
- Choose one of the rhyming words from the spelled differently list, and try to come up with several additional rhymes. Look especially for varied spellings.

Language Logic

GRAMMAR TERMS & DEFINITIONS

◯ Ask your teacher to quiz you with the grammar flashcards. Alternately, use the test feature in the Cottage Press *Bards & Poets I* Quizlet Classroom for an online or printed quiz for Lesson 18.

Writer's Journal

DICTATION: POETRY

◯ Work in your Writer's Journal. Write as your teacher dictates a passage to you from your Commonplace Book. When you are done, check your work carefully, word by word, against the original. Check for accurate spelling, capitalization, and punctuation.

Classical Composition

Writer's Journal

POETRY

◯ In your Writer's Journal, write two to four rhyming lines that summarize the action of "The Farmer Hero." If you wish, include a poetic **moral** at the end. Consider including them at the end of your retelling as a brief summary of the story. You may find it easiest to imitate the rhyme and meter of a few lines of the poetic selection for this lesson or a previous lesson.

NARRATIVE RETELLING – FINAL DRAFT

◯ Read over the final version of your retelling one last time and make any needed changes. Save it on your computer; print and file with all the other drafts in your writing binder.

Commonplace

FROM YOUR READING

Find selections in a book or poem to add to your Commonplace Book. Include the name of the book or poem, properly formatted. Label the entry with the grammar or poetry feature, the figure of speech, or as a favorite passage. Aim for a minimum of three entries, with at least one from each category.

Commonplace Book

Grammar Features (choose any)

- ◆ A sentence that has an interesting or descriptive noun, a strong and fitting verb, a well-chosen adjective, and/or a vivid adverb
- ◆ A sentence with one or more prepositional phrases or indirect objects
- ◆ A sentence that has a possessive noun or pronoun and/or an appositive
- ◆ A sentence that has a conjunction to join words, phrases, or clauses
- ◆ A sentence that has a participle or participial phrase
- ◆ An interesting dialogue tag (add to your Dialogue Tags list)
- ◆ An interrogative, exclamatory, or imperative sentence

Figures (choose any)

- ◆ Figures of Speech: simile, onomatopoeia, anastrophe, alliteration, and/or metaphor
- ◆ Figures of Description: anemographia and/or hydrographia

Poetry Features (choose any)

- ◆ Rhyme (note name of the rhyme scheme)
- ◆ Iambic, anapestic, dactylic, or trochaic meter (note name of the meter)
- ◆ Stanza (note name of stanza form)

Favorite Passage: Add at least one passage of one to three sentences or several lines of poetry that captured your attention in your reading this week. It may be something you found beautiful, thought-provoking, funny, or interesting.

❧

THE STORIES OF ALBION AND BRUTUS
from OUR ISLAND STORY by Henrietta Marshall

Once upon a time there was a giant called Neptune. When he was quite a tiny boy, Neptune loved the sea. All day long he played in it, swimming, diving, and laughing gleefully as the waves dashed over him.

As he grew older he came to know and love the sea so well that the sea and the waves loved him too, and acknowledged him to be their king. At last people said he was not only king of the waves, but god of the sea.

Neptune had a very beautiful wife who was called Amphitrite. He had also many sons. As each son became old enough to reign, Neptune made him king over an island.

Neptune's fourth son was called Albion. When it came to his turn to receive a kingdom, a great council was called to decide upon an island for him.

Now Neptune and Amphitrite loved Albion more than any of their other children. This made it very difficult to chose which island should be his.

The mermaids and mermen, as the wonderful people who live in the sea are called, came from all parts of the world with news of beautiful islands. But after hearing about them, Neptune and Amphitrite would shake their heads and say, "No, that is not good enough for Albion."

At last a little mermaid swam into the pink and white coral cave in which the council was held. She was more beautiful than any mermaid who had yet come to the council. Her eyes were merry and honest, and they were blue as the sky and the sea. Her hair was as yellow as fine gold, and in her cheeks a lovely pink came and went. When she spoke, her voice sounded as clear as a bell and as soft as the whisper of the waves, as they ripple upon the shore.

"O Father Neptune," she said, "let Albion come to my island. It is a beautiful little island. It lies like a gem in the bluest of waters. There the trees and the grass are green, the cliffs are white and the sands are golden. There the sun shines and the birds sing. It is a land of beauty. Mountains and valleys, broad lakes and swift-flowing rivers, all are there. Let Albion come to my island."

"Where is this island?" said Neptune and Amphitrite both at once. They thought it must indeed be a beautiful land if it were only half as lovely as the little mermaid said.

"Oh, come, and I will show it to you," replied she. Then she swam away in a great hurry to show her beautiful island, and Neptune, Amphitrite, and all the mermaids and mermen followed.

It was a wonderful sight to see them as they swam along. Their white arms gleamed in the sunshine, and their golden hair floated out over the water like fine seaweed. Never before had so many of the sea-folk been gathered together at one place, and the noise of their tails flapping through the water brought all the little fishes and great sea monsters out, eager to know what was happening. They swam and swam until they came to the little green island with the white cliffs and yellow sands.

As soon as it came in sight, Neptune raised himself on a big wave, and when he saw the little island lying before him, like a beautiful gem in the blue water, just as the mermaid had said, he cried out in joy, "This is the island of my love. Albion shall rule it and Albion it shall be called."

So Albion took possession of the little island, which until then had been called Samothea, and he changed its name to Albion, as Neptune had said should be done.

For seven years Albion reigned over his little island. At the end of that time he was killed in a fight with the hero Hercules. This was a great grief to Neptune and Amphitrite. But because of the love they bore to their son Albion, they continued to love and watch over the little green island which was called by his name.

For many years after the death of Albion the little island had no ruler. At last, one day there came sailing from the far-off city of Troy a prince called Brutus. He, seeing the fair island, with white cliffs and golden sands, landed with all his mighty men of war. There were many giants in the land in those days, but Brutus fought and conquered them. He made himself king, not only over Albion, but over all the islands which lay around. He called them the kingdom of Britain or Britannia after his own name, Brutus, and Albion he called Great Britain because it was the largest of the islands.

Although after this the little island was no longer called Albion, Neptune still loved it. When he grew old and had no more strength to rule, he gave his sceptre to the islands called Britannia, for we know—

"Britannia rules the waves."

This is a story of many thousand years ago. Some people think it is only a fairy tale. But however that may be, the little island is still sometimes called Albion, although it is nearly always called Britain.

In this book you will find the story of the people of Britain. The story tells how they grew to be a great people, till the little green island set in the lonely sea was no longer large enough to contain them all. Then they sailed away over the blue waves to far-distant countries. Now the people of the little island possess lands all over the world. These lands form the empire of Greater Britain.

Many of these lands are far, far larger than the little island itself. Yet the people who live in them still look back lovingly to the little island, from which they or their fathers came, and call it "Home."

CR

Lesson 19.1

Prose & Poetry

A LOOK AT LITERARY ELEMENTS IN THE NARRATIVE

1 Read
- Listen carefully as your teacher reads the selection aloud. **Delight** in the story.

2 Inquire
- Does the **title** give any hint as to the content or message of the story? If this story was published by the author in a larger book or an anthology, does that title give any hint?
- Discuss the meaning of these words in the context of the story: *acknowledged, kingdom, council, mermaids (and mermen), gem, possession,* and any unfamiliar words.

3 Observe the Content
- **Setting** When and where does this story take place?
- **Characters** Who is (are) the main character(s) in this story?
- **Conflict** What is the main problem or crisis for the character(s)?
- **Resolution** Is the problem solved? If so, how? If not, why not?
- **Point of View** Who is telling the story? Is it first-person or third-person?
- **Figures** Can you identify any examples of simile, onomatopoeia, anemographia, anastrophe, alliteration, hydrographia, or metaphor in this narrative?

4 Investigate the Context
Several wonderful legends about the founding of England were told by authors and historians from ancient to medieval times, continuing into the modern age. The British Isles were certainly known to the ancient Romans; this map was made by Greek cartographer Claudius Ptolemy of Alexandria, c. AD 150, about the time some of the earliest tales begin.

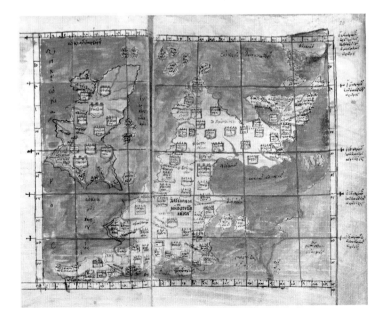

Contrary to popular opinion, though stories may be called a *legends*, this does not always mean that they are completely fictional. Of course, some legends are fanciful and clearly fictional, but others may have some element of fact mixed with fiction. Our story is a prime example of this. Thomas Bulfinch writes,

> According to the earliest accounts, Albion, a giant, and son of Neptune, a contemporary of Hercules, ruled over the island, to which he gave his name. Presuming to oppose the progress of Hercules in his western march, he was slain by him. Another story is that Histion, the son of Japhet, the son of Noah, had four sons, Francus, Romanus, Alemannus, and Britto, from whom descended the French, Roman, German, and British people.
>
> Rejecting these and other like stories, [John] Milton gives more regard to the story of Brutus, the Trojan, which, he says, is supported by "descents of ancestry long continued, laws and exploits not plainly seeming to be borrowed or devised, which on the common belief have wrought no small impression; defended by many, denied utterly by few." The principal authority is Geoffrey of Monmouth, whose history, written in the twelfth century, purports to be a translation of a history of Britain brought over from the opposite shore of France, which, under the name of Brittany, was chiefly peopled by natives of Britain who, from time to time, emigrated thither, driven from their own country by the inroads of the Picts and Scots. According to this authority, Brutus was the son of Silvius, and he of Ascanius, the son of Aeneas, whose flight from Troy and settlement in Italy are narrated in "Stories of Gods and Heroes." — Thomas Bulfinch, *The Age of Fable*

Henrietta (H.E.) Marshall was born in 1867 in Scotland. She wrote many books for children, primarily dealing with British national history and literature, but she also wrote about the history of other countries, including the United States. She did not marry or have children, and very little is known about her life. She died in 1941. Her most famous book is *Our Island Story, A History of England for Boys and Girls*.

5 Connect the Thoughts

◆ Does this story remind you of other stories with similar plots, messages, or characters?

◆ Does this story remind you of any fables?

◆ Does this story remind you of any proverbs or other well-known quotations? If so, enter these in your Commonplace Book.

Commonplace Book

6 Profit and Delight

- ◆ **Delight** What are the sources of delight in this story?
- ◆ **Wisdom** What wisdom does this story furnish?
- ◆ **Read** the narrative aloud to your teacher with expression and with proper pauses.

PLOT OBSERVATION: IDENTIFYING ACTIONS

Observe the plot of "The Stories of Albion and Brutus." Work in pencil on the original narrative at the beginning of this lesson, marking and making notes in the margin as instructed below.

A. Quickly read through the narrative once more. Number the paragraphs, and then mark the story as you have learned to do. Divide the narrative into actions.

B. Mark an x beside the sections that do not detail an action, and note what these are: **Prologue, Epilogue, Explanation, Description, Summary, Author Comments**.

C. Mark the major actions. Then, mark in the left margin if the action is made up of **Dialogue** or **Thoughts**. Consider Theon's Six. Remember that action can change even in the middle of a paragraph. Feel free to change your mind often as you work through the entire narrative—this is why you must use a pencil! Keep in mind that there is not just one right way to divide narratives into actions Just make sure you can explain why you divide them as you do, using Theon's Six.

D. Review the narrative. Make notes in the margin indicating if any of the rest of Theon's Six changed with each action. You should definitely have notes about Person. Ask the questions for the other four, but do not worry too much if you can only add notes for two or three others.

E. Discuss your work with your teacher.

Language Logic

GRAMMAR
FLASHCARDS

GRAMMAR TERMS & DEFINITIONS

Review all flashcards according to tabs.

GRAMMAR PRACTICE AND REVIEW

In your Writer's Journal, copy these sentences. Analyze each sentence by marking the simple subject (who or what the sentence is about) with a single underline, and the verb or verb phrase with a double underline. Write DO over the direct object, or LV over the linking verb; write PA over a predicate adjective and PN over a predicate nominative. Put parentheses around each prepositional phrase. Then diagram the sentence. Refer to *Sentence Sense* as needed.

1. Neptune had a very beautiful wife, Amphitrite.

2. The little mermaid's hair was as yellow as fine gold, and in her cheeks a lovely pink came and went.

3. The noise of their tails flapping through the water brought all the little fishes and great sea monsters out.

4. He saw the little island lying before him, like a beautiful gem in the blue water.

5. Brutus, seeing the fair island, with white cliffs and golden sands, landed with all his mighty men of war.

Writer's Journal

Eloquent Expression

COPIA OF WORDS: VOCABULARY STUDY

Conduct a vocabulary study for "The Stories of Albion and Brutus."

Writer's Journal

A. Choose at least two unfamiliar words to study. If you need suggestions, see the list under **Inquire** in Literary Elements above. Work in your Writer's Journal.

B. Complete Vocabulary Study steps A-G for each word (see Appendix).

Commonplace

NARRATIVE

Session one of three commonplace sessions for this lesson. Literary selection: "The Stories of Albion and Brutus."

Commonplace Book

❦ Set your timer and begin copying. When you finish, check your work carefully, word by word, against the original.

Lesson 19.2

Prose & Poetry

PLOT OBSERVATION: OUTLINE WITH CAPTIONS

❦ In your Writer's Journal, create an outline to capture your observations with parallel captions.

Writer's Journal

A. Jot down a quick caption for each major action, as well as any of the following: Prologue, Epilogue, Explanation, Description, Summary, Author Comments.

B. Review your captions, and choose a parallel format.

C. Revise all captions to conform to the format you have chosen.

Language Logic

GRAMMAR FLASHCARDS

GRAMMAR TERMS & DEFINITIONS

❦ Review all flashcards according to tabs.

THE GERUND

❦ Read and discuss the following sections in *Sentence Sense* with your teacher.

I.   Etymology – The Verb
  ◆ 3.11A Verbals *Review this lesson*
  ◆ 3.11 B Verbal Classes *Review this lesson*
V.   Exercises
  ◆ Oral exercise: Identify each gerund or participle in *Harvey's* 91,
    Sentences 1, 2, 3, 4, 5, and 7.

Classical Composition

PLOT OBSERVATION: ORAL NARRATION

 Without reading "The Stories of Albion and Brutus" again, retell the **plot** orally to your
teacher. Refer to your plot observation of the narrative with Theon's Six if needed.

Commonplace

NARRATIVE

Session two of three commonplace sessions for this lesson. Literary
selection: "The Stories of Brutus and Albion."

 Set your timer and begin copying. When you finish, check
your work carefully, word by word, against the original. Check
spelling, capitalization, and punctuation for accuracy.

Commonplace
Book

Lesson 19.3

Language Logic

GRAMMAR
FLASHCARDS

GRAMMAR TERMS & DEFINITIONS
 Review all flashcards according to tabs.

SENTENCE DIAGRAMMING

 Read and discuss the following sections in *Sentence Sense* with your teacher.

III. Sentence Diagrammming: Verbals as Nouns
- ◆ 18.1 Participial Nouns (Gerunds)
- ◆ 18.2 Gerund Phrases

 In your Writer's Journal, copy these sentences. Analyze each sentence by marking the simple subject (who or what the sentence is about) with a single underline, and the verb or verb phrase with a double underline. Write DO over a direct object, LV over a linking verb, PA over a predicate adjective, and PN over a predicate nominative. Put parentheses around each prepositional phrase. Then diagram the sentence. Refer to *Sentence Sense* as needed.

1. Gambling is a crime.

2. Boys like running, jumping, and skating.

3. The burning of the capitol was a wanton outrage.

4. Your remaining here would ruin us all.

5. This was Cincinnatus, an old retired soldier; he spent all his time in plowing, sowing, and reaping.

Writer's Journal

Eloquent Expression

SENTENCE STYLE – COPIA OF CONSTRUCTION: PHRASE PLACEMENT

Participial phrases modifying nouns can also be moved within a sentence. Relocating a participle to the beginning of a sentence is an effective device to vary your sentence opening words.

Erasmus, having received your letter, was filled with great joy.

Having received your letter, Erasmus was filled with great joy.

Usually it is best to keep participles and participial phrases near the noun or pronoun they modify. Otherwise, you may end up with *dangling participles*:

I saw an accident walking down the street.

Driving like a maniac, the deer was hit and killed.

Although these sentences are amusing, they do not give us a clear understanding of the action. In your writing, make sure it is clear what noun or pronoun your participles are modifying.[1]

Prepositional phrases functioning as adverbs can also be moved within the sentence quite freely, but you should always read the sentence carefully to make sure that you have not changed the meaning by moving the modifer.

I received your letter with great joy.

With great joy, I received your letter.

Complete these exercises in your Writer's Journal.

Writer's Journal

◉ Paraphrase these sentences, moving the underlined participles or participle phrases to a different position. Be careful to check that the resulting sentences retain the same sense and are grammatically correct.

1. He saw the little island lying before him.

2. He, seeing the fair island, landed with all his mighty men of war.

◉ Paraphrase each sentence twice, changing the position of the underlined adverbs and/or prepositional phrases each time.

3. Then she swam away in a great hurry.

4. He gave his sceptre to the islands called Britannia.

Classical Composition

NARRATIVE RETELLING – FIRST DRAFT

You will have two sessions to work on this retelling. Begin here, and plan to finish in Lesson 19.4. As you write your retelling, do your best to use proper grammar and spelling, but keep in mind that you will have opportunity to edit before you finalize it.

1. Teacher Note: For a classroom activity, find some sentences with dangling modifiers in your newspaper or on the internet. Write them on the board and have students correct.

◉ Retell "The Stories of Albion and Brutus" in writing, keeping the
same characters, setting, and sequence of action. Choose either
first or third person point of view, but be consistent throughout.
This means you need to make sure that the pronouns are
consistent, and pay close attention attention to subject/verb
agreement. Refer to your plot observation of the narrative with
Theon's Six, but do not review the original narrative before you
write. Include:

- ◆ a heading, properly formatted
- ◆ at least one instance of alliteration
- ◆ at least one instance of metaphor
- ◆ (optional figure of speech) simile, onomatopoeia, anastrophe
- ◆ (optional figure of description) anemographia, hydrographia

Lesson 19.4

Language Logic

GRAMMAR
FLASHCARDS

GRAMMAR TERMS & DEFINITIONS
◉ Review all flashcards according to tabs.

SENTENCE DIAGRAMMING

◉ In your Writer's Journal, copy these sentences. Analyze each sentence by marking the simple
subject (who or what the sentence is about) with a single underline, and the verb or verb
phrase with a double underline. Write DO over a direct object, LV over a linking verb, PA
over a predicate adjective, and PN over a predicate nominative. Put parentheses around
each prepositional phrase. Then diagram the sentence. Refer to *Sentence Sense* as needed.

1. Albion shall rule it and Albion it shall be called.

2. By walking all night, Cincinnatus brought his men in the rear
   of the Æquians.

3. Give me two good men to help me, and I will hold the bridge
   and stop the enemy from coming over.

4. The quarreling had been much more violent than usual and each of the Sons was moping in a surly manner.

5. The Jabberwock, with eyes of flame, came whiffling through the tulgey wood.

Classical Composition

Writer's Journal

NARRATIVE RETELLING – FINISH FIRST DRAFT

Finish the first draft of your narrative retelling. Review the instructions in Lesson 19.3 as needed.

Commonplace

NARRATIVE

Session three of three commonplace sessions for this lesson. Literary selection: "The Stories of Albion and Brutus."

Commonplace Book

Set your timer. Begin where you stopped in the last session. When you finish, check your work carefully against the original for accuracy.

Lesson 19.5

Prose & Poetry

POETRY APPRECIATION

Read and enjoy a few poems in your poetry anthology. Identify rhyme schemes and stanza forms of one or two. Look for poems with iambic, trochaic, dactylic, or anapestic meter. Look for figures of speech and figures of description in the poems you read, and make note of any you find for future Commonplace Book entries. Read one or two poems aloud with expression and proper pauses. Pause at punctuation, but not necessarily at the ends of lines. Finally, choose a rhyming poem with trochaic meter to observe.

Language Logic

GRAMMAR TERMS & DEFINITIONS

◆ Ask your teacher to quiz you with the grammar flashcards. Alternately, use the test feature in the Cottage Press *Bards & Poets I* Quizlet Classroom for an online or printed quiz for Lesson 19.

DICTATION: NARRATIVE PASSAGE

◆ Work in your Writer's Journal. Write as your teacher dictates a passage to you from your Commonplace Book. When you are done, check your work carefully, word by word, against the original. Check for accurate spelling, capitalization, and punctuation.

Classical Composition

NARRATIVE RETELLING: TYPE FINAL DRAFT

◆ Type your retelling on the computer with spell-check turned off, or ask your writing mentor to type it exactly as you wrote it. Save, print, and file this draft in your writing binder.

Commonplace

FROM YOUR READING

Find selections in a book or poem to add to your Commonplace Book. Include the name of the book or poem, properly formatted. Label the entry with the grammar or poetry feature, the figure of speech, or as a favorite passage. Aim for a minimum of three entries, with at least one from each category.

Commonplace Book

❀ Grammar Features (choose any)

- ◆ A sentence that has an interesting or descriptive noun, a strong and fitting verb, a well-chosen adjective, and/or a vivid adverb
- ◆ A sentence with one or more prepositional phrases or indirect objects
- ◆ A sentence that has a possessive noun or pronoun and/or an appositive
- ◆ A sentence that has a conjunction to join words, phrases, or clauses
- ◆ A sentence that has a participle or participial phrase
- ◆ An interesting dialogue tag (add to your Dialogue Tags list)
- ◆ An interrogative, exclamatory, or imperative sentence

❀ Figures (choose any)

- ◆ Figures of Speech: simile, onomatopoeia, anastrophe, alliteration, and/or metaphor
- ◆ Figures of Description: anemographia and/or hydrographia

❀ Poetry Features (choose any)

- ◆ Rhyme (note name of the rhyme scheme)
- ◆ Iambic, anapestic, dactylic, or trochaic meter (note name of the meter)
- ◆ Stanza (note name of stanza form)

❀ Favorite Passage: Add at least one passage of one to three sentences or several lines of poetry that captured your attention in your reading this week. It may be something you found beautiful, thought-provoking, funny, or interesting.

❧

OLD IRONSIDES

Aye tear her tattered ensign down
Long has it waved on high,
And many an eye has danced to see
That banner in the sky;
Beneath it rung the battle shout,
And burst the cannon's roar;—
The meteor of the ocean air
Shall sweep the clouds no more.

Her deck, once red with heroes' blood,
Where knelt the vanquished foe,
When winds were hurrying o'er the flood,
And waves were white below,
No more shall feel the victor's tread,
Or know the conquered knee;—
The harpies of the shore shall pluck
The eagle of the sea!

Oh, better that her shattered hulk
Should sink beneath the wave;
Her thunders shook the mighty deep,
And there should be her grave;
Nail to the mast her holy flag,

Set every threadbare sail,

And give her to the god of storms,

The lightning and the gale!

— OLIVER WENDELL HOLMES

℞

Lesson 20.1

Prose & Poetry

A LOOK AT LITERARY ELEMENTS IN THE POEM

1 Read

◆ Follow along and listen carefully as the poem is read aloud, OR read it aloud yourself. Read it at least two or three times. **Delight** in the meter, the rhyme, and the images.

2 Inquire

◆ Does the **title** give any hint as to the content or message of the poem?

◆ Are there any other unfamiliar persons, places, or things mentioned in the poem? Discuss these with your teacher.

◆ Discuss the meaning of these words in the context of the story: *ensign, banner, meteor, vanquished, tread, harpies, threadbare, gale,* and any unfamiliar words.

◆ Was there any part of the poem you did not understand? If so, discuss this with your teacher and classmates.

3 Observe the Content

◆ **Lyrical Elements** What does the poet describe?

   ▪ What does the poet describe?

   ▪ Does the poet make you see, hear, smell, taste, or touch anything?

   ▪ Does the poet compare something in the poem to some other thing?

◆ **Narrative Elements** Does this poem tell a story? If so, observe the

   ▪ **Setting** When and where does this story take place?

   ▪ **Characters** Who is (are) the main character(s) in this story?

   ▪ **Conflict** What is the main problem or crisis for the character(s)?

   ▪ **Resolution** Is the problem solved? If so, how? If not, why not?

◆ **Point of View** Who is speaking in the poem? Is it first-person or third-person?

◆ **Figures** Can you identify any examples of simile, onomatopoeia, anemographia, anastrophe, alliteration, hydrographia, or metaphor in this poem?

4 Investigate the Context

Oliver Wendell Holmes, Sr. (1809-1894), another of the Fireside Poets, along with Whittier and Holmes, was born in the city of Cambridge Massachusetts He was a true *polymath*. (If you do not know what this means, conduct a Vocabulary Study!) Trained at Harvard as medical doctor, he was a professor of medicine at both Dartmouth and Harvard, and a popular lecturer. He was also a gifted poet, as our selection demonstrates. His pen saved the venerable old frigate, the *U.S.S. Constitution*, better known as "Old Ironsides." George Washington had commissioned her in 1797, and she had served the United

States nobly in the wars against the Barbary Pirates, and in the War of 1812. One morning, Holmes picked up his newspaper to find that the Constitution had been slated to be scrapped by the U. S. Navy. In his dismay, Holmes quickly penned "Old Ironsides"; it was published the next day in several East Coast newspapers, arousing so much public sentiment that the Navy relented and preserved the ship. She is harbored as a museum ship in Boston to this day. Make sure you visit if you are ever in Boston! The painting below is *Chase of the Constitution, July 1812* by Anton Fischer, painted in the early 20th century.

5 Connect the Thoughts

- ◆ Does this poem remind you of other poems, or of stories with similar plots, messages, or characters?
- ◆ Does this poem remind you of any proverbs or other well-known quotations? If so, enter these in your Commonplace Book.

Commonplace Book

6 Profit and Delight

- ◆ **Delight** What are the sources of delight in this poem?
- ◆ **Wisdom** What wisdom does this poem furnish?
- ◆ **Read** the poem aloud to your teacher with expression and with proper pauses.
- ◆ **Record** in your Book of Centuries: Oliver Wendell Holmes, Old Ironsides Commissioned.
- ◆ **Memorize** this poem and **recite** it before an audience.

Language Logic

GRAMMAR FLASHCARDS

GRAMMAR TERMS & DEFINITIONS

Review all flashcards according to tabs.

GRAMMAR PRACTICE AND REVIEW

In your Writer's Journal, copy these sentences. Analyze each sentence by marking the simple subject (who or what the sentence is about) with a single underline, and the verb or verb phrase with a double underline. Write DO over the direct object, or LV over the linking verb; write PA over a predicate adjective and PN over a predicate nominative. Put parentheses around each prepositional phrase. Then diagram the sentence. Refer to *Sentence Sense* as needed.

1. Aye, tear her tattered ensign down!

   Long has it waved on high.

2. The harpies of the shore shall pluck

   The eagle of the sea!

Writer's Journal

3. Her thunders shook the mighty deep,

    And there should be her grave;

    Nail to the mast her holy flag,

    Set every threadbare sail,

    And give her to the god of storms,

    The lightning and the gale!

Classical Composition

EDITOR'S PEN – THE BIG PICTURE

 Edit your retelling from Lesson 19:

Editor's Pen – The Big Picture

✓ All important plot elements included
✓ All characters represented correctly
✓ Sequence: *same as the original*
✓ Length: *similar to the original*
✓ Point of View: *3rd person or 1st person*
✓ Figure of Speech: *alliteration, metaphor;* optional: *simile, onomatopoeia, anastrophe*
✓ Figure of Description, optional: *anemographia, hydrographia*

A. Read aloud exactly what you have written—not what you THINK you have written! Mark any corrections on your first draft.

B. Next, work through the Big Picture checklist above with your writing mentor.

C. Transfer all additions and corrections from your print copy of the retelling to your file on the computer. Print and file this edited version in your binder along with your marked-up editing copy of the first draft.

Commonplace

Commonplace
Book

POETRY

Session one of three commonplace sessions for this lesson. Literary
selection: "Old Ironsides."

 Set your timer and begin copying. When finished, check your
work carefully against the original for accuracy.

Lesson 20.2

Prose & Poetry

RHYME SCHEME AND STANZA FORM

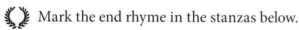 Mark the end rhyme in the stanzas below.

> Aye, tear her tattered ensign down!
>
> Long has it waved on high,
>
> And many an eye has danced to see
>
> That banner in the sky;
>
> Beneath it rung the battle shout,
>
> And burst the cannon's roar;——
>
> The meteor of the ocean air
>
> Shall sweep the clouds no more.
>
> Her deck, once red with heroes' blood,
>
> Where knelt the vanquished foe,
>
> When winds were hurrying o'er the flood,
>
> And waves were white below,
>
> No more shall feel the victor's tread,
>
> Or know the conquered knee;——
>
> The harpies of the shore shall pluck
>
> The eagle of the sea!

Oh, better that her shattered hulk

Should sink beneath the wave;

Her thunders shook the mighty deep,

And there should be her grave;

Nail to the mast her holy flag,

Set every threadbare sail,

And give her to the god of storms,

The lightning and the gale!

⚜ Name the predominant rhyme scheme and the stanza form of this poem.

Language Logic

GRAMMAR TERMS & DEFINITIONS
⚜ Review all flashcards according to tabs.

THE INFINITIVE
 Read and discuss the following sections in *Sentence Sense* with your teacher.

I.   Etymology – The Verb
- ◆ 3.11A Verbals *Review this lesson*
- ◆ 3.11B Verbal Classes *Review this lesson*

V.   Exercises
- ◆ Oral exercise: Identify each infinitive used as a modifier in *Harvey's* 187, Sentences 2, 6, 7, and 8.

Eloquent Expression

FIGURE OF SPEECH: PERSONIFICATION
Personification is another **figure of speech** that is found very often in prose, poetry, and everyday speech. Here are some examples:

A <u>wise old owl</u> . . .

The brook <u>chatters</u>.

Little soft clouds <u>played happily</u> in a blue sky, <u>skipping</u> from time to time in front of the sun. — A. A. Milne, *Winnie-the-Pooh*

As you can see, **personification** can give living characteristics to an abstract idea or non-living thing, or it can give human characteristics to a non-human thing. Sometimes a thing or idea is addressed directly as if it were a person, as in this familiar poem:

Twinkle, twinkle, <u>little star</u>,
How I wonder what you are. — Jane Taylor

⚜ Study and review figures of speech with your teacher.

A. Discuss the examples of personification with your teacher.

B. Look in "Old Ironsides" for examples of personification and discuss them with your teacher. In your Writer's Journal, list the figures of personfication you find in this poem.

Writer's Journal

C. Look through other poems we have studied in *Bards & Poets I* for more examples of personification. Make note of some that you may wish to copy into your Commonplace Book.

Classical Composition

EDITOR'S PEN – ZOOM 5X: PARAGRAPHS

⚜ Now that the Big Picture is set, begin to zoom in for a close look at the paragraph(s) in your retelling with your writing mentor.

Editor's Pen – Zoom 5x: Paragraphs
✔ Formatting: *proper indentation*
✔ Length: *neither too wordy nor too short*
✔ Sentence class by use: *effective use*
✔ Sentence openers: *varied*

✔ Dialogue: *effective use*
✔ Verb Tense: *consistent*
✔ Pronouns: *consistent with chosen point of view*

A. Read aloud your most recently edited version. Check each item in the Editor's Pen checklist to identify possible changes. Mark these on your print copy.

B. Transfer all additions and corrections from your print copy to the computer file. Print this version and file it in your binder along with your other versions.

Lesson 20.3

Prose & Poetry

SCANSION

 Scan these stanzas, following the three steps you have learned.

Step 1 Mark each syllable as either stressed (/) or unstressed (∪). Say the line aloud several times to "get" the meter. Next, say the line aloud emphasizing the stresses as you mark the stresses only. Then go back and mark the unstressed syllables, saying the line aloud once more to check your work. Pronounce *meteor* and *hurrying* with two syllables. There is one extra unstressed syllabe in the first stanza, third line, second foot.

Step 2 Insert dividers (|) to mark off the feet.

Step 3 Name the poem's predominant meter:

Aye, tear her tattered ensign down!

Long has it waved on high,

And many an eye has danced to see

That banner in the sky;

Beneath it rung the battle shout,

And burst the cannon's roar;—

The meteor of the ocean air

Shall sweep the clouds no more.

Her deck, once red with heroes' blood,

Where knelt the vanquished foe,

When winds were hurrying o'er the flood,

And waves were white below,

No more shall feel the victor's tread,

Or know the conquered knee;—

The harpies of the shore shall pluck

The eagle of the sea!.

Language Logic

GRAMMAR TERMS & DEFINITIONS
Review all flashcards according to tabs.

SENTENCE DIAGRAMMING
Read and discuss the following sections in *Sentence Sense* with your teacher.

III. Sentence Diagrammming: Verbals as Modifiers
   ◆ 17.3 Infinitive Phrases Used as Modifiers

III. Sentence Diagrammming: Verbals as Nouns
   ◆ 18.4 Infinitive Phrases Used as Nouns

In your Writer's Journal, copy these sentences. Analyze each sentence by marking the simple subject (who or what the sentence is about) with a single underline, and the verb or verb phrase with a double underline. Write DO over a direct object, LV over a linking verb, PA over a predicate adjective, and PN over a predicate nominative. Put parentheses around each prepositional phrase. Then diagram the sentence. Refer to *Sentence Sense* as needed.

1. To doubt the promise of a friend is a sin.

2. He has gone to his office to write a letter.

3. Music hath charms to soothe the savage breast.

4. He intended to call for you.

5. *Challenge (classroom exercise):* I believe him to be an honest

   man.

Eloquent Expression

SENTENCE STYLE – YOUR STYLE!

Craft copia for sentences from your own retelling using Sentence Style devices we have studied.

A. Work with your writing mentor to choose three sentences from your retelling that could be improved.

B. Copy the first in your Writer's Journal. Underline every important word in the sentence and jot down synonyms for each.

C. Use the list of Sentence Style devices below as you write several new versions of the sentence. New devices from this lesson are listed in bold type. You may use more than one device in each sentence.

D. Repeat the instructions above for the second and third sentences.

E. Choose your favorite paraphrase of each sentence. Replace the original sentences in your retelling before you edit again.

COPIA OF WORDS	COPIA OF CONSTRUCTION

COPIA OF WORDS
- ✓ Synonyms and Antonyms
- ✓ Opening Words
- ✓ Dialogue Tags
- ✓ Point of View
- ✓ Nouns – varied and descriptive
  - ◆ switch noun/pronouns
- ✓ Verbs – strong and fitting
- ✓ Modifiers
  - ◆ add adjective
  - ◆ add adverb

COPIA OF CONSTRUCTION
- ✓ Sentence class by use
- ✓ Dialogue
  - ◆ Tag line position
- ✓ Verb Tense
- ✓ Sentence Structure
  - ◆ switch possessive/'of' phrases
  - ◆ **change position of phrases**
- ✓ Sentence Combination
  - ◆ compound elements

Classical Composition

EDITOR'S PEN – ZOOM 10X: SENTENCES

Now it is time to zoom in even closer as you check the sentences in your retelling. Work with your writing mentor.

Editor's Pen – Zoom 10x: Sentences
- ✓ Complete thought expressed
- ✓ Subject and predicate agree in number
- ✓ Correct capitalization and punctuation
  - ◆ Commas correctly used for words in a series
  - ◆ No comma splices or run-on sentences!

A. Read aloud your your most recently edited version. Use the Editor's Pen checklist to identify changes you need to make. Mark all changes on your print copy.

B. Transfer all additions and corrections from your print copy to the computer file. Print this version and file it in your binder along with your other versions.

Commonplace

POETRY

Session two of three commonplace sessions for this lesson. Literary selection: "Old Ironsides."

Commonplace Book

 Set your timer. Begin where you stopped in the last session. When you finish, check your work carefully against the original for accuracy.

Lesson 20.4

Prose & Poetry

SCANSION

 Scan these stanzas, following the three steps you have learned.

Step 1 Mark each syllable as either stressed (/) or unstressed (∪). Say the line aloud several times to "get" the meter. Next, say the line aloud emphasizing the stresses as you mark the stresses only. Then go back and mark the unstressed syllables, saying the line aloud once more to check your work. Pronounce *meteor* and *every* with two syllables. There is one extra unstressed syllabe in the first stanza, second line.

Step 2 Insert dividers (|) to mark off the feet.

Step 3 Name the poem's predominant meter:

Oh, better that her shattered hulk

Should sink beneath the wave;

Her thunders shook the mighty deep,

And there should be her grave;

Nail to the mast her holy flag,

Set every threadbare sail,

And give her to the god of storms,

The lightning and the gale!

Language Logic

GRAMMAR TERMS & DEFINITIONS

Review all flashcards according to tabs.

SENTENCE DIAGRAMMING

In your Writer's Journal, copy these sentences. Analyze each sentence by marking the simple subject (who or what the sentence is about) with a single underline, and the verb or verb phrase with a double underline. Write DO over a direct object, LV over a linking verb, PA over a predicate adjective, and PN over a predicate nominative. Put parentheses around each prepositional phrase. Then diagram the sentence. Refer to *Sentence Sense* as needed.

Writer's Journal

1. They were not prepared to fight so powerful a force.

2. At last, like a great fledgling, Daedalus learned to fly.

3. Then the three hurried over to the other end of the bridge, and stood ready to keep off the enemy.

4. Never again did he attempt to fly.

5. And many an eye has danced to see

   That banner in the sky.

Eloquent Expression

PARAGRAPH STYLE – PARAPHRASE WITH COPIA

For this exercise, choose from all of the copia devices you have learned so far. See the copia chart in Lesson 20.3. New devices are in bold type.

In your Writer's Journal, paraphrase this paragraph. Change each sentence opener, and change at least one sentence class by use. Use as many synonym substitutions as possible. Use as many of the other copia devices as you are able. Make notes on the paragraph below before you begin.

"O Father Neptune," she said, "let Albion come to my island. It

is a beautiful little island. It lies like a gem in the bluest of waters.

There the trees and the grass are green, the cliffs are white and the

sands are golden. There the sun shines and the birds sing. It is a land of

beauty. Mountains and valleys, broad lakes and swift-flowing rivers,

all are there. Let Albion come to my island."

Classical Composition

EDITOR'S PEN – FINE FOCUS: WORDS

The final checks dwell on the details of your word usage. Continue to compile your personal editing checklist to use in editing all of your work across the curriculum.

Editor's Pen – Fine Focus: Words
✓ Word choices varied; word meanings clear
- ◆ Verbs: *strong, fitting; appropriate adverbs if needed*
- ◆ Nouns: *clear, descriptive; appropriate adjectives if needed*
- ◆ Dialogue: *dialogue tags varied if appropriate*

✓ Correct spelling
✓ Final read-through

A. Read aloud your most recent version. Identify changes you need to make with the Editor's Pen checklist. Mark these on your print copy.

B. Transfer all additions and corrections from your print copy to the computer file. Print this final version and file it in your binder along with your other versions.

Commonplace

POETRY

Commonplace Book

Session three of three commonplace sessions for this lesson. Literary selection: "Old Ironsides."

 Set your timer and begin copying. When you finish, check your work carefully against the original for accuracy.

Lesson 20.5

Prose & Poetry

POETRY APPRECIATION

 Read and enjoy a few poems in your poetry anthology. Identify rhyme schemes and stanza forms of one or two. Look for figures of speech and figures of description in the poems you read, and make note of any you find for future Commonplace Book entries. Read one or two poems aloud with expression and proper pauses. Pause at punctuation, but not necessarily at the ends of lines. Finally, choose a rhyming poem with iambic, trochaic, dactylic, or anapestic meter to observe.

Writer's Journal

- In your Writer's Journal, write the title of the poem and the author. Make note of its meter, rhyme scheme, and stanza form.

- Write the rhyming words from the poem in two lists: one list for those spelled the same, and one list for those spelled differently.

- Choose one of the rhyming words from the spelled differently list, and try to come up with several additional rhymes. Look especially for varied spellings.

Language Logic

GRAMMAR TERMS & DEFINITIONS

◆ Ask your teacher to quiz you with the grammar flashcards. Alternately, use the test feature in the Cottage Press *Bards & Poets I* Quizlet Classroom for an online or printed quiz for Lesson 20.

DICTATION: POETRY

◆ Work in your Writer's Journal. Write as your teacher dictates a passage to you from your Commonplace Book. When you are done, check your work carefully, word by word, against the original. Check for accurate spelling, capitalization, and punctuation.

Classical Composition

POETRY

◆ In your Writer's Journal, write two to four rhyming lines that summarize the action of "Stories of Albion and Brutus." If you wish, include a poetic **moral** at the end. Consider including them at the end of your retelling as a brief summary of the story. You may find it easiest to imitate the rhyme and meter of a few lines of the poetic selection for this lesson or a previous lesson.

NARRATIVE RETELLING – FINAL DRAFT

◆ Read over the final version of your retelling one last time and make any needed changes. Save it on your computer; print and file with all the other drafts in your writing binder.

Commonplace

FROM YOUR READING

Find selections in a book or poem to add to your Commonplace Book. Include the name of the book or poem, properly formatted. Label the entry with the grammar or poetry feature, the figure of speech, or as a favorite passage. Aim for a minimum of three entries, with at least one from each category.

Commonplace Book

Grammar Features (choose any)

- A sentence that has an interesting or descriptive noun, a strong and fitting verb, a well-chosen adjective, and/or a vivid adverb
- A sentence with one or more prepositional phrases or indirect objects
- A sentence that has a possessive noun or pronoun and/or an appositive
- A sentence that has a conjunction to join words, phrases, or clauses
- A sentence with a participle or participial phrase, and/or an infinitive or infinitive phrase
- An interesting dialogue tag (add to your Dialogue Tags list)
- An interrogative, exclamatory, or imperative sentence

Figures (choose any)

- Figures of Speech: simile, onomatopoeia, anastrophe, alliteration, metaphor, and/or personification
- Figures of Description: anemographia and/or hydrographia

Poetry Features (choose any)

- Rhyme (note name of the rhyme scheme)
- Iambic, anapestic, dactylic, or trochaic meter (note name of the meter)
- Stanza (note name of stanza form)

Favorite Passage: Add at least one passage of one to three sentences or several lines of poetry that captured your attention in your reading this week. It may be something you found beautiful, thought-provoking, funny, or interesting.

Lesson 21

☙

from THE COMING OF THE ROMANS
from OUR ISLAND STORY by Henrietta Marshall

Julius Cæsar had been fighting in Gaul, or France as we now call it. While there, he heard of the little island with white cliffs over the sea. He was told that the people were very big and brave and fierce. He also heard that it was a rich land full of tin, lead, and other useful metals, and that the shores were strewn with precious pearls. So he resolved to conquer this land and add it to the Roman Empire.

Cæsar gathered together about eighty ships, twelve thousand men, and a great many horses. These he thought would be enough with which to conquer the wild men of Britain. One fine day he set sail from France and soon came in sight of the island. The Britons in some way or other had heard of his coming and had gathered to meet him. As he drew near, Cæsar saw with surprise that the whole shore was covered with men ready for battle. He also saw that the place which he had chosen for landing was not good, for there were high, steep cliffs upon which the Britons could stand and shower darts upon his soldiers. So he turned his ships and sailed along the coast until he came to a place where the shore was flat.

The Roman ships were called galleys. They had sails, but were also moved by oars. The rowers sat in long lines down each side of the galley. Sometimes there were two or three tiers of them sitting one above the other. These rowers were generally slaves and worked in chains. They were often soldiers who had been taken prisoner in war, or wicked men who were punished for their misdeeds by being made to row in these galleys.

It was a dreadful life. The work was very hard, and in a storm if the vessel was wrecked, as often happened, the poor galley slaves were almost sure to be drowned, because their heavy chains prevented them from swimming.

As the Roman galleys sailed along the coast, the British warriors with their horses and war chariots followed on land.

The war chariots of the British were very terrible. They were like light carts and held several men; one to drive the horses and the others to fight. On either side, from the centre of the wheels, swords stuck out. As the wheels went round these swords cut down, killed, or wounded every one who came within reach. The Britons trained their horses so well, that they would rush madly into battle or stand stock still in a moment. It was a fearful sight to see these war chariots charge an enemy.

After sailing along the coast a little way, Cæsar found a good place at which to land, and turned his vessels inshore. But the great galleys required so much water in which to sail that they could not come quite close to land.

Seeing this, Cæsar told his soldiers to jump into the water. But the soldiers hesitated, for the Britons had rushed into the water to meet them and the Romans did not like the idea of fighting in the sea.

Although the Romans were very good soldiers, they were not such good sailors as might have been expected. They did not love the water as the Britons did.

These fierce "barbarians," as the Romans called the Britons, urging their horses into the waves, greeted the enemy with loud shouts. Every inch of the shore was known to them. They knew exactly where it was shallow and where it was deep, so they galloped through the water without fear.

Suddenly a brave Roman, when he saw how the soldiers hesitated, seized a standard and leaped overboard crying, "Leap forth now, soldiers, if you will not betray your ensign to the enemy, for I surely will bear myself as is my duty."

The Romans did not have flags such as we have in our army. Their standard was an eagle which was carried upon a pole. The eagle was of gold, or gilded to look like gold. Wherever the eagle led, there the soldiers followed, for it was the emblem of their honour, and they fought for and guarded it as their most precious possession.

So now, when the Roman soldiers saw their standard in the midst of the enemy, they followed with all haste. Their fear was great lest it should be taken. It was counted as a terrible disgrace to the Romans if they returned from battle without their standard. Death was better than disgrace, so they leaped into the water to meet the fierce Britons.

A fearful fight followed. The Romans could not keep their proper order, neither could they find firm footing. Weighed down with their heavy armour, they sank in the sand or slipped upon the rocks. All the while the Britons showered darts upon them and struck at them fiercely with their battle-axes and swords.

The Britons were very brave, but they had not learned the best ways of fighting as the Romans had. So after a terrible struggle the Romans reached the land. On shore they formed in close ranks and charged the Britons.

The Britons in their turn charged the Romans with their war chariots. The horses tore wildly along, neighing and champing their bits, and trampling underfoot those who were not cut down with the swords on the wheels. As they galloped, the fighting men in the cars threw darts and arrows everywhere among the enemy. When they were in the thickest of the fray the horses would suddenly stand still. Then the soldiers, springing out of the chariot, would fight fiercely for a few minutes with their battle-axes, killing every one within reach. Again they would leap into the cart, the horses would start forward and once more gallop wildly through the ranks of the enemy, leaving a track of dead behind them wherever they passed. But in spite of all their wild bravery the Britons were beaten at last and fled before the Romans.

Thus Cæsar first landed upon the shores of Britain. But so many of his soldiers were killed and wounded that he was glad to make peace with these brave islanders.

He sailed away again in such of his ships as had not been destroyed. For fierce storms had arisen a few days after his landing and wrecked many of his vessels.

Cæsar did not gain much glory from this fight. Indeed, when he went away, it seemed rather as if he were fleeing from a foe than leaving a conquered land.

CR

Lesson 21.1

Prose & Poetry

A LOOK AT LITERARY ELEMENTS IN THE NARRATIVE

1 **Read**
  ◆ Listen carefully as your teacher reads the selection aloud. **Delight** in the story.

2 **Inquire**
  ◆ Does the **title** give any hint as to the content or message of the story? If this story was published by the author in a larger book or an anthology, does that title give any hint?
  ◆ Discuss the meaning of these words in the context of the story:
  fierce, steep, galleys, tiers, misdeeds, prevented, hesitated, barbarians, standard, and any unfamiliar words.

3 **Observe the Content**
  ◆ **Setting** When and where does this story take place?
  ◆ **Characters** Who is (are) the main character(s) in this story?
  ◆ **Conflict** What is the main problem or crisis for the character(s)?
  ◆ **Resolution** Is the problem solved? If so, how? If not, why not?
  ◆ **Point of View** Who is telling the story? Is it first-person or third-person?
  ◆ **Figures** Can you identify any examples of simile, onomatopoeia, anemographia, anastrophe, alliteration, hydrographia, metaphor, or personification in this narrative?

4 Investigate the Context

Henrietta Marshall continues the history of Britain which we studied in Lesson 19. This story comes to us from the primary source of Caesar's own account in *The Gallic Wars* and from Roman historian Valerius Maximus's *Memorable Words and Deeds*. British historians Bede, Nennius, and Geoffrey of Monmouth, writing in the eighth, ninth, and twelfth centuries, respectively.

5 Connect the Thoughts

Commonplace Book

- ◆ Does this story remind you of other stories with similar plots, messages, or characters?
- ◆ Does this story remind you of any fables?
- ◆ Does this story remind you of any proverbs or other well-known quotations? If so, enter these in your Commonplace Book.

6 Profit and Delight

- ◆ **Delight** What are the sources of delight in this story?
- ◆ **Wisdom** What wisdom does this story furnish?
- ◆ **Read** the narrative aloud to your teacher with expression and with proper pauses.
- ◆ **Record** in your Book of Centuries: Julius Caesar, Julius Caesar's First Visit to Britain.

PLOT OBSERVATION: IDENTIFYING ACTIONS

Observe the plot of "The Coming of the Romans." Work in pencil on the original narrative at the beginning of this lesson, marking and making notes in the margin as instructed below.

A. Quickly read through the narrative once more. Number the paragraphs, and then mark the story as you have learned to do. Divide the narrative into actions.

B. Mark an x beside the sections that do not detail an action, and note what these are: **Prologue, Epilogue, Explanation, Description, Summary, Author Comments**.

C. Mark the major actions. Then, mark in the left margin if the action is made up of **Dialogue** or **Thoughts**. Consider Theon's Six. Remember that action can change even in the middle of a paragraph. Feel free to change your mind often as you work through the entire narrative—this is why you must use a pencil! Keep in mind that there is not just one right way to divide narratives into actions. Just make sure you can explain why you divide them as you do, using Theon's Six.

D. Review the narrative. Make notes in the margin indicating if any of the rest of Theon's Six changed with each action. You should definitely have notes about Person. Ask the questions for the other four, but do not worry too much if you can only add notes for two or three others.

E. Discuss your work with your teacher.

Language Logic

GRAMMAR FLASHCARDS

GRAMMAR TERMS & DEFINITIONS
Review all flashcards according to tabs.

GRAMMAR PRACTICE AND REVIEW

In your Writer's Journal, copy these sentences. Analyze each sentence by marking the simple subject (who or what the sentence is about) with a single underline, and the verb or verb phrase with a double underline. Write DO over the direct object, or LV over the linking verb; write PA over a predicate adjective and PN over a predicate nominative. Put parentheses around each prepositional phrase. Then diagram the sentence. Refer to *Sentence Sense* as needed.

1. So Julius Caesar resolved to conquer this land and to add it to the Roman Empire.

2. The Britons had heard of his coming and had gathered to meet him.

3. The Britons were very brave, but they had not learned the best ways of fighting.

4. The eagle was gilded to look like gold.

Writer's Journal

Eloquent Expression

COPIA OF WORDS: VOCABULARY STUDY

Writer's Journal

❦ Conduct a vocabulary study for "The Coming of the Romans."

   A. Choose at least two unfamiliar words to study. If you need suggestions, see the list under **Inquire** in Literary Elements above. Work in your Writer's Journal.

   B. Complete Vocabulary Study steps A-G for each word (see Appendix).

Commonplace

NARRATIVE

Commonplace Book

Session one of three commonplace sessions for this lesson. Literary selection: "The Coming of the Romans."

❦ Set your timer and begin copying. When you finish, check your work carefully, word by word, against the original.

Lesson 21.2

Prose & Poetry

PLOT OBSERVATION: OUTLINE WITH CAPTIONS

Writer's Journal

❦ In your Writer's Journal, create an outline to capture your observations with parallel captions.

   A. Jot down a quick caption for each major action, as well as any of the following: Prologue, Epilogue, Explanation, Description, Summary, Author Comments.

   B. Review your captions, and choose a parallel format.

   C. Revise all captions to conform to the format you have chosen.

Language Logic

GRAMMAR TERMS & DEFINITIONS

Review all flashcards according to tabs.

SENTENCE DIAGRAMMING

Read and discuss the following section in *Sentence Sense* with your teacher.

III. Sentence Diagrammming: Independent Elements
- ◆ 24.3 Expletives

In your Writer's Journal, copy these sentences. Analyze each sentence by marking the simple subject (who or what the sentence is about) with a single underline, and the verb or verb phrase with a double underline. Write DO over a direct object, LV over a linking verb, PA over a predicate adjective, and PN over a predicate nominative. Put parentheses around each prepositional phrase. Then diagram the sentence. Refer to *Sentence Sense* as needed.

1. It was gloomy to be inside that house.

2. How pleasant it is to see the sun.

3. There is a balm in Gilead.

4. 'Tis not in mortals to command success.

5. To everything there is a season. – Eccleiastes 3:1

Writer's Journal

Classical Composition

PLOT OBSERVATION: ORAL NARRATION

Without reading "The Coming of the Romans" again, retell the **plot** orally to your teacher. Refer to your plot observation of the narrative with Theon's Six if needed.

Commonplace

NARRATIVE

Session two of three commonplace sessions for this lesson. Literary selection: "The Coming of the Romans."

Commonplace Book

🏵 Set your timer and begin copying. When you finish, check your work carefully, word by word, against the original. Check spelling, capitalization, and punctuation for accuracy.

Lesson 21.3

Language Logic

GRAMMAR FLASHCARDS

GRAMMAR TERMS & DEFINITIONS
🏵 Review all flashcards according to tabs.

SENTENCE DIAGRAMMING

🏵 In your Writer's Journal, copy these sentences. Analyze each sentence by marking the simple subject (who or what the sentence is about) with a single underline, and the verb or verb phrase with a double underline. Write DO over a direct object, LV over a linking verb, PA over a predicate adjective, and PN over a predicate nominative. Put parentheses around each prepositional phrase. Then diagram the sentence. Refer to *Sentence Sense* as needed.

1. There were high, steep cliffs.

2. Suddenly there was heard a violent knocking at the door, and the old King, the Prince's father, went out to open it.

3. It was a wonderful sight to see the mermaids and mermen swimming along.

4. It seems so easy to be strong.

Writer's Journal

5. Challenge (classroom): It seems so easy to be strong,

So simple to be true.

Eloquent Expression

SENTENCE STYLE – COPIA OF WORDS: VERB/VERBAL SWITCH

We have already practiced adding appropriate adjectives as modifiers. But remember that nouns and pronouns may also be used as adjective elements.

If your sentence contains a participle or participle phrase, you can often exchange it for the main verb:

> <u>Receiving</u> your letter, Erasmus <u>was pleased</u>.

> <u>Pleased</u>, Erasmus <u>received</u> your letter.

SENTENCE STYLE – COPIA OF WORDS: GERUND/INFINITIVE SWITCH

If your sentence contains an infinitive used as a noun, you can sometimes exchange it for a gerund, and vice versa:

> <u>The receiving of your letter</u> brought me great joy.

> <u>To receive your letter</u> brought me great joy.

Note that there are some sentences that will not work for this, such as *These would be enough with which <u>to conquer</u> the wild men of Britain*. Also, while this may not yield the best sentences in the world, the practice is beneficial, and may occasionally turn up a gem in your own writing.

Complete these exercises in your Writer's Journal.

Writer's Journal

❦ Paraphrase these sentences, exchanging the participle and the main verb in each.

1. The Britons, <u>urging their horses into the waves</u>, greeted the enemy with loud shouts.

2. The horses tore wildly along, <u>neighing and champing their bits</u>.

❦ Paraphrase these sentences, changing the underlined infinitive to a gerund, and the underlined gerund to an infinitive.

3. It was fearful <u>to see</u> these war chariots charge an enemy.

4. The Romans did not like <u>fighting</u> in the sea.

Classical Composition

NARRATIVE RETELLING – FIRST DRAFT

You will have two sessions to work on this retelling. Begin here, and plan to finish in Lesson 21.4. As you write your retelling, do your best to use proper grammar and spelling, but keep in mind that you will have opportunity to edit before you finalize it.

Writer's Journal

◉ Retell "The Coming of the Romans" in writing, keeping the same characters, setting, and sequence of action. Choose either first or third person point of view, but be consistent throughout. This means you need to make sure that the pronouns are consistent, and pay close attention attention to subject/verb agreement. Refer to your plot observation of the narrative with Theon's Six, but do not review the original narrative before you write. Include:

- ◆ a heading, properly formatted
- ◆ at least one instance of metaphor
- ◆ at least one instance of personification
- ◆ (optional figure of speech) simile, onomatopoeia, anastrophe, alliteration
- ◆ at least one figure of description: anemographia, hydrographia

Lesson 21.4

Language Logic

GRAMMAR FLASHCARDS

GRAMMAR TERMS & DEFINITIONS
◉ Review all flashcards according to tabs.

Classical Composition

Writer's Journal

NARRATIVE RETELLING – FINISH FIRST DRAFT

Finish the first draft of your narrative retelling. Review the instructions in Lesson 21.3 as needed.

Commonplace

NARRATIVE

Session three of three commonplace sessions for this lesson. Literary selection: "The Coming of the Romans."

Commonplace Book

Set your timer. Begin where you stopped in the last session. When you finish, check your work carefully against the original for accuracy.

Lesson 21.5

Prose & Poetry

POETRY APPRECIATION

Read and enjoy a few poems in your poetry anthology. Identify rhyme schemes and stanza forms of one or two. Look for poems with iambic, trochaic, dactylic, or anapestic meter. Look for figures of speech and figures of description in the poems you read, and make note of any you find for future Commonplace Book entries. Read one or two poems aloud with expression and proper pauses. Pause at punctuation, but not necessarily at the ends of lines. Finally, choose a rhyming poem with trochaic meter to observe.

Language Logic

GRAMMAR TERMS & DEFINITIONS

 Ask your teacher to quiz you with the grammar flashcards. Alternately, use the test feature in the Cottage Press *Bards & Poets I* Quizlet Classroom for an online or printed quiz for Lesson 21.

DICTATION: NARRATIVE PASSAGE

 Work in your Writer's Journal. Write as your teacher dictates a passage to you from your Commonplace Book. When you are done, check your work carefully, word by word, against the original. Check for accurate spelling, capitalization, and punctuation.

Writer's Journal

Classical Composition

NARRATIVE RETELLING: TYPE FINAL DRAFT

 Type your retelling on the computer with spell-check turned off, or ask your writing mentor to type it exactly as you wrote it. Save, print, and file this draft in your writing binder.

Commonplace

FROM YOUR READING

Find selections in a book or poem to add to your Commonplace Book. Include the name of the book or poem, properly formatted. Label the entry with the grammar or poetry feature, the figure of speech, or as a favorite passage. Aim for a minimum of three entries, with at least one from each category.

Commonplace Book

 Grammar Features (choose any)

- ◆ A sentence that has an interesting or descriptive noun, a strong and fitting verb, a well-chosen adjective, and/or a vivid adverb
- ◆ A sentence with one or more prepositional phrases or indirect objects
- ◆ A sentence that has a possessive noun or pronoun and/or an appositive
- ◆ A sentence that has a conjunction to join words, phrases, or clauses
- ◆ A sentence with a participle or participial phrase, and/or an infinitive or infinitive phrase
- ◆ An interesting dialogue tag (add to your Dialogue Tags list)
- ◆ An interrogative, exclamatory, or imperative sentence

Figures (choose any)

- ◆ Figures of Speech: simile, onomatopoeia, anastrophe, alliteration, metaphor, and/or personification
- ◆ Figures of Description: anemographia and/or hydrographia

Poetry Features (choose any)

- ◆ Rhyme (note name of the rhyme scheme)
- ◆ Iambic, anapestic, dactylic, or trochaic meter (note name of the meter)
- ◆ Stanza (note name of stanza form)

Favorite Passage: Add at least one passage of one to three sentences or several lines of poetry that captured your attention in your reading this week. It may be something you found beautiful, thought-provoking, funny, or interesting.

☙

PAUL REVERE'S RIDE

Listen, my children, and you shall hear
Of the midnight ride of Paul Revere,
On the eighteenth of April, in Seventy-five;
Hardly a man is now alive
Who remembers that famous day and year.

He said to his friend, "If the British march
By land or sea from the town to-night,
Hang a lantern aloft in the belfry arch
Of the North Church tower as a signal light,—
One, if by land, and two, if by sea;
And I on the opposite shore will be,
Ready to ride and spread the alarm
Through every Middlesex village and farm,
For the country-folk to be up and to arm."

Then he said, "Good night!" and with muffled oar
Silently rowed to the Charlestown shore,
Just as the moon rose over the bay,
Where swinging wide at her moorings lay
The Somerset, British man-of-war;
A phantom ship, with each mast and spar
Across the moon like a prison bar,
And a huge black hulk, that was magnified

By its own reflection in the tide.

Meanwhile, his friend, through alley and street,
Wanders and watches with eager ears,
Till in the silence around him he hears
The muster of men at the barrack door,
The sound of arms, and the tramp of feet,
And the measured tread of the grenadiers,
Marching down to their boats on the shore.

Then he climbed to the tower of the Old North Church,
Up the wooden stairs, with stealthy tread,
To the belfry-chamber overhead,
And startled the pigeons from their perch
On the sombre rafters, that round him made
Masses and moving shapes of shade,—
Up the trembling ladder, steep and tall,
To the highest window in the wall,
Where he paused to listen and look down
A moment on the roofs of the town,
And the moonlight flowing over all.

Beneath, in the churchyard, lay the dead,
In their night-encampment on the hill,
Wrapped in silence so deep and still
That he could hear, like a sentinel's tread,
The watchful night-wind, as it went
Creeping along from tent to tent,
And seeming to whisper, "All is well!"
A moment only he feels the spell
Of the place and the hour, and the secret dread

Of the lonely belfry and the dead;

For suddenly all his thoughts are bent

On a shadowy something far away,

Where the river widens to meet the bay,—

A line of black that bends and floats

On the rising tide, like a bridge of boats.

Meanwhile, impatient to mount and ride,

Booted and spurred, with a heavy stride

On the opposite shore walked Paul Revere.

Now he patted his horse's side,

Now gazed at the landscape far and near,

Then, impetuous, stamped the earth,

And turned and tightened his saddle-girth;

But mostly he watched with eager search

The belfry-tower of the Old North Church,

As it rose above the graves on the hill,

Lonely and spectral and sombre and still.

And lo! as he looks, on the belfry's height

A glimmer, and then a gleam of light!

He springs to the saddle, the bridle he turns,

But lingers and gazes, till full on his sight

A second lamp in the belfry burns!

A hurry of hoofs in a village street,

A shape in the moonlight, a bulk in the dark,

And beneath, from the pebbles, in passing, a spark

Struck out by a steed flying fearless and fleet;

That was all! And yet, through the gloom and the light,

The fate of a nation was riding that night;

And the spark struck out by that steed, in his flight,

Kindled the land into flame with its heat.

He has left the village and mounted the steep,

And beneath him, tranquil and broad and deep,

Is the Mystic, meeting the ocean tides;

And under the alders, that skirt its edge,

Now soft on the sand, now loud on the ledge,

Is heard the tramp of his steed as he rides.

It was twelve by the village clock

When he crossed the bridge into Medford town.

He heard the crowing of the cock,

And the barking of the farmer's dog,

And felt the damp of the river fog,

That rises after the sun goes down.

It was one by the village clock,

When he galloped into Lexington.

He saw the gilded weathercock

Swim in the moonlight as he passed,

And the meeting-house windows, blank and bare,

Gaze at him with a spectral glare,

As if they already stood aghast

At the bloody work they would look upon.

It was two by the village clock,

When he came to the bridge in Concord town.

He heard the bleating of the flock,

And the twitter of birds among the trees,

And felt the breath of the morning breeze

Blowing over the meadows brown.

And one was safe and asleep in his bed

Who at the bridge would be first to fall,

Who that day would be lying dead,

Pierced by a British musket-ball.

You know the rest. In the books you have read,
How the British Regulars fired and fled,—
How the farmers gave them ball for ball,
From behind each fence and farm-yard wall,
Chasing the red-coats down the lane,
Then crossing the fields to emerge again
Under the trees at the turn of the road,
And only pausing to fire and load.

So through the night rode Paul Revere;
And so through the night went his cry of alarm
To every Middlesex village and farm,—
A cry of defiance and not of fear,
A voice in the darkness, a knock at the door,
And a word that shall echo forevermore!
For, borne on the night-wind of the Past,
Through all our history, to the last,
In the hour of darkness and peril and need,
The people will waken and listen to hear
The hurrying hoof-beats of that steed,
And the midnight message of Paul Revere.

— HENRY WADSWORTH LONGFELLOW

℘

Lesson 22.1

Prose & Poetry

A LOOK AT LITERARY ELEMENTS IN THE POEM

1 Read

◆ Follow along and listen carefully as the poem is read aloud, OR read it aloud yourself. Read it at least two or three times. **Delight** in the meter, the rhyme, and the images.

2 Inquire

◆ Does the **title** give any hint as to the content or message of the poem?

◆ Are there any other unfamiliar persons, places, or things mentioned in the poem? Discuss these with your teacher.

◆ Discuss the meaning of these words in the context of the story: *belfry, phantom, hulk, magnified, barrack, grenadiers, sentinel, spectral, sombre, tranquil, gilded, defiance, borne.* and any unfamiliar words.

◆ Was there any part of the poem you did not understand? If so, discuss this with your teacher and classmates.

3 Observe the Content

◆ **Lyrical Elements**
- What does the poet describe?
- Does the poet make you see, hear, smell, taste, or touch anything?
- Does the poet compare something in the poem to some other thing?

◆ **Narrative Elements** Does this poem tell a story? If so, observe the
- **Setting** When and where does this story take place?
- **Characters** Who is (are) the main character(s) in this story?
- **Conflict** What is the main problem or crisis for the character(s)?
- **Resolution** Is the problem solved? If so, how? If not, why not?

◆ **Point of View** Who is speaking in the poem? Is it first-person or third-person?

◆ **Figures** Can you identify any examples of simile, onomatopoeia, anemographia, anastrophe, alliteration, hydrographia, metaphor, or personification in this poem?

4 Investigate the Context

Nineteenth century American poet Henry Wadsworth Longfellow (1807-1882) is beloved of young and old alike, and *Paul Revere's Ride* has been memorized and recited by generations of American school-children. The events which inspired it were practically in the poet's backyard:

Across the Charles River from Boston, and some twenty miles from Concord, lay the quiet old city of Cambridge, with its splendid, wide-spreading elms and all the rosy brick buildings of Harvard University. Here, in an old wooden house where Washington had stayed when he took command of the American army, lived a young Harvard professor, Henry Wadsworth Longfellow. He was scholarly and gentle, his home was simple and elegant, and he traveled now and then in Europe. Life for him was pleasant and peaceful as was life in Cambridge generally, where rooms were full of books, conversations were of bookish things, and

the sharpest sounds to be heard were the musical tinkling of bells as cows ambled home at twilight, the lullaby of the crickets, or the creaking of sleds in the snow . . . His house was full of children. Every evening at twilight he heard, in the room above him, the patter of little feet. Then he saw by the lamplight his children on the stairs. A rush and a raid from the doorway, they were climbing over his chair – Alice, laughing Allegra, and Edith with golden hair. — *My Book House: Halls of Fame,* Olive Beaupré Miller

As you will remember, Longfellow was one of the Fireside Poets of New England, along with Holmes and Whittier. He was also close friends with other literary lights of the day such as Ralph Waldo Emerson and Henry David Thoreau.

5 Connect the Thoughts

◆ Does this poem remind you of other poems, or of stories with similar plots, messages, or characters?

◆ Does this poem remind you of any proverbs or other well-known quotations? If so, enter these in your Commonplace Book.

Commonplace Book

6 Profit and Delight

◆ **Delight** What are the sources of delight in this poem?

◆ **Wisdom** What wisdom does this poem furnish?

◆ **Read** the poem aloud to your teacher with expression and with proper pauses.

◆ **Record** in your Book of Centuries: Henry Wadsworth Longfellow, Paul Revere, Battles of Lexington and Concord.

◆ **Memorize** this poem and **recite** it before an audience.

Language Logic

GRAMMAR TERMS & DEFINITIONS

Review all flashcards according to tabs.

GRAMMAR PRACTICE AND REVIEW

In your Writer's Journal, copy these sentences. Analyze each sentence by marking the simple subject (who or what the sentence is about) with a single underline, and the verb or verb phrase with a double underline. Write D.O. over the direct object, or L.V. over the linking verb; write PA over a predicate adjective and PN over a predicate nominative. Put parentheses around each prepositional phrase. Then diagram the sentence. Refer to *Sentence Sense* as needed.

1. *Challenge (classroom):*

   And I on the opposite shore will be,

   Ready to ride and spread the alarm

   Through every Middlesex village and farm,

   For the country-folk to be up and to arm.

2. Beneath, in the churchyard, lay the dead,

   In their night-encampment on the hill,

   Wrapped in silence so deep and still.

3. Booted and spurred, with a heavy stride

   On the opposite shore walked Paul Revere.

4. He heard the bleating of the flock,

   And the twitter of birds among the trees,

And felt the breath of the morning breeze

Blowing over the meadows brown.

Eloquent Expression

COPIA OF WORDS: VOCABULARY STUDY

Writer's
Journal

Conduct a vocabulary study for "Paul Revere's Ride."

A. Choose at least two unfamiliar words to study. If you need suggestions, see the list under **Inquire** in Literary Elements above. Work in your Writer's Journal.

B. Complete Vocabulary Study steps A-G for each word (see Appendix).

Classical Composition

EDITOR'S PEN – THE BIG PICTURE

Edit your retelling from Lesson 21:

Editor's Pen – The Big Picture
- ✓ All important plot elements included
- ✓ All characters represented correctly
- ✓ Sequence: *same as the original*
- ✓ Length: similar to the original
- ✓ Point of View: 3rd person or 1st person
- ✓ Figure of Speech: *metaphor, personification*; optional: *simile, onomatopoeia, anastrophe, alliteration*
- ✓ Figure of Description: *chronographia* (will be added in Lesson 22.2); optional: *anemographia, hydrographia*

A. Read aloud exactly what you have written—not what you THINK you have written! Mark any corrections on your first draft.

B. Next, work through the Big Picture checklist above with your writing mentor.

C. Transfer all additions and corrections from your print copy of the retelling to your file on the computer. Print and file this edited version in your binder along with your marked-up editing copy of the first draft.

Commonplace

Commonplace Book

POETRY

Session one of three commonplace sessions for this lesson. Literary selection: "Paul Revere's Ride."

☙ Set your timer and begin copying. When finished, check your work carefully against the original for accuracy.

Lesson 22.2

Prose & Poetry

RHYME SCHEME AND STANZA FORM

☙ Mark the end rhyme in the stanzas below.

Listen, my children, and you shall hear

Of the midnight ride of Paul Revere,

On the eighteenth of April, in Seventy-five;

Hardly a man is now alive

Who remembers that famous day and year.

He said to his friend, "If the British march

By land or sea from the town to-night,

Hang a lantern aloft in the belfry arch

Of the North Church tower as a signal light,—

One, if by land, and two, if by sea;

And I on the opposite shore will be,

Ready to ride and spread the alarm

Through every Middlesex village and farm,

For the country-folk to be up and to arm."

Then he said, "Good night!" and with muffled oar

Silently rowed to the Charlestown shore,

Just as the moon rose over the bay,

Where swinging wide at her moorings lay

The Somerset, British man-of-war;

A phantom ship, with each mast and spar

Across the moon like a prison bar,

And a huge black hulk, that was magnified

By its own reflection in the tide.

Meanwhile, his friend, through alley and street,

Wanders and watches with eager ears,

Till in the silence around him he hears

The muster of men at the barrack door,

The sound of arms, and the tramp of feet,

And the measured tread of the grenadiers,

Marching down to their boats on the shore.

Name the rhyme schemes in these stanzas. Look at the original selection and make note of the rest. Longfellow uses differing stanza forms. Go back to the original selection, and list the stanza forms in order. Remember that not only the words, but the form of the poem communicates the poet's message. What do you think Longfellow might be communicating with the irregular rhyme scheme and arrangement of stanzas?

Language Logic

PHRASES, CLAUSES, AND RELATIVE PRONOUNS

🏵 Read and discuss the following sections in *Sentence Sense* with your teacher.

II. Syntax – The Sentence

- ◆ 9.2 Elements of a Sentence *Just read the opening sentence to this section. We study sentence elements in a future book.*
- ◆ 9.6A Phrases
- ◆ 9.7A Clauses
- ◆ 9.7B Types of Clauses

🏵 Move the flashcards that you have mastered backwards in your file system. Leave any that you have not mastered behind the **Daily** tab. Add these flashcards to your box behind the Daily tab, and begin to memorize them:

- ◆ Phrase
- ◆ Clause
- ◆ Principal Clause
- ◆ Subordinate Clause

Eloquent Expression

FIGURE OF DESCRIPTION: CHRONOGRAPHIA

Chronos is the Greek word for *time*. **Chronographia**, then, is the vivid description of a particular time. This may be a historical time period, or it may be a recurring time period, such as a season or a particular time of day.

Recall that figures of speech are often used to produce figures of description. Look for **simile** and **personification,** and other figures in these examples of chronographia from literature:

> There was once a king of Scotland whose name was Robert Bruce. He had need to
> be both brave and wise, for the times in which he lived were wild and rude. — James
> Baldwin, *Fifty Famous Stories*

Old Mother West Wind came down from the Purple Hills in the shadowy coolness of the early morning, before even jolly, round, red Mr. Sun had thrown off his rosy coverlids for his daily climb up through the blue sky. — Thorton Burgess, *Mother West Wind's Children*

One autumn when the nuts were ripe, and the leaves on the hazel bushes were golden and green. — Beatrix Potter, *The Tale of Squirrel Nutkin*

Chill December brings the sleet
Blazing fire, and Christmas treat. — Sara Coleridge, "A Calendar"

"I believe the nicest and sweetest days are not those on which anything very splendid or wonderful or exciting happens but just those that bring simple little pleasures, following one another softly, like pearls slipping off a string." — Lucy Maude Montgomery, *Anne of Avonlea*

⚜ Study and practice the figure of chronographia with your teacher.

A. Discuss the examples of chronographia with your teacher.

B. Look in this week's poem for examples of chronorographia. Discuss this with your teacher. Look through other poems we have studied in *Bards & Poets I* for more examples of chronographia. Make note of some that you may wish to copy into your Commonplace Book.

C. In your Writer's Journal, write a sentence or two of your own chronographia, vividly describing the time of year in which this story is set (you will have to do a little research!) Or, choose a time of day that you imagine the landing to have occured.

D. Add your figure of chronographia to the narrative retelling by writing it in the appropriate place on your print copy of our current draft.

Classical Composition

EDITOR'S PEN – ZOOM 5X: PARAGRAPHS

⚜ Now that the Big Picture is set, begin to zoom in for a close look at the paragraph(s) in your retelling with your writing mentor.

Editor's Pen – Zoom 5x: Paragraphs

✓ Formatting: *proper indentation*
✓ Length: *neither too wordy nor too short*
✓ Sentence class by use: *effective use*

✓ Sentence openers: *varied*
✓ Dialogue: *effective use*
✓ Verb Tense: *consistent*
✓ Pronouns: *consistent with chosen point of view*

A. Read aloud your most recently edited version. Check each item in the Editor's Pen checklist to identify possible changes. Mark these on your print copy.

B. Transfer all additions and corrections from your print copy to the computer file. Print this version and file it in your binder along with your other versions.

Lesson 22.3

Prose & Poetry

SCANSION

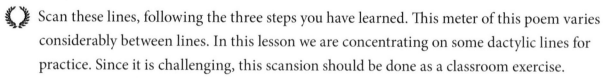 Scan these lines, following the three steps you have learned. This meter of this poem varies considerably between lines. In this lesson we are concentrating on some dactylic lines for practice. Since it is challenging, this scansion should be done as a classroom exercise.

Step 1 Mark each syllable as either stressed (/) or unstressed (∪). Say the line aloud several times to "get" the meter. Next, say the line aloud emphasizing the stresses as you mark the stresses only. Then go back and mark the unstressed syllables, saying the line aloud once more to check your work. Pronounce *every* with two syllables.

Step 2 Insert dividers (|) to mark off the feet. These lines are dactylic. Remember that you will only have one stress in each foot. Remember that dactylic lines often will insert some trochees, and the unstressed syllable is often dropped in the final foot of the line.

Listen, my children, and you shall hear

One, if by land, and two, if by sea;

Through every Middlesex village and farm,

Ready to ride and spread the alarm

Un der the trees at the turn of the road,

You know the rest. In the books you have read,

Language Logic

GRAMMAR TERMS & DEFINITIONS
🏵 Review all flashcards according to tabs.

RELATIVE PRONOUNS AND ADJECTIVE CLAUSES
🏵 Read and discuss the following sections in *Sentence Sense* with your teacher.

   I. Etymology: Pronouns
      ◆ 2.8 Relative Pronouns
  III. Sentence Diagrammming: Clauses
      ◆ 21.1 Adjective Clauses
  V. Exercises
      ◆ Oral Exercise: Point out the relative pronouns in the sentences from *Harvey's* 74, Sentences 1-5. Tell the antecedent of each, and its function in the clause it introduces.

🏵 In your Writer's Journal, copy these sentences. Analyze each sentence by marking the simple subject (who or what the sentence is about) with a single underline, and the verb or verb phrase with a double underline. Write DO over a direct object, LV over a linking verb, PA over a predicate adjective, and PN over a predicate nominative. Put parentheses around each prepositional phrase. Bracket the clauses (see Nota Bene in *Sentence Sense* 21.1, and example brackets in the first two sentences below). Then diagram the sentence. Refer to *Sentence Sense* as needed.

1. [Those [who sow] will reap.]

2. [This is the dog [that worried the cat] [that ate the malt] [that lay in the house] [that Jack built.]]

3. They that forsake the law praise the wicked.

4. The house which you admire so much belongs to the man whom we see yonder.

5. The Lord God planted a garden eastward in Eden; and there he put the man whom He had formed. – Genesis 2:8

Eloquent Expression

SENTENCE STYLE – YOUR STYLE!

Craft copia for sentences from your own retelling using Sentence Style devices we have studied.

A. Work with your writing mentor to choose three sentences from your retelling that could be improved.

B. Copy the first in your Writer's Journal. Underline every important word in the sentence and jot down synonyms for each.

C. Use the list of Sentence Style devices below as you write several new versions of the sentence. New devices from this lesson are listed in bold type. You may use more than one device in each sentence.

D. Repeat the instructions above for the second and third sentences.

E. Choose your favorite paraphrase of each sentence. Replace the original sentences in your retelling before you edit again.

COPIA OF WORDS

✓ Synonyms and Antonyms

✓ Opening Words

✓ Dialogue Tags - synonyms for *said*

✓ Point of View

✓ Nouns – varied and descriptive
   ◆ switch noun/pronouns
   ◆ **switch gerund/infinitve**

✓ Verbs – strong and fitting
   ◆ **switch verb/verbal**

✓ Modifiers
   ◆ add adjective
   ◆ add adverb

COPIA OF CONSTRUCTION

✓ Sentence class by use

✓ Dialogue
   ◆ Tag line position

✓ Verb Tense

✓ Sentence Structure
   ◆ switch possessive/*of* phrases
   ◆ change position of phrases

✓ Sentence Combination
   ◆ compound elements

Classical Composition

EDITOR'S PEN – ZOOM 10X: SENTENCES

Now it is time to zoom in even closer as you check the sentences in your retelling. Work with your writing mentor.

Editor's Pen – Zoom 10x: Sentences

✓ Complete thought expressed

✓ Subject and predicate agree in number

✓ Correct capitalization and punctuation
   ◆ Commas correctly used for words in a series
   ◆ No comma splices or run-on sentences!

A. Read aloud your your most recently edited version. Use the Editor's Pen checklist to identify changes you need to make. Mark all changes on your print copy.

B. Transfer all additions and corrections from your print copy to the computer file. Print this version and file it in your binder along with your other versions.

Commonplace

POETRY

Session two of three commonplace sessions for this lesson. Literary selection: "Paul Revere's Ride."

Commonplace Book

 Set your timer. Begin where you stopped in the last session. When you finish, check your work carefully against the original for accuracy.

Lesson 22.4

Prose & Poetry

SCANSION

 Scan these lines, following the three steps you have learned. In this lesson we are concentrating on some anapestic lines for practice. Note that all of these lines also contains some iambs. Since it is challenging, this scansion should be done as a classroom exercise.

Step 1 Mark each syllable as either stressed (/) or unstressed (∪). Say the line aloud several times to "get" the meter. Next, say the line aloud emphasizing the stresses as you mark the stresses only. Then go back and mark the unstressed syllables, saying the line aloud once more to check your work.

Step 2 Insert dividers (|) to mark off the feet. Remember that you will only have one stress in each foot.

On the eigh teenth of A pril, in Sev en ty-five;

Who re mem bers that fa mous day and year.

He said to his friend, "If the Bri tish march

By land or sea from the town to-night,

In the hour of dark ness and pe ril and need,

The peo ple will wa ken and lis ten to hear

The hur ry ing hoof-beats of that steed,

And the mid night mes sage of Paul Re vere.

Language Logic

GRAMMAR TERMS & DEFINITIONS
❀ Review all flashcards according to tabs.

SENTENCE DIAGRAMMING

❀ In your Writer's Journal, copy these sentences. Analyze each sentence by marking the simple subject (who or what the sentence is about) with a single underline, and the verb or verb phrase with a double underline. Write DO over a direct object, LV over a linking verb, PA over a predicate adjective, and PN over a predicate nominative. Put parentheses around each prepositional phrase. Bracket the clauses. Then diagram the sentence. Refer to *Sentence Sense* as needed.

1. Cincinnatus laid aside the title of dictator, which he had

    borne for only a few days.

2. Neptune had a very beautiful wife who was called Amphitrite.

3. The horses tore wildly along, neighing and champing their

    bits, and trampling underfoot those who were not cut down

    with the swords on the wheels.

Writer's Journal

Eloquent Expression

PARAGRAPH STYLE – PARAPHRASE WITH COPIA
For this exercise, choose from all of the copia devices you have learned so far. See the copia chart in Lesson 22.3. New devices are in bold type.

In your Writer's Journal, paraphrase this paragraph. Change each sentence opener, and change at least one sentence class by use. Use as many synonym substitutions as possible. Use as many of the other copia devices as you are able. Make notes on the paragraph below before you begin.

The war chariots of the British were very terrible. They were like light carts and held several men; one to drive the horses and the others to fight. On either side, from the centre of the wheels, swords stuck out. As the wheels went round these swords cut down, killed, or wounded every one who came within reach. The Britons trained their horses so well, that they would rush madly into battle or stand stock still in a moment. It was a fearful sight to see these war chariots charge an enemy.

Classical Composition

EDITOR'S PEN – FINE FOCUS: WORDS

The final checks dwell on the details of your word usage. Continue to compile your personal editing checklist to use in editing all of your work across the curriculum.

Editor's Pen – Fine Focus: Words

✓ Word choices varied; word meanings clear
  ◆ Verbs: *strong, fitting; appropriate adverbs if needed*
  ◆ Nouns: *clear, descriptive; appropriate adjectives if needed*
  ◆ Dialogue: *dialogue tags varied if appropriate*
✓ Correct spelling
✓ Final read-through

A. Read aloud your most recent version. Identify changes you need to make with the Editor's Pen checklist. Mark these on your print copy.

B. Transfer all additions and corrections from your print copy to the computer file. Print this final version and file it in your binder along with your other versions.

Commonplace

Commonplace Book

POETRY

Session three of three commonplace sessions for this lesson. Literary selection: "Paul Revere's Ride."

 Set your timer and begin copying. When you finish, check your work carefully against the original for accuracy.

Lesson 22.5

Prose & Poetry

POETRY APPRECIATION

 Read and enjoy a few poems in your poetry anthology. Identify rhyme schemes and stanza forms of one or two. Look for figures of speech and figures of description in the poems you read, and make note of any you find for future Commonplace Book entries. Read one or two poems aloud with expression and proper pauses. Pause at punctuation, but not necessarily at the ends of lines. Finally, choose a rhyming poem with iambic, trochaic, dactylic, or anapestic meter to observe.

Writer's Journal

- In your Writer's Journal, write the title of the poem and the author. Make note of its meter, rhyme scheme, and stanza form.
- Write the rhyming words from the poem in two lists: one list for those spelled the same, and one list for those spelled differently.

◆ Choose one of the rhyming words from the spelled differently list, and try to come up with several additional rhymes. Look especially for varied spellings.

Language Logic

GRAMMAR TERMS & DEFINITIONS

🏛 Ask your teacher to quiz you with the grammar flashcards. Alternately, use the test feature in the Cottage Press *Bards & Poets I* Quizlet Classroom for an online or printed quiz for Lesson 22.

DICTATION: POETRY

🏛 Work in your Writer's Journal. Write as your teacher dictates a passage to you from your Commonplace Book. When you are done, check your work carefully, word by word, against the original. Check for accurate spelling, capitalization, and punctuation.

Classical Composition

POETRY

🏛 In your Writer's Journal, write two to four rhyming lines that summarize the action of "Coming of the Romans." If you wish, include a poetic **moral** at the end. Consider including them at the end of your retelling as a brief summary of the story. You may find it easiest to imitate the rhyme and meter of a few lines of the poetic selection for this lesson or a previous lesson.

NARRATIVE RETELLING – FINAL DRAFT

🏛 Read over the final version of your retelling one last time and make any needed changes. Save it on your computer; print and file with all the other drafts in your writing binder.

Commonplace

FROM YOUR READING

Find selections in a book or poem to add to your Commonplace Book. Include the name of the book or poem, properly formatted. Label the entry with the grammar or poetry feature, the figure of speech, or as a favorite passage. Aim for a minimum of three entries, with at least one from each category.

Commonplace Book

🏵 Grammar Features (choose any)

- ◆ A sentence that has an interesting or descriptive noun, a strong and fitting verb, a well-chosen adjective, and/or a vivid adverb
- ◆ A sentence with one or more prepositional phrases or indirect objects
- ◆ A sentence that has a possessive noun or pronoun and/or an appositive
- ◆ A sentence that has a conjunction to join words, phrases, or clauses
- ◆ A sentence with a participle or participial phrase, and/or an infinitive or infinitive phrase
- ◆ An interesting dialogue tag (add to your Dialogue Tags list)
- ◆ An interrogative, exclamatory, or imperative sentence

🏵 Figures (choose any)

- ◆ Figures of Speech: simile, onomatopoeia, anastrophe, alliteration, metaphor, and/or personification
- ◆ Figures of Description: anemographia, hydrographia, and/or chronographia

🏵 Poetry Features (choose any)

- ◆ Rhyme (note name of the rhyme scheme)
- ◆ Iambic, anapestic, dactylic, or trochaic meter (note name of the meter)
- ◆ Stanza (note name of stanza form)

🏵 Favorite Passage: Add at least one passage of one to three sentences or several lines of poetry that captured your attention in your reading this week. It may be something you found beautiful, thought-provoking, funny, or interesting.

CR

THE CITY OF DESTRUCTION

from PILGRIM'S PROGRESS by John Bunyan

As I walked through the wilderness of this world, I lighted on a
certain place where was a den, and laid me down in that place to sleep;
and as I slept, I dreamed a dream. I dreamed, and behold, I saw a man
clothed with rags, standing in a certain place, with his face from his own
house, a book in his hand, and a great burden upon his back. I looked,
and saw him open the book, and read therein; and as he read, he wept
and trembled; and, not being able longer to contain, he brake out with a
lamentable cry, saying, "What shall I do?"

In this plight, therefore, he went home, and restrained himself as long
as he could, that his wife and children should not perceive his distress; but
he could not be silent long, because that his trouble increased. Wherefore
at length he brake his mind to his wife and children; and thus he began
to talk to them: "Oh my dear wife," said he, "and you my sweet children,
I, your dear friend, am in myself undone by reason of a burden that
lieth hard upon me; moreover, I am told to a certainty that this our city
will be burned with fire from heaven; in which fearful overthrow, both
myself, with thee, my wife, and you, my sweet babes, shall miserably
come to ruin, except some way of escape can be found whereby we may
be delivered." At this all his family were sore amazed; not for that they
believed that what he had said to them was true, but because they thought
that some frenzy or madness had got into his head; therefore, it drawing
towards night, and they hoping that sleep might settle his brain, with all
haste they got him to bed. But the night was as troublesome to him as
the day; wherefore, instead of sleeping, he spent it in sighs and tears. So
when the morning was come, they would know how he did. He told them,
Worse and worse: he also set to talking to them again; but they began to
be hardened. They also thought to drive away his madness by harsh and
surly treatment of him: sometimes they would ridicule, sometimes they

would chide, and sometimes they would quite neglect him. Wherefore he began to retire himself to his chamber, to pray for and pity them, and also to sorrow over his own misery; he would also walk solitary in the fields, sometimes reading, and sometimes praying; and thus for some days he spent his time.

Now, I saw, upon a time, when he was walking in the fields, that he was (as he was wont) reading in his book, and greatly distressed in his mind; and as he read, he burst out as he had done before, crying, "What shall I do to be saved?"

I saw also that he looked this way and that way, as if he would run; yet he stood still, because (as I perceived) he could not tell which way to go. I looked then, and saw a man named Evangelist coming to him, who asked, "Wherefore dost thou cry?"

He answered, "Sir, I read in the book in my hand, that I am condemned to die, and after that to come to judgment; and I find that I am not willing to do the first, nor able to do the second."

Then said Evangelist, "Why not willing to die, since this life is troubled with so many evils?" The man answered, "Because I fear that this burden that is upon my back will sink me lower than the grave, and I shall fall into Tophet. And, sir, if I be not fit to go to prison, I am not fit to go to judgment, and from thence to death; and the thoughts of these things make me cry."

Then said Evangelist, "If this be thy condition, why standest thou still?"

He answered, "Because I know not whither to go." Then he gave him a parchment roll, and there was written within, "Flee from the wrath to come."

The man, therefore, read it, and looking upon Evangelist very carefully, said, "Whither must I fly?" Then said Evangelist (pointing with his finger over a very wide field), "Do you see yonder wicket-gate?" The man said, "No." Then said the other, "Do you see yonder shining light?" He said, "I think I do." Then said Evangelist, "Keep that light in your eye, and go up directly thereto; so shalt thou see the gate; at which, when thou knockest, it shall be told thee what thou shalt do." So I saw in my dream that the man began to run. Now, he had not run far from his own door, when his wife and children perceiving it, began to cry after him to return; but the man put his fingers in his ears, and ran on, crying, "Life! life! eternal life!" So he looked not behind him, but fled towards the middle of the plain.

The neighbors also came out to see him run; and as he ran, some mocked, others threatened, and some cried after him to return; and among those that did so there were two that resolved to fetch him back by force. The name of the one was Obstinate, and the name of the other Pliable. Now, by this time the man was got a good distance from them; but, however, they were resolved to pursue him, which they did, and in a little time they overtook him. Then said the man, "Neighbors, wherefore are ye come?" They said, "To persuade you to go back with us." But he said, "That can by no means be: you dwell," said he, "in the City of Destruction, the place also where I was born: I see it to be so; and, dying there, sooner or later, you will sink lower than the grave, into a place that burns with fire and brimstone. Be content, good neighbors, and go along with me."

Obst. "What!" said Obstinate, "and leave our friends and comforts behind us?"

Chris. "Yes," said Christian (for that was his name), "because that all which you forsake is not worthy to be compared with a little of that I am seeking to enjoy; and if you would go along with me, and hold it, you shall fare as I myself; for there, where I go, is enough and to spare. Come away, and prove my words."

Obst. What are the things you seek, since you leave all the world to find them?

Chris. I seek a place that can never be destroyed, one that is pure, and that fadeth not away, and it is laid up in heaven, and safe there, to be given, at the time appointed, to them that seek it with all their heart. Read it so, if you will, in my book.

Obst. "Tush!" said Obstinate, "away with your book; will you go back with us or no?"

Chris. "No, not I," said the other, "because I have put my hand to the plough."

Obst. Come, then, neighbor Pliable, let us turn again, and go home without him: there is a company of these crazy-headed fools, that, when they take a fancy by the end, are wiser in their own eyes than seven men that can render a reason.

Pli. Then said Pliable, "Don't revile; if what the good Christian says is true, the things he looks after are better than ours; my heart inclines to go with my neighbor."

Obst. What! more fools still? Be ruled by me, and go back; who knows whither such a brain-sick fellow will lead you? Go back, go back, and be wise.

Chris. Nay, but do thou come with thy neighbor Pliable; there are such things to be had which I spoke of, and many more glories besides. If you believe not me, read here in this book; and for the truth of what is told therein, behold, all is made by the blood of Him that made it.

Pli. "Well, neighbor Obstinate," said Pliable, "I begin to come to a point; I intend to go along with this good man, and to cast in my lot with him. But, my good companion, do you know the way to this desired place?"

Chris. I am directed by a man, whose name is Evangelist, to speed me to a little gate that is before us, where we shall receive directions about the way.

Pli. Come, then, good neighbor, let us be going. Then they went both together.

   "And I will go back to my place," said Obstinate; "I will be no companion of such misled, fantastical fellows."

—edited by REV. JESSE LYMAN HURLBUT

CR

Lesson 23.1

Prose & Poetry

A LOOK AT LITERARY ELEMENTS IN THE NARRATIVE

1 **Read**
  ◆ Listen carefully as your teacher reads the selection aloud. **Delight** in the story.

2 **Inquire**
  ◆ Does the **title** give any hint as to the content or message of the story? If this story was published by the author in a larger book or an anthology, does that title give any hint?
  ◆ Discuss the meaning of these words in the context of the story: *den, plight, burden, ruin, wrath, obstinate, pliable,* and any unfamiliar words.

3 **Observe the Content**
  ◆ **Setting** When and where does this story take place?
  ◆ **Characters** Who is (are) the main character(s) in this story?
  ◆ **Conflict** What is the main problem or crisis for the character(s)?
  ◆ **Resolution** Is the problem solved? If so, how? If not, why not?
  ◆ **Point of View** Who is telling the story? Is it first-person or third-person?
  ◆ **Figures** Can you identify any examples of simile, onomatopoeia, anemographia, anastrophe, alliteration, hydrographia, metaphor, personification, or chronographia in this narrative?

4 **Investigate the Context**
John Bunyan was born the son of an impoverished tinker in 1628 near Bedford, England. His sparse education ended early when he went to work in his father's shop. He was not a pious young man; in fact,

Bunyan tells us that he swore and told lies and that he was the ringleader in all the wickedness of the village. But perhaps he was not so bad as he would have us believe, for he was always very severe in his judgments of himself. Perhaps he was not worse than many other boys who did not feel that they had sinned beyond all forgiveness. And in spite of his awful thoughts and terrifying dreams Bunyan still went on being a naughty boy; he still told lies and swore.

. . . while he was still very young, he married. Both he and his wife were, he says, "as poor as poor might be, not having so much household stuff as a dish or a spoon betwixt us both . . . He began now to go a great deal to church, and one of his chief pleasures was helping to ring the bells. To him the services were a joy. He loved the singing, the altar with its candles, the rich robes, the white surplices, and everything that made the service beautiful. Yet the terrible struggle between good and evil in his soul went on. He seemed to hear voices in the air, good voices and bad voices, voices that accused him, voices that tempted. He was a most miserable man. . . But at last the long struggle ended and his tortured mind found rest in the love of Christ.

. . . Bunyan's friends found out his great gift of speech. They begged him to preach, but he was so humble and modest that at first he refused. At length, however, he was over-persuaded. He began his career as a minister and soon became famous. People came from long distances to hear him, and he preached not only in Elstow and Bedford but in all the country round. He preached, not only in churches, but in barns and in fields, by the roadside or in the market-place, anywhere, in fact, where he could gather an audience. — Henrietta Marshall, *English Literature for Boys and Girls*

But Bunyan was not licensed to preach in England, so eventually he was arrested and jailed at Bedford.

. . . He would not promise to cease from preaching . . . Seeing there was no help for it, Bunyan set himself bravely to endure his imprisonment. And, in truth, this was not very severe. Strangely enough he was allowed to preach to his fellow- prisoners, he was even at one time allowed to go to church. But the great thing for us is that he wrote books. Already, before his imprisonment, he had written several books, and now he wrote that for which he is most famous, the *Pilgrim's Progress*.

It is a book so well known and so well loved that I think I need say little about it. In the form of a dream Bunyan tells, as you know, the story of Christian who set out on his long and difficult pilgrimage from the City of Destruction to the City of the Blest. He tells of all Christian's trials and adventures on the way, of how he encounters giants and lion, of how he fights with a great demon, and of how at length he arrives at his journey's end in safety. A great writer [Macaulay] has said, "There is no book in our literature on which we would so readily stake the fame of the old unpolluted English language, no book which shows so well how rich that language is in its own proper wealth, and how little it has been improved by all that it has borrowed."— Henrietta Marshall, *English Literature for Boys and Girls*

5 Connect the Thoughts

- ◆ Does this story remind you of other stories with similar plots, messages, or characters?
- ◆ Does this story remind you of any fables?
- ◆ Does this story remind you of any proverbs or other well-known quotations? If so, enter these in your Commonplace Book.

Commonplace Book

6 Profit and Delight

- ◆ **Delight** What are the sources of delight in this story?
- ◆ **Wisdom** What wisdom does this story furnish?
- ◆ **Read** the narrative aloud to your teacher with expression and with proper pauses.
- ◆ **Record** in your Book of Centuries: John Bunyan.

PLOT OBSERVATION: IDENTIFYING ACTIONS

Observe the plot of "The City of Destruction." Work in pencil on the original narrative at the beginning of this lesson, marking and making notes in the margin as instructed below.

A. Quickly read through the narrative once more. Number the paragraphs, and then mark the story as you have learned to do. Divide the narrative into actions.

B. Mark an x beside the sections that do not detail an action, and note what these are: **Prologue, Epilogue, Explanation, Description, Summary, Author Comments.**

C. Mark the major actions. Then, mark in the left margin if the action is made up of **Dialogue** or **Thoughts**. Consider Theon's Six. Remember that action can change even in the middle of a paragraph. Feel free to change your mind often as you work through the entire narrative—this is why you must use a pencil! Keep in mind that there is not just one right way to divide narratives into actions. Just make sure you can explain why you divide them as you do, using Theon's Six.

D. Review the narrative. Make notes in the margin indicating if any of the rest of Theon's Six changed with each action. You should definitely have notes about Person. Ask the questions for the other four, but do not worry too much if you can only add notes for two or three others.

E. Discuss your work with your teacher.

Language Logic

GRAMMAR
FLASHCARDS

GRAMMAR TERMS & DEFINITIONS
Review all flashcards according to tabs.

GRAMMAR PRACTICE AND REVIEW

In your Writer's Journal, copy these sentences. Analyze each sentence by marking the simple subject (who or what the sentence is about) with a single underline, and the verb or verb phrase with a double underline. Write DO over the direct object, or LV over the linking verb; write PA over a predicate adjective and PN over a predicate nominative. Put parentheses around each prepositional phrase. Mark the subjects and verbs. Bracket the clauses. Then diagram the sentence. Refer to *Sentence Sense* as needed.

1. I dreamed, and behold, I saw a man clothed with rags, standing in a certain place.

   Challenge (classroom): I dreamed, and behold, I saw a man clothed with rags, standing in a certain place, with his face from his own house, a book in his hand, and a great burden upon his back.

Writer's
Journal

2. There were two that resolved to fetch him back by force.

   Challenge (classroom): Among those that did so there were two that resolved to fetch him back by force.

3. I seek a place that can never be destroyed.

   Challenge (classroom): I seek a place that can never be destroyed, that is pure, and that fadeth not away.

Eloquent Expression

COPIA OF WORDS: VOCABULARY STUDY

Writer's Journal

⚜ Conduct a vocabulary study for "The City of Destruction."

A. Choose at least two unfamiliar words to study. If you need suggestions, see the list under **Inquire** in Literary Elements above. Work in your Writer's Journal.

B. Complete Vocabulary Study steps A-G for each word (see Appendix).

Commonplace

NARRATIVE

Commonplace Book

Session one of three commonplace sessions for this lesson. Literary selection: "The City of Destruction."

 Set your timer and begin copying. When you finish, check your work carefully, word by word, against the original.

Lesson 23.2

Prose & Poetry

PLOT OBSERVATION: OUTLINE WITH CAPTIONS

Writer's Journal

⚜ In your Writer's Journal, create an outline to capture your observations with parallel captions.

A. Jot down a quick caption for each major action, as well as any of the following: Prologue, Epilogue, Explanation, Description, Summary, Author Comments.

B. Review your captions, and choose a parallel format.

C. Revise all captions to conform to the format you have chosen.

Language Logic

COORDINATE AND SUBORDINATE CONJUNCTIONS

◉ Read and discuss the following sections in *Sentence Sense* with your teacher.

I. Etymology - The Conjunction

- ◆ 7.2 Classes of Conjunctions
- ◆ 7.3 - 7.4 Coordinate and Subordinate Conjunction Subclasses

  Our aim in having you read these lessons is to familiarize you with the most common coordinate and subordinate conjunctions. You do not need to learn the subclasses themselves at this point.

V. Exercises

- ◆ Oral Exercise: Point out the conjunctions in the sentences from *Harvey's* 146, Sentences 1, 3, 5, 7, and 9. Tell whether each is coordinate or subordinate.

◉ Move the flashcards that you have mastered backwards in your file system. Leave any that you have not mastered behind the **Daily** tab. Add this flashcard to your box behind the Daily tab, and begin to memorize it:

- ◆ Conjunction Classes

◉ Review all flashcards according to tabs.

Classical Composition

PLOT OBSERVATION: ORAL NARRATION

◉ Without reading "The City of Destruction" again, retell the **plot** orally to your teacher. Refer to your plot observation of the narrative with Theon's Six if needed.

Commonplace

NARRATIVE

Session two of three commonplace sessions for this lesson. Literary selection: "The City of Destruction."

Commonplace
Book

 Set your timer and begin copying. When you finish, check your work carefully, word by word, against the original. Check spelling, capitalization, and punctuation for accuracy.

Lesson 23.3

Language Logic

GRAMMAR
FLASHCARDS

GRAMMAR TERMS & DEFINITIONS
 Review all flashcards according to tabs.

SENTENCE DIAGRAMMING
 Read and discuss the following section in *Sentence Sense* with your teacher.

SENTENCE
SENSE

III. Sentence Diagrammming: Clauses
 ◆ 21.2 Adverb Clauses

 In your Writer's Journal, copy these sentences. Analyze each sentence by marking the simple subject (who or what the sentence is about) with a single underline, and the verb or verb phrase with a double underline. Write DO over the direct object, or LV over the linking verb; write PA over a predicate adjective and PN over a predicate nominative. Put parentheses around each prepositional phrase. Mark the subjects and verbs. Bracket the clauses (see Nota Bene in *Sentence Sense* 21.2, and example brackets in the first two sentences below). Then diagram the sentence. Refer to *Sentence Sense* as needed.

Hint: In Sentence #1, *for* is a subordinate conjunction, so diagram accordingly.

1. [There was no reply, [for [a slight fear was upon every man.]]]

2. [Men must be taught [as if you taught them not.]]

Writer's Journal

4. As I walked through the wilderness of this world, I lighted on certain place.

5. If you believe not me, read here in this book.

Eloquent Expression

SENTENCE STYLE – COPIA OF CONSTRUCTION: WORDS, PHRASES, AND CLAUSES

An adjective element is a word or group of words that modifies a noun or pronoun. Adjective elements can be constructed as words, phrases, or clauses. Study the underlined adjective elements in the sentences below. Notice how the same thought can be expressed with a word, a phrase, or a clause.

Erasmus, joyful, received your letter.

Filled with joy, Erasmus received your letter.

Erasmus, who was filled with joy, received your letter.

An adverb element is a word or group of words that modifies a verb (or verbal!), an adjective, or another adverb. Adverb elements may also be constructed as words, phrases, or clauses.

Your letter brought Erasmus joy immediately.

Your letter brought Erasmus joy upon its arrival.

Your letter brought Erasmus joy when it arrived.

So here is yet another tool for writing excellent sentences and adding interest to your narrative: experiment with switching words, phrases, and clauses for adjective and adverb elements. The lists below show the different types of words, phrases, and clauses that can be adjective and adverb elements.

ADJECTIVE ELEMENTS	ADVERB ELEMENTS
Words	**Words**
✓ Adjective	✓ Adverb
✓ Possessive Noun or Pronoun	
✓ Appositive	
✓ Participle	
Phrases	**Phrases**
✓ Prepositional Phrase	✓ Prepositional Phrase
✓ Appositive Phrase	✓ Infinitive Phrase
✓ Participial Phrase	
✓ Infinitive Phrase	
Clauses	**Clauses**
✓ Relative Clause	✓ Adverbial Clause

Complete these exercises in your Writer's Journal.

Paraphrase each sentence twice, first changing the underlined adjective or adverb element to a phrase and then changing it to a clause.

1. I saw a <u>ragged</u> man.

2. He brake out with a <u>lamentable</u> cry.

3. He could not be silent <u>long</u>.

3. You shall <u>miserably</u> come to ruin.

Classical Composition

NARRATIVE RETELLING – FIRST DRAFT

You will have two sessions to work on this retelling. Begin here, and plan to finish in Lesson 23.4. As you write your retelling, do your best to use proper grammar and spelling, but keep in mind that you will have opportunity to edit before you finalize it.

Retell "The City of Destruction" in writing, keeping the same characters, setting, and sequence of action. Choose either first or third person point of view, but be consistent throughout. This means you need to make sure that the pronouns are consistent, and pay close attention attention to subject/verb agreement. Refer to your plot observation of the narrative with Theon's Six, but do not review the original narrative before you write. Include:

- ◆ a heading, properly formatted
- ◆ at least two figures of speech: simile, onomatopoeia, anastrophe, alliteration, metaphor
- ◆ at least one figure of description: anemographia, hydrographia, choronographia

Lesson 23.4

Language Logic

GRAMMAR TERMS & DEFINITIONS

Review all flashcards according to tabs.

SENTENCE DIAGRAMMING

In your Writer's Journal, copy these sentences. Analyze each sentence by marking the simple subject (who or what the sentence is about) with a single underline, and the verb or verb phrase with a double underline. Write D.O. over the direct object, or L.V. over the linking verb; write PA over a predicate adjective and PN over a predicate nominative. Put parentheses around each prepositional phrase. Mark the subjects and verbs. Bracket the clauses. Then diagram the sentence. Refer to *Sentence Sense* as needed.

1. Joyfully hastening back to his farm, Cincinnatus took up his plowing where he had dropped it; and he went on living quietly and simply.

2. All day he played in it, swimming, diving, and laughing gleefully as the waves dashed over him.

Writer's Journal

3. For suddenly all his thoughts are bent

    On a shadowy something far away,

    Where the river widens to meet the bay.

4. Her deck, once red with heroes' blood,

    Where knelt the vanquished foe,

    When winds were hurrying o'er the flood,

    And waves were white below,

    No more shall feel the victor's tread.

Classical Composition

Writer's
Journal

NARRATIVE RETELLING – FINISH FIRST DRAFT

🏵 Finish the first draft of your narrative retelling. Review the instructions in Lesson 23.3 as needed.

Commonplace

Commonplace
Book

NARRATIVE

Session three of three commonplace sessions for this lesson. Literary selection: "The City of Destruction."

🏵 Set your timer. Begin where you stopped in the last session. When you finish, check your work carefully against the original for accuracy.

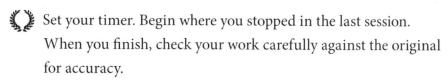

Lesson 23.5

Prose & Poetry

POETRY APPRECIATION

Read and enjoy a few poems in your poetry anthology. Identify rhyme schemes and stanza forms of one or two. Look for poems with iambic, trochaic, dactylic, or anapestic meter. Look for figures of speech and figures of description in the poems you read, and make note of any you find for future Commonplace Book entries. Look for figures of speech and figures of description in the poems you read, and make note of any you find for future Commonplace Book entries. Read one or two poems aloud with expression and proper pauses. Pause at punctuation, but not necessarily at the ends of lines. Finally, choose a rhyming poem with trochaic meter to observe.

Language Logic

GRAMMAR TERMS & DEFINITIONS

Ask your teacher to quiz you with the grammar flashcards. Alternately, use the test feature in the Cottage Press *Bards & Poets I* Quizlet Classroom for an online or printed quiz for Lesson 23.

DICTATION: NARRATIVE PASSAGE

Writer's Journal

Work in your Writer's Journal. Write as your teacher dictates a passage to you from your Commonplace Book. When you are done, check your work carefully, word by word, against the original. Check for accurate spelling, capitalization, and punctuation.

Classical Composition

NARRATIVE RETELLING: TYPE FINAL DRAFT

Type your retelling on the computer with spell-check turned off, or ask your writing mentor to type it exactly as you wrote it. Save, print, and file this draft in your writing binder.

Commonplace

FROM YOUR READING

Find selections in a book or poem to add to your Commonplace Book. Include the name of the book or poem, properly formatted. Label the entry with the grammar or poetry feature, the figure of speech, or as a favorite passage. Aim for a minimum of three entries, with at least one from each category.

Commonplace
Book

Grammar Features (choose any)

- A sentence that has an interesting or descriptive noun, a strong and fitting verb, a well-chosen adjective, and/or a vivid adverb
- A sentence with one or more prepositional phrases or indirect objects
- A sentence that has a possessive noun or pronoun and/or an appositive
- A sentence that has a conjunction to join words, phrases, or clauses
- A sentence with a participle or participial phrase, and/or an infinitive or infinitive phrase
- An interesting dialogue tag (add to your Dialogue Tags list)
- An interrogative, exclamatory, or imperative sentence

Figures (choose any)

- Figures of Speech: simile, onomatopoeia, anastrophe, alliteration, metaphor, and/or personification
- Figures of Description: anemographia, hydrographia, and/or chronographia

Poetry Features (choose any)

- Rhyme (note name of the rhyme scheme)
- Iambic, anapestic, dactylic, or trochaic meter (note name of the meter)
- Stanza (note name of stanza form)

Favorite Passage: Add at least one passage of one to three sentences or several lines of poetry that captured your attention in your reading this week. It may be something you found beautiful, thought-provoking, funny, or interesting.

Lesson 24

CR

THE NEW COLOSSUS

Not like the brazen giant of Greek fame,
With conquering limbs astride from land to land;
Here at our sea-washed, sunset gates shall stand
A mighty woman with a torch, whose flame
Is the imprisoned lightning, and her name
Mother of Exiles. From her beacon-hand
Glows world-wide welcome; her mild eyes command
The air-bridged harbor that twin cities frame.
"Keep, ancient lands, your storied pomp!" cries she
With silent lips. "Give me your tired, your poor,
Your huddled masses yearning to breathe free,
The wretched refuse of your teeming shore.
Send these, the homeless, tempest-tost to me,
I lift my lamp beside the golden door!"

— EMMA LAZARUS

CR

Lesson 24.1

Prose & Poetry

A LOOK AT LITERARY ELEMENTS IN THE POEM

1 Read
- ◆ Follow along and listen carefully as the poem is read aloud, OR read it aloud yourself. Read it at least two or three times. **Delight** in the meter, the rhyme, and the images.

2 Inquire
- ◆ Does the **title** give any hint as to the content or message of the poem? Here is a description of the "old" Colossus of Rhodes:

> This marvelous brazen statue, which was so fine that it was one of the seven wonders of the ancient world, represented the sun god, with his head surrounded by rays, and with his feet resting one on each side of the entrance of the port. We are told that the *Colossus of Rhodes*, as this statue was generally called, was so tall that ships under full sail easily passed under its spreading legs in and out of the harbor.
>
> It stood there for about sixty years, when it was overthrown by an earthquake. After lying in ruins for a long time, the brass was sold as old metal. It was carried off on the backs of camels, and we are told that nine hundred of these animals were required for the work.
>
> Thus vanished one of the much talked of wonders of the ancient world. The others were Diana's Temple at Ephesus, the Tomb of Mausolus (which was so fine that any handsome tomb is sometimes called a mausoleum), the Pharos or Lighthouse of Alexandria or Messina, the Walls and Hanging Gardens of Babylon, the Labyrinth of Crete, and the Pyramids of Egypt. To these is often added the Parthenon at Athens, which, as you have seen, was decorated by the carvings of Phidias. — Helene Guerber, *The Story of the Greeks*

- ◆ Are there any unfamiliar persons, places, or things mentioned in the poem? Discuss these with your teacher.
- ◆ Discuss the meaning of these words in the context of the story: *brazen, limbs, astride, exiles, welcome, storied, pomp, yearning, refuse, teeming,* and any unfamiliar words.

◆ Was there any part of the poem you did not understand? If so, discuss this with your
teacher and classmates.

3 Observe the Content

◆ **Lyrical Elements**

  ▪ What does the poet describe?

  ▪ Does the poet make you see, hear, smell, taste, or touch anything?

  ▪ Does the poet compare something in the poem to some other thing?

◆ **Narrative Elements** Does this poem tell a story? If so, observe the

  ▪ **Setting** When and where does this story take place?

  ▪ **Characters** Who is (are) the main character(s) in this story?

  ▪ **Conflict** What is the main problem or crisis for the character(s)?

  ▪ **Resolution** Is the problem solved? If so, how? If not, why not?

◆ **Point of View** Who is speaking in the poem? Is it first-person or third-person?

◆ **Figures** Can you identify any examples of simile, onomatopoeia, anemographia,
anastrophe, alliteration, hydrographia, metaphor, personification, or chronographia in
this poem?

4 Investigate the Context

Emma Lazarus (1849-1887), an American from New
York City, began writing poetry in her early teens;
her first volume of poems was published when she
was just 18. She became a successful author and
poet, a notable accomplishment for a woman of her
day, and all the more so because she was descended
from Jewish immigrants. Her appreciation for her
cultural heritage—inspired by reading a George
Eliot novel—led her to charity work on behalf of
Russian Jews who were being persecuted in the
pogroms. many of whom were making their way to
New York as refugees. She wrote "The New
Colossus" in 1883 at the request of a friend, and
donated it to be auctioned to raise money to

construct a pedestal on which to place the newly gifted and dedicated Statue of Liberty. That
statue had been a gift from the people of France as recognition of the contributions of the
United States to the cause of freedom and democracy. Eventually, the final lines of "The New
Colossus" were engraved on that pedestal, and have become a byword identifying the
promise of America to millions of immigrants.

5 **Connect the Thoughts**
- ◆ Does this poem remind you of other poems, or of stories with similar plots, messages, or characters?
- ◆ Does this poem remind you of any proverbs or other well-known quotations? If so, enter these in your Commonplace Book.

Commonplace Book

6 **Profit and Delight**
- ◆ **Delight** What are the sources of delight in this poem?
- ◆ **Wisdom** What wisdom does this poem furnish?
- ◆ **Read** the poem aloud to your teacher with expression and with proper pauses.
- ◆ **Record** in your Book of Centuries: Emma Lazarus, Statue of Liberty.
- ◆ **Memorize** this poem and **recite** it before an audience.

Language Logic

GRAMMAR FLASHCARDS

GRAMMAR TERMS & DEFINITIONS
❀ Review all flashcards according to tabs.

GRAMMAR PRACTICE AND REVIEW
❀ In your Writer's Journal, copy these sentences. Analyze each sentence by marking the simple subject (who or what the sentence is about) with a single underline, and the verb or verb phrase with a double underline. Write DO over the direct object, or LV over the linking verb; write PA over a predicate adjective and PN over a predicate nominative. Put parentheses around each prepositional phrase. Mark the subjects and verbs. Bracket the clauses. Then diagram the sentence. Refer to *Sentence Sense* as needed.

1. Here at our sea-washed, sunset gates shall stand

    A mighty woman with a torch, whose flame

    Is the imprisoned lightning.

Writer's Journal

2. From her beacon-hand

Glows world-wide welcome; her mild eyes command

The air-bridged harbor that twin cities frame.

Classical Composition

EDITOR'S PEN – THE BIG PICTURE

 Edit your retelling from Lesson 23:

Editor's Pen – The Big Picture

✓ All important plot elements included

✓ All characters represented correctly

✓ Sequence: *same as the original*

✓ Length: similar to the original

✓ Point of View: 3rd person or 1st person

✓ Figures of Speech – at least two of the following: *metaphor, personification, simile, onomatopoeia, anastrophe, alliteration*

✓ Figure of Description: *astrothesia* (will be added in Lesson 24.2); optional: *anemographia, hydrographia, chronographia*

A. Read aloud exactly what you have written—not what you THINK you have written! Mark any corrections on your first draft.

B. Next, work through the Big Picture checklist above with your writing mentor.

C. Transfer all additions and corrections from your print copy of the retelling to your file on the computer. Print and file this edited version in your binder along with your marked-up editing copy of the first draft.

Eloquent Expression

COPIA OF WORDS: VOCABULARY STUDY

Conduct a vocabulary study for "The New Colossus."

Writer's Journal

A. Choose at least two unfamiliar words to study. If you need suggestions, see the list under **Inquire** in Literary Elements above. Work in your Writer's Journal.

B. Complete Vocabulary Study steps A-G for each word (see Appendix).

Commonplace

Commonplace Book

POETRY

Session one of three commonplace sessions for this lesson. Literary selection: "The New Colossus."

Set your timer and begin copying. When finished, check your work carefully against the original for accuracy.

Lesson 24.2

Prose & Poetry

RHYME SCHEME AND STANZA FORM

Mark the end rhyme in the stanza below.

Not like the brazen giant of Greek fame,

With conquering limbs astride from land to land;

Here at our sea-washed, sunset gates shall stand

A mighty woman with a torch, whose flame

Is the imprisoned lightning, and her name

Mother of Exiles. From her beacon-hand

Glows world-wide welcome; her mild eyes command

The air-bridged harbor that twin cities frame.

"Keep, ancient lands, your storied pomp!" cries she

With silent lips. "Give me your tired, your poor,

Your huddled masses yearning to breathe free,

The wretched refuse of your teeming shore.

Send these, the homeless, tempest-tost to me,

I lift my lamp beside the golden door!"

◆ Name the predominant rhyme scheme and the stanza form of this poem.

Language Logic

GRAMMAR TERMS & DEFINITIONS
◆ Review all flashcards according to tabs.

SENTENCE DIAGRAMMING

◆ Read and discuss the following section in *Sentence Sense* with your teacher.

III. Sentence Diagrammming: Clauses
  ◆ 21.3 Noun Clauses

◆ In your Writer's Journal, copy these sentences. Analyze each sentence by marking the simple subject (who or what the sentence is about) with a single underline, and the verb or verb phrase with a double underline. Write DO over the direct object, or LV over the linking verb; write PA over a predicate adjective and PN over a predicate nominative. Put parentheses around each prepositional phrase. Mark the subjects and verbs. Bracket the clauses. (see Nota Bene in *Sentence Sense* 21.3, and example brackets in the first sentence below). Then diagram the sentence. Refer to *Sentence Sense* as needed.

Writer's
Journal

1. [They soon saw [that resistance would be useless.]]

   Challenge (classroom): [They soon saw [that resistance would
   be useless] and offered to sursrender.]

   Extra Challenge (classroom): [They soon saw [that resistance
   would be useless] and, without striking a single blow, offered
   to surrender.]

2. The Æquians, at dawn, found that the tables were turned.

   Challenge (classroom): The Æquians, at dawn, found that the tables were turned, and that
   they were now between two armies of angry Romans.

Eloquent Expression

FIGURE OF DESCRIPTION: ASTROTHESIA

Astro is the Greek word for *star*; **astrothesia** is the vivid description of the stars or the night sky.

Recall that figures of speech are often used to produce figures of description. Look for
personification and **alliteration** in these examples of astrothesia from literature:

> Now the bright morning-star, Day's harbinger, comes dancing from the East... — John
> Milton, "Song of a May Morning"

> It's lovely to live on a raft. We had the sky up there, all speckled with stars, and we used
> to lay on our backs and look up at them, and discuss about whether they was made or
> only just happened.   — Mark Twain, *The Adventures of Huckleberry Finn*

> Marilla, look at that big star over Mr. Harrison's maple grove, with all that holy hush
> of silvery sky about it. I gives me a feeling that is like a prayer. After all, when one can
> see stars and skies like that, little disappointments and accidents can't matter so much,
> can they? — L. M. Montgomery, *Anne of Avonlea*

Study and practice the figure of astrothesia with your teacher.

A. Discuss the examples of astrothesia with your teacher.

B. Look in "God of Our Fathers" (Lesson 12) for examples of astrothesia. Discuss this with your teacher. Look through other poems we have studied in *Bards & Poets I* for more examples of astrothesia. Make note of some that you may wish to copy into your Commonplace Book.

C. In your Writer's Journal, write a sentence or two of your own astrothesia, vividly describing the stars over the City of Destruction.

D. Add your figure of astrothesia to the narrative retelling by writing it in the appropriate place on your print copy of our current draft.

Classical Composition

EDITOR'S PEN – ZOOM 5X: PARAGRAPHS

Now that the Big Picture is set, begin to zoom in for a close look at the paragraph(s) in your retelling with your writing mentor.

Editor's Pen – Zoom 5x: Paragraphs

✓ Formatting: *proper indentation*
✓ Length: *neither too wordy nor too short*
✓ Sentence class by use: *effective use*
✓ Sentence openers: *varied*
✓ Dialogue: *effective use*
✓ Verb Tense: *consistent*
✓ Pronouns: *consistent with chosen point of view*

A. Read aloud your most recently edited version. Check each item in the Editor's Pen checklist to identify possible changes. Mark these on your print copy.

B. Transfer all additions and corrections from your print copy to the computer file. Print this version and file it in your binder along with your other versions.

Lesson 24.3

Prose & Poetry

SCANSION

 Scan these stanzas, following the three steps you have learned.

Step 1 Mark each syllable as either stressed (/) or unstressed (∪). Say the line aloud several times to "get" the meter. Next, say the line aloud emphasizing the stresses as you mark the stresses only. Then go back and mark the unstressed syllables, saying the line aloud once more to check your work. This poem is predominately iambic, but you will need to "force" several lines to fit by stressing words/syllables you would not usually stress. It is often a good idea to begin scanning in the middle of a poem, because the beginning and ending of stanzas are most likely to have metrical variations. In this case, do lines one, five, six, and nine last.

Step 2 Insert dividers (|) to mark off the feet. Remember that you will only have one stress in each foot. Pronounce *conquering* with two syllables.

Step 3 Name the poem's predominant meter:

Not like the brazen giant of Greek fame,

With conquering limbs astride from land to land;

Here at our sea-washed, sunset gates shall stand

A mighty woman with a torch, whose flame

Is the imprisoned lightning, and her name

Mother of Exiles. From her beacon-hand

Glows world-wide welcome; her mild eyes command

The air-bridged harbor that twin cities frame.

"Keep, ancient lands, your storied pomp!" cries she

With silent lips. "Give me your tired, your poor,

Your huddled masses yearning to breathe free,

The wretched refuse of your teeming shore.

Send these, the homeless, tempest-tost to me,

I lift my lamp beside the golden door!"

Language Logic

GRAMMAR TERMS & DEFINITIONS

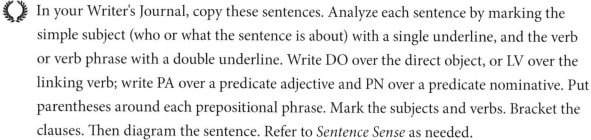 Review all flashcards according to tabs.

SENTENCE DIAGRAMMING

 In your Writer's Journal, copy these sentences. Analyze each sentence by marking the simple subject (who or what the sentence is about) with a single underline, and the verb or verb phrase with a double underline. Write DO over the direct object, or LV over the linking verb; write PA over a predicate adjective and PN over a predicate nominative. Put parentheses around each prepositional phrase. Mark the subjects and verbs. Bracket the clauses. Then diagram the sentence. Refer to *Sentence Sense* as needed.

Writer's Journal

1. But when the face of Sextus

   Was seen among the foes,

   A yell that rent the firmament

   From all the town arose.

2. Sir, I read in the book in my hand, that I am condemned to die.

   Challenge (classroom): Sir, I read in the book in my hand, that I am condemned to die, and after that to come to judgment.

Extra Challenge (classroom): Sir, I read in the book in my hand, that I am condemned to die, and after that to come to judgment; and I find that I am not willing to do the first, nor able to do the second.

Classical Composition

EDITOR'S PEN – ZOOM 10X: SENTENCES

Now it is time to zoom in even closer as you check the sentences in your retelling. Work with your writing mentor.

> ### Editor's Pen – Zoom 10x: Sentences
> ✓ Complete thought expressed
> ✓ Subject and predicate agree in number
> ✓ Correct capitalization and punctuation
>   ◆ Commas correctly used for words in a series
>   ◆ No comma splices or run-on sentences!

A. Read aloud your your most recently edited version. Use the Editor's Pen checklist to identify changes you need to make. Mark all changes on your print copy.

B. Transfer all additions and corrections from your print copy to the computer file. Print this version and file it in your binder along with your other versions.

Commonplace

POETRY

Session two of three commonplace sessions for this lesson. Literary selection: "The New Colossus."

Set your timer. Begin where you stopped in the last session. When you finish, check your work carefully against the original for accuracy.

Commonplace Book

Lesson 24.4

Language Logic

GRAMMAR TERMS & DEFINITIONS
🏅 Review all flashcards according to tabs.

Eloquent Expression

SENTENCE STYLE – YOUR STYLE!

🏅 Craft copia for sentences from your own retelling using Sentence Style devices we have studied.

A. Work with your writing mentor to choose three sentences from your retelling that could be improved.

B. Copy the first in your Writer's Journal. Underline every important word in the sentence and jot down synonyms for each.

C. Use the list of Sentence Style devices below as you write several new versions of the sentence. New devices from this lesson are listed in bold type. You may use more than one device in each sentence.

D. Repeat the instructions above for the second and third sentences.

E. Choose your favorite paraphrase of each sentence. Replace the original sentences in your retelling before you edit again.

COPIA OF WORDS	COPIA OF CONSTRUCTION
✓ Synonyms and Antonyms	✓ Sentence class by use
✓ Opening Words	✓ Dialogue
✓ Dialogue Tags - synonyms for *said*	◆ Tag line position
✓ Point of View	✓ Verb Tense

✓ Nouns – varied and descriptive
   ◆ switch noun/pronouns
   ◆ **switch gerund/infinitve**
✓ Verbs – strong and fitting
   ◆ **switch verb/verbal**
✓ Modifiers
   ◆ add adjective
   ◆ add adverb

✓ Sentence Structure
   ◆ switch possessive/*of* phrases
   ◆ change position of phrases
   ◆ **switch words/phrases/clauses**
✓ Sentence Combination
   ◆ compound elements

Classical Composition

EDITOR'S PEN – FINE FOCUS: WORDS

The final checks dwell on the details of your word usage. Continue to compile your personal editing checklist to use in editing all of your work across the curriculum.

Editor's Pen – Fine Focus: Words

✓ Word choices varied; word meanings clear
   ◆ Verbs: *strong, fitting; appropriate adverbs if needed*
   ◆ Nouns: *clear, descriptive; appropriate adjectives if needed*
   ◆ Dialogue: *dialogue tags varied if appropropriate*
✓ Correct spelling
✓ Final read-through

A. Read aloud your most recent version. Identify changes you need to make with the Editor's Pen checklist. Mark these on your print copy.

B. Transfer all additions and corrections from your print copy to the computer file. Print this final version and file it in your binder along with your other versions.

Commonplace

Commonplace Book

POETRY

Session three of three commonplace sessions for this lesson. Literary selection: "The New Colossus."

 Set your timer and begin copying. When you finish, check your work carefully against the original for accuracy.

Lesson 24.5

Prose & Poetry

POETRY APPRECIATION

 Read and enjoy a few poems in your poetry anthology. Identify rhyme schemes and stanza forms of one or two. Look for figures of speech and figures of description in the poems you read, and make note of any you find for future Commonplace Book entries. Read one or two poems aloud with expression and proper pauses. Pause at punctuation, but not necessarily at the ends of lines. Finally, choose a rhyming poem with trochaic meter to observe. Finally, choose a rhyming poem with iambic, trochaic, dactylic, or anapestic meter to observe.

Writer's Journal

- In your Writer's Journal, write the title of the poem and the author. Make note of its meter, rhyme scheme, and stanza form.
- Write the rhyming words from the poem in two lists: one list for those spelled the same, and one list for those spelled differently.
- Choose one of the rhyming words from the spelled differently list, and try to come up with several additional rhymes. Look especially for varied spellings.

Language Logic

GRAMMAR TERMS & DEFINITIONS

♔ Ask your teacher to quiz you with the grammar flashcards. Alternately, use the test feature in the Cottage Press *Bards & Poets I* Quizlet Classroom for an online or printed quiz for Lesson 24.

DICTATION: POETRY

♔ Work in your Writer's Journal. Write as your teacher dictates a passage to you from your Commonplace Book. When you are done, check your work carefully, word by word, against the original. Check for accurate spelling, capitalization, and punctuation.

Eloquent Expression

PARAGRAPH STYLE – PARAPHRASE WITH COPIA

For this exercise, choose from all of the copia devices you have learned so far. See the copia chart in Lesson 24.4. New devices are in bold type.

♔ In your Writer's Journal, paraphrase this paragraph. Change each sentence opener, and change at least one sentence class by use. Use as many synonym substitutions as possible. Use as many of the other copia devices as you are able. Make notes on the paragraph below before you begin.

As I walked through the wilderness of this world, I lighted on a

certain place where was a den, and laid me down in that place to sleep;

and as I slept, I dreamed a dream. I dreamed, and behold, I saw a man

clothed with rags, standing in a certain place, with his face from his own house, a book in his hand, and a great burden upon his back. I looked, and saw him open the

book, and read therein; and as he read, he wept and trembled; and, not being able longer to con-

tain, he brake out with a lamentable cry, saying, "What shall I do?"

Classical Composition

POETRY

Writer's Journal

🏵 In your Writer's Journal, write two to four rhyming lines that summarize the action of "The City of Destruction." If you wish, include a poetic **moral** at the end. Consider including them at the end of your retelling as a brief summary of the story. You may find it easiest to imitate the rhyme and meter of a few lines of the poetic selection for this lesson or a previous lesson.

NARRATIVE RETELLING – FINAL DRAFT

🏵 Read over the final version of your retelling one last time and make any needed changes. Save it on your computer; print and file with all the other drafts in your writing binder.

Commonplace

FROM YOUR READING

Find selections in a book or poem to add to your Commonplace Book. Include the name of the book or poem, properly formatted. Label the entry with the grammar or poetry feature, the figure of speech, or as a favorite passage. Aim for a minimum of three entries, with at least one from each category.

Commonplace Book

🏵 Grammar Features (choose any)

- ◆ A sentence that has an interesting or descriptive noun, a strong and fitting verb, a well-chosen adjective, and/or a vivid adverb
- ◆ A sentence with one or more prepositional phrases or indirect objects

- ◆ A sentence that has a possessive noun or pronoun and/or an appositive
- ◆ A sentence that has a conjunction to join words, phrases, or clauses
- ◆ A sentence with a participle or participial phrase, and/or an infinitive or infinitive phrase
- ◆ An interesting dialogue tag (add to your Dialogue Tags list)
- ◆ An interrogative, exclamatory, or imperative sentence

Figures (choose any)

- ◆ Figures of Speech: simile, onomatopoeia, anastrophe, alliteration, metaphor, and/or personification
- ◆ Figures of Description: anemographia, hydrographia, chronographia, and/or astrothesia

Poetry Features (choose any)

- ◆ Rhyme (note name of the rhyme scheme)
- ◆ Iambic, anapestic, dactylic, or trochaic meter (note name of the meter)
- ◆ Stanza (note name of stanza form)

Favorite Passage: Add at least one passage of one to three sentences or several lines of poetry that captured your attention in your reading this week. It may be something you found beautiful, thought-provoking, funny, or interesting.

Lesson 25

CR

THE SLOUGH OF DESPOND

from PILGRIM'S PROGRESS by John Bunyan

Now, I saw in my dream, that, when Obstinate was gone back, Christian and Pliable went talking over the plain; and thus they began:

Chris. Come, neighbor Pliable, how do you do? I am glad you are persuaded to go along with me. Had even Obstinate himself but felt what I have felt of the powers and terrors of what is yet unseen, he would not thus lightly have given us the back.

Pli. Come, neighbor Christian, since there are none but us two here, tell me now further what the things are, and how to be enjoyed, whither we are going.

Chris. I can better understand them with my mind than speak of them with my tongue; but yet, since you are desirous to know, I will read of them in my book.

Pli. And do you think that the words of your book are certainly true?

Chris. Yes, verily; for it was made by Him that cannot lie.

Pli. Well said; what things are they?

Chris. There is an endless kingdom to be enjoyed, and everlasting life to be given us, that we may live in that kingdom forever.

Pli. Well said; and what else?

Chris. There are crowns of glory to be given us, and garments that will make us shine like the sun in the sky.

Pli. This is very pleasant; and what else?

Chris. There shall be no more crying, nor sorrow; for he that is owner of the place will wipe all tears from our eyes.

Pli. And what company shall we have there?

Chris. There we shall be with seraphims and cherubims, creatures that shall dazzle your eyes to look on them. There also you shall meet with thousands and ten thousands that have gone before us to that place; none of them are hurtful, but all loving and holy; every one walking in the sight of God, and standing in His presence with acceptance for ever. In a word, there we shall see the elders with their golden crowns; there we shall see the holy women with their golden harps; there we shall see men that by the world were cut in pieces, burnt in flames, eaten of beasts, drowned in the seas, for the love they bear to the Lord of the place, all well, and clothed with everlasting life as with a garment.

Pli. The hearing of this is enough to delight one's heart. But are these things to be enjoyed? How shall we get to be sharers thereof?

Chris. The Lord, the Governor of the country, hath written that in this book; the substance of which is, If we be truly willing to have it, He will bestow it upon us freely.

Pli. Well, my good companion, glad am I to hear of these things; come on, let us mend our pace.

Chris. I cannot go so fast as I would, by reason of this burden that is on my back.

Now, I saw in my dream, that just as they had ended this talk, they drew nigh to a very miry slough or swamp, that was in the midst of the plain; and they, being heedless, did both fall suddenly into the bog. The name of the slough was Despond. Here, therefore, they wallowed for a time, being grievously bedaubed with the dirt; and Christian, because of the burden that was on his back, began to sink into the mire.

Pli. Then said Pliable, "Ah! neighbor Christian where are you now?"

Chris. "Truly," said Christian, "I do not know."

Pli. At this Pliable began to be offended, and angrily said to his fellow, "Is this the happiness you have told me all this while of? If we have such

ill speed at our first setting out, what may we expect between this and
our journey's end? May I get out again with my life, you shall possess the
brave country alone for me." And with that, he gave a desperate struggle
or two, and got out of the mire on that side of the swamp which was next
to his own house: so away he went, and Christian saw him no more.

Wherefore Christian was left to tumble in the Slough of Despond
alone; but still he tried to struggle to that side of the slough which was
farthest from his own house, and next to the wicket-gate; the which, he
did but could not get out because of the burden that was upon his back;
but I beheld in my dream, that a man came to him whose name was Help,
and asked him, What he did there?

Chris. "Sir," said Christian, "I was bid to go this way by a man called
Evangelist, who directed me also to yonder gate, that I might escape the
wrath to come; and as I was going there I fell in here."

Help. But why did you not look for the steps?

Chris. Fear followed me so hard, that I fled the next way and fell in.

Help. Then said he, "Give me thine hand." So he gave him his hand, and
he drew him out, and set him upon solid ground, and bade him go on his
way.

Then I stepped to him that plucked him out, and said, "Sir, wherefore,
since over this place is the way from the City of Destruction to yonder
gate, is it that this place is not mended, that poor travelers might go
thither with more safety?" And he said unto me, "This miry slough is
such a place as cannot be mended; it is the hollow whither the scum and
filth that go with the feeling of sin, do continually run, and therefore it
is called the Slough of Despond; for still, as the sinner is awakened by
his lost condition, there arise in his soul many fears, and doubts, and
discouraging alarms, which all of them get together and settle in this
place; and this is the reason of the badness of the ground.

"It is not the pleasure of the King that this place should remain so
bad. His laborers also have, by the direction of His Majesty's surveyors,
been for about these sixteen hundred years employed about this patch

of ground, if perhaps it might have been mended; yea, and to my knowledge," said he, "here have been swallowed up at least twenty thousand cart-loads, yea, millions, of wholesome teachings, that have at all seasons been brought from all places of the King's dominions (and they that can tell say they are the best materials to make good ground of the place), if so be it might have been mended; but it is the Slough of Despond still, and so will be when they have done what they can.

"True, there are, by the direction of the Lawgiver, certain good and substantial steps, placed even through the very midst of this slough; but at such time as this place doth much spew out its filth, as it doth against change of weather, these steps are hardly seen; or, if they be, men, through the dizziness of their heads, step aside, and then they are bemired to purpose, notwithstanding the steps be there; but the ground is good when they are got in at the gate."

—edited by REV. JESSE LYMAN HURLBUT

ᚲᚱ

Lesson 25.1

Prose & Poetry

A LOOK AT LITERARY ELEMENTS IN THE NARRATIVE

1 Read
◆ Listen carefully as your teacher reads the selection aloud. **Delight** in the story.

2 Inquire
◆ Does the **title** give any hint as to the content or message of the story? If this story was published by the author in a larger book or an anthology, does that title give any hint?
◆ Discuss the meaning of these words in the context of the story: *desirous, certainly, slough, despond, scum, alarms, wholesome, spew* and any unfamiliar words.

3 **Observe the Content**
  ◆ **Setting** When and where does this story take place?
  ◆ **Characters** Who is (are) the main character(s) in this story?
  ◆ **Conflict** What is the main problem or crisis for the character(s)?
  ◆ **Resolution** Is the problem solved? If so, how? If not, why not?
  ◆ **Point of View** Who is telling the story? Is it first-person or third-person?
  ◆ **Figures** Can you identify any examples of simile, onomatopoeia, anemographia, anastrophe, alliteration, hydrographia, metaphor, personification, chronographia, or astrothesia in this narrative?

4 **Investigate the Context**
Review the context of Pilgrim's Progress from Lesson 23.1. If you have time, read the entire biography of Bunyan in *English Literature for Boys and Girls*, by Henrietta E. Marshall. It is available to read for free online at mainlesson.com.

5 **Connect the Thoughts**
  ◆ Does this story remind you of other stories with similar plots, messages, or characters?
  ◆ Does this story remind you of any fables?
  ◆ Does this story remind you of any proverbs or other well-known quotations? If so, enter these in your Commonplace Book.

Commonplace Book

6 **Profit and Delight**
  ◆ **Delight** What are the sources of delight in this story?
  ◆ **Wisdom** What wisdom does this story furnish?
  ◆ **Read** the narrative aloud to your teacher with expression and with proper pauses.

PLOT OBSERVATION: IDENTIFYING ACTIONS

Observe the plot of "The Slough of Despond." Work in pencil on the original narrative at the beginning of this lesson, marking and making notes in the margin as instructed below.

A. Quickly read through the narrative once more. Number the paragraphs, and then mark the story as you have learned to do. Divide the narrative into actions.

B. Mark an x beside the sections that do not detail an action, and note what these are: **Prologue, Epilogue, Explanation, Description, Summary, Author Comments**.

C. Mark the major actions. Then, mark in the left margin if the action is made up of **Dialogue** or **Thoughts**. Consider Theon's Six. Remember that action can change even in the middle of a paragraph. Feel free to change your mind often as you work through the entire narrative—this is why you must use a pencil! Keep in mind that there is not just one right way to divide narratives into actions. Just make sure you can explain why you divide them as you do, using Theon's Six.

D. Review the narrative. Make notes in the margin indicating if any of the rest of Theon's Six changed with each action. You should definitely have notes about Person. Ask the questions for the other four, but do not worry too much if you can only add notes for two or three others.

E. Discuss your work with your teacher.

Language Logic

GRAMMAR TERMS & DEFINITIONS
❦ Review all flashcards according to tabs.

GRAMMAR PRACTICE AND REVIEW
❦ In your Writer's Journal, copy these sentences. Analyze each sentence by marking the simple subject (who or what the sentence is about) with a single underline, and the verb or verb phrase with a double underline. Write DO over the direct object, or LV over the linking verb; write PA over a predicate adjective and PN over a predicate nominative. Put parentheses around each prepositional phrase. Bracket the clauses. hen diagram the sentence. Refer to *Sentence Sense* as needed. (Hints: for #3, see *Sentence Sense* 24.3. Also, in #4, *remain* is a linking verb. See explanation in *Bards & Poets I* Teaching Helps.)

Writer's Journal

1. They drew nigh to a very miry slough or swamp, that was in the midst of the plain; and they, being heedless, did both fall suddenly into the bog.

2. Ah! neighbor Christian where are you now?

3. Still he tried to struggle to that side of the slough which was farthest from his own house, and next to the wicket-gate.

4. It is not the pleasure of the King that this place should remain so bad.

Eloquent Expression

COPIA OF WORDS: VOCABULARY STUDY

Writer's Journal

❡ Conduct a vocabulary study for "The Slough of Despond."

A. Choose at least two unfamiliar words to study. If you need suggestions, see the list under **Inquire** in Literary Elements above. Work in your Writer's Journal.

B. Complete Vocabulary Study steps A-G for each word (see Appendix).

Commonplace

NARRATIVE

Commonplace Book

Session one of three commonplace sessions for this lesson. Literary selection: "The Slough of Despond."

 Set your timer and begin copying. When you finish, check your work carefully, word by word, against the original.

Lesson 25.2

Prose & Poetry

PLOT OBSERVATION: OUTLINE WITH CAPTIONS

Writer's Journal

❡ In your Writer's Journal, create an outline to capture your observations with parallel captions.

A. Jot down a quick caption for each major action, as well as any of the following: Prologue, Epilogue, Explanation, Description, Summary, Author Comments.

B. Review your captions, and choose a parallel format.

C. Revise all captions to conform to the format you have chosen.

Language Logic

SENTENCE DIAGRAMMING

◯ Read and discuss the following sections in *Sentence Sense* with your teacher.

III. Sentence Diagrammming: Sentence Classes by Form
   ◆ 20.1 Simple Sentences
   ◆ 20.2 Compound Sentences
   ◆ 20.3 Complex Sentences
   ◆ 20.4 Compound-Complex Sentences

◯ Move the flashcards that you have mastered backwards in your file system. Leave any that you have not mastered behind the **Daily** tab. Add these flashcards to your box behind the Daily tab, and begin to memorize them:

   ◆ Simple Sentence
   ◆ Compound Sentence
   ◆ Complex Sentence
   ◆ Compound-Complex Sentence

◯ Review all flashcards according to tabs.

◯ In your Writer's Journal, copy these sentences. Analyze each sentence by marking the simple subject (who or what the sentence is about) with a single underline, and the verb or verb phrase with a double underline. Write DO over the direct object, or LV over the linking verb; write PA over a predicate adjective and PN over a predicate nominative. Put parentheses around each prepositional phrase. Mark the subjects and verbs. Bracket the clauses. Classify the sentence as simple, compound, complex, or compound-complex. Then diagram the sentence. Refer to *Sentence Sense* as needed. If you need help on #3, see *Sentence Sense* 24.3.

Writer's Journal

1. The name of the one was Obstinate, and the name of the

    other was Pliable.

2. So he gave him his hand, and he drew him out, and set him upon solid ground, and told
   him to go on his way.

3. It was twelve by the village clock

   When he crossed the bridge into Medford town.

Classical Composition

PLOT OBSERVATION: ORAL NARRATION

Without reading "The Slough of Despond" again, retell the **plot** orally to your teacher. Refer
to your plot observation of the narrative with Theon's Six if needed.

Commonplace

NARRATIVE

Session two of three commonplace sessions for this lesson. Literary
selection: "The Slough of Despond."

Commonplace
Book

Set your timer and begin copying. When you finish, check
your work carefully, word by word, against the original. Check
spelling, capitalization, and punctuation for accuracy.

Lesson 25.3

Language Logic

GRAMMAR
FLASHCARDS

GRAMMAR TERMS & DEFINITIONS

Review all flashcards according to tabs.

SENTENCE DIAGRAMMING

In your Writer's Journal, copy these sentences. Analyze each sentence by marking the simple
subject (who or what the sentence is about) with a single underline, and the verb or verb

phrase with a double underline. Write DO over a direct object, LV over a linking verb, PA over a predicate adjective, and PN over a predicate nominative. Put parentheses around each prepositional phrase. Bracket the clauses. Classify the sentence as simple, compound, complex, or compound-complex Then diagram the sentence. Refer to *Sentence Sense* as needed.

In the first subordinate clause, *as* is used as a relative pronoun. See B*ards & Poets I* Teaching Helps for an explanation.

Writer's Journal

1. This miry slough is such a place as cannot be mended; it is the hollow whither the scum and filth that go with the feeling of sin, do continually run, and therefore it is called the Slough of Despond.

2. There are, by the direction of the Lawgiver, certain good and substantial steps, placed even through the very midst of this slough.

Eloquent Expression

SENTENCE STYLE – COPIA OF CONSTRUCTION: INDIRECT QUOTATIONS

When you are writing a narrative, using dialogue can add a great deal of interest. But there are times when using direct quotations is not appropriate or expedient, such as when you empasizing the action, or when you are writing a summary of the action. Direct quotations can easily be switched to indirect quotations.

Erasmus said, "Thank you for your letter."

Erasmus thanked him for his letter.

Erasmus cried, "This letter brings me great joy!"

Erasmus expressed great joy on reading the letter. OR Erasmus read the letter with joy.

Use the dialogue tag *said* sparingly when you write indirect quotations. Refer to your Synonyms for Said list to find appropriate substitutes, or paraphrase the sentence entirely as in the last example above.

Paraphrase each sentence below, changing direct quotations to indirect quotations.

Writer's Journal

1. "Truly," said Christian, "I do not know."

2. Then said Help, "Give me thine hand."

Classical Composition

NARRATIVE RETELLING – FIRST DRAFT

You will have two sessions to work on this retelling. Begin here, and plan to finish in Lesson 25.4. As you write your retelling, do your best to use proper grammar and spelling, but keep in mind that you will have opportunity to edit before you finalize it.

Retell "The Slough of Despond" in writing, keeping the same characters, setting, and sequence of action. Choose either first or third person point of view, but be consistent throughout. This means you need to make sure that the pronouns are consistent, and pay close attention attention to subject/verb agreement. Refer to your plot observation of the narrative with Theon's Six, but do not review the original narrative before you write. Include:

Writer's Journal

- a heading, properly formatted
- at least two figures of speech: simile, onomatopoeia, anastrophe, alliteration, metaphor
- at least one figure of description: anemographia, hydrographia, choronographia, astrothesia

Lesson 25.4

Language Logic

GRAMMAR FLASHCARDS

GRAMMAR TERMS & DEFINITIONS

Review all flashcards according to tabs.

SENTENCE DIAGRAMMING

 In your Writer's Journal, copy these lines. Analyze each sentence by marking the simple subject (who or what the sentence is about) with a single underline, and the verb or verb phrase with a double underline. Write DO over a direct object, LV over a linking verb, PA over a predicate adjective, and PN over a predicate nominative. Put parentheses around each prepositional phrase. Bracket the clauses. Classify the sentence as simple, compound, complex, or compound-complex Then diagram the sentence. Refer to *Sentence Sense* as needed.

Hint: Diagram *from behind* as a compound preposition. See *Bards & Poets I* Teaching Helps for an explanation.

Writer's Journal

In the books you have read,

How the British Regulars fired and fled,—

How the farmers gave them ball for ball,

From behind each fence and farm-yard wall,

Chasing the red-coats down the lane,

Then crossing the fields to emerge again

Under the trees at the turn of the road,

And only pausing to fire and load.

Classical Composition

Writer's Journal

NARRATIVE RETELLING – FINISH FIRST DRAFT

 Finish the first draft of your narrative retelling. Review the instructions in Lesson 25.3 as needed.

Commonplace

NARRATIVE

Session three of three commonplace sessions for this lesson. Literary selection: "The Slough of Despond."

Commonplace Book

 Set your timer. Begin where you stopped in the last session. When you finish, check your work carefully against the original for accuracy.

Lesson 25.5

Prose & Poetry

POETRY APPRECIATION

 Read and enjoy a few poems in your poetry anthology. Identify rhyme schemes and stanza forms of one or two. Look for poems with iambic, trochaic, dactylic, or anapestic meter. Look for figures of speech and figures of description in the poems you read, and make note of any you find for future Commonplace Book entries. Read one or two poems aloud with expression and proper pauses. Pause at punctuation, but not necessarily at the ends of lines. Finally, choose a rhyming poem with trochaic meter to observe.

Language Logic

GRAMMAR TERMS & DEFINITIONS

GRAMMAR FLASHCARDS

 Ask your teacher to quiz you with the grammar flashcards. Alternately, use the test feature in the Cottage Press *Bards & Poets I* Quizlet Classroom for an online or printed quiz for Lesson 25.

DICTATION: NARRATIVE PASSAGE

 Work in your Writer's Journal. Write as your teacher dictates a passage to you from your Commonplace Book. When you are done, check your work carefully, word by word, against the original. Check for accurate spelling, capitalization, and punctuation.

Writer's Journal

Classical Composition

NARRATIVE RETELLING: TYPE FINAL DRAFT

 Type your retelling on the computer with spell-check turned off, or ask your writing mentor to type it exactly as you wrote it. Save, print, and file this draft in your writing binder.

Commonplace

FROM YOUR READING

Find selections in a book or poem to add to your Commonplace Book. Include the name of the book or poem, properly formatted. Label the entry with the grammar or poetry feature, the figure of speech, or as a favorite passage. Aim for a minimum of three entries, with at least one from each category.

Commonplace Book

Grammar Features (choose any)

- ◆ A sentence that has an interesting or descriptive noun, a strong and fitting verb, a well-chosen adjective, and/or a vivid adverb
- ◆ A sentence with one or more prepositional phrases or indirect objects
- ◆ A sentence that has a possessive noun or pronoun and/or an appositive
- ◆ A sentence that has a conjunction to join words, phrases, or clauses
- ◆ A sentence with a participle or participial phrase, and/or an infinitive or infinitive phrase
- ◆ A complex, compound, or compound-complex sentence
- ◆ An indirect quotation

- ◆ An interesting dialogue tag (add to your Dialogue Tags list)
- ◆ An interrogative, exclamatory, or imperative sentence

Figures (choose any)

- ◆ Figures of Speech: simile, onomatopoeia, anastrophe, alliteration, metaphor, and/or personification
- ◆ Figures of Description: anemographia, hydrographia, chronographia, and/or astrothesia

Poetry Features (choose any)

- ◆ Rhyme (note name of the rhyme scheme)
- ◆ Iambic, anapestic, dactylic, or trochaic meter (note name of the meter)
- ◆ Stanza (note name of stanza form)

Favorite Passage: Add at least one passage of one to three sentences or several lines of poetry that captured your attention in your reading this week. It may be something you found beautiful, thought-provoking, funny, or interesting.

Lesson 26

ℭℛ

CONCORD HYMN

By the rude bridge that arched the flood,

Their flag to April's breeze unfurled,

Here once the embattled farmers stood,

And fired the shot heard round the world.

The foe long since in silence slept;

Alike the conqueror silent sleeps;

And Time the ruined bridge has swept

Down the dark stream which seaward creeps.

On this green bank, by this soft stream,

We set to-day a votive stone;

That memory may their deed redeem,

When, like our sires, our sons are gone.

Spirit, that made those heroes dare,

To die, and leave their children free,

Bid Time and Nature gently spare

The shaft we raise to them and thee.

— RALPH WALDO EMERSON

ℭℛ

Lesson 26.1

Prose & Poetry

A LOOK AT LITERARY ELEMENTS IN THE POEM

1 **Read**
 ◆ Follow along and listen carefully as the poem is read aloud, OR read it aloud yourself. Read it at least two or three times. **Delight** in the meter, the rhyme, and the images.

2 **Inquire**
 ◆ Does the **title** give any hint as to the content or message of the poem?
 ◆ Are there any unfamiliar persons, places, or things mentioned in the poem? Discuss these with your teacher. Why does the poem mention April's breeze when it was written for a July celebration?
 ◆ Discuss the meaning of these words in the context of the story: *embattled, ruined, creeps, votive, redeem, sires, dare, spare,* and any unfamiliar words.
 ◆ Was there any part of the poem you did not understand? If so, discuss this with your teacher and classmates.

3 **Observe the Content**
 ◆ **Lyrical Elements**
   ▪ What does the poet describe?
   ▪ Does the poet make you see, hear, smell, taste, or touch anything?
   ▪ Does the poet compare something in the poem to some other thing?
 ◆ **Narrative Elements** Does this poem tell a story? If so, observe the
   ▪ **Setting** When and where does this story take place?
   ▪ **Characters** Who is (are) the main character(s) in this story?
   ▪ **Conflict** What is the main problem or crisis for the character(s)?
   ▪ **Resolution** Is the problem solved? If so, how? If not, why not?
 ◆ **Point of View** Who is speaking in the poem? Is it first-person or third-person?
 ◆ **Figures** Can you identify any examples of simile, onomatopoeia, anemographia, anastrophe, alliteration, hydrographia, metaphor, personification, chronographia, or astrothesia in this poem?

4 **Investigate the Context**
Ralph Waldo Emerson (1803-1882) was another of the influential literary New Englanders, a friend of Longfellow and Holmes, and another Harvard graduate. He served as Class Poet

while at Harvard, although his class standing was in the precise middle of the 59 students. Still, he is one of America's most famous philosophers, essayists, and poets. He traveled abroad and met Wordsworth and Coleridge, both of whom had a great impact on his philosophy and poetry, which in turn influenced Emerson's American literary friends, including those he mentored, such as Henry David Thoreau, author of *On Walden Pond*, and Lousia May Alcott, author of *Little Women*.

Emerson wrote "Concord Hymn" for the town's Independence Day dedication of a monument near the Old North Bridge in 1837, in commemoration of the Battle of Concord, the second battle of the American War for Independence. This hymn was originally sung to the very familiar tune "Old Hundredth." (Students who completed *Primer One* will remember this as the tune for "All People That On Earth Do Dwell.") The closing line of the first stanza has become a descriptor for the Battles of Lexington and Concord, and for the American War for Independence itself, which unquestionably set off worldwide repercussions in the struggle for liberty; it subsequently has come to be used for any historical event initiating a global chain of events.

5 Connect the Thoughts
- Does this poem remind you of other poems, or of stories with similar plots, messages, or characters?
- Does this poem remind you of any proverbs or other well-known quotations? If so, enter these in your Commonplace Book.

6 Profit and Delight
- **Delight** What are the sources of delight in this poem?
- **Wisdom** What wisdom does this poem furnish?
- **Read** the poem aloud to your teacher with expression and with proper pauses.
- **Record** in your Book of Centuries: Ralph Waldo Emerson.
- **Memorize** this poem and **recite** it before an audience.

Commonplace Book

Language Logic

GRAMMAR FLASHCARDS

GRAMMAR TERMS & DEFINITIONS

⚜ Review all flashcards according to tabs.

GRAMMAR PRACTICE AND REVIEW

⚜ In your Writer's Journal, copy this sentence. Analyze the sentence by marking the simple subject (who or what the sentence is about) with a single underline, and the verb or verb phrase with a double underline. Write DO over the direct object, or LV over the linking verb; write PA over a predicate adjective and PN over a predicate nominative. Put parentheses around each prepositional phrase. Bracket the clauses. Classify the sentence as simple, compound, complex, or compound-complex. Then diagram the sentence. Refer to *Sentence Sense* as needed. Then diagram the sentence. Refer to *Sentence Sense* as needed.

Challenge (classroom):

By the rude bridge that arched the flood,

Their flag to April's breeze unfurled,

Here once the embattled farmers stood,

And fired the shot heard round the world.

Writer's Journal

Classical Composition

EDITOR'S PEN – THE BIG PICTURE

⚜ Edit your retelling from Lesson 25:

Editor's Pen – The Big Picture
- ✓ All important plot elements included
- ✓ All characters represented correctly

✓ Sequence: *same as the original*

✓ Length: *similar to the original*

✓ Point of View: *3rd person or 1st person*

✓ Figures of Speech – at least two of the following: *metaphor, personification, simile, onomatopoeia, anastrophe, alliteration*

✓ Figure of Description: *topographia* (will be added in Lesson 26.2); optional: *anemographia, hydrographia, chronographia, astrothesia*

A. Read aloud exactly what you have written—not what you THINK you have written! Mark any corrections on your first draft.

B. Next, work through the Big Picture checklist above with your writing mentor.

C. Transfer all additions and corrections from your print copy of the retelling to your file on the computer. Print and file this edited version in your binder along with your marked-up editing copy of the first draft.

Eloquent Expression

COPIA OF WORDS: VOCABULARY STUDY

Conduct a vocabulary study for "Concord Hymn."

Writer's Journal

A. Choose at least two unfamiliar words to study. If you need suggestions, see the list under **Inquire** in Literary Elements above. Work in your Writer's Journal.

B. Complete Vocabulary Study steps A-G for each word (see Appendix*)*.

Commonplace

Commonplace Book

POETRY

Session one of three commonplace sessions for this lesson. Literary selection: "Concord Hymn."

Set your timer and begin copying. When finished, check your work carefully against the original for accuracy.

Lesson 26.2

Prose & Poetry

RHYME SCHEME AND STANZA FORM

 Mark the end rhyme in the stanzas below.

By the rude bridge that arched the flood,

Their flag to April's breeze unfurled,

Here once the embattled farmers stood,

And fired the shot heard round the world.

The foe long since in silence slept;

Alike the conqueror silent sleeps;

And Time the ruined bridge has swept

Down the dark stream which seaward creeps.

On this green bank, by this soft stream,

We set to-day a votive stone;

That memory may their deed redeem,

When, like our sires, our sons are gone.

Spirit, that made those heroes dare,

To die, and leave their children free,

Bid Time and Nature gently spare

The shaft we raise to them and thee.

 Name the predominant rhyme scheme and the stanza form of this poem.

Language Logic

GRAMMAR TERMS & DEFINITIONS

Review all flashcards according to tabs.

SENTENCE DIAGRAMMING

In your Writer's Journal, copy these lines. Analyze the sentence by marking the simple subject (who or what the sentence is about) with a single underline, and the verb or verb phrase with a double underline. Write D.O. over the direct object, or L.V. over the linking verb; write PA over a predicate adjective and PN over a predicate nominative. Put parentheses around each prepositional phrase. Mark the subjects and verbs. Bracket the clauses. Classify the sentence as simple, compound, complex, or compound-complex. Then diagram the sentence. Refer to *Sentence Sense* as needed.

Writer's Journal

> The foe long since in silence slept;
>
> Alike the conqueror silent sleeps;
>
> And Time the ruined bridge has swept
>
> Down the dark stream which seaward creeps.

Eloquent Expression

FIGURE OF DESCRIPTION: TOPOGRAPHIA

Topos is the Greek word for *a place*; **topographia** is the vivid description of a place. Recall that figures of speech are often used to produce figures of description. Look for figures of speech in these examples of topographia from literature:

> Mr. McGregor's rubbish heap was a mixture. There were jam pots and paper bags, and mountains of chopped grass from the mowing machine (which always tasted oily), and some rotten vegetable marrows and an old boot or two. — Beatrix Potter, *The Tale of the Flopsy Bunnies*

> There were no rocky cliffs like those of England. Before them rose tall, green pine trees, and great oaks still wearing their dress of reddish brown. Not a town or a single house

could they see. No smoke rose from the forest to tell them where a village lay hidden. Not a sound was heard but the whistling of the cold wind through the ropes and masts, and the lapping of the water about the boat. — Margraret Pumphrey, *Stories of the Pilgrims*

Study and practice the figure of topographia with your teacher.

A. Discuss the examples of topographia with your teacher.

B. Look in this week's poem for examples of topographia. Discuss this with your teacher. Look through other poems we have studied in *Bards & Poets I* for more examples of topographia. Make note of some that you may wish to copy into your Commonplace Book.

C. In your Writer's Journal, write a sentence or two of your own topographia, vividly describing the Slough of Despond.

D. Add your figure of topographia to the narrative retelling by writing it in the appropriate place on your print copy of our current draft.

Classical Composition

EDITOR'S PEN – ZOOM 5X: PARAGRAPHS

Now that the Big Picture is set, begin to zoom in for a close look at the paragraph(s) in your retelling with your writing mentor.

> Editor's Pen – Zoom 5x: Paragraphs
> ✔ Formatting: *proper indentation*
> ✔ Length: *neither too wordy nor too short*
> ✔ Sentence class by use: *effective use*
> ✔ Sentence openers: *varied*
> ✔ Dialogue: *effective use*
> ✔ Verb Tense: *consistent*
> ✔ Pronouns: *consistent with chosen point of view*

A. Read aloud your most recently edited version. Check each item in the Editor's Pen checklist to identify possible changes. Mark these on your print copy.

B. Transfer all additions and corrections from your print copy to the computer file. Print this version and file it in your binder along with your other versions.

Lesson 26.3

Prose & Poetry

SCANSION

 Scan these stanzas, following the three steps you have learned.

Step 1 Mark each syllable as either stressed (/) or unstressed (∪). Say the line aloud several times to "get" the meter. Next, say the line aloud emphasizing the stresses as you mark the stresses only. Then go back and mark the unstressed syllables, saying the line aloud once more to check your work. Here, we also recommend that you do not start scanning with the first line!

Step 2 Insert dividers (|) to mark off the feet. Remember that you will only have one stress in each foot. Pronounce *conqueror* with two syllables. There is one extra unstressed syllable in the first stanza, second foot.

Step 3 Name the poem's predominant meter:

By the rude bridge that arched the flood,

Their flag to April's breeze unfurled,

Here once the embattled farmers stood,

And fired the shot heard round the world.

The foe long since in silence slept;

Alike the conqueror silent sleeps;

And Time the ruined bridge has swept

Down the dark stream which seaward creeps.

Language Logic

GRAMMAR FLASHCARDS

GRAMMAR TERMS & DEFINITIONS
◯ Review all flashcards according to tabs.

SENTENCE DIAGRAMMING

◯ In your Writer's Journal, copy these lines. Analyze the sentence by marking the simple subject (who or what the sentence is about) with a single underline, and the verb or verb phrase with a double underline. Write DO over a direct object, LV over a linking verb, PA over a predicate adjective, and PN over a predicate nominative. Put parentheses around each prepositional phrase. Bracket the clauses. Classify the sentence as simple, compound, complex, or compound-complex Then diagram the sentence. Refer to *Sentence Sense* as needed.

In this sentence, *that* is used as a conjunction rather than a relative pronoun. Check the dictionary to prove it!

On this green bank, by this soft stream,

We set to-day a votive stone;

That memory may their deed redeem,

When, like our sins, our sons are gone.

Writer's Journal

Eloquent Expression

SENTENCE STYLE – YOUR STYLE!

◯ Craft copia for sentences from your own retelling using Sentence Style devices we have studied.

A. Work with your writing mentor to choose three sentences from your retelling that could be improved.

B. Copy the first in your Writer's Journal. Underline every important word in the sentence and jot down synonyms for each.

Writer's Journal

C. Use the list of Sentence Style devices below as you write several new versions of the sentence. You may use more than one device in each sentence.

D. Repeat the instructions above for the second and third sentences.

E. Choose your favorite paraphrase of each sentence. Replace the original sentences in your retelling before you edit again.

COPIA OF WORDS	COPIA OF CONSTRUCTION
✓ Synonyms and Antonyms	✓ Sentence class by use
✓ Opening Words	✓ Dialogue
✓ Dialogue Tags - synonyms for *said*	◆ Tag line position
✓ Point of View	✓ Verb Tense
✓ Nouns – varied and descriptive	✓ Sentence Structure
◆ switch noun/pronouns	◆ switch possessive/*of* phrases
◆ switch gerund/infinitve	◆ change position of phrases
✓ Verbs – strong and fitting	◆ **switch words/phrases/clauses**
◆ switch verb/verbal	✓ Sentence Combination
✓ Modifiers	◆ compound elements
◆ add adjective	
◆ add adverb	

Classical Composition

EDITOR'S PEN – ZOOM 10X: SENTENCES

Now it is time to zoom in even closer as you check the sentences in your retelling. Work with your writing mentor.

Editor's Pen – Zoom 10x: Sentences

✓ Complete thought expressed

✓ Subject and predicate agree in number

✓ Correct capitalization and punctuation

◆ Commas correctly used for words in a series

◆ No comma splices or run-on sentences!

A. Read aloud your your most recently edited version. Use the Editor's Pen checklist to identify changes you need to make. Mark all changes on your print copy.

B. Transfer all additions and corrections from your print copy to the computer file. Print this version and file it in your binder along with your other versions.

Commonplace

POETRY

Session two of three commonplace sessions for this lesson. Literary selection: "Concord Hymn."

Commonplace Book

 Set your timer. Begin where you stopped in the last session. When you finish, check your work carefully against the original for accuracy.

Lesson 26.4

Prose & Poetry

SCANSION

 Scan these stanzas, following the three steps you have learned.

Step 1 Mark each syllable as either stressed (/) or unstressed (∪). Say the line aloud several times to "get" the meter. Next, say the line aloud emphasizing the stresses as you mark the stresses only. Then go back and mark the unstressed syllables, saying the line aloud once more to check your work.

Step 2 Insert dividers (|) to mark off the feet. Remember that you will only have one stress in each foot. Pronounce *memory* with two syllables.

Step 3 Name the poem's predominant meter:

On this green bank, by this soft stream,

We set to-day a votive stone;

That memory may their deed redeem,

When, like our sires, our sons are gone.

Spirit, that made those heroes dare,

To die, and leave their children free,

Bid Time and Nature gently spare

The shaft we raise to them and thee.

Language Logic

GRAMMAR
FLASHCARDS

GRAMMAR TERMS & DEFINITIONS
❀ Review all flashcards according to tabs.

Classical Composition

EDITOR'S PEN – FINE FOCUS: WORDS
The final checks dwell on the details of your word usage. Continue to compile your personal editing checklist to use in editing all of your work across the curriculum.

Editor's Pen – Fine Focus: Words
✓ Word choices varied; word meanings clear
  ◆ Verbs: *strong, fitting; appropriate adverbs if needed*
  ◆ Nouns: *clear, descriptive; appropriate adjectives if needed*
  ◆ Dialogue: *dialogue tags varied if appropropriate*
✓ Correct spelling
✓ Final read-through

A. Read aloud your most recent version. Identify changes you need to make with the Editor's Pen checklist. Mark these on your print copy.

B. Transfer all additions and corrections from your print copy to the computer file. Print this final version and file it in your binder along with your other versions.

Eloquent Expression

PARAGRAPH STYLE – PARAPHRASE WITH COPIA

For this exercise, choose from all of the copia devices you have learned so far. See the copia chart in Lesson 26.3. New devices are in bold type.

In your Writer's Journal, paraphrase this paragraph. Change each sentence opener, and change at least one sentence class by use. Use as many synonym substitutions as possible. Use as many of the other copia devices as you are able. Make notes on the paragraph below before you begin.

Wherefore Christian was left to tumble in the Slough of Despond alone; but still he tried to struggle to that side of the slough which was farthest from his own house, and next to the wicket-gate; the which, he did but could not get out because of the burden that was upon his back; but I beheld in my dream, that a man came to him whose name was Help, and asked him, What he did there?

Writer's Journal

Commonplace

Commonplace
Book

POETRY

Session three of three commonplace sessions for this lesson. Literary
selection: "Concord Hymn."

 Set your timer and begin copying. When you finish, check your
work carefully against the original for accuracy.

Lesson 26.5

Prose & Poetry

POETRY APPRECIATION

 Read and enjoy a few poems in your poetry anthology. Identify rhyme schemes and stanza
forms of one or two. Look for figures of speech and figures of description in the poems you
read, and make note of any you find for future Commonplace Book entries. Read one or two
poems aloud with expression and proper pauses. Pause at punctuation, but not necessarily
at the ends of lines. Finally, choose a rhyming poem with iambic, trochaic, dactylic, or
anapestic meter to observe.

Writer's
Journal

- In your Writer's Journal, write the title of the poem and the
  author. Make note of its meter, rhyme scheme, and stanza
  form.
- Write the rhyming words from the poem in two lists: one
  list for those spelled the same, and one list for those spelled
  differently.
- Choose one of the rhyming words from the spelled differently
  list, and try to come up with several additional rhymes. Look especially for varied
  spellings.

Language Logic

GRAMMAR TERMS & DEFINITIONS

◌ Ask your teacher to quiz you with the grammar flashcards. Alternately, use the test feature in the Cottage Press *Bards & Poets I* Quizlet Classroom for an online or printed quiz for Lesson 26.

DICTATION: POETRY

◌ Work in your Writer's Journal. Write as your teacher dictates a passage to you from your Commonplace Book. When you are done, check your work carefully, word by word, against the original. Check for accurate spelling, capitalization, and punctuation.

Classical Composition

POETRY

◌ In your Writer's Journal, write two to four rhyming lines that summarize the action of "The Slough of Despond." If you wish, include a poetic **moral** at the end. Consider including them at the end of your retelling as a brief summary of the story. You may find it easiest to imitate the rhyme and meter of a few lines of the poetic selection for this lesson or a previous lesson.

NARRATIVE RETELLING – FINAL DRAFT

◌ Read over the final version of your retelling one last time and make any needed changes. Save it on your computer; print and file with all the other drafts in your writing binder.

Commonplace

Commonplace
Book

FROM YOUR READING

Find selections in a book or poem to add to your Commonplace Book.
Include the name of the book or poem, properly formatted. Label the
entry with the grammar or poetry feature, the figure of speech, or as a
favorite passage. Aim for a minimum of three entries, with at least one
from each category.

 Grammar Features (choose any)

- ◆ A sentence that has an interesting or descriptive noun, a strong and fitting verb, a well-chosen adjective, and/or a vivid adverb
- ◆ A sentence with one or more prepositional phrases or indirect objects
- ◆ A sentence that has a possessive noun or pronoun and/or an appositive
- ◆ A sentence that has a conjunction to join words, phrases, or clauses
- ◆ A sentence with a participle or participial phrase, and/or an infinitive or infinitive phrase
- ◆ A complex, compound, or compound-complex sentence
- ◆ An indirect quotation
- ◆ An interesting dialogue tag (add to your Dialogue Tags list)
- ◆ An interrogative, exclamatory, or imperative sentence

Figures (choose any)

- ◆ Figures of Speech: simile, onomatopoeia, anastrophe, alliteration, metaphor, and/or personification
- ◆ Figures of Description: anemographia, hydrographia, chronographia, astrothesia, and/or topographia

Poetry Features (choose any)

- ◆ Rhyme (note name of the rhyme scheme)
- ◆ Iambic, anapestic, dactylic, or trochaic meter (note name of the meter)
- ◆ Stanza (note name of stanza form)

Favorite Passage: Add at least one passage of one to three sentences or several lines of poetry
that captured your attention in your reading this week. It may be something you found
beautiful, thought-provoking, funny, or interesting.

CR

GEORGE WASHINGTON

from HERO TALES IN AMERICAN HISTORY by Henry Cabot Lodge

Born of a distinguished family in the days when the American colonies were still ruled by an aristocracy, Washington started with all that good birth and tradition could give. Beyond this, however, he had little. His family was poor, his mother was left early a widow, and he was forced after a very limited education to go out into the world to fight for himself. He had strong within him the adventurous spirit of his race. He became a surveyor, and in the pursuit of this profession plunged into the wilderness, where he soon grew to be an expert hunter and backwoodsman. Even as a boy the gravity of his character and his mental and physical vigor commended him to those about him, and responsibility and military command were put in his hands at an age when most young men are just leaving college. As the times grew threatening on the frontier, he was sent on a perilous mission to the Indians, in which, after passing through many hardships and dangers, he achieved success. When the troubles came with France it was by the soldiers under his command that the first shots were fired in the war which was to determine whether the North American continent should be French or English. In his earliest expedition he was defeated by the enemy. Later he was with Braddock, and it was he who tried, to rally the broken English army on the stricken field near Fort Duquesne. On that day of surprise and slaughter he displayed not only cool courage but the reckless daring which was one of his chief characteristics. He so exposed himself that bullets passed through his coat and hat, and the Indians and the French who tried to bring him down thought he bore a charmed life. He afterwards served with distinction all through the French war, and when peace came he went back to the estate which he had inherited from his brother, the most admired man in Virginia.

At that time he married, and during the ensuing years he lived the
life of a Virginia planter, successful in his private affairs and serving the
public effectively but quietly as a member of the House of Burgesses.
When the troubles with the mother country began to thicken he was
slow to take extreme ground, but he never wavered in his belief that all
attempts to oppress the colonies should be resisted, and when he once took
up his position there was no shadow of turning. He was one of Virginia's
delegates to the first Continental Congress, and, although he said but
little, he was regarded by all the representatives from the other colonies
as the strongest man among them. There was something about him even
then which commanded the respect and the confidence of every one who
came in contact with him.

It was from New England, far removed from his own State, that
the demand came for his appointment as commander-in-chief of the
American army. Silently he accepted the duty, and, leaving Philadelphia,
took command of the army at Cambridge. There is no need to trace him
through the events that followed. From the time when he drew his sword
under the famous elm tree, he was the embodiment of the American
Revolution, and without him that revolution would have failed almost at
the start. How he carried it to victory through defeat and trial and every
possible obstacle is known to all men.

When it was all over he found himself facing a new situation. He
was the idol of the country and of his soldiers. The army was unpaid,
and the veteran troops, with arms in their hands, were eager to have
him take control of the disordered country as Cromwell had done in
England a little more than a century before. With the army at his back,
and supported by the great forces which, in every community, desire
order before everything else, and are ready to assent to any arrangement
which will bring peace and quiet, nothing would have been easier than
for Washington to have made himself the ruler of the new nation. But
that was not his conception of duty, and he not only refused to have
anything to do with such a movement himself, but he repressed, by his
dominant personal influence, all such intentions on the part of the army.
On the 23d of December, 1783, he met the Congress at Annapolis, and
there resigned his commission. What he then said is one of the two most

memorable speeches ever made in the United States, and is also memorable for its meaning and spirit among all speeches ever made by men. He spoke as follows:

"Mr. President:—The great events on which my resignation depended having at length taken place, I have now the honor of offering my sincere congratulations to Congress, and of presenting myself before them, to surrender into their hands the trust committed to me and to claim the indulgence of retiring from the service of my country.

Happy in the confirmation of our independence and sovereignty and pleased with the opportunity afforded the United States of becoming a respectable nation, I resign with satisfaction the appointment I accepted with diffidence; a diffidence in my abilities to accomplish so arduous a task, which, however, was superseded by a confidence in the rectitude of our cause, the support of the supreme power of the Union, and the patronage of Heaven.

The successful termination of the war has verified the most sanguine expectations, and my gratitude for the interposition of Providence and the assistance I have received from my countrymen increases with every review of the momentous contest.

While I repeat my obligations to the Army in general, I should do injustice to my own feelings not to acknowledge, in this place, the peculiar services and distinguished merits of the Gentlemen who have been attached to my person during the war. It was impossible that the choice of confidential officers to compose my family should have been more fortunate. Permit me, sir, to recommend in particular those who have continued in service to the present moment as worthy of the favorable notice and patronage of Congress.

I consider it an indispensable duty to close this last solemn act of my official life by commending the interests of our dearest country to the protection of Almighty God, and those who have the superintendence of them to His holy keeping.

Having now finished the work assigned me, I retire from the great theatre of action, and, bidding an affectionate farewell to this august body, under whose orders I have so long acted, I here offer my commission and take my leave of all the employments of public life."

The great master of English fiction, writing of this at Annapolis, says: "Which was the most splendid spectacle ever witnessed—the opening feast of Prince George in London, or the resignation of Washington? Which is the noble character for after ages to admire—yon fribble dancing in lace and spangles, or yonder hero who sheathes his sword after a life of spotless honor, a purity unreproached, a courage indomitable and a consummate victory?"

❦

Lesson 27.1

Prose & Poetry

A LOOK AT LITERARY ELEMENTS IN THE NARRATIVE

1 **Read**
   ◆ Listen carefully as your teacher reads the selection aloud. **Delight** in the story.

2 **Inquire**
   ◆ Does the **title** give any hint as to the content or message of the story? If this story was published by the author in a larger book or an anthology, does that title give any hint?
   ◆ Discuss the meaning of these words in the context of the story: *inspiration, assurance, scrutiny, distinguished, gravity, vigor, expedition, embodiment, resigned,* and any unfamiliar words. From Washington's farewell address, you might also want to study: *satisfaction, diffidence, arduous, rectitude, superseded, sanguine, merits, patronage, august, unreproached, consummate.*

3 **Observe the Content**
   ◆ **Setting** When and where does this story take place?
   ◆ **Characters** Who is (are) the main character(s) in this story?
   ◆ **Conflict** What is the main problem or crisis for the character(s)?
   ◆ **Resolution** Is the problem solved? If so, how? If not, why not?
   ◆ **Point of View** Who is telling the story? Is it first-person or third-person?
   ◆ **Figures** Can you identify any examples of simile, onomatopoeia, anemographia,

anastrophe, alliteration, hydrographia, metaphor, personification, chronographia, astrothesia or topographia in this narrative?

4 Investigate the Context

Like many of the literary lights of our country's earlier years, Henry Cabot Lodge (1850-1924) was a Massachusetts native, and a graduate of Harvard. A statesman and historian, Lodge served in the U.S. Senate from 1893-1924, and was a close friend of President Theodore Roosevelt. Athough they did not always see eye-to-eye politically, they were fast friends from the day they met:

>According to Roosevelt's wife, Edith, the two men were "like brothers." She said they "talked a blue streak" and often "lost themselves in the deep canyons of their wild intellectual pursuits" . . . Roosevelt's son Kermit . . . commented that Lodge knew his father better than anyone alive, save Mother. At some deep level, they were soul mates" . . .

In 1895, just a few years after [Roosevelt and Lodge] met, they co-wrote a collection of historical profiles and vignettes, *Hero Tales of American History*. This was their favorite project and remained so throughout their lives. Reading it today reveals much about the strength that both men drew from their relationship. Ted, the firstborn of Roosevelt's brood, asserted, "That book not only provides portraits of a fistful of American heroes, it portrays the way a collaborative friendship can shape the destiny of a nation."

. . .This book was their attempt to revive a venerable old Christian tradition of charting the topography of that forgotten foreign land called the past. It was an effort to make the tales of the American heroes of yore a narrative worthy to be told at home and around the hearth, appealing to the heroic heart of all generations and reinvigorating the eternal infancy of mankind. Thus it was essentially a story, not a study. It was comprised of true tales, to be sure, but they hoped that it would read like valiant fables and not like vapid facts. — Dr. George Grant, Introduction to *Hero Tales of American History*

5 Connect the Thoughts

◆ Does this story remind you of other stories with similar plots, messages, or characters?

◆ Does this story remind you of any fables?

◆ Does this story remind you of any proverbs or other well-known quotations? If so, enter these in your Commonplace Book.

Commonplace Book

6 Profit and Delight

◆ **Delight** What are the sources of delight in this story?

◆ **Wisdom** What wisdom does this story furnish?

◆ **Read** the narrative aloud to your teacher with expression and with proper pauses.

◆ **Record** in your Book of Centuries: Henry Cabot Lodge, George Washington.

PLOT OBSERVATION: IDENTIFYING ACTIONS

Observe the plot of "George Washington." Work in pencil on the original narrative at the beginning of this lesson, marking and making notes in the margin as instructed below.

A. Quickly read through the narrative once more. Number the paragraphs, and then mark the story as you have learned to do. Divide the narrative into actions.

B. Mark an x beside the sections that do not detail an action, and note what these are: **Prologue, Epilogue, Explanation, Description, Summary, Author Comments**.

C. Mark the major actions. Then, mark in the left margin if the action is made up of **Dialogue** or **Thoughts**. Consider Theon's Six. Remember that action can change even in the middle of a paragraph. Feel free to change your mind often as you work through the entire narrative—this is why you must use a pencil! Keep in mind that there is not just one right way to divide narratives into actions. Just make sure you can explain why you divide them as you do, using Theon's Six.

D. Review the narrative. Make notes in the margin indicating if any of the rest of Theon's Six changed with each action. You should definitely have notes about Person. Ask the questions for the other four, but do not worry too much if you can only add notes for two or three others.

E. Discuss your work with your teacher.

Language Logic

GRAMMAR TERMS & DEFINITIONS
Review all flashcards according to tabs.

GRAMMAR PRACTICE AND REVIEW

In your Writer's Journal, copy these sentences. Analyze each sentence by marking the simple subject (who or what the sentence is about) with a single underline, and the verb or verb phrase with a double underline. Write DO over the direct object, or LV over the linking verb; write PA over a predicate adjective and PN over a predicate nominative. Put parentheses around each prepositional phrase. Bracket the clauses. Classify the sentence as simple, compound, complex, or compound-complex. Then diagram the sentence. Refer to *Sentence Sense* as needed.

1. Born of a distinguished family in the days when the American colonies were still ruled by an aristocracy, Washington started with all that good birth and tradition could give.

2. He so exposed himself that bullets passed through his coat and hat, and the Indians and the French who tried to bring him down thought he bore a charmed life.

Writer's Journal

Eloquent Expression

COPIA OF WORDS: VOCABULARY STUDY

Conduct a vocabulary study for "George Washington."

A. Choose at least two unfamiliar words to study. If you need suggestions, see the list under **Inquire** in Literary Elements above. Work in your Writer's Journal.

B. Complete Vocabulary Study steps A-G for each word (see Appendix).

Writer's Journal

Commonplace

NARRATIVE

Session one of three commonplace sessions for this lesson. Literary
selection: "George Washington."

Commonplace
Book

🏵 Set your timer and begin copying. When you finish, check your
work carefully, word by word, against the original.

Lesson 27.2

Prose & Poetry

PLOT OBSERVATION: OUTLINE WITH CAPTIONS

🏵 In your Writer's Journal, create an outline to capture your
observations with parallel captions.

Writer's
Journal

A. Jot down a quick caption for each major action, as well
    as any of the following: Prologue, Epilogue, Explanation,
    Description, Summary, Author Comments.

B. Review your captions, and choose a parallel format.

C. Revise all captions to conform to the format you have chosen.

Language Logic

GRAMMAR
FLASHCARDS

GRAMMAR TERMS & DEFINITIONS
🏵 Review all flashcards according to tabs.

SENTENCE DIAGRAMMING

🏵 In your Writer's Journal, copy these sentences. Analyze each sentence by marking the
simple subject (who or what the sentence is about) with a single underline, and the verb
or verb phrase with a double underline. Write DO over the direct object, or LV over the
linking verb; write PA over a predicate adjective and PN over a predicate nominative. Put
parentheses around each prepositional phrase. Mark the subjects and verbs. Bracket the

clauses. Classify the sentence as simple, compound, complex, or compound-complex. Then diagram the sentence. Refer to *Sentence Sense* as needed.

Hint: Before you begint to diagram #2, identify the objective complement in the principal clause. See *Bards & Poets I* Teaching Helps for an explanation.

Writer's Journal

1. From the time when he drew his sword under the famous elm tree, he was the embodiment of the American Revolution, and without him that revolution would have failed almost at the start.

2. With the army at his back, and supported by the great forces which, in every community, desire order before everything else, and are ready to assent to any arrangement which will bring peace and quiet, Washington could have made himself the ruler of the new nation.

Classical Composition

PLOT OBSERVATION: ORAL NARRATION

 Without reading "George Washington" again, retell the **plot** orally to your teacher. Refer to your plot observation of the narrative with Theon's Six if needed. Note that the letter at the end will not be part of the retelling.

Commonplace

NARRATIVE

Session two of three commonplace sessions for this lesson. Literary selection: "George Washington."

Commonplace Book

Set your timer and begin copying. When you finish, check your work carefully, word by word, against the original. Check spelling, capitalization, and punctuation for accuracy.

Lesson 27.3

Language Logic

GRAMMAR TERMS & DEFINITIONS
Review all flashcards according to tabs.

SENTENCE DIAGRAMMING

In your Writer's Journal, copy these sentences. Analyze each sentence by marking the simple subject (who or what the sentence is about) with a single underline, and the verb or verb phrase with a double underline. Write DO over a direct object, LV over a linking verb, PA over a predicate adjective, and PN over a predicate nominative. Put parentheses around each prepositional phrase. Bracket the clauses. Classify the sentence as simple, compound, complex, or compound-complex Then diagram the sentence. Refer to *Sentence Sense* as needed.

Hint: Note the relative clause with no introductory relative pronoun (*I have received from my country*).

1. The successful termination of the war has verified the most sanguine expectations, and my gratitude for the interposition of Providence and the assistance I have received from my countrymen increases with every review of the momentous contest.

Writer's Journal

2. *Challenge (classroom):* I have now the honor of offering my sincere congratulations to Congress, and of presenting myself before them, to surrender into their hands the trust committed to me and to claim the indulgence of retiring from the service of my country.

Eloquent Expression

SENTENCE STYLE – COPIA OF CONSTRUCTION: PRINCIPAL AND SUBORDINATE
CLAUSES

Clauses can sometimes be switched by classification. The principal clause can be made subordinate, and vice versa.

When it arrived, your letter brought joy to Erasmus.

Your letter, which brought joy to Erasmus, arrived today.

Your letter, which was filled with glad tidings, brought joy to Erasmus.

Your letter was filled with glad tidings that brought joy to Erasmus.

As you can see in the examples above, and the meaning or emphasis of the sentence may change a little (or a lot!), which may or may not be a good thing. Check the meaning of the rewritten sentence carefully to make sure it says what you want it to say.

 Paraphrase each sentence, switching principal and subordinate clauses.

Writer's Journal

1. As the times grew threatening on the frontier, he was sent on a perilous mission to the Indians.

2. Washington plunged into the wilderness, where he soon grew to be an expert hunter and backwoodsman.

Classical Composition

NARRATIVE RETELLING – FIRST DRAFT

You will have two sessions to work on this retelling. Begin here, and plan to finish in Lesson 27.4. As you write your retelling, do your best to use proper grammar and spelling, but keep in mind that you will have opportunity to edit before you finalize it.

Writer's Journal

 Retell "George Washington" in writing, keeping the same characters, setting, and sequence of action. Choose either first or third person point of view, but be consistent throughout. This means you need to make sure that the pronouns are consistent, and pay close attention attention to subject/verb agreement. Refer to your plot observation of the narrative with Theon's Six, but do not review the original narrative before you write. Include:

- ◆ a heading, properly formatted
- ◆ at least two figures of speech: simile, onomatopoeia, anastrophe, alliteration, metaphor
- ◆ at least one figure of description: anemographia, hydrographia, choronographia, astrothesia, topographia

Lesson 27.4

Language Logic

GRAMMAR TERMS & DEFINITIONS
 Review all flashcards according to tabs.

Classical Composition

Writer's Journal

NARRATIVE RETELLING – FINISH FIRST DRAFT
 Finish the first draft of your narrative retelling. Review the instructions in Lesson 27.3 as needed.

Commonplace

NARRATIVE
Session three of three commonplace sessions for this lesson. Literary selection: "George Washington."

Commonplace Book

 Set your timer. Begin where you stopped in the last session. When you finish, check your work carefully against the original for accuracy.

Lesson 27.5

Prose & Poetry

POETRY APPRECIATION

Read and enjoy a few poems in your poetry anthology. Identify rhyme schemes and stanza forms of one or two. Look for poems with iambic, trochaic, dactylic, or anapestic meter. Look for figures of speech and figures of description in the poems you read, and make note of any you find for future Commonplace Book entries. Read one or two poems aloud with expression and proper pauses. Pause at punctuation, but not necessarily at the ends of lines. Finally, choose a rhyming poem with trochaic meter to observe.

Language Logic

GRAMMAR TERMS & DEFINITIONS

Ask your teacher to quiz you with the grammar flashcards. Alternately, use the test feature in the Cottage Press *Bards & Poets I* Quizlet Classroom for an online or printed quiz for Lesson 27.

DICTATION: NARRATIVE PASSAGE

Work in your Writer's Journal. Write as your teacher dictates a passage to you from your Commonplace Book. When you are done, check your work carefully, word by word, against the original. Check for accurate spelling, capitalization, and punctuation.

Classical Composition

NARRATIVE RETELLING: TYPE FINAL DRAFT

Type your retelling on the computer with spell-check turned off, or ask your writing mentor to type it exactly as you wrote it. Save, print,

and file this draft in your writing binder.

Commonplace

FROM YOUR READING

Find selections in a book or poem to add to your Commonplace Book. Include the name of the book or poem, properly formatted. Label the entry with the grammar or poetry feature, the figure of speech, or as a favorite passage. Aim for a minimum of three entries, with at least one from each category.

Commonplace Book

 Grammar Features (choose any)

- ◆ A sentence that has an interesting or descriptive noun, a strong and fitting verb, a well-chosen adjective, and/or a vivid adverb
- ◆ A sentence with one or more prepositional phrases or indirect objects
- ◆ A sentence that has a possessive noun or pronoun and/or an appositive
- ◆ A sentence that has a conjunction to join words, phrases, or clauses
- ◆ A sentence with a participle or participial phrase, and/or an infinitive or infinitive phrase
- ◆ A complex, compound, or compound-complex sentence
- ◆ An indirect quotation
- ◆ An interesting dialogue tag (add to your Dialogue Tags list)
- ◆ An interrogative, exclamatory, or imperative sentence

Figures (choose any)

- ◆ Figures of Speech: simile, onomatopoeia, anastrophe, alliteration, metaphor, and/or personification
- ◆ Figures of Description: anemographia, hydrographia, chronographia, astrothesia, and/or topographia

Poetry Features (choose any)

- ◆ Rhyme (note name of the rhyme scheme)
- ◆ Iambic, anapestic, dactylic, or trochaic meter (note name of the meter)
- ◆ Stanza (note name of stanza form)

Favorite Passage: Add at least one passage of one to three sentences or several lines of poetry that captured your attention in your reading this week. It may be something you found beautiful, thought-provoking, funny, or interesting.

ↂ

MY NATIVE LAND

from LAY OF THE LAST MINSTREL, CANTO VI

I

Breathes there the man, with soul so dead,

Who never to himself hath said,

   This is my own, my native land!

Whose heart hath ne'er within him burn'd,

As home his footsteps he hath turn'd,

   From wandering on a foreign strand!

If such there breathe, go, mark him well;

For him no Minstrel raptures swell;

High though his titles, proud his name,

Boundless his wealth as wish can claim;

Despite those titles, power, and pelf,

The wretch, concentred all in self,

Living, shall forfeit fair renown,

And, doubly dying, shall go down

To the vile dust, from whence he sprung,

Unwept, unhonour'd, and unsung.

II

O Caledonia! stern and wild,

Meet nurse for a poetic child!

Land of brown heath and shaggy wood,

Land of the mountain and the flood,

Land of my sires! what mortal hand

Can e'er untie the filial band,

That knits me to thy rugged strand!

Still as I view each well-known ,

Think what is now, and what hath been,

Seems as, to me of all bereft,

Sole friends thy woods and streams were left;

And thus I love them better still,

Even in extremity of ill.

By Yarrow's streams still let me stray,

Though none should guide my feeble way;

Still feel the breeze down Ettrick break,

Although it chill my wither'd cheek;

Still lay my head by Teviot Stone,

Though there, forgotten and alone,

The Bard may draw his parting groan.

— SIR WALTER SCOTT

ℭℛ

Lesson 28.1

Prose & Poetry

A LOOK AT LITERARY ELEMENTS IN THE POEM

1 **Read**
- Follow along and listen carefully as the poem is read aloud, OR read it aloud yourself. Read it at least two or three times. **Delight** in the meter, the rhyme, and the images.

2 **Inquire**
- Does the **title** give any hint as to the content or message of the poem?
- Are there any other unfamiliar persons, places, or things mentioned in the poem? Discuss these with your teacher.

- Discuss the meaning of these words in the context of the story: *native, strand, Minstrel, boundless, pelf, wretch, forfeit, renown, vile, Caledonia, filial, bereft, extremity,* and any unfamiliar words.

- Was there any part of the poem you did not understand? If so, discuss this with your teacher and classmates.

3 Observe the Content

- **Lyrical Elements**
  - What does the poet describe?
  - Does the poet make you see, hear, smell, taste, or touch anything?
  - Does the poet compare something in the poem to some other thing?

- **Narrative Elements** Does this poem tell a story? If so, observe the
  - **Setting** When and where does this story take place?
  - **Characters** Who is (are) the main character(s) in this story?
  - **Conflict** What is the main problem or crisis for the character(s)?
  - **Resolution** Is the problem solved? If so, how? If not, why not?

- **Point of View** Who is speaking in the poem? Is it first-person or third-person?

- **Figures** Can you identify any examples of simile, onomatopoeia, anemographia, anastrophe, alliteration, hydrographia, metaphor, personification, chronographia, astrothesia or topographia in this poem?

4 Investigate the Context

Sir Walter Scott 1771-1832), a beloved Scottish author and poet, is credited with the invention of the historical novel. If you have not already read them, you must put at least his novels *Ivanhoe* and *The Talisman* on your reading list!

Scott's "Marmion" and "Lady of the Lake" aroused a whole nation to enthusiasm, and for the first time romantic poetry became really popular. So also, the novel had been content to paint men and women of the present, until the wonderful series of Waverley novels appeared, when suddenly, by the magic of this "Wizard of the North," all history seemed changed. The past, which had hitherto appeared as a dreary region of dead heroes, became alive again, and filled with a multitude of men and women who had the surprising charm of reality. — William J. Long, *English Literature, Its History and Its Significance for the English Speaking World*

Scott was greatly influenced by Robert Burns; the poetry and storytelling of these two brought about a renaissance of national spirit in Scotland after years of British attempts to extinguish Scottish lore. In a tribute to Burns, Scott said, "When I want to express a sentiment I feel strongly, I find the phrase in Shakespeare—or thee."

Our selection is taken from one of his early poems, *Lay of the Last Minstrel*. This book-length narrative poem is written in six cantos. In the preface to the 1805 edition of his poem, Scott says:

> The Poem, now offered to the Public, is intended to illustrate the customs and manners which anciently prevailed on the Borders of England and Scotland. …As the description of ry and manners was more the object of the Author than a combined and regular narrative, the plan of the Ancient Metrical Romance was adopted, which allows greater latitude, in this respect, than would be consistent with the dignity of a regular Poem. …For these reasons, the Poem was put into the mouth of an ancient Minstrel, the last of the race, who, as he is supposed to have survived the Revolution, might have caught somewhat of the refinement of modern poetry, without losing the simplicity of his original model. The date of the Tale itself is about the middle of the sixteenth century, when most of the personages actually flourished. The time occupied by the action is Three Nights and Three Days.

5 Connect the Thoughts

◆ Does this poem remind you of other poems, or of stories with similar plots, messages, or characters?

◆ Does this poem remind you of any proverbs or other well-known quotations? If so, enter these in your Commonplace Book.

Commonplace Book

6 Profit and Delight

◆ **Delight** What are the sources of delight in this poem?

◆ **Wisdom** What wisdom does this poem furnish?

◆ **Read** the poem aloud to your teacher with expression and with proper pauses.

◆ **Record** in your Book of Centuries: Sir Walter Scott.

◆ **Memorize** this poem and **recite** it before an audience.

Language Logic

GRAMMAR TERMS & DEFINITIONS
Review all flashcards according to tabs.

GRAMMAR PRACTICE AND REVIEW

In your Writer's Journal, copy these lines, which are taken from the Introduction to *Lay of the Last Minstrel*, and they will offer some valuable review in diagramming. Analyze each sentence by marking the simple subject (who or what the sentence or clause is about) with a single underline, and the verb or verb phrase with a double underline. Write DO over the direct object, or LV over the linking verb; write PA over a predicate adjective and PN over a predicate nominative. Put parentheses around each prepositional phrase. Bracket the clauses. Classify the sentence as simple, compound, complex, or compound-complex. Then diagram the sentence. Refer to *Sentence Sense* as needed.

Hint: Notice that the first three clauses are connected by commas, with no conjunction. See *Bards & Poets I Teaching Helps* for an explanation.

Writer's Journal

The way was long, the wind was cold,

The Minstrel was infirm and old;

His wither'd cheek, and tresses gray,

Seem'd to have known a better day;

The harp, his sole remaining joy,

Was carried by an orphan boy.

The last of all the Bards was he,

Who sung of Border chivalry.

Classical Composition

EDITOR'S PEN – THE BIG PICTURE

 Edit your retelling from Lesson 27:

Editor's Pen – The Big Picture

✓ All important plot elements included

✓ All characters represented correctly

✓ Sequence: *same as the original*

✓ Length: similar to the original

✓ Point of View: 3rd person or 1st person

✓ Figures of Speech – at least two of the following: *metaphor, personification, simile, onomatopoeia, anastrophe, alliteration*

A. Read aloud exactly what you have written—not what you THINK you have written! Mark any corrections on your first draft.

B. Next, work through the Big Picture checklist above with your writing mentor.

C. Transfer all additions and corrections from your print copy of the retelling to your file on the computer. Print and file this edited version in your binder along with your marked-up editing copy of the first draft.

Commonplace

Commonplace Book

POETRY

Session one of three commonplace sessions for this lesson. Literary selection: "My Native Land."

 Set your timer and begin copying. When finished, check your work carefully against the original for accuracy.

Lesson 28.2

Prose & Poetry

RHYME SCHEME AND STANZA FORM

Mark the end rhyme in the stanzas below.

I

Breathes there the man, with soul so dead,

Who never to himself hath said,

   This is my own, my native land!

Whose heart hath ne'er within him burn'd,

As home his footsteps he hath turn'd,

   From wandering on a foreign strand!

If such there breathe, go, mark him well;

For him no Minstrel raptures swell;

High though his titles, proud his name,

Boundless his wealth as wish can claim;

Despite those titles, power, and pelf,

The wretch, concentred all in self,

Living, shall forfeit fair renown,

And, doubly dying, shall go down

To the vile dust, from whence he sprung,

Unwept, unhonour'd, and unsung.

II

O Caledonia! stern and wild,

Meet nurse for a poetic child!

Land of brown heath and shaggy wood,

Land of the mountain and the flood,

Land of my sires! what mortal hand

Can e'er untie the filial band,

That knits me to thy rugged strand!

Still as I view each well-known ,

Think what is now, and what hath been,

Seems as, to me of all bereft,

Sole friends thy woods and streams were left;

And thus I love them better still,

Even in extremity of ill.

By Yarrow's streams still let me stray,

Though none should guide my feeble way;

Still feel the breeze down Ettrick break,

Although it chill my wither'd cheek;

Still lay my head by Teviot Stone,

Though there, forgotten and alone,

The Bard may draw his parting groan.

 Name the predominant rhyme scheme and the stanza form of this poem.

Language Logic

GRAMMAR TERMS & DEFINITIONS
 Review all flashcards according to tabs.

SENTENCE DIAGRAMMING

 In your Writer's Journal, copy these sentences. Analyze each sentence by marking the simple subject (who or what the sentence is about) with a single underline, and the verb or verb phrase with a double underline. Write DO over the direct object, or LV over the linking verb; write PA over a predicate adjective and PN over a predicate nominative. Put parentheses around each prepositional phrase. Mark the subjects and verbs. Bracket the clauses. Classify the sentence as simple, compound, complex, or compound-complex. Then diagram the sentence. Refer to *Sentence Sense* as needed.

Hint: There are quite a few appositives at the beginning of this sentence. Once you have identified and diagrammed those, the diagram is fairly simple. See *Bards & Poets I* Teaching Helps for a full explanation.

O Caledonia! stern and wild,

Meet nurse for a poetic child!

Land of brown heath and shaggy wood,

Land of the mountain and the flood,

Land of my sires! what mortal hand

Can e'er untie the filial band,

That knits me to thy rugged strand!

Eloquent Expression

COPIA OF WORDS: VOCABULARY STUDY

Ⓠ Conduct a vocabulary study for "My Native Land."

A. Choose at least two unfamiliar words to study. If you need suggestions, see the list under **Inquire** in Literary Elements above. Work in your Writer's Journal.

B. Complete Vocabulary Study steps A-G for each word (see Appendix).

Classical Composition

EDITOR'S PEN – ZOOM 5X: PARAGRAPHS

Ⓠ Now that the Big Picture is set, begin to zoom in for a close look at the paragraph(s) in your retelling with your writing mentor.

Editor's Pen – Zoom 5x: Paragraphs

✓ Formatting: *proper indentation*

✓ Length: *neither too wordy nor too short*

✓ Sentence class by use: *effective use*

✓ Sentence openers: *varied*

✓ Dialogue: *effective use*

✓ Pronouns: *consistent with chosen point of view*

A. Read aloud your most recently edited version. Check each item in the Editor's Pen checklist to identify possible changes. Mark these on your print copy.

B. Transfer all additions and corrections from your print copy to the computer file. Print this version and file it in your binder along with your other versions.

Lesson 28.3

Prose & Poetry

SCANSION

 Scan these stanzas, following the three steps you have learned.

Step 1 Mark each syllable as either stressed (/) or unstressed (∪). Say the line aloud several times to "get" the meter. Next, say the line aloud emphasizing the stresses as you mark the stresses only. Then go back and mark the unstressed syllables, saying the line aloud once more to check your work.

Step 2 Insert dividers (|) to mark off the feet. Remember that you will only have one stress in each foot. Pronounce *wandering* with two syllables.

Step 3 Name the poem's predominant meter:

Breathes there the man, with soul so dead,

Who never to himself hath said,

This is my own, my native land!

Whose heart hath ne'er within him burn'd,

As home his footsteps he hath turn'd,

　　From wandering on a foreign strand!

If such there breathe, go, mark him well;

For him no Minstrel raptures swell;

High though his titles, proud his name,

Boundless his wealth as wish can claim;

Despite those titles, power, and pelf,

The wretch, concentred all in self,

Living, shall forfeit fair renown,

And, doubly dying, shall go down

To the vile dust, from whence he sprung,

Unwept, unhonour'd, and unsung.

Language Logic

GRAMMAR TERMS & DEFINITIONS
🏆 Review all flashcards according to tabs.

SENTENCE DIAGRAMMING
🏆 In your Writer's Journal, copy these sentences. Analyze each sentence by marking the simple subject (who or what the sentence is about) with a single underline, and the verb or verb phrase with a double underline. Write DO over a direct object, LV over a linking verb, PA

over a predicate adjective, and PN over a predicate nominative. Put parentheses around each prepositional phrase. Bracket the clauses. Classify the sentence as simple, compound, complex, or compound-complex Then diagram the sentence. Refer to *Sentence Sense* as needed.

Hint: Note that *all, down,* and *whence* are all used as adverbs. See *Bards & Poets I* Teaching Helps for a full explanation. We definitely recommend this sentence as a collaborative classroom exercise!

Despite those titles, power, and pelf,

The wretch, concentred all in self,

Living, shall forfeit fair renown,

And, doubly dying, shall go down

To the vile dust, from whence he sprung,

Unwept, unhonour'd, and unsung.

Eloquent Expression

SENTENCE STYLE – YOUR STYLE!

Craft copia for sentences from your own retelling using Sentence Style devices we have studied.

A. Work with your writing mentor to choose three sentences from your retelling that could be improved.

B. Copy the first in your Writer's Journal. Underline every important word in the sentence and jot down synonyms for each.

C. Use the list of Sentence Style devices below as you write several new versions of the sentence. You may use more than one device in each sentence.

D. Repeat the instructions above for the second and third sentences.

E.   Choose your favorite paraphrase of each sentence. Replace the original sentences in your retelling before you edit again.

COPIA OF WORDS

✓ Synonyms and Antonyms

✓ Opening Words

✓ Dialogue Tags - synonyms for *said*
   ◆ switch direct/indirect quotations

✓ Point of View

✓ Nouns – varied and descriptive
   ◆ switch noun/pronouns
   ◆ switch gerund/infinitve

✓ Verbs – strong and fitting
   ◆ switch verb/verbal

✓ Modifiers
   ◆ add adjective
   ◆ add adverb

COPIA OF CONSTRUCTION

✓ Sentence class by use

✓ Dialogue
   ◆ Tag line position
   ◆ switch direct/indirect quotations

✓ Verb Tense

✓ Sentence Structure
   ◆ switch possessive/*of* phrases
   ◆ change position of phrases
   ◆ switch words/phrases/clauses
   ◆ switch subordinate/principal clauses

✓ Sentence Combination
   ◆ compound elements

Classical Composition

EDITOR'S PEN – ZOOM 10X: SENTENCES

Now it is time to zoom in even closer as you check the sentences in your retelling. Work with your writing mentor.

Editor's Pen – Zoom 10x: Sentences

✓ Complete thought expressed

✓ Subject and predicate agree in number

✓ Correct capitalization and punctuation
   ◆ Commas correctly used for words in a series
   ◆ No comma splices or run-on sentences!

A.   Read aloud your your most recently edited version. Use the Editor's Pen checklist to identify changes you need to make. Mark all changes on your print copy.

B.   Transfer all additions and corrections from your print copy to the computer file. Print this version and file it in your binder along with your other versions.

Commonplace

POETRY

Session two of three commonplace sessions for this lesson. Literary selection: "My Native Land."

 Set your timer. Begin where you stopped in the last session. When you finish, check your work carefully against the original for accuracy.

Commonplace Book

Lesson 28.4

Prose & Poetry

SCANSION

 Scan these stanzas, following the three steps you have learned.

Step 1 Mark each syllable as either stressed (/) or unstressed (∪). Say the line aloud several times to "get" the meter. Next, say the line aloud emphasizing the stresses as you mark the stresses only. Then go back and mark the unstressed syllables, saying the line aloud once more to check your work.

Step 2 Insert dividers (|) to mark off the feet. Remember that you will only have one stress in each foot. Pronounce *even* with one syllable (e'en); pronounce *filial* and *Teviot* with two syllables; pronounce *Caledonia* with three syllables.

Step 3 Name the poem's predominant meter:

O Caledonia! stern and wild,

Meet nurse for a poetic child!

Land of brown heath and shaggy wood,

Land of the mountain and the flood,

Land of my sires! what mortal hand

Can e'er untie the filial band,

That knits me to thy rugged strand!

Still as I view each well-known ,

Think what is now, and what hath been,

Seems as, to me of all bereft,

Sole friends thy woods and streams were left;

And thus I love them better still,

Even in extremity of ill.

By Yarrow's streams still let me stray,

Though none should guide my feeble way;

Still feel the breeze down Ettrick break,

Although it chill my wither'd cheek;

Still lay my head by Teviot Stone,

Though there, forgotten and alone,

The Bard may draw his parting groan.

Language Logic

GRAMMAR TERMS & DEFINITIONS
() Review all flashcards according to tabs.

Eloquent Expression

PARAGRAPH STYLE – PARAPHRASE WITH COPIA

For this exercise, choose from all of the copia devices you have learned so far. See the copia chart in Lesson 28.3. New devices are in bold type.

() In your Writer's Journal, paraphrase this paragraph. Change each sentence opener, and change at least one sentence class by use. Use as many synonym substitutions as possible. Use as many of the other copia devices as you are able. Make notes on the paragraph below before you begin.

While I repeat my obligations to the Army in general, I should do

njustice to my own feelings not to acknowledge, in this place, the

peculiar services and distinguished merits of the Gentlemen who have

been attached to my person during the war. It was impossible that the

choice of confidential officers to compose my family should have been

more fortunate. Permit me, sir, to recommend in particular those who have continued in service

to the present moment as worthy of the favorable notice and patronage of Congress.

Writer's
Journal

Classical Composition

EDITOR'S PEN – FINE FOCUS: WORDS

The final checks dwell on the details of your word usage. Continue to compile your personal editing checklist to use in editing all of your work across the curriculum.

Editor's Pen – Fine Focus: Words
✓ Word choices varied; word meanings clear
   ◆ Verbs: *strong, fitting; appropriate adverbs if needed*
   ◆ Nouns: *clear, descriptive; appropriate adjectives if needed*
   ◆ Dialogue: *dialogue tags varied if appropropriate*
✓ Correct spelling
✓ Final read-through

A. Read aloud your most recent version. Identify changes you need to make with the Editor's Pen checklist. Mark these on your print copy.

B. Transfer all additions and corrections from your print copy to the computer file. Print this final version and file it in your binder along with your other versions.

Commonplace

Commonplace
Book

POETRY

Session three of three commonplace sessions for this lesson. Literary
selection: "My Native Land."

 Set your timer and begin copying. When you finish, check your
work carefully against the original for accuracy.

Lesson 28.5

Prose & Poetry

POETRY APPRECIATION

 Read and enjoy a few poems in your poetry anthology. Identify rhyme schemes and stanza
forms of one or two. Look for figures of speech and figures of description in the poems you
read, and make note of any you find for future Commonplace Book entries. Read one or two
poems aloud with expression and proper pauses. Pause at punctuation, but not necessarily
at the ends of lines. Finally, choose a rhyming poem with iambic, trochaic, dactylic, or
anapestic meter to observe.

Writer's
Journal

- In your Writer's Journal, write the title of the poem and the
  author. Make note of its meter, rhyme scheme, and stanza
  form.
- Write the rhyming words from the poem in two lists: one
  list for those spelled the same, and one list for those spelled
  differently.
- Choose one of the rhyming words from the spelled differently
  list, and try to come up with several additional rhymes. Look
  especially for varied spellings.

Language Logic

GRAMMAR TERMS & DEFINITIONS

◉ Ask your teacher to quiz you with the grammar flashcards. Alternately, use the test feature in the Cottage Press *Bards & Poets I* Quizlet Classroom for an online or printed quiz for Lesson 28.

DICTATION: POETRY

◉ Work in your Writer's Journal. Write as your teacher dictates a passage to you from your Commonplace Book. When you are done, check your work carefully, word by word, against the original. Check for accurate spelling, capitalization, and punctuation.

Classical Composition

POETRY

◉ In your Writer's Journal, write two to four rhyming lines that summarize the action of "George Washington." If you wish, include a poetic **moral** at the end. Consider including them at the end of your retelling as a brief summary of the story. You may find it easiest to imitate the rhyme and meter of a few lines of the poetic selection for this lesson or a previous lesson.

NARRATIVE RETELLING – FINAL DRAFT

◉ Read over the final version of your retelling one last time and make any needed changes. Save it on your computer; print and file with all the other drafts in your writing binder.

Commonplace

Commonplace Book

FROM YOUR READING

Find selections in a book or poem to add to your Commonplace Book. Include the name of the book or poem, properly formatted. Label the entry with the grammar or poetry feature, the figure of speech, or as a favorite passage. Aim for a minimum of three entries, with at least one from each category.

 Grammar Features (choose any)

- ◆ A sentence that has an interesting or descriptive noun, a strong and fitting verb, a well-chosen adjective, and/or a vivid adverb
- ◆ A sentence with one or more prepositional phrases or indirect objects
- ◆ A sentence that has a possessive noun or pronoun and/or an appositive
- ◆ A sentence that has a conjunction to join words, phrases, or clauses
- ◆ A sentence with a participle or participial phrase, and/or an infinitive or infinitive phrase
- ◆ A complex, compound, or compound-complex sentence
- ◆ An indirect quotation
- ◆ An interesting dialogue tag (add to your Dialogue Tags list)
- ◆ An interrogative, exclamatory, or imperative sentence

Figures (choose any)

- ◆ Figures of Speech: simile, onomatopoeia, anastrophe, alliteration, metaphor, and/or personification
- ◆ Figures of Description: anemographia, hydrographia, chronographia, astrothesia, and/or topographia

Poetry Features (choose any)

- ◆ Rhyme (note name of the rhyme scheme)
- ◆ Iambic, anapestic, dactylic, or trochaic meter (note name of the meter)
- ◆ Stanza (note name of stanza form)

Favorite Passage: Add at least one passage of one to three sentences or several lines of poetry that captured your attention in your reading this week. It may be something you found beautiful, thought-provoking, funny, or interesting.

Appendix

Writer's Journal

This composition book will be the place to put exercises, vocabulary studies, outlines and first drafts, dictation, and most other exercises. When you see an image like the one to the right, you are to do the work in your Writer's Journal. This notebook is simple to use. Start at the beginning of the book with Lesson 1. At the top of the first page, write the title:

Lesson 1 – The Reading Mother

Then, just add the exercises as you get to them in the text. The final few pages of the book will be reserved for several lists you will be prompted to make over the course of *Bards & Poets I*.

Commonplace Book

Sir, if you will be so good as to favor me with a blank book, I will transcribe the most remarkable occurrences I meet with in my reading, which will serve to fix them upon my mind. — John Quincy Adams, age 10, in a letter to his father

The Commonplace Book is the place to record beautiful literary passages in books that you are reading or studying. *Primer* and *Fable & Song* students keep a copybook, and the Commonplace Book is very similar. You will enter parts of every narrative and poem you study in *Bards & Poets I* in your Commonplace Book. In addition, any time you are asked to find an example of a particular grammar structure or figure of speech in your reading, the Commonplace Book is the place to put it.

When you see an image like the one to the right, you are make an entry in your Commonplace Book as instructed. A habit of reading with a pen in hand will make this much easier. Mark passages that you may wish to add to your commonplace directly in the book (with your parents' permission). If you would rather not write in the book, you could use a few index cards as bookmarks that you may make notes on, or stick 10-12 sticky notes to the back cover, and mark pages with passages that you might add to your Commonplace Book with a flag

and a note.

Later, transfer entries into your commonplace book in your best handwriting, and with appropriate attribution. Begin your Commonplace Book right at the beginning of the notebook, and add entries straight through from front to back. If you like, you may make a title page that includes the date you begin it (and later you can add the date you complete it). You might also copy the quote above from John Quincy Adams on the title page.

Commonplace entries should include the date of entry. In the attribution, include the title of the story or poem, the author, and the book in which the passage is found. Note that for handwritten entries, the title of a book will be underlined; chapter, fable, and poem titles will be placed in quotes. For a Scripture passage, include the verse reference. Sometimes you will be instructed to make a note or label a particular type of passage.

Leave the left-hand page blank, partly because it is neater, and partly because it allows you to go back and make notes on previous entries. Consider also developing your own personal flourish to place between entries, as in the sample entries below. Make your Commonplace Book attractive and neat, and make commonplacing a lifelong habit.

September 8, 2019

A thirsty Crow found a Pitcher with some water in it, but so little was there that, try as she might, she could not reach it with her beak, and it seemed as though she would die of thirst within sight of the remedy. At last she hit upon a clever plan. She began dropping pebbles into the Pitcher, and with each pebble the water rose a little higher until at last it reached the brim, and the knowing bird was enabled to quench her thirst.

Necessity is the mother of invention.

— Aesop's Fables, "The Crow and the Pitcher," by V.S. Jones

℘

September 22, 2019

Dark brown is the river,
    Golden is the sand.
It flows along for ever,
    With trees on either hand.
—Robert Louis Stevenson, "Where Go the Boats?" A Child's Garden of Verses

ↂ

October 23, 2020

Therefore whosoever heareth these sayings of mine, and doeth them, I will liken him unto a wise man, which built his house upon a rock: And the rain descended, and the floods came, and the winds blew, and beat upon that house; and it fell not: for it was founded upon a rock.

And every one that heareth these sayings of mine, and doeth them not, shall be likened unto a foolish man, which built his house upon the sand: And the rain descended, and the floods came, and the winds blew, and beat upon that house; and it fell: and great was the fall of it.

— A parable of Jesus, Matthew 7:24-27, King James Version

ↂ

January 18, 2020

There is no frigate like a book — Emily Dickinson, "A Book" [simile]

ↂ

March 25, 2020

There were stars staring in a black frosty sky overhead.

— C. S. Lewis, The Silver Chair [personification]

ↂ

There is a time for work and a time for play. — moral from "The Ants and the Grasshopper. (Similar messages: Ecclesiates 3, Pilgrims at Plymouth and the settlers at Jamestown)

ↂ

Vocabulary Study

Our knowledge is proportional to the number of words we understand, each conveying
a different thought, and our own power of producing thought and feeling in others
depends on the number of words that we can properly and promptly use.

— Erastus Otis Haven, *Rhetoric: A Textbook*

Practice Vocabulary Study not just in *Bards & Poets I*, but in all of your school subjects, and
with all of your reading. This is an excellent study skill to use in every area that you study, as
vocabulary is often the key to understanding a given subject.

STEPS FOR VOCABULARY STUDY

A. **Literary Context** Write the sentence (or at least the clause) containing the word to be
   studied. Underline the word.

B. **Spelling Analysis** Print the word again, dividing it into syllables, and including
   spelling markings based on the phonics method you have learned. If you have not
   learned a phonics marking method, copy the dictionary pronunciation.

C. **Part of Speech Identification** Note the part of speech according to the context of the
   word in the literary selection. For example, *trust* is listed in the dictionary as both a
   noun and a verb; determine how it is being used in the selection to know which word to
   enter.

D. **Definition** Write the dictionary definition that best fits the word in the context of the
   literary selection.

E. **Etymology** On the next line, note the etymology of the word from the dictionary. In
   the front of the dictionary, there should be a key to the abbreviations and symbols used
   to note etymology. These will vary from dictionary to dictionary. For example, you may
   see something like <*ME pleasaunt* <*OF plaisant*. This means the word as it is used today
   was derived from a Middle English word that was in turn derived from an Old French
   word.

F. **Synonyms** and **Antonyms** On the next line write *syn:* and then make a list of
   synonyms (words having the same or nearly the same meaning) for the word from
   the dictionary. Below that, write *ant:*, and make a list of antonyms (words having an
   opposite meaning). You may find many synonyms and/or antonyms for a given word,
   but try to choose the ones that relate to the context as the vocabulary word.

A good dictionary will usually list several synonyms for each entry. For additional synonyms, ask your teacher to show you how to use a thesaurus. Keep one handy on your desk at all times! If you do not have a print thesaurus, there are some good ones available online, like thesaurus.com. Always use caution with online resources, and ask your teacher at home to help you avoid internet dangers and temptations.

G. **Literary Quotation** On the next line, copy a quotation from a different source that uses this word. Some good sources would include: the Bible, literary works, or the speeches, prayers, and letters of historical figures. Be sure to include an attribution.

A bible concordance is always a good place to start. Try the King James Version for lovely literary quotations. Some dictionaries, like Webster's 1828 Dictionary, include a quality literary quotation for most words. A reference like like Bartlett's Quotations is handy for this as well – and you can probably find a free or inexpensive one on Paperback Swap or Amazon Marketplace.

If you do not have a print resource, ask your teacher at home for permission and help in using an online resource like biblegateway.org, or bartleby.com. I cannot repeat this too often—always use caution with online resources!

After completing these steps, discuss your findings with your teacher, and review the Word Usage notes in the dictionary for each word. Some possibilities for consideration include:

✓ Is this a word that is frequently misspelled or misunderstood? Does this word have any **homonyms** (words that sound the same but have a different spelling)? Does this word have any words that are frequently confused with it, such as *affect* and *effect*, or *then* and *than*? Are there any tips to help you remember the correct spelling and usage?

✓ Did you learn anything new about this word?

✓ Is the way the word is used in the literary selection "artfully varied from ordinary speech"? If so, it may be a figure of speech, and you should consider the literal meaning vs. the figural meaning of the word.

✓ Can this word be used as other parts of speech? If so, how does the meaning change?

✓ Discuss the synonyms and antonyms for the word. What effect would it have if one of the synonyms you have chosen was used in the literary selection in place of the original? What if you used an antonym with a negative expression before it in place of the original?

EXAMPLE VOCABULARY STUDY

Oh I do think it the pleasantest thing ever a child can do! — "The Swing" by Robert Louis Stevenson

Note: The dictionary does not have an entry for *pleasantest*, so it is necessary to remove the suffix -est, and define the root word)

plea sant, adj, giving or affording pleasure; enjoyable

syn: agreeable, delightful, pleasing amusing enjoyable

ant: disagreeable, gloomy, sad, unpleasant

late 14th century, <ME plesaunt <OF plaisant "pleasant, pleasing agreeable"

"The lines have fallen for me in pleasant places; indeed, I have a beautiful inheritance." — Psalm 16:6, KJV

EXAMPLE VOCABULARY STUDY DISCUSSION

For this word, you might want to discuss the spelling. How can you remember that pleasant uses **ea** to spell the short sound of **e** /ĕ/? Perhaps if you think about the verb from which this adjective is derived, *to please*, it will be easier to remember.

You might also discuss the suffix -**est**. Usually when we want to make the superlative form of a multi-syllable adjective, we use the adverb *most* in front of the positive form of the adjective: *most pleasant*. Try that out in the poem. Think about why Robert Louis Stevenson might have chosen to use *pleasantest* instead. Think about who is speaking in this poem: young children often might not pick up little nuances in language usage, so the word *pleasantest* lends child-likeness to the language of the poem.

Grammar Flashcards

Grammar concepts and definitions should be reviewed regularly. Flashcards are the best way to achieve this. In *Bards & Poets I,* new grammar terms are introduced in the poetry lessons, and you will be prompted to add flashcards to your review system. You may either make your own flashcards, or use print the free *Bards & Poets I* Flashcards PDF on cardstock. To download the PDF, visit the Cottage Press website.

Some of the first flashcards you will add are review from *Fable & Song.* New terms and concepts will be added as you proceed through the lessons. Both daily and periodic review are needed because systematic, regular review promotes mastery.

My tried and true system for reviewing flashcards requires only an index card box, nine dividers, and index cards. Make your own dividers: turn index cards on end and cut them short enough to fit in the box but taller than the height of the flashcards in the box. For 3" x 5" index cards, your finished size will be about 3" x 3.5." Write the following headers across the top of the divider:

Daily	Wednesday
Even	Thursday
Odd	Friday
Monday	Review
Tuesday	

In Lesson 1, you will be instructed to make or print out several flashcards. Put these behind the Daily tab, and review them every day. In a subsequent lesson, you will move these (assuming you have mastered them) back to the Even tab. You will place new flashcards behind the Daily tab. The first flashcards will now be reviewed only on even numbered days of the month. The new flashcards will now be reviewed every day.

Continue to move the current cards back as you add new ones. The cards behind the Even tab get moved back to the Odd tab, and these will be reviewed on the odd numbered days of the month. The cards behind the Odd tab get moved back to the Monday tab, and these will be reviewed only on Monday. Keep moving them back in this fashion until flashcards reach the Review section. By the time flashcards make it back there, they should only need to be reviewed occasionally. If students need extra review on a previously learned flashcard, move it back to the Daily tab, and when it is mastered, move it back through the tabs for review.

So, for example, on Wednesday, October 15, you would review the flashcards in the Daily, Odd, and Wednesday tabs.

Quizlet Quizzes

Cottage Press has a Quizlet Classroom with sets of flashcards corresponding with the lessons in *Bards & Poets I*. This is a wonderful free resource for reviewing, quizzing, and having fun with the flashcards. You can even make and take tests there. In addition to the online site, Quizlet has free apps for smartphones and tablets that are very well done. Visit the *Bards & Poets I* Quizlet classroom:

https://quizlet.com/class/7398171/

Note: Some of the information contained on a single flashcard in the Cottage Press pdf was broken into two or more flashcards on Quizlet. The testing and quizzing features on Quizlet work better that way.

Theon's Six Narrative Elements

This chart lists questions and prompts to help you analyze the elements that Theon identified as fundamental to a narrative. Not every question will be answered in every narrative, but the questions are designed to help you thoroughly observe a narrative.[1]

PERSON   Who are the characters in this narrative? Make notes of anything significant you learn about each one, such as:

      ✓ Place of birth and parents or ancestors

      ✓ Physical appearance

      ✓ Personality

      ✓ Education

      ✓ Age

      ✓ Situation in life (social standing, job, etc.)

ACTION   What happened? List the actions in this narrative.

PLACE   Where does this narrative (or action) take place? Inside or outside? Country, continent, planet, universe? Does the author describe its physical appearance?

TIME   When does this narrative (or action) take place?

      ✓ Date

      ✓ Season or time of year

      ✓ Time of day

      ✓ Other things happening in the same place at the same time

      ✓ Other things happening in other places at the same time

MANNER   How was the action done? Was it done willingly or unwillingly?

      ✓ If unwillingly – was it done in ignorance, by accident, or from necessity?

      ✓ If willingly – was it done by force, by deceit, or in secret?

CAUSE   Why was the action done?

      ✓ To acquire goods?

      ✓ To escape evil?

      ✓ From friendship?

      ✓ Because of relationship: wife, husband, children, father, mother, friend, etc.?

      ✓ Out of the passions: love, hate, envy, pity, drunkenness, etc.?

1 Theon's Six Narrative Elements taken from Kennedy, *Progymnasmata*, 28.

Eloquent Expression Through Copia

COPIA OF WORDS

✓ Synonyms (Lesson 2) and Antonyms (Lesson 3)

✓ Dialogue Tags – synonyms for *said* (Lesson 2)

✓ Nouns – varied and descriptive (Lesson 4)
- ◆ switch nouns/pronouns (Lesson 4)
- ◆ switch gerund/infinitive (Lesson 21)

✓ Verbs – fitting and strong (Lesson 3)
- ◆ switch verb/verbal (Lesson 21)

✓ Modifiers
- ◆ add adjective (Lesson 5)
- ◆ add adverb (Lesson 7)

COPIA OF CONSTRUCTION

✓ Sentence Class by Use (Lesson 1)

✓ Opening Word (Lesson 15)

✓ Dialogue
- ◆ tag line position (Lesson 2)
- ◆ switch direct/indirect quotations (Lesson 25)

✓ Point of View (Lesson 13)

✓ Verb Tense (Lesson 7)

✓ Sentence Structure
- ◆ switch possessive/*of* phrases (Lesson 17)
- ◆ change position of phrases (Lesson 19)
- ◆ switch words/phrases/clauses (Lesson 20)
- ◆ switch subordinate/principal clauses (Lesson 27)

✓ Sentence Combination
- ◆ compound elements (Lessons 9 and 11)

Grammar Terms & Definitions

Parts of Speech

Parts of Speech	1. Noun, 2. Pronoun, 3. Verb, 4. Adjective, 5. Adverb, 6. Preposition, 7. Conjunction, 8. Interjection	**Lesson 2**
Noun	names a person, place, thing, or idea	**Lesson 3**
Classes	common, proper	
common	a name common to a class of persons, places, things, or ideas	**Lesson 4**
proper	names a particular person, place, thing, or idea	
Properties	gender, person, number, case	
Property – Number	singular (only one), plural (more than one)	
Verb	shows action, being, or state	**Lesson 3**
Linking	joins the subject to a noun or adjective in the predicate	
	forms of be: am, is, are, was, be, being, been	**Lesson 6**
	verbs of sensing: taste, feel, smell, sound, look, appear	
Auxiliaries	forms of be: am, is, are, was, be, being, been	
	3 D's: do, does, did	
	3 H's: have, has, had	**Lesson 3**
	3 M's: may, might, must	
Verbal	derived from a verb; has both properties of a verb and of an adjective, a noun, or an adverb	
Classes	participle, gerund, infinitive	
Participle	verbal adjective	**Lesson 18**
Gerund	verbal noun	
Infinitive	verbal noun, adjective, or adverb; *to* + verb	
Adjective	describes or defines a noun or pronoun	
Adjective Questions	what kind? which one? how many?	
Classes	descriptive, definitive	**Lesson 5**
Descriptive Adjective	describes a noun; telling what kind?	
Definitive Adjective	limits or defines; telling which one? or how many?	
Pronoun	"stands in" for a noun	
Classes	personal, possessive, relative, interrogative	**Lesson 6**
Antecedent	noun for which the pronoun "stands in"	
Adverb	modifies a verb, an adjective, or another adverb	
Adverb Questions	where? when? why? how? to what extent?	**Lesson 7**
Preposition	connects a noun or a pronoun to another word in the sentence	**Lesson 8**

Common Prepositions

aboard	among	between	from	over	underneath
above	around	beyond	in	past	until
about	at	but	into	since	unto
across	before	by	like	through	up
after	behind	down	near	throughout	upon
against	below	during	of	to	with
along	beneath	except	off	toward	within
amid	beside	for	on	under	without

Conjunction	connects words, phrases, clauses, or sentences	**Lesson 9**

Classes	coordinate, subordinate, correlative	
coordinate	joins elements of same rank or name	Lesson 23
subordinate	joins elements of different ranks or names	
correlative	coordinates or subordinates used in pairs	
Interjection	shows sudden or strong emotion	**Lesson 10**

Sentence Terms

Sentence	begins with a capital letter, ends with end punctuation, expressses a complete thought, has both a subject and a predicate	**Lesson 1**
Subject	who or what the sentence is about	**Lesson 3**
Predicate	what the subject is or does	
Sentence Class by Use	declarative, interrogative, imperative, exclamatory	
Declarative Sentence	makes a statement or gives information	**Lesson 1**
Interrogative Sentence	asks a question	
Imperative Sentence	tells or commands someone to do something	
Exclamatory Sentence	expresses strong or sudden emotion	
Phrase	a group of words working together in a sentence; does not have both a subject and a predicate	
Clause	a group of words working together in a sentence; has both a subject and a predicate	**Lesson 22**
Principal Clause	still makes complete sense if separated from the rest of the sentence	
Subordinate Clause	does not make complete sense if separated from the rest of the sentence	
Sentence Class by Form	simple, compound, complex, compound-complex	
Simple Sentence	has one principal clause	
Compound Sentence	has two or more principal clauses	**Lesson 25**
Complex Sentence	has a principal clause and one or more subordinate clauses	
Compound-Complex Sentence	has two or more principal clauses and one or more subordinate clauses	
Basic Comma Rules	separate by commas: a series, a direct quotation, the salutation of an informal letter	**Lesson 1**
Capitalization Rules	capitalize the first word of every sentence, proper nouns, titles, I, O!, dates and days of the week	**Lesson 1**
Direct Quotation	relates what a speaker did or thought, repeating his/her actual words	**Lesson 2**

Bibliography
℘

This Bibliography lists works that we have used in researching and creating this curriculum. Most of these are cited by short footnotes throughout the text. Most selections at the beginning of lessons are in the public domain, besides the full length excerpts of the progymnasmata translations, which are used by permission of the Society for Biblical Literature in Atlanta, Georgia. The article "Why Read Plutarch?" is used by permission of the author, Dr. George Grant.

Erasmus, *On Copia of Words and Ideas,* trans. Donald B. King. Milwaukee: The Marquette University Press, 1963.

Gayley, Young, and Kurtz, *English Poetry: Its Principles and Progress.* New York: The Macmillan Company, 1921.

Gideon O. Burt. Silva Rhetoricae, rhetoric.byu.edu/

Gibson, Craig A. *Libanius' Progymnasmata: Model Exercises in Greek Prose Composition and Rhetoric.* Atlanta, Society for Biblical Literature, 2008.

Grant, George. "Why Read Plutarch?" Ambleside Online, 2002-2019. Accessed July 25, 2019. amblesideonline.org/WhyPlutarch.shtml

Harvey, Thomas W. *A Practical Grammar of the English Language: Revised Edition.* New York: Van Antwerp, Bragg & Co., 1868.

Harvey, Thomas W. *Elementary Grammar and Composition.* New York: American Book Company, 1880.

Hock, Ronald F., and O'Neil, Edward N. *The Chreia and Ancient Rhetoric: Classroom Exercises.* Atlanta, Society for Biblical Literature, 2002.

Kennedy, George A. *Progymnasmata: Greek Textbooks of Prose Composition and Rhetoric.* Atlanta: Society of Biblical Literature, 2003.

℘

COTTAGE PRESS

Classical Curriculum
with a
Charlotte Mason foundation
for Language Arts & more
— toward a life well-read

Language Lessons for Children
Primer One & Primer Two

Charlotte Mason style gentle lessons in grammar and composition for early elementary students—the perfect preparation for more rigorous language arts in later years. Features copywork and narration lessons drawn from classic children's literature and poetry. Includes nature and picture study lessons each week.

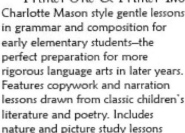

Language Arts for Grammar Students
Language Arts for Intermediate Students

Grammar and composition lessons structured around the fable and narrative stages of the progymnasmata. Features selections for imitation from classic children's literature as well as a gentle introduction to several classics as well. Includes strong sentence diagramming component along with basic studies in poetry, literary terms, figures of speech, and figures of description.

Language Arts for Upper School
Poetics & Progym I, II, and III

Composition and introductory rhetoric structured around the classical progymnasmata. Selections from the classical literature are central to each lesson for imitation, comprehension, and literary analysis. Includes in-depth study of grammar, sentence diagramming, poetry, literary terms, figures of speech, and figures of description.

Historical Timeline Notebook
Book of Centuries

A blank timeline book for students to record the major events and people they encounter in their study of history, literature, science, art, and music. Each page has lined sections for lists and blank sections for sketching.

Cottage Press Classics
Poetry Readers

Based on Charlotte Mason's method of poetry study, each volume of the Poetry Readers series includes three or four poets, along with several selections from Shakespeare's sonnets and plays, providing more than enough poems for a full year's poetry study. Our six year cycle of poets will introduce students to many of the most beautiful and well-known poems in the English tongue.

Visit *cottagepresspublishing.net* to see our complete offerings.

Revised and updated January 2020.

Made in United States
North Haven, CT
12 July 2024